DOUBLE
JEOPARDY

SUNY series, The Social Context of Education
Christine E. Sleeter, editor

DOUBLE JEOPARDY

Addressing Gender Equity in Special Education

edited by

HARILYN ROUSSO
and
MICHAEL L. WEHMEYER

State University
of New York
Press

Published by
State University of New York Press, Albany

For information, address State University of New York Press,
90 State Street, Suite 700, Albany, NY 12207

Production by Susan Geraghty
Marketing by Patrick Durocher

Library of Congress Cataloging-in-Publication Data

Double jeopardy : addressing gender equity in special education /
[edited by] Harilyn Rousso, Michael L. Wehmeyer.
     p. cm. — (SUNY series, the social context of education)
   Includes bibliographical references and index.
   ISBN 0-7914-5075-9 (alk. paper) — ISBN 0-7914-5076-7 (pbk. : alk. paper)
     1. Handicapped women—Education—United States. 2. Sex differences in
education—United States. 3. Educational equalization—United States. I. Rousso, Harilyn,
1946– II. Wehmeyer, Michael L. III. SUNY series, social context of education.

LC4019 .D75 2000
306.43—dc21

                                                                                00-050480

10 9 8 7 6 5 4 3 2 1

CONTENTS

CONTRIBUTORS

Adrienne Asch, Ph.D., Henry R. Luce Professor of Biology, Ethics and the Politics of Human Reproduction, Wellesley College

Michael Benz, Ph.D., Professor, College of Education, University of Oregon

Bonnie Doren, Ph.D., Assistant Professor, College of Education, University of Oregon

Estelle Eskenazi, LCSW, Project Director, Health Futures for Youth with Disabilities, Progressive Research and Training for Action

Nancy Ferreyra, Independent Consultant

Michelle Fine, Ph.D., Professor of Social/Personality Psychology, The Graduate School and University Center of the City University of New York

Craig P. Flood, Ed.D., Educational Equity Consultant

Merle Froschl, Co-Director, Educational Equity Concepts, Inc.

Dolores A. Grayson, Ph.D., Executive Director, GrayMill

Katherine Hanson, Director, Gender and Diversities Institute, Education Development Center, Inc.

Taran Jefferies, Research Associate, Program in Biology, Ethics and the Politics of Human Reproduction, Wellesley College

Eric Jolly, Ph.D., Vice President, Education Development Center, Inc.

Melissa Keyes, Ph.D., K2 Associates, LLC

Eleanor Linn, Senior Associate Director, Programs for Educational Opportunity, School of Education, University of Michigan

Theresa Mickey McCormick, Ph.D., Professor, Curriculum and Instruction Department, Iowa State University

Harilyn Rousso, Co-Editor, Executive Director, Disabilities Unlimited Consulting Services

Ellen Rubin, Coordinator of Disability Programs, Educational Equity Concepts, Inc.

Michelle Schwartz, M.A., Domestic Violence/Caregiver Violence Educator, Disability Services ASAP, SafePlace, Domestic Violence and Sexual Assault Survival Center

Susan Shaffer, Deputy Director, Mid-Atlantic Equity Center

Linda Shevitz, Educational Equity Specialist, Division of Instruction and Staff Development/ Equity Assurance and Compliance Branch, Maryland State Department of Education

Susan J. Smith, Project Director, Gender Healthy Schools, Education Development Center, Inc.

Ellen Wahl, Director of Youth, Family and Community Programs, American Museum of Natural History

Michael Wehmeyer, Ph.D., Co-Editor, Research Associate Professor, Director, Self-Determination Projects, Beach Center on Families and Disability, University of Kansas

Maryann Wickett, third- and fourth-grade teacher, Carrillo Elementary School, San Marcos Unified School District, San Marcos, CA

FOREWORD

Michelle Fine

I spent an afternoon, recently, at a private residential school for children who are blind or visually impaired. This facility serves youth, largely African American and Latino, from a range of social economic classes, largely poor and working class, boys and girls with "dual diagnoses." Teaching ranged from awesome to awful, from imaginative to insulting. Blind children get the short end of the pedagogical stick more often than not. Differences mattered and often became treated as deficits. Gender and race were adamantly not discussed. Those of us doing the research considered the institution to be *segregated* by disability status; educators within considered it *specialized*.

It has been well over a decade since Adrienne Asch and I co-edited *Women with Disabilities* (Temple University Press, 1988). In that time much more has come to be known, understood, litigated, and achieved in the field of disability rights, critical race theory, and feminism. Yet, as a field, special education remains plagued with ongoing questions about equity, access, "difference," and potential. Gender is but one axis of difference that deserves interrogation. An institute like the one I visited remains persistently at the bottom of class, race, and disability politics.

This book enters the question of differences between students receiving special education services not as deficit but as a question of power. Gender and disability are the analytic lense that pierce each chapter, but intersecting questions of race and class fill the pages. Over a quarter century since Public Law 94–142, the Education for All Handicapped Children Act, we still witness institutions like the one I have described, and we can witness segregation within presumably mainstreamed schools. We can look at the numbers of students receiving special education services and ask profound questions about labeling, discrimination, African American males being targeted, and girls across racial and ethnic groups perhaps being neglected. As the male numbers swell, we still don't know if we should worry more about the overidentified boys or the under-identified girls.

Race, class, and gender matter for students receiving special education services, as everywhere else. These three vectors of social experience affect one's health status, access to care, likelihood of being labeled, treatment within education, and the economic, social, and psychological aftermath of schooling. The chapters in this book powerfully address these intersections with a collective passion, a bright eye toward theory, and a strident focus on policy and practice.

Harilyn Rousso (as always) and Michael L. Wehmeyer have brought together a set of scholars, teachers, activists, and administrators who share a serious concern for the intellectual and social well-being of youth with disabilities. All of these authors write through gender, race, ethnicity, and class as seriously as they engage questions of the body, (dis)ability accommodations, and expectations. They force readers not to pigeonhole, to recognize there are many genders, disabilities, racial and ethnic groups, and yet to insist that readers recognize the deep and persistent impact of each on human relations, expectations, possibilities, and imposed limitations.

The entire volume and each chapter within amazingly accomplishes five ends, with grace and provocation. First, each chapter theoretically and empirically advances our understandings of how gender, disability, race, and class intersect, with attention to both males and females. There are no simple formulations, essentialisms or reductions to slogans. There is close analytic work at the intersections with some profound findings about double and triple jeopardizes. Second, the language of the book moves elegantly among scholarship, practice, social policy, on-the-ground activism, and often personal reflections. This blend of evidence and persuasion makes for a teary, painful, delicious read. Third, the chapters rise to responsible occasion in their offering of political horror stories. The authors are insistent that in the glee of legislation and policy reform, we not forget that in the day to day, children with disabilities continue to endure and have to learn to resist empty expectations, the spears of stereotypes, the terrors of the temporarily able bodied, as we continue to spew our anxieties into the bodies, minds, and spirits of these youth. Fourth, the text fundamentally challenges the growing movement toward biological determinism and sociobiology. These chapters shift the "common sense" and demonstrate that the limitations imposed on youths with disabilities are largely social and political, not so much in the body or mind as in the cruel refusal of the larger society to take them at their most serious, most capable, most loving, and most potential filled. And, fifth, not a chapter can be read without readers enjoying an enlivened sense of possibility for "what could be," an activist nudge toward "what must become." The reader will finish this book with a sense of outrage and an understanding of the political project that must be undertaken in order for children with disabilities to have access not only to a full education but also to social justice.

ACKNOWLEDGMENTS

This book is a product of a grant (PR/Award No. H029K60173) originally awarded to The Arc of the United States by the U.S. Department of Education Women's Educational Equity Act Program. We are particularly grateful to Judith Heumann, Assistant Secretary, Office of Special Education and Rehabilitative Services, U.S. Department of Education, who directed that the project continue to receive funding from OSEP after the WEEA program had been "zero-funded." Several program officers at OSEP were supportive and instrumental in bringing the project and this book to fruition, particularly Renee Bradley. We would note, however, that the opinions expressed in this text do not necessarily represent that of the federal government and endorsement of the federal government should not be assumed. The editors are grateful to the many highly qualified authors who contributed to this effort and to Michelle Fine for taking time from her busy schedule to contribute a foreword to the book. We are also grateful to Christine Sleeter, editor of the SUNY series on The Social Context of Education for including this text in that excellent series, and to SUNY Press for their support throughout the process. The editors would also like to acknowledge our deep gratitude to our colleague Michelle Schwartz. Michelle was coordinator for the project and was instrumental in pulling the text together and in manuscript preparation. Above all, however, Michelle was a talented colleague whose work informed us and kept us on track. On a personal note, Harilyn would like to thank Gene Brown for his loving support, wisdom about the ebbs and flows of the writing life, and willingness to read, edit and inspire; to her sister Sandy Izhakoff for always being there; to Linda Nathan Marks, Nancy Barnes, and Diane Goodstein for their guidance about the creative process; and to her sisters, friends, and colleagues in the disabled women's, disability rights and Disability Studies communities for their support, catalytic ideas and leadership. Michael Wehmeyer would like to acknowledge the support of his colleagues at both The Arc and the University of Kansas and to his family (Kathy, Geoff, and Graham) for once again tolerating late night edits and deadlines that impinged on weekends.

INTRODUCTION

Harilyn Rousso
and Michael L. Wehmeyer

INTERVIEWER (to a group of adolescent girls with disabilities): Is there anything you want the world to know about you?

ANNA: Most people just see my disability. They forget I'm also a girl. So tell them, will you?

MARIE: Yeah, that's it. Tell them we're girls, like all the other girls.

INTERVIEWER: Is that good, being a girl?

DEIRDRE: Mostly I like it. But sometimes it sucks. (Everyone laughs)

INTERVIEWER: Why?

DEIRDRE: Boys have it easier.

MARIE: Tell me about it.

INTERVIEWER: In school?

DEIRDRE: Not just school. At home, everywhere. It's not fair.

MARIE: Yeah, tell them we want, no, we demand equal rights. Or else.

—Rousso, 1993

WHY THIS BOOK?

This book exists for the simple reason that there is, to our knowledge, no similar resource available. Educators trained to teach students with disabilities rarely receive information about gender equity (or the lack thereof) in the educational process. As is amply illustrated in the chapters that follow, there is abundant evidence that being female is often a disadvantage at school, negatively impacting the quality of education

1

that a student receives. There is a growing body of evidence that being disabled and female is a double disadvantage, placing young women with disabilities in *double jeopardy* for poverty, unemployment, and a bleak future upon leaving school. Despite this potential dual risk, issues related to disability, gender, and education are rarely discussed. This text is an attempt to begin that dialogue. It is intended to summarize what we know about gender bias, both in general education and for students receiving special education services, to offer strategies to promote gender equity and to identify the gaps that exist in knowledge and practice.

In discussing issues of gender inequity and disability, we want to clearly articulate that we believe that any "disadvantaged status" associated with being female and/or disabled is rooted not in biology, but rather in society through pervasive biases, stereotypes, and discrimination. Stereotypes about women combine with stereotypes about people with disabilities so that disabled women are perceived less favorably than either nondisabled women or disabled men. They are often viewed as sick, childlike, dependent, asexual, or incompetent, and their talents and assets are overlooked. These complex stereotypes translate into patterns of double discrimination that pervade the home, school, workplace, and community. The presence of discriminatory patterns in schools is particularly disheartening because education offers such promise to provide all students with the tools to survive and thrive and to promote the values of equality and justice that are part of the foundation of this country.

Fundamentally, this book is intended to enable educators to fulfill the promise of a quality education for their students with disabilities who are female and, by extension, all students. It probably cannot be stated often enough that gender equitable educational practices are good educational practices from which all students benefit, male or female, disabled or nondisabled. The text enables teachers to identify gender bias and its interaction with disability bias in their schools, in their classrooms, and in themselves and to develop tools and strategies to develop gender equitable education, which is an essential ingredient of excellent education.

ACHIEVING EQUITY FOR ALL STUDENTS

The concept of gender equity undergirds all aspects of this text, so it is important to understand what we mean by this construct. According to gender equity experts David Sadker and Phyllis Lerner, "gender equity in education is teaching and treating students based on individual needs, abilities and characteristics rather than on gender-based assumptions and stereotypes" (personal communication, 8 September 1999).[1] Equity doesn't *necessarily* mean treating female and male students identically, but rather involves treating each student individually. Gender equity has more to do with fairness than with sameness, and in that respect differs from equality (Kreinberg, 1997). For example, some groups of girls and boys may come to school with a different range of experiences due to their dissimilar socialization. Despite considerable progress, parents and society continue to set different expectations for girls and boys and provide them with disparate opportunities. Girls may have had less access to computers or hands-on science at home, boys less exposure to literature, the arts, or writing opportunities. To work with boys and girls in identical ways to expand their computer or language arts skills may unwittingly privilege one gender over the other, whereas to choose varied methodologies reflecting differing, individualized needs will help insure that both groups leave school with similar levels of competence in each area. This is equitable education. However, to work with boys and girls differently based on stereotypical assumptions rather than first hand knowledge of their varied needs is inequitable.

Gender equity in education involves all aspects of learning, including access to opportunities, treatment, and educational outcomes.[2] In contrast, gender bias, or sexism, involves discriminating against or stereotyping a student based on gender so that a student's gender predicts course placement, teacher expectations and attitudes, or test scores. Gender bias does not affect all students in the same way. Other student characteristics such as disability status, race, ethnicity, or family income often influence the extent and nature of gender bias; such characteristics often evoke their own forms of bias, such as ableism, racism, and classism, that may interact with gender bias, producing unique compounding effects. As a result, understanding gender bias requires understanding the various ways it reveals itself among diverse students, and eliminating gender bias needs to be seen within the larger goal of eliminating all forms of bias in school.

There have been a number of broad trends in the gender equity field in the past twenty-five years that have relevance to this text and warrant a brief mention.[3] Among the most important is the recognition that "girls" or "females" do not form a homogeneous group, all of whom have the same needs. While this seems fairly self-evident, policy and practice with regard to equity have not always shown an appreciation of girls' heterogeneity across race, ethnicity, socioeconomic class, language, disability status, or other factors. There are considerable differences in gender equity issues both *within* each gender and *between* the two genders. For example, some educational needs of African American girls are likely to differ from those of Hispanic girls, and needs of both groups of girls living in urban settings may differ from those of their racial or ethnic counterparts in rural or suburban settings. This recognition of heterogeneity has highlighted the importance of considering the interactive effects of *multiple* forms of bias, as has already been suggested above, and the complex interaction of environment with educational need. It has encouraged the disaggregation of data in research, so progress for varied groups of girls can be assessed and compared, and the development of diverse program models to promote gender equity in education that reflect diverse needs. We note that despite this trend toward appreciating the heterogeneity of girls, girls with disabilities have not necessarily been recognized and embraced as a component of the rich tapestry of girls. While below we will suggest a possible reason for this exclusion, we note here one further intricacy that the dimension of disability adds. The needs of girls with different disabling conditions may differ. The instructional needs of girls with mental retardation, for example, may vary significantly from those of girls with a noncognitive disability. Thus, the interaction between gender and disability is not simply a two-factor, single-level issue. It involves multiple levels of each of those factors.

A second trend has been a shift in focus from the view of girls as "victims" of gender bias and other problems in adolescence to one of girls who are often resilient, creative, and strong in the face of sexism and other societal barriers; they are active agents rather than passive victims. This has followed a similar trend involving students with disabilities, which focuses on student ability and self-determination rather than the oft noted deficit model that has pervaded special education services. The implications of this shift in focus have led to the development of programs and services that empower girls and students with disabilities, that build on their strengths and resilience, rather than to "fix" them or "fit" them into the male or nondisabled norm.

Related to this is the notion that gender bias doesn't always or only put girls at a disadvantage, that sometimes it works against boys and in favor of girls, resulting in a wider recognition that gender bias hurts all students. Flood (chapter 9, this volume) addresses how schools fail boys as well. This broader focus on boys (and on the heterogeneity of girls) has emerged partly as a result of successful efforts to reduce the gender gap in areas such as math and science, where boys have historically been privileged (see Wahl, chapter 6, this volume). As the gender gap has been reduced, it has become clear that (1) there still are other types of previously unacknowledged gender gaps where girls are privileged, like the language arts, and (2) the gender gap has not necessarily been reduced for all girls, that for certain groups the gaps remain, and hence there is need to look beyond gender and consider intragender groups.

GIRLS WITH DISABILITIES

Lest we fall into the trap of using the term *girls with disabilities*, as if they were a homogenous population with identical needs, it is worth briefly discussing issues pertaining to disability and girls with disabilities. Numerically, this is a relatively large group. The Twentieth Annual Report to Congress on the implementation of IDEA (U.S. Department of Education, 1998) identified 5,235,952 students ages six to twenty-one who were provided special education services in the 1996–1997 school year. Half of these students were between the ages of six and eleven, 44 percent were ages twelve through seventeen, and between 4 and 9 percent were ages eighteen through twenty-one. IDEA defines twelve categories of disability, but more than 90 percent of school-age students were classified in one of four categories: learning disabilities (n = 51 percent), speech or language impairment (n = 20 percent), mental retardation (n = 11 percent), and emotional disturbance (n = 9 percent). The distribution of students by disability varies across age groups, with specific learning disability being the largest category across all the ages. The sheer number of students receiving special education services has been increasing in recent years, with the largest increases in other health impairments, partly due to increased identification of students with attention deficit disorders. The percentage of students with orthopedic or specific learning disabilities has also increased, while students classified as having mental retardation or deaf-blindness have decreased in numbers.

While this report does not disaggregate data by gender, a prevalent characteristic of special education services has been that boys outnumber girls almost two to one (see Wehmeyer and Schwartz, this volume, for detailed examination of disproportionate representation). This circumstance is a good illustration of the need to examine issues pertaining to gender equity through the lens of a wide array of factors, since there is also a disproportionate number of African American and Hispanic males receiving special education services. When examining issues of disproportionate access to services, there is a need to consider all components, be they gender, race, or language competency issues. In fact, however, the presence of a disability is often perceived as such a dominant factor in the lives of students with disabilities and their families that other characteristics that we know influence the lives of nondisabled students—such as gender, race, ethnicity, and class—often get overlooked. This tunnel vision has discouraged parents from advocating for issues beyond disability and special education teachers from recognizing the compounding issues that their students face. It has also prevented the gender-equity-in-education movement from recognizing that disabled students have a gender, and disabled girls are part of the community of girls, which may help explain why they have often been excluded from the heterogeneity-of-girls trend described above. The one exception to the tunnel vision has come from the civil rights community, which has spoken out against the previously mentioned disproportionate numbers of African American students, particularly boys, receiving special education services. Here there has been concern about racism and its interaction with sexism but only with regard to the identification of students receiving special education services. Perhaps ironically, the concern itself reflects a form of disability bias, in that the concern is that students receiving special education services inevitably receive an inferior education, so by placing boys of color in special education, their future is compromised. While misidentification is a real problem, it would be far less so if students labeled as disabled received a quality education similar to their nondisabled peers. But the inferior education model for disabled students is in itself rarely if ever challenged in this discussion.

Getting back to girls, we wish to highlight that based on the figures and percentages presented in the *Twentieth Annual Report to Congress* (U.S. Department of Education, 1998), more than 1.7 million students in the 1996–1997 school year were girls and young women with disabilities receiving special education services. In addition, we can assume that there were a considerable number of disabled girls whose need for special education services went unrecognized. By this writing, the numbers most likely have risen. Girls with disabilities are a large, diverse group; they need us to pay close attention to who they are, with their commonalities and their differences.

DOES IT MATTER?

There has been progress over the last two decades to include people with disabilities in the discussion about gender equity. We see this book as part of that progress and as a vehicle to continue the discussion. Is there a need for such an effort? The answer lies in understanding the damaging consequences of bias due to the double jeopardy of disability and gender. Those consequences are glimpsed in the outcomes experienced by women with disabilities, particularly vocational and employment outcomes. Doren and Benz (chapter 13, this volume) provide a comprehensive look at these findings, but even a summary of them is discouraging. Research indicates that males with disabilities are more likely to be employed, work full-time and remain so than are females. When employed, females with disabilities are more likely to be employed in unskilled jobs than males in spite of a lack of differences between sexes in I.Q., achievement, and basic job skills. Does gender equity matter for girls with disabilities? Unequivocally, yes.

This litany of less positive outcomes for girls with disabilities has been a fairly consistent way to address issues of gender equity, yet we prefer instead to focus our attention on the possibilities that exist. Although girls and young women with disabilities do face gender bias in combination with disability bias, and they pay a price for this in terms of what happens after school, they are not helpless victims in this process. That is the stereotype, not the reality. Girls with disabilities, by virtue of their disability experience, gender, and a host of other characteristics, bring a range of assets to the classroom that they can and do use to confront bias. And with these assets, girls with disabilities can and do enhance and inform not only their own learning but also the learning experiences of other students, both disabled and nondisabled, particularly if teachers know how to recognize and support their unique talents and sources of resilience. Many of the young women with disabilities we met have much to teach, for example, about how to engage in creative problem solving and accomplish tasks in nontraditional ways—an excellent tool for scientific inquiry—and how to detect and challenge prejudice of all types, an essential tool for citizenship in our society. We have learned from them. In part, we, as editors of this text, want to challenge the deficit model of students with disabilities and instead to emphasize the resilience and assets of girls (and boys) with disabilities. Marie, one of the young women in the dialogue that began our introduction, warns us that she demands equality or else. She and her friends are perfectly willing to take up the fight and take on the world. As educators, isn't it our job to join them?

OVERVIEW OF THE BOOK

The text is organized into four sections. The first section includes two chapters that introduce and provide an overview of issues pertaining to gender and disability at a societal level; they also foster an awareness of the complexity and diversity of young women and young men with disabilities. The second section, chapters 3 through 11, addresses gender equity issues affecting the education of all students; several of these chapters draw on the extensive body of research on gender bias in general education, offering implications for students with disabilities. The third section, chapters 12 through 16, focuses on the extant knowledge of gender issues specifically and, to some degree, uniquely related to the education of students with disabilities or to students receiving special education services and supports; this section also describes some innovative programs for girls and/or youth with disabilities that promote equity. The final section presents a chapter summarizing some of the key findings in the book and making recommendations for the future. We believe that the future of the nascent field of gender and disability is in the hands of our readers. We encourage you to infuse a combined gender and disability consciousness into your work and to consider undertaking new research and program and curriculum development to address gender bias for young people with disabilities and/or those receiving special education services so that none of our students are in double or even single jeopardy in school.

NOTES

1. Their more official definition that appeared in print is as follows: "Gender equity in school means that educational employees teach, help, and interact with students on the basis of their individual needs, abilities and characteristics rather than on gender-based assumptions and stereotypes." *Gender Equity Digest* (resources on gender equity in education), NEA, Human and Civil Rights, Washington, D.C., March 1998.

2. Another definition we might consider, although slightly more complex, is from WEEA Equity Resource Center web site (*www.edc.org/WomensEquity/genderdef.html*): "Gender equity is a set of actions, attitudes, and assumptions that provide opportunities and create expectations about individuals, regardless of gender. Gender equity is an equal chance for females and males at: 1) learning regardless of subject; 2) preparing for future education, jobs, and careers; 3) high expectations; 4) developing, achieving, and learning; 5) equitable treatment and outcomes in school and beyond."

3. A fuller discussion of trends in gender equity can be found in AAUW, 1998, *Gender gaps: Where schools still fail our children,* Washington, D.C.: Author; and L. Phillips, 1998, *The girls report: What we know and need to know about growing up female,* New York: National Council for Research on Women.

REFERENCES

Kreinberg, N. 1997. How much time do we have? In *Thoughts and Deeds: Equity in Mathematics and Science Education.* Edited by N. Kreinberg and E. Wahl. Washington, D.C.: American Association for the Advancement of Science, 11–16.

Rousso, H. 1993. *Conversations with girls with disabilities in New York City.* Transcripts. Unpublished paper.

U.S. Department of Education. 1998. *To assure the free appropriate public education of all children with disabilities. The Twentieth Annual Report to Congress on the implementation of IDEA.* Washington, D.C.: Author.

SECTION I

Gender and Disability

CHAPTER 1

Beyond Pedestals: The Lives of Girls and Women with Disabilities

Adrienne Asch, with Harilyn Rousso and Taran Jefferies

INTRODUCTION

This chapter is based on a previous chapter (Asch and Fine, 1988) that introduced a co-edited volume on women with disabilities (Fine and Asch, 1988). A decade later, many of the ideas in that essay still aid those thinking about questions of how biology and society interact in the lives of girls and women with disabilities. This chapter seeks to introduce the topic of being female and disabled to those who will work with young people in schools. Like families, schools convey cultural and societal norms that can influence how people live. Thus, how teachers and administrators relate to today's young people, and what they expect of today's students, ground self-perceptions and social interactions for tomorrow's citizens. It is crucial for educators to attend to the particular circumstances of their students who face not only the social disadvantages of gender but also the pervasive awkwardness and misunderstanding replete in the lives of people with disabilities.

"DISCOVERING" THE DISABLED WOMAN

Women with disabilities face more than double the discrimination of other girls and women in our society. Despite the prevalence of disability in this society, disabled persons tend to be invisible. While most people's lives will be touched by disability in some way, our society avoids the topic in much the same way it avoids encounters with disabled individuals. Indeed, public reluctance to deal with disability as a potential in one's life or the lives of loved ones is reflected in the lack of information about it. Despite the penchant for data collection, our society and its major institutions know little about the extent and experience of disability.

In 1995, it was estimated that nearly 54 million citizens of the United States had disabilities: 10 percent of the population age twenty-one and younger, slightly under 20 percent of all working age people, and over half of all people age sixty-five and older (McNeil, 1997). Of the 134 million women and girls in this country, it is estimated that over one-fifth (21.3 percent) have disabilities that affect their daily lives (Jans and Stoddard, 1999). How do being female and having a disability interact? How do women with disabilities view their experience? What can we learn about disability from literature, folklore, social science, law, and public policy? Does it matter at what age or stage in life disability occurs? How do race, social class, social circumstances, and sexual orientation influence the lives of women with disabilities? These are a few of the questions that spawned the last twenty years of research and writing discussed in the following pages and in this new book. Only in the last two decades has there been any effort to examine such questions, and much remains to be learned.

In 1981 Fine and Asch wrote the article "Disabled Women: Sexism without the Pedestal" (Fine and Asch, 1981). They reviewed what was known about the economic, social, and psychological circumstances of women with disabilities and suggested explanations for why these women found themselves significantly more disadvantaged than either nondisabled women or disabled men. Disabled women, they found, experience much the same oppression as nondisabled women, without receiving the ostensible rewards of the "pedestal" upon which some (white) women traditionally have been placed. The article concluded by proposing directions for research, policy, and politics.

The passage of nearly two decades has seen growth in the new genre of writing on and by disabled women, including edited compilations of personal narrative, sensitive autobiography, collections of research, and trenchant philosophical and political essays. Jo Campling (1981) brought to public discourse the private lives and stories of British women with disabilities, a book hailed here too, because it spoke for long-silent U.S. women. That same year Duffy (1981) offered a valuable discussion of sexuality as a key arena of both oppression and expression for women with disabilities. Subsequent work includes valuable personal accounts and interviews of women with disabilities from Canada (Matthews, 1983); the United States (Browne, Connors, and Stern, 1985; Willmuth and Holcomb, 1993); and throughout the globe (Driedger and Gray, 1992; Keith, 1996; Lonsdale, 1990; Morris, 1989; Stewart, Percival and Epperly, 1992). (See also Deborah Kent's reviews of several books on women with disabilities 1993; 1994; 1996; 1999.) Several women have written in depth about how disability has affected their lives (Grealy, 1994; Heppner, 1992; Kaysen, 1993; Klein, 1997; Mairs, 1996; Panzarino, 1994; Seinkowicz-Mercer and Kaplan, 1989; Tucker, 1995; Williams, 1992). In addition, there have been works of research and theory on several aspects of disabled women's lives (Deegan and Brooks, 1985; Fine and Asch, 1988; *Journal of Disability Policy Studies*, 1997); and a few feminist theorists with disabilities have offered explicitly feminist accounts of the meaning of disability for women and men (Hannaford, 1985; Morris, 1993; Wendell, 1996). The last several editions including the 1998 revision of the Boston Women's Health Book Collective classic on women's health attend sensitively and in detail to the concerns of girls and women with disabilities (Boston Women's Health Book Collective, 1998).

In addition to the growing body of literature, there has recently been an upsurge of events and conferences that involve or revolve around issues of interest to disabled girls and women, including the NGO Forum that preceded the Fourth World Conference on Women (Beijing, 1995); the International Leadership Forum for Women with Disabilities (Washington, D.C., 1997); regional conferences on women and employment sponsored by World Institute on Disability and Rehabilitation International (Berkeley, San Antonio, and Laughlin, 1999, 2000); the Centers for Disease Control's conference Promoting the Health and Wellness of Women with Disabilities (San Antonio, 1999); and Funding for all Women: Including Women and Girls with Disabilities (Oakland, 1999). This activity reveals that there is a need for action in addition to words and that people are becoming sensitive to the issues that specifically affect women and girls with disabilities.

Before examining the data available on girls and women with disabilities, one must note that there is still relatively little information. Previously, almost all research on disabled men and women seemed to assume the irrelevance of gender, race, ethnicity, sexual orientation, or social class. Having a disability presumably eclipsed these dimensions of social experience. Even sensitive students of disability (for example, Becker, 1980; Davis, 1961, 1963; Darling, 1979; Gliedman and Roth, 1980; Goffman, 1963; Higgins, 1980; Roskies, 1972; Wright, 1960, 1983) focused on disability as a unitary concept and took it to be not merely the "master" status but apparently the exclusive status for disabled people. Alongside the growth of studies about women with disabilities is continuing research on "disability" as a unitary concept. Valuable data on the "quality of life" of people who have spinal cord injuries and on adolescents who were disabled from birth indicate overall life satisfaction that surprises most nondisabled people, who continue to expect that a disability prevents a rewarding life. Nonetheless, if there are sex differences in attitudes of these respondents, we cannot learn this from the research (Eisenberg and Salz, 1991; Gerhart et al., 1994; Ray and West, 1984). Moreover, in the most recent national survey assessing life satisfaction of adults with disabilities eight years after the passage of the Americans with Disabilities Act, almost no attention is given to sex differences in social participation or life satisfaction (National Organization on Disability, 1998). Paralleling what Eisenstein (1983) described as the "false universalism" of feminist writing of the 1970s, the disability rights literature stresses commonalities among all disabled people rather than differences based on gender. More disability data are being disaggregated by factors including gender, race, and class. However, these considerations are not consistently applied and remain piecemeal and unintegrated in both research studies and practices.

The meaning of gender has been neglected by many rehabilitation and medical professionals, social scientists, and disability rights activists. When disability research and policy have attended to gender, they have usually focused on the concerns of males. For many years the thrust of rehabilitation and government study and policy was on the war-wounded or work-injured disabled person, who was, invariably, male. Having a disability was seen as synonymous with being dependent, childlike, and helpless—an image challenging all that is embodied in the ideal male: virility, autonomy, and independence. Yet this image replicated, if in caricature, all that is embodied in the ideal female: emotionality, passivity, and dependence (Broverman et al., 1972). Concerns with "emasculation" may promote efforts directed toward those at the locus of the masculinity/dependence contradiction, not toward those at the redundant intersection of femininity and dependence. Certainly, the social imperative seems to have been to study and rehabilitate the "wounded male" (Rose, 1984). While there are now more frequent references to disability as a characteristic among others to be considered, often this is included only in name. As has been the experience of other minorities, token quotes from disability scholars and activists and superficial treatment of disabled women's issues are not adequate substitutions for informed and interested discussion and study.

Women with disabilities traditionally have been ignored not only by those concerned about disability but also by those examining women's experiences. Even the feminist scholars to whom we owe great intellectual and political debts have perpetuated this neglect. The popular view of women with disabilities has been one mixed with repugnance. Perceiving disabled women as childlike, helpless, and victimized, nondisabled feminists have severed them from the sisterhood in an effort to advance more powerful, competent, and appealing female icons. As one feminist academic said to Michelle Fine, the nondisabled coeditor of the 1988 volume on women with disabilities: "Why study women with disabilities? They reinforce traditional stereotypes of women being dependent, passive, and needy."

Feminist anthologies, including key works that mindfully integrate racial and minority group concerns with gender analyses, have usually ignored women with disabilities (Cox, 1981; Eisenstein and Jardine, 1985; Freeman, 1984; Hansen and Philipson, 1990; Jordan, 1997; Jordan et al., 1991; Sargent, 1981; Snitow, Stansell, and Thompson, 1983). In 1983, Eisenstein chronicled major feminist thought since 1970, noting how feminist writings and politics sought to learn from and unite women of the working and middle classes, married women and single women, mothers and nonmothers, lesbians and heterosexual women, women of color and white women, women of all ages. Yet, her otherwise excellent book completely omits comment on the absence of women with disabilities from women's groups and women's writing. Her call for renewed attention to differences among women nowhere recognizes disabled women as a group whose voice needs to be heard. Such omissions by feminists through the 1980s and 1990s are especially distressing when one recalls that disabled women have appeared at political gatherings since the 1977 Houston Conference on Women and were present by the hundreds at the 1995 Fourth World Conference on Women in Beijing. Moreover, despite their occasional presence in anthologies, scholarly publications, and the feminist popular press since the 1980s, most nondisabled women scholars have joined men in relegating disabled women to a realm beneath their intellectual and political ken. With the advent of "political correctness" in the early 1990s, one might be tempted to believe that disability would come out of the closet of invisibility. However, even the PC culture of the 1990s has ignored women with disabilities including them—if at all—in a kind of laundry list of the oppressed and victimized. Nondisabled academics and activists who have fought hard for women's right to autonomy may fear disability in parents, friends, children, or themselves. Accepting the widespread, if inaccurate, belief that disability inevitably threatens independence, women know that it is they, as women, who will be called upon to care for the disabled individual. As Miller (1976, 1987) noted, it is women who do the culture's nurturing work. Perhaps the conviction

that disabled people are burdensome and that women will be so bur-
dened accounts for feminist resistance to involvement in the disability
rights movement.

DISABLED WOMEN: FACT AND SOCIAL CONSTRUCT

Over the past thirty-five years, feminist researchers have unhooked
notions of gender from those of sex. The socially acquired aspects of the
female—presumably the loving, caretaking, and cooperative work—
have been separated from the biological aspects. The "maternal
instinct," along with women's ostensible inability to compete effectively
or to be sexually assertive, has been demystified and tracked to socially
constructed origins (Chodorow, 1978; Ruddick, 1980).

Likewise, in the past thirty years, both the study and the politics of
disability have been transformed. Activists and scholars have insisted
that the "impairment" (the biological condition) and the "disability"
(the functional limitation) be conceptually disentangled from the handicap (the social ramifications) of the condition. The nine-year-old girl
with fused or missing fingers has a biological impairment; her difficulty
in grasping a pen or in turning the pages of a book is a functional limitation or disability; yet with the proper alternatives, such as using her
other hand or using an adapted computer and page-turner, she has no
handicap to her educational progress.

Using arguments of the 1960s civil rights and women's movements,
disability activists and scholars sought to demonstrate that anatomy
need not be destiny. Obstacles to education, community and political
participation, independent living, employment, and personal relationships derived not from the incapacities, for example, of individuals in
wheelchairs to walk stairs but in the existence of the stairs themselves.
If people with mobility impairments could not enter buildings without
ramps or ride inaccessible buses, the fault was in the structures and the
transportation system, not their bodies. If people who wished to work
could not because of medical standards that barred anyone with a history of heart disease, epilepsy, or obesity, or with diabetes or visual or
hearing impairments, the problem might be one of arbitrary medical
standards and not of a person's inherent incapacity to perform specific
job tasks. If men and women with disabilities suffered social isolation or
discovered that former friends no longer had time for them, perhaps the
problem was not in their psychology but in others' attitudes toward disability and expectations of friendship.

During the 1970s grassroots groups of disabled people organized
along single- and cross-disability lines, formed statewide and national

membership organizations and coalitions, founded legal advocacy centers, and published newsletters. They worked along with parents of disabled children and with nondisabled advocates to obtain laws guaranteeing rights of access to education, employment, government services, and community life. By the end of the decade, although disabled people still had far fewer civil rights than those available to people fighting race or sex discrimination, their situation had begun to improve. On 26 July 1990, another ten years of activism culminated in the signing into law of the Americans with Disabilities Act, legislation hailed by people with disabilities as their civil rights law. Congressional recognition of disabled people as constituting a discriminated-against minority inspires its provisions forbidding discrimination in employment and requiring that all government agencies, nonprofit organizations, and private businesses modify their physical structures and ways of providing services to be usable to those with disabilities. Much the same spirit of enabling inclusion in all of society by changing institutions to make participation feasible permeates the Individuals with Disabilities Education Act (IDEA) that is changing where and how disabled students learn. (For discussions of civil rights legislation, see Bowe, 1980, Funk, 1987; West, 1996; for disabled people as a minority group, see Funk, 1987, Hahn, 1987; and for the disability rights and independent living movements, see Russel, 1998; Scotch, 1984; Shapiro, 1994).

Feminist scholars and disability activists, then, have demonstrated that the experiences of being female or of having a disability are socially constructed; that the biological cannot be understood outside of those contexts and relationships that shape and give meaning to femaleness and to disability. In what follows, we use the tools of feminist and disability scholarship and politics to explore the situation of disabled women. Finding, as we did earlier, that disabled women still are more disadvantaged than either nondisabled women or disabled men, we discuss the relative impacts of sexism and of disability discrimination and examine their interaction.

It is ironic to note that the very category that integrates this text, "disabled girls and women," exists wholly as a social construct. Why should a limb-deficient girl, a teenager with Down syndrome, a girl with cystic fibrosis, or her classmate who is blind have anything in common with each other or with a woman with breast cancer or another woman who is recovering from a stroke? What they share is similar treatment by a sexist and disability-phobic society, one which creates categories of "normal" and "other" and makes hierarchies based on categories of difference (Minow, 1990; Wendell, 1996). It is their categorization as other and the resulting invidious treatment they receive that makes it likely that any or all will be thrown together in school, in the unemployment line, in segregated recreation programs, and in legislation.

The Americans with Disabilities Act defines disability as "a physical or mental impairment that substantially limits one or more of the major life activities," a record of such impairment, or being regarded as having such impairment (Americans with Disabilities Act, 1990, sec. 3). As defined in the Individuals with Disabilities Education Act (IDEA) Amendments of 1997, a child with a disability is a child with mental retardation, hearing impairments (including deafness), speech or language impairments, visual impairment (including blindness), serious emotional disturbance (hereinafter referred to as "emotional disturbance"), orthopedic impairments, autism, traumatic brain injury, other health impairments, or specific learning disabilities, who, by reason thereof, needs special education and related services (IDEA, 1997).

These definitions are broad, encompassing conditions not commonly thought of as disabilities but rather as chronic illnesses, health problems, or the like. Note that neither law defines "disability" in strictly biological terms. The ADA speaks of impairments that limit the performance of a major life activity or are regarded by others as doing so. The IDEA describes a child with a disability as one whose condition requires the receipt of special education services; thus, different children with the same diagnoses—cerebral palsy or diabetes—might be perceived by one teacher as needing such services and by another as in no need of any special services. Disabilities both readily apparent and invisible can interfere with daily activities: mobility, for example, can be affected not only by polio or amputation but also by arthritis, a heart condition, or respiratory or back problems. Reading print may be difficult because of vision impairment or some types of learning disabilities. People with histories of institutionalization for mental illness or mental retardation may in fact not be hindered in any life task but may carry records that haunt them and impede their access to education and employment. People with cancer in remission, epilepsy, cosmetic disfigurements, or obesity may find themselves regarded as impaired when they are able to perform in any social role. Thus, the social construction of disability, like that of gender, underscores that it is the attitudes and institutions of the nondisabled, even more than the biological characteristics of the disabled, that turn characteristics into handicaps.

The following data must be preceded by an acknowledgment that throughout, biology is confounded by the social constructions of disability, gender, and their interaction. If twice as many boys as girls are classified in need of and are enrolled in special-education services (Gillespie and Fink, 1974; Hobbs, 1975; Jans and Stoddard, 1999), the causes cannot be attributed solely to more frequent incidence of biological limitation in boys. Similarly, although it may appear straightforward to determine the numbers of working-age women and men with disabilities, the difficulties in obtaining reliable data are manifold.

Obtaining sensitive, accurate data on persons with disabilities requires asking questions that do not confound health status with social role performance. Up until 1990, the U.S. Census Bureau solely assessed disability in the following way: "Does this person have a physical, mental, or other health condition which has lasted for six or more months and which (1) limits the kind or amount of work this person can do at a job? (2) prevents this person from working at a job?" (Haber and McNeil, 1983, p. 6). Not only does such questioning fail to pick up those who do not perceive themselves to be limited in work because of a health condition, but it fails to obtain any information about people with health impairments who, for whatever reason, do not choose to work. The 1990 census included an additional question to try to compensate for the individuals the previous question missed. Respondents were asked, "Because of a health condition that has lasted for six or more months, does this person have any difficulty (a) going outside the home alone, for example, to shop or visit a doctor's office? (b) taking care of his or her own personal needs, such as bathing, dressing, or getting around inside the home?" This question more directly addresses those who choose not to work; however, it also bases disability in a frame of dependency and inability. The more recent census question still fails to disentangle the biological impairment and functional disability from the social handicap. The inability to go outside the home alone might stem from the lack of a wheelchair for someone with multiple sclerosis or arthritis, or it might arise because someone with deteriorating vision has not been taught how to use a cane or guide dog. It is important to ask the right questions to get accurate data. The Health Interview Survey, another often-used source of disability data, asks about "usual activities" in the past twelve months. As Haber and McNeil (1983) point out, "The 'usual activity' screen reduces disability reporting for women whose 'usual activity' was keeping house, but should not affect reporting by men" (p. 3). Do women tend not to report themselves as disabled if they can perform what they consider their primary social roles of homemaker and caretaker? Do women overreport because traditionally they are more willing than men to admit health problems and are more likely to consult health professionals? Notwithstanding these serious qualifications, there is value in outlining the situation of today's disabled female.

The Disabled Girl in Family and School

Growing up in families where they are usually the only one with a disability, disabled girls stand out from peers and even intimates. In that disabled youngsters are of all races, cultures, and economic strata, they might be expected to feel connected to others of their class and race rather than to disabled people of another class or race. Yet they may be barred from the intimacy, security, and place that define community. Within what they consider to be "their own group," they may feel ostracized and may turn to others with disabilities as their only source of acceptance, affirmation, companionship, and strength (Johnson, 1987). Disabled boys and young men may appreciate such contact as well, but we suspect that socialization differs somewhat for disabled boys and girls. A study conducted by SRI International finds that while in high school disabled girls are less likely to participate in social activities or employment and are more socially isolated upon leaving school (Wagner, 1992). Accounts of the lives of disabled women and men reveal that boys are more often encouraged to meet the world, whereas girls are more often kept from it (Asch and Sacks, 1983; Brightman, 1984; Hahn, 1983b; Heinrich and Kriegel, 1961; Roth, 1981).

Reactions of the disabled women interviewed by Asch and Fine (1988) confirm this. Maria, age fifteen, testifies: "My brother has the same hearing problem as I do. Growing up, he was encouraged in school, sports, and to learn to work. I was protected and kept at home." We know less than we should about the familial, educational, and social experiences of girls and young women with disabilities. Are Maria's parents typical in sheltering their disabled daughter? Certainly disability will not have the same meaning for all parents, and thus will differ for their daughters. Class, race, ethnicity, values, and the medical professionals with whom they interact influence parental response to the disabled girl, influencing her options.

Social class can alleviate or exacerbate the impact of a disability, just as class and race influence access to decent housing, schooling, cultural activities, and recreational opportunities for nondisabled youth. For the educated and economically comfortable parent willing to assist a disabled youngster, these resources may reduce what could otherwise be serious deprivations. Yet Darling's (1979) literature review of the impact of disabled children on family life, as well as interviews conducted by Rapp (1987), caution against assuming that the disabled child born to middle-class parents will have an easier time in life. Cultures and classes that place high value on autonomy, intellect, or appearance may thwart their disabled child or reject the child altogether. Rapp corroborates the finding of Darling's earlier review, that middle-class and educated parents are more likely to reject cognitive or intellectual disabilities in their children, whereas working-class people and poor people may be more hostile to one whose physical condition may render the child vulnerable.

Such findings do not differentiate parental response based on the child's gender. Harris and Wideman (1988) wonder whether a girl's early diagnosis of disability prevents her mother from connecting with her and communicating the continuity of identity often observed between mothers and daughters. If these authors are correct, the psychological development of girls with disabilities may differ markedly from nondisabled girls and the formulations of Chodorow (1978) and Miller (1976, 1987) that have influenced current theory and research about the relationality of "women" may need to be refined to understand the experiences and relationships of girls and women whose disabilities occur early in life. Future research on disabled children and their families needs to examine what it means for a mother or father, rich or poor, to have a son or daughter with a disability.

More than two decades after the passage of the Education for All Handicapped Children Act, now IDEA, mandated access to a free, appropriate public education in the most least restrictive setting, a significant number of disabled students still spend the majority of their school day in special classes, outside integrated general education classes (U.S. Department of Education 1998). Disabled young people still do not benefit from equal opportunities in school (U.S. Department of Education, 1987), but what about the role of gender? This volume describes in depth what is known about harmful effects of gender bias on disabled girls (and boys), so we will not elaborate here; but we do stress the need for considerably more research.

Disabled Women of Working Age

Because the government's efforts in behalf of disabled people historically have been aimed at economic productivity and self-support, more is known about disabled women of working age, and better comparisons can be made with both nondisabled women and disabled men. One must be wary of comparisons between women with and without disabilities, however, because age is a confounding variable. For both sexes, disability increases dramatically with age. Work disability has been reported fairly equally by males at 10.2 percent and 9.9 percent of females. The distribution of work disability is not as evenly reported among different races and ethnicities: whites report 9.4 percent; blacks report 15.4 percent; Hispanics report 9.6 percent; and all other races report 8.5 percent (LaPlante et al., 1996). Disabled men are more likely than disabled women to participate in the labor force, as is true with both men and women without disabilities. Among women with work disabilities, there was only a 28.5 percent participation rate in 1998; for men with work disabilities, the participation rate was higher at 32.3

percent. For women and men without work disabilities, the labor force participation rates were considerably higher: 75.8 percent and 89.1 percent respectively (Jans and Stoddard, 1999). Across groups, men are more likely than women to be employed or to own a business. Disability compounds this factor, and as a result disabled women are less likely to be employed than disabled men and both men and women without disabilities.

Among those who are employed, disabled women tend to be tracked in lower wage positions. From 1994 through 1995, the median monthly earnings for all women were less than the median monthly earnings for all men. Where nondisabled men earned 49 percent more than nondisabled women, disabled men earned an even greater percentage (55 percent) of disabled women's median monthly income. Severely disabled women earned the least of these groups, with an average median monthly income of only $1000, less than half of that of a nondisabled man, who averaged $2190 (Jans and Stoddard, 1999). To understand this significant gap between women with disabilities and men without, first remember that more than half of all women with disabilities who are working are employed less than full time; whereas nondisabled men tend to work full time, and the median monthly earnings reflect their longer working hours (U.S. Census Bureau, 1999). This is despite the findings of a recent survey of disabled Americans, which showed that of the two-thirds of disabled people between the ages of sixteen and sixty-four who are out of work, more than three-quarters would prefer to be employed (LaPlante et al., 1996). Thus, we must conclude that relatively few disabled men or women perceive their disabilities as precluding economically productive activity.

Through the 1980s, it was clear that disabled men and women were poorer than those without disabilities. Disabled women were at the bottom of the ladder, with black disabled women having less income than any other race/gender/disability category. For example, using median income figures for black and white males and females with and without work disabilities, the median income for black disabled females in 1984 was twenty-two cents to the white nondisabled male dollar (Bowe, 1984).

While identical updated statistics have proven unobtainable in our searches, there are indications that although this picture has improved somewhat, it remains a reality—one's race, gender, and disability factor into one's earnings. Both men and women with work disabilities are more likely to live in poverty than both women and men without work disabilities (Jans and Stoddard, 1999). Women with work disabilities more often live in poverty than men with work disabilities, and women with severe disabilities that keep them from working have a poverty rate of over 40 percent (Jans and Stoddard, 1999). An overwhelming majority (72.9 percent) of disabled single mothers with children under the age of six are found among those in poverty (LaPlante et al., 1996). We have noted above that women of different races report disability at different rates (LaPlante et al., 1996); therefore, we can extrapolate that races and ethnicities that report higher rates of disability, such as black women, may be disproportionately affected. Why this relationship—between gender, disability and poverty—exists must be the focus of further investigation.

High rates of unemployment for women with disabilities contribute to the large numbers in poverty. This year's Current Population Survey data reveal that even for women with disabilities between ages sixteen and thirty-four, only one-third have jobs, and not even half (42.7 percent) of women with disabilities who have a college or graduate education are employed; almost twice as many (82.5 percent) similarly educated nondisabled women have jobs (U.S. Census Bureau, 1999). Disabled women are slightly less likely than disabled men to have a college education. College-educated men with work disabilities are also more successful than disabled women in obtaining employment. Why are women less likely than men to obtain a college education if a disability is involved for both, when for the general population, more college students are female than male? And even more important, why are college-educated women with disabilities out of the workforce, whereas disabled men with similar educational attainment are employed? Is the explanation gender and disability discrimination, and if so, what accounts for employer attitudes? Or is the unemployed college graduate a woman who acquired a disability in midlife and decided that she preferred to leave the workforce rather than juggle the demands of paid work, domestic work, childcare, and new disability? Perhaps disability in midlife for a college-educated male is less overwhelming if his wife still handles "the second shift" in the home (Hochschild, 1997). Disabled women's generally low levels of education cannot be ascribed to disability factors, whether inherent in biology or discrimination. Most women become disabled after education and training have been completed. In fact, it is likely that the women's predisability work and living arrangements contribute to disability. Unskilled manual labor, substandard living conditions, poor nutrition, and inadequate medical care all take a toll.

Unfortunately, once she has a disability, a woman is likely to discover that such factors as age, gender, predisability education, occupation, and income work to deny her the help she needs. Established to reduce the economic burdens of disabled people, the rehabilitation system has historically aided society's haves in disproportionate numbers: those who are male, under forty-five, white, better-educated, middle class, articulate, aggressive, "motivated" (Kirchner, 1987; Stone, 1986). In the 1980s, rehabilitated women's cases were substantially more likely to be closed in a nonwage-earning capacity (Vash, 1982). Women were more likely to be denied such services entirely (Nagi, 1969); they were less likely to be referred to vocational training or on-the-job training, more likely to be trained as homemakers, and more likely to be channeled into traditionally female occupations than were men with equivalent skills and aptitudes (Packer, 1983). Perhaps in light of these observations, the rehabilitation system has better served women in recent years, although it is not clear if they are yet being served equally. In the Vocational Rehabilitation Program in 1996, disabled women made up less than half (45.1 percent) of the cases closed with an employment outcome (Jans and Stoddard, 1999). While women with disabilities have moved into more managerial and professional positions in the past decade and a half, compared to men with disabilities they are underrepresented as computer equipment operators and computer programmers (Jans and Stoddard, 1999). This may indicate that women with disabilities are not being instructed in sufficiently equal numbers to compete for today's more cutting-edge, high-tech professions. More research needs to be conducted to determine the interaction of gender and the rehabilitation system.

Given that disabled women are more likely than disabled men to live in poverty and rely on government income support, the allocation of public resources, while providing little relief for either disabled men or women, does exacerbate gender disparities; the amount of a Social Security recipient's benefits under the Disability Insurance Program is tied to predisability earnings. In 1997, more men than women received Social Security monies through the Old Age, Survivors, and Disability Insurance Program. Also, men receive more money on average than women, and this benefits gap has been widening since 1970 (Jans and Stoddard, 1999).

In this context of extreme educational and economic disadvantage, worsened for women of color, women with disabilities not only are systematically cut off from productive work but also are denied access to the traditional (if now disputed) responsibilities of women: to nurture and reproduce. In what follows, we offer some hypotheses about the disabled woman's exclusion from either the productive role of paid work or the nurturant, reproductive role. To do so, we discuss the meanings of attractiveness and sexuality, nurturance, and reproduction as they affect women in the spheres of work and love.

NURTURANCE, SEXUALITY, AND REPRODUCTION:
THE EXEMPT WOMAN

Disabled Women as Partners

The income-earning opportunities of women with disabilities are constrained. So, too, are their opportunities to be nurtured and to nurture, to be lovers and be loved, to be mothers if they desire. Women with disabilities are less likely than nondisabled women or disabled men to fulfill roles customarily reserved for their respective sexes. Exempted from the "male" productive role and the "female" nurturing one, having the glory of neither, disabled women are arguably doubly oppressed—or, perhaps, "freer" to be nontraditional. Should they pursue what has been thought nontraditional, however, the decision to work, to be a single mother, to be involved in a lesbian relationship, or to enter politics may be regarded as a default rather than a preference. We recognize that many women have no desire to marry, mother, or be sexual with men, and that marriage and childbearing statistics must not be used to measure "social success." Nonetheless, while many nondisabled and disabled women are choosing nontraditional lifestyles, some disabled women go other routes not by choice alone.

Franklin (1977) reported that disabled women were less likely than nondisabled women to be married, more likely to marry later, and more likely to be divorced. Bowe (1984) and Hanna and Rogovsky (1986) report similar findings from the Current Population Survey's data of the early 1980s. Whereas 60 percent of men with disabilities and women without them are married, only 49 percent of disabled women are married. The picture has not changed all that much in the 1990s for women with disabilities; 50 percent of women with activity limitations are married, as compared to the marriage rates for other groups—64 percent of women with no activity limitations, 68 percent of men with activity limitations, and 69 percent of men with no activity limitations (Jans and Stoddard, 1999). As with employment and earnings data, actual disparities between disabled and nondisabled women may be greater when the age factor previously cited is taken into account. Nearly 60 percent of nondisabled women are under forty-five years of age, with half under age twenty-two. It can be expected that many of these nondisabled younger women who show up in census data as unmarried will marry. These data alone do not reveal how much the presence of a woman's disability affects her choices, chances, or inclinations to marry or be involved in a loving relationship with a woman or a man. That more disabled women are unmarried than nondisabled women might be explained by demographic differences: being older they have had more time for their marriages to sour. Many are widowed, as are women of comparable age without disabilities.

When disabled women are compared with nondisabled women and disabled men on rates of divorce and separation, differences again surface between the situation of disabled women and either other group. Hanna and Rogovsky (1993) analyzed 1985 Current Population Survey data on marital status, dividing a subsample of ever-married but not widowed men and women into three categories: nondisabled, mildly disabled, and severely disabled. They found that more women than men in all categories were divorced, but significant differences emerged between "severely disabled women" and other groups. Only 14 percent of men termed "severely disabled" were divorced, but 26 percent of severely disabled women were. While men's rates of separation were 3 percent, 5 percent, and 7 percent for each category of disability status, women's rates of separation were 4 percent, 6 percent, and 11 percent. Thirty-seven percent of "severely disabled" women, as contrasted with 22 percent of severely disabled men who were once married, are no longer married, for reasons other than death of a spouse. These differences have been observed in a comparison of the marital status of women and men with no, some, or severe activity limitations. It was found that women with severe activity limitations had the highest rate of divorce, followed by women with less limitation, women with no activity limitation, and all men (Jans and Stoddard, 1999).

Anecdote, interview, and autobiography corroborate the census data and the stereotype of the disabled woman as alone. For both men and women whose disabilities occur before marriage, literature reveals considerable apprehension about finding a mate. Hahn (1983b) and Asch and Sacks (1983) reviewed published autobiographies and noted how little could be found about intimate relationships; of those who did live with adult partners, nearly all were men. In personal accounts and interviews reported in Bowe (1981), Brightman (1984), Duffy (1981), Heinrich and Kriegel (1961), Matthews (1983), and Roth (1981), we discover how difficult it is for disabled men or women to find a partner relationship. Nonetheless, many more men than women eventually established satisfying relationships. Matthews (1983) found that only five of the forty-five women she interviewed were married, and half reported no sexual relationship since becoming disabled. Only half of the seventy-five orthopedically disabled women who responded to Duffy's (1981) questionnaire had ever been married. Bonwich (1985) recounts that twenty-nine of the thirty-six rural, spinal-cord-injured women she interviewed had been romantically involved or married prior to their becoming disabled; fifteen saw these relationships end after onset of disability.

A growing body of literature has emerged since these studies were conducted; the 1990s have seen more books and articles dealing with the topic of disability and both reproductive and nonreproductive sexuality. In 1997, Mobility International USA produced a manual on disabled women and global development that included extensive resource sections on parenting, reproductive rights, and sexuality. However, this increase in literature is perhaps unduly optimistic; while a step in the right direction, this literature is often focused on barriers to, and not examples of, successful, mutual, happy relationships. Also, most of the sources focus on parenting and the right to reproduce, which may be easier topics to address since there is no equivalent "right to a long, lasting, loving relationship." One notable exception is *The Sexual Politics of Disability*, described by its authors as "the first book to look at the sexual politics of disability from a disability rights perspective. We attempt to explore the emotional and sexual experiences of disabled people in a variety of key areas, relying predominantly on the verbatim accounts of disabled people themselves" (Shakespeare, Gillespie-Sells, and Davies, 1996, p. 1).

The only group of disabled adults in which women are more likely than men to be married is women with mental retardation. Safilios-Rothschild (1977) suggested that the "retarded" wife may fit all too well the criteria of the "good wife": one who is docile, passive, loyal, and dependent, not likely to show her husband up. How can we explain these data? If disability is thought to reinforce the customary female characteristics of passivity, compliance, and good nature, why should women with disabilities frequently be without partners?

The literature on the views of the nondisabled toward persons with disabilities reveals that the attitudes of nondisabled women and men are overwhelmingly negative. Men's attitudes, however, are the more extreme (Siller et al., 1976). These researchers found that disabled children and adults were more likely to be rejected as family members than as acquaintances or workmates by both men and women, but rates of rejection were greater for nondisabled men. Hanna and Rogovsky (1993) suggest that a disabled woman may be more negatively viewed by both women and men than a disabled man. Surveying nondisabled college students, they found that images of "disabled woman," "disabled man," and "woman" differed markedly. When asked how women and men using wheelchairs became disabled, nondisabled students attributed male disability to external situations such as war, work injury, or accident and female disability to internal causes, such as disease. The authors suggest that attributing disability to disease may foster more negative attitudes because disease stimulates fears of contagion or of the person's inherent moral badness. Thus, the disabled woman may be viewed as more dangerous than a similarly disabled male, more morally suspect, or more deserving of her fate. When these same students were asked to draw associations for "woman," and "disabled woman," the associations cited for the two could not have been more different. "Woman" drew associations of worker (intelligent, leader, career); of sexuality (soft, lovable, orgasm); of mother or wife (wife, mother, mom, married, childbearer). When asked to associate to "disabled woman," students described her in terms of dependence and impairment (crippled, almost lifeless); of age (gray, old, white hair); of despair (someone to feel sorry for, pity, sorry, lonely, ugly). She was virtually never depicted as wife, mother, or worker by the more than one hundred students.

Attractiveness and Nurturance

To understand these phenomena and their consequences for disabled women, we examine the implications of cultural views of attractiveness and of nurturance. First, it is important to note that a pervasive "attractiveness stereotype" enables people to believe that those who are attractive are also "more sensitive, kind, interesting, strong, poised, modest, sociable, outgoing, and exciting, sexually warm and responsive," and will "hold better jobs, have more successful marriages, and happier and more fulfilling lives" (Berscheid and Walster, 1972, pp. 46, 74). In short, attractiveness is linked to virtue, to all that is desired, especially by men of women. In the cultural imagination, beauty is linked to goodness and nurturance, the traits most sought after in women both as lovers and as workers. Ample evidence substantiates that perceptions of women's attractiveness influence women's educational and work opportunities (Unger, 1985; Unger, Hilderbrand, and Mador, 1982). Unfortunately for the disabled woman, only a few attributes count toward attractiveness in the United States, and a woman's bodily integrity is one such requirement (Hahn, 1983a; Lakoff and Scherr, 1984). Furthermore, a woman's beauty is seen as a reflection of a male partner's social status. As Lakoff and Scherr (1984) note, "The message we are given daily by the myriad images of beauty is that women must look a certain way to be loved and admired, to be worth anything" (p. 114).

In a discussion of male notions of attractiveness, these authors note that physical grace and ease are also important in the assessment of what is desirable in women. The woman with a disability, whether apparent or invisible, may display less than the norm or the fantasied ideal of bodily integrity, grace, and ease. The devices she values for enhancing free movement and communication (braces, crutches, hearing aids, or canes) may repel men seeking the fantasied flawlessness. Given that disabled women are found unattractive by college students as well as by clinicians (Hanna and Rogovsky, 1993; Unger 1985; Unger, Hilderbrand, and Mardor, 1982), and given that men value physical attractiveness in a partner significantly more than women do, it is little wonder that heterosexual women with disabilities are more likely than disabled men to be alone.

The argument of women's attractiveness as a display of male status is not sufficient, however, to explain the underinvolvement of disabled women in intimate relationships with men (and women). To pursue the heterosexual question first, it may be that men's unacknowledged needs and dependencies—satisfied often in relationships with women—reduce men's desire to become connected in work or in love with disabled women. Drawing on the writing of Miller (1976, 1987), we contend that if a woman's role in heterosexual relationships has been to accommodate a man emotionally while not exposing his vulnerabilities, the disabled woman may be thought unfit. If men desired only the passive, doll-like female of the stereotype, disabled women might do, but the doll must be functional as well as decorative. Feminist theorists such as Hartmann (1981) and Eisenstein (1984) have argued that the smooth functioning of advanced capitalism requires the illusion, if not reality, of a heterosexual nuclear home warmed and nurtured by an all-giving and all-comforting woman.

Brownmiller (1984) characterizes nurturance when applied to women as "warmth, tenderness, compassion, sustained emotional involvement in the welfare of others, and a weak or nonexistent competitive drive. Nurturant labor includes child care, spouse care, cooking and feeding, soothing and patching, straightening out disorder and cleaning up dirt, little considerations like sewing a button on a grown man's raincoat, major considerations like nursing relationships and mending rifts, putting the demands of family and others before one's own, and dropping one's work to minister to the sick, the troubled, and the lonely in their time of need" (pp. 221–22). Men may assume incorrectly that a disabled woman could not contribute either physical or emotional housekeeping to a spouse and children. If a woman cannot sew on a button because she cannot use her hands, she may be thought unfit to help with the mending of emotional fences as well.

Disabled persons (men and women) often elicit in nondisabled others powerful existential anxieties about their own helplessness, needs, and dependencies (Hahn, 1983a). For a man who may have such emotional residues well buried, their activation in the presence of a disabled woman may stimulate reflexively his rejection of her. Even if a man believed that a particular disabled woman could manage to run her own life and master the details of helping him with his, how could he accept help from an unwhole, "sick" woman? How can she minister to his needs when a disabled woman epitomizes all that is needy herself? Might it be that taking help from such a presumably helpless woman arouses guilt or shame in any man who might consider it? If men can accept emotional sustenance only from women who can provide the maximum in physical caretaking, the woman with limitations may be viewed as inadequate to give the warmth, companionship, and shelter men traditionally expect from their mates. If men fear both their own and another's dependency and intimacy to the extent that Chodorow (1978) has argued, if disabled persons awaken such feelings, and if men desire women who can satiate their own emotional needs without either publicly acknowledging them or requiring reciprocity, disabled women are likely to be rejected forcefully as lovers/partners.

The view of the disabled woman as limited emotionally because she may be limited physically may account for the preference of disabled men for nondisabled partners. In their review of the autobiographies of blind women and men, Asch and Sacks (1983) discovered that men sought sighted wives to complement them; to confer upon them a status of normal, successful, integrated; and to ensure their smooth navigation literally and figuratively through the world. In a study of the coping strategies of disabled scientists, a group that was overwhelmingly male, many reported that one major strategy was acquisition of a wife (Redden, personal communication, 1980). In a *New York Times* article enshrining negative stereotypes about nondisabled women who marry disabled men and the men they marry, Rose (1984) postulated that the disabled man is the perfect outlet for nurturance and competence for nondisabled women who could not fulfill themselves or demonstrate their full capacity in a relationship with a truly competent male. Here, disabled men are perceived as lacking all capacities for self-direction merely because they cannot walk or see; nondisabled women are pictured as dominating their disabled spouses. The reverse situation of a disabled woman with a nondisabled male partner is omitted altogether from the discussion. Although he comes to very different conclusions about the relative status of disabled men and women, Shakespeare (1998) suggests that disabled men are perceived as less than the "normal" male in nearly every aspect of stereotypical masculinity—strength, sexuality, self-dependence. If Shakespeare is correctly capturing the psychological world of men with disabilities, he may help explain why they, too, prefer nondisabled partners to show that they can be found acceptable and worthy to "perfect" "whole" women—ones who do not share disability status.

We suggest that men spurn disabled women as workers and partners because they fail to measure up on grounds of appearance or of perceived abilities in physical and emotional caretaking. Although this argument aids understanding of her marginality in the arenas of hetero-sexual love and male-controlled work, it fails to fully explain the situa-tion of disabled lesbians. In the 1980s, there were no data to be found on the numbers of lesbians with disabilities or on their acceptance by nondisabled or disabled lesbians as partners, but comments made by many disabled lesbians indicated that within the community of lesbians the disabled woman is still in search of love. Disabled lesbians have described being dismissed, shunned, or relegated to the status of friend and confidante rather than lover, just as have heterosexual disabled women. We still do not have numbers of disabled lesbians, but there are increasing numbers of writings and publications by and for this popula-tion, largely based on experience and interview. The internet is one safe gathering space that has recently been tapped into as a resource and mode of connection. A quarterly, *Dykes, Disability and Stuff* is offered through the Gay Canada website (www.gaycanada.com/womonspace/april.htm). There have also been a few collections of gay disabled writ-ings, including Raymond Luczak's *Eyes of Desire: A Deaf Gay and Les-bian Reader* (1993).

Chodorow (1978), Gilligan (1982) Miller (1976; 1987), and Jordan and colleagues (1991) have much to say about women's capacity for relatedness. At its best, that relational potential renders women well-suited to cooperate, empathize, affiliate, examine the interpersonal dimensions of moral questions, anticipate others' needs—all those qual-ities current feminists at once struggle against and delight in. Cultivated by the culture to perpetuate male dominance and now seen as the source of women's potential strength for our own and the world's betterment (Eisenstein 1983; Miller 1976; Ruddick 1989), these very qualities may be stimulated when a woman confronts a disabled woman as a potential lover. If the dark, problematic side of a capacity for relatedness is a too-ready potential for merger with another, stereotypes about the presumed dependency and neediness of a disabled woman could easily send women scurrying in the other direction. There has been some recent talk in feminist circles about the burden of disability for nondisabled women (Hillyer, 1993). Indeed, women often are the caretakers, in families, friendships, and paid work. Women are nearly three times as likely to be the primary caregivers for elderly people with disabilities (Jans and Stod-dard, 1999). This experiential and anecdotal evidence perpetuates a view of disability as a uniform state rather than as a diverse experience that is subject to change in the individual, in society, and over time. As Wright first argued forty years ago (1960; 1983), functional incapacity in one area "spreads" to perceived incapacity in all facets of life. The woman with a hearing impairment may be imagined unable to understand or communicate, and someone who cannot carry fifty pounds because of a back problem may be imagined unable to shoulder the emotional work of a loving relationship. So long as nondisabled women hold these stereotypes, the thought of a disabled woman as a lover may engender fears of merger, exaggerate lack of boundaries, and spawn fantasies of endless responsibility, of unremitting care. Until nondisabled men and women recognize that disabled people can contribute to others' well-being, contemplating "taking on" such a woman as friend or lover will tend to activate such fears.

These arguments, admittedly, are speculative and have not been critically examined in feminist writing since first advanced (Asch and Fine, 1988). However, they receive some theoretical support in discussions of the tensions in friendships between women with and without disabilities (Fisher and Galler, 1988) and in Hillyer's (1993) emphasis on caretaking in her relationship with her teenage, disabled daughter. Whether or not these dynamics operate in intimate heterosexual or lesbian couples involving a disabled partner remains to be explored. So, too, must we inquire about interdependence, reciprocity, and gender roles in couples where both partners have disabilities. Although some disabled people shun other disabled people as intimates, others do not. From our interviews, observations at disability conferences, and conversations with scores of women, we suspect that disabled women who marry after onset of disability are more likely than similarly disabled men to have a disabled spouse. Because disability, unlike race or ethnicity, has not necessarily created natural cultures or communities wherein people customarily look to one another to create intimacy and family, one wonders whether those women whose partners are also disabled consider this a positive choice, a default option, or an irrelevant characteristic. What is crucial is that readers understand that why disabled women encounter difficulty in establishing nurturing relations is a significant question and not one with an "obvious answer."

Sexuality and Motherhood

Often deprived of the chance for long-term intimacy, disabled women also have been historically considered unfit as sexual partners and as mothers. Many women have spoken angrily of the unavailability of adequate counseling on sexuality, birth control, pregnancy, and childbirth from either gynecologists or rehabilitation professionals. Ignorant of the adverse consequences of some birth control devices for women with particular conditions, many gynecologists prescribed unsafe methods. In 1977, Safilios-Rothschild noted that since coronary research has been conducted almost exclusively on men, it has produced data relevant only to men. Women who sought information about resuming sexual activity after a heart attack were provided with male standards or with no answers at all. So astonishing is it to some physicians that disabled women might be sexual that Galler (1984) reported completely unnecessary abdominal surgery for one woman because no one believed that someone with cerebral palsy could have the symptoms of venereal disease.

Presently, there is a heightened awareness of and sensitivity to disabled women's reproductive health needs; as of yet, there has not been enough research or increases in accessibility. For example, since 1994, two major conferences have been federally sponsored, one by the Centers for Disease Control and one by the National Center for Medical Rehabilitation Research, to better understand the health care issues that affect disabled women and to develop resources to that end. Despite these efforts, disabled women in comparison to nondisabled women still experience serious problems when seeking reproductive health care, such as being refused health care because of their disability; difficulty finding physicians knowledgeable about specific disabilities and pregnancy; having higher incidence of chronic urinary tract infections, heart disease, depression, and osteoporosis, and experiencing these conditions at younger ages; using public health clinics, specialists, and hospital emergency departments at higher rates than nondisabled women (Nosek et al., 1997).

Motherhood, the institution and experience that perhaps has dominated all cultural conceptions of women—eclipsing even expectations of beauty, softness, or ever-present sexuality—often has been proscribed for a woman with a disability. Many states have had laws forbidding people with histories of epilepsy, mental retardation, and psychiatric disability from marrying. Fears that disabled women would produce children with similar conditions (nearly always groundless since most disabilities are not hereditary) have mingled with convictions that they would harm, deprive, or burden children they attempted to rear. Distressingly, the recent volumes recounting the richness and diversity of women's experiences of motherhood omit any discussion of mothers with disabilities. If disability is discussed at all, it is in the account of a nondisabled woman raising an "exceptional" child, and the "extraordinary" work involved. Perhaps unacknowledged notions that no woman with a disability can be a true feminist mother explain the absence of the voices of these mothers from an otherwise fascinating and insightful literature of women's experience (Coll, Surrey, and Weingarten, 1998; Hanigsberg and Ruddick, 1999; Klein, 1998). The absence of the disabled mother from mainstream feminist and medical literature leads to ignorance and prejudice on the part of midwives, physicians, social service agencies, and courts. Many obstetricians and midwives refuse to deal with women whose disabilities may complicate their pregnancies (Nosek et al., 1997). Social service agencies still decline to let disabled women keep children they have borne (Matthews, 1992), and adoption agencies and courts insist that a parent's disability—even if it is not life-threatening—may harm a child and is thus relevant to adoption decisions (National Public Radio, 1999). There have been at least two published incidents in the 1990s where a disabled woman was assumed unfit to mother and nearly lost her child; once as a result of inaction of bystanders to assist a disabled mother whose child was injured, and the other as a result of court action (Jacobson, 1999; Matthews, 1992).

Self-esteem, Resistance, and Identity

Tom Shakespeare (1999) writes, "The traditional account, such as it is, of disabled masculinity rests therefore on the notion of contradiction: femininity and disability reinforce each other, masculinity and disability conflict with each other" (p. 51). If our culture views being female and disabled as "redundant," but being male and disabled is a contradiction, we must ponder on the effects of such role definitions on the self-concept of disabled women. Some women accommodate societal projections, becoming the dependent creatures their parents, teachers, and others expected. In fact, the psychological literature suggests this response to be the norm. Consider this in relation to findings that disabled girls and women perceive themselves and are perceived by others more negatively than do disabled boys and men. They report more negative self-images (Weinberg, 1976), are viewed in less favorable ways (Miller, 1970), and are more likely to be victims of hostility than are disabled men (Titley and Viney, 1969). The Asch and Sacks (1983) analysis of autobiographies of blind women and men indicated that women internalized negative messages more than men, seeing themselves as burdensome, unwanted, and unlovable, whereas men rarely did. More recently, Nosek and Collegaues (1997) reported that physically disabled women's self-esteem is influenced more by social and environmental factors, such as work, relationships, and abuse, and less by the fact of having a disability.

Such findings about self-esteem need to be analyzed. It may be that males with disabilities can escape some of the trap of the disability role by aspiring to male characteristics of mastery, competence, and autonomy; disabled women and girls, however, forsake their gender role if they use such means of escape. We believe that such role contradictions can plague the female seeking to affirm her identity in the presence of a disability. Particularly for the disabled girl (and the self-esteem literature generally concentrates on children and adolescents), becoming socialized in a family and school unclear about norms or future expectations for her, self-esteem may be a serious problem.

A look at current discussions of male and female paths of development suggests ideas about the sense of self and of socialization of the disabled girl (Harris and Wideman, 1988). What happens to a disabled girl growing up in a family where her mother perceives that because the daughter is disabled, she is fundamentally different from the mother and thus is not expected to develop into the kind of woman the mother aspired to be? Friedman (1980) suggests that a mother's major task is to "hand down the legacy of womanhood . . . to share it and be an example of it" (p. 90). If the mother's definition of womanhood is based upon being attractive to and caring for a mate, she may inculcate in her daughter the belief that disability renders such a life impossible.

Thus, the disabled girl's best hope may be to turn to the male norms of achievement for establishing a sense of self. Although she may acquire many skills and psychological resources to assist her in the productive world, she is not becoming the typical girl and young woman for whom establishing affiliative ties is of paramount importance (Person, 1982). Autobiographies of many disabled women emphasize their quest for independence, work, and escape out of the stereotype of disability as helplessness. As one disabled woman put it: "I was raised to be a nondisabled son." However proud she may be of her accomplishments, the disabled girl knows she is not becoming like other women. Unless she likes that difference, it may lead to the lowered self-esteem found in psychological studies and in some autobiographical literature (Asch and Sacks, 1983).

At the other end of the spectrum are disabled females who resist all the gender-based and disability-based stereotypes and take pride in the identities they forge. Because of or despite their parents, they get an education and a job. They live independently, enjoy sex with men or women, become pregnant and carry to term if they choose, or abort if they prefer. They relish their friendships, intimacies, lovers, activities. Some determine that they will play by the rules of achievement and succeed at meeting standards that are often deemed inaccessible to them. Some accept societal norms of attractiveness and enjoy the challenge of living up to them, disability notwithstanding. Others choose to disregard anything that seems like "passing" (Goffman, 1963). Some women demand that the world accept them on their terms, whether those terms be insisting upon signing rather than speaking, not covering their burn scars, not wearing clothing to hide parts of their bodies others may see as "ugly" or "deformed," or rejecting prostheses that inhibit and do not help.

Following her mastectomy, Lorde (1980) refused to wear a prosthetic breast: "On the day after the stitches came out . . . I got so furious with the nurse who told me I was bad for the morale of the office because I did not wear a prosthesis" (p. 52). Diane, a quadri-amputee interviewed by Gelya Frank, refused her prostheses because "I knew it was going on my body. And that would add more sweat, and more asthma, because I would have to work harder with it. So I always saw my body as something that was mine, and something that was free, and I hated anything kind of binding" (Frank 1981, p. 84).

Having incorporated her disability into her identity during her childhood, Harilyn Rousso (1984) resisted her mother's attempts to make her appear more typical. She explains: "She [her mother] made numerous attempts to have me go for physical therapy and to practice walking more 'normally' at home. I vehemently refused. She could not understand why I would not walk straight. . . . My disability, with my different walk and talk and my involuntary movements, having been with me all of my life, was part of me, part of my identity. With these disability features, I felt complete and whole. My mother's attempt to change my walk felt like an assault on myself, an incomplete acceptance of all of me, an attempt to make me over" (p. 9).

From these and many other examples, we know that some disabled girls and women flourish in spite of the pressures from family and the distortions and discrimination meted out by society. Today, women with disabilities hold major government posts, speak out on behalf of others with disabilities, and demonstrate competence in business and the professions. Despite difficulties, more women with disabilities alone or with partners care for children they bear or adopt, and they participate in spreading the word that achievement in work, love, and parenting are possible (Jacobson, 1999; Wates, 1999).

RECOMMENDATIONS FOR
EDUCATORS AND RESEARCHERS

Although legislation, the disability rights movement, and public education have ended much of the worst of segregation for today's girls and women with disabilities, educators should not be sanguine about the lives of their disabled students—either male or female. Amidst the discussions of low self-esteem for girls at puberty, of teachers in the 1990s persisting in favoring boys in co-ed classes, of plummeting academic performance and increasing disaffection of young girls of all races and classes, no attention has been paid to how budding sexuality and adolescence affect girls who may already feel marginal and ostracized because their bodies do not resemble those of the idealized form featured in television, fashion magazines, and Hollywood. If schools are places in which students of diverse backgrounds, temperaments, and talents must discover how to excel at social as well as academic skills, they are crucial institutions for inculcating values for and expectations of an adult future. Consistently, disabled youth—especially if their impairments are noticeable—feel in but not of their class, grade, or school. All too many leave school with no experience of membership in an after-school club, a role in a group project, an invitation to a sleep-over, a dance, or a spontaneous trip to a shopping mall or movie.

Teachers must be leaders in expecting excellent work habits, cooperation, peer involvement, and responsibility from their disabled students, and they must help all students find ways to discover that a girl's speech impairment does not mean that she has no ideas to contribute or jokes to tell. She may need more time to tell them, and she must be in a classroom that gives her that time, as it gives time to others. Teachers must be creative in showing the disabled girl and her nondisabled classmates that she has talents as well as problems, just as they do. If these girls are consistently made to feel that their disabling characteristic is the only thing that adults or children notice about them, they will remain as isolated and segregated as if they were in special classes or special schools. The classroom must become a vehicle for disabled students to demonstrate their similarities with those around them. Without such early learning that cooperation, performance, and contribution are possible, disabled girls will continue to be failed by their schools. They will leave with only academic skills at best and will have no sense that their experiences of cooperation, play, friendship, carrying out classroom tasks prepares them for adult roles as friend, partner, caretaker, or worker.

While girls with disabilities may need help overcoming barriers to mutual friendships in and out of the classroom, they may also profit from discovering they are not the only one with a disability, and they may value organized activity that brings them into contact with peers and adults living life with similar disabilities. For the young girl and her parents who imagine that disability precludes typical adult responsibilities and relationships, discovering others who can assure them that disability does not forestall adulthood. Regrettably, the only way to reduce what seems like ubiquitous shame at having a disability may be to recognize that disability is actually common in life if not frequent in any one school or neighborhood. Students and families must discover the network of self-help and political groups that comprise the disability rights movement and must have the opportunity to expand their school, faith, and cultural world to include those with the commonality of disability. Only when it is seen as equally legitimate to affiliate with people who have disabilities as it is to enjoy the company of other chess players, Peruvians, or Moslems will disabled and nondisabled people recognize that impairment is simply one acceptable form of human variation.

Just as young girls yearn for time with other girls their age and with those who are older and can show them how to experiment with becoming women, young people who have disabilities deserve to carve out time and space to explore that part of their identity. Along with ensuring participation for disabled students in clubs based on a love of sports, games, photography, computers, or the arts, the school can foster peer groups of support around disability as a life issue, as they are coming to do for young people facing moving, family changes, or the like.

Many of these recommendations may apply as much to boys who have disabilities as to girls. We need to know much more than we now do about similarities and differences in the psychological and social development of girls and boys who have disabilities. In general, for teenagers and adults with disabilities, the discrimination they face based on disability has eclipsed their sense of commonality with nondisabled people of their race, religion, or gender. Many conferences geared to women with disabilities focus almost exclusively on the "disability" component of life and have often neglected discussions of gender identity. What permits some women with disabilities to comfortably affiliate with nondisabled women for social or political purposes, and what prevents others from believing that they can be known or understood by anyone without a disability? What helps some students create meaningful relationships with classmates and teachers, whereas other students with similar types of impairments remain isolated and alienated? What classroom climate, size, or teaching style best permits students with disabilities to develop their talents and become valued members of a peer group? Rousso (1988) argued convincingly that the adolescent years of girls with disabilities were powerfully influenced for good or ill based on parental views of their daughters as either "defective" women or members of a minority group. Parents who conveyed to their daughters that the young women had reason to try for and expect the friendship and romance of others their age differentiated women who ultimately experienced a measure of social and sexual success during their school years from those who did not. What factors in parents permit some to see their daughters' strengths, while others communicate that disability is a social deficit?

If some parents are so imbued with the belief that a child's impairment spells a bleak, unproductive, and isolated life, how can schools work to promote new views for the student her/himself, attempting to muffle or eradicate such parental psychological abuse, even if unintended? As our nation continues to experiment with the best ways to reward teachers and students for excellence in communicating and absorbing necessary knowledge and critical thinking tools, and as communities create climates to promote healthy self-esteem, intergroup cooperation, and respect, we must remember to reform the practices that have made school an often lonely and humiliating experience for millions of young women—and men—with disabilities. This is in keeping with our goal to eliminate the hostility and alienation that engender school violence. We hope that this book adds to the resources of scholarship and practical guidance that will empower educators to believe in their students with disabilities. Imbued with such conviction, educators can work to empower those students to believe in themselves and others to believe in them.

NOTE

Acknowledgment: Portions of this chapter, including many of the quotes from women and girls with disabilities, were taken from the original article by Asch and Fine, 1988, which the current chapter updates; they appear here with permission from the publisher. Also, we would like to thank Deborah Kent Stein for her many excellent suggestions of sources and ideas that have improved this revision.

REFERENCES

Alexander, V. 1985, Fall. Black women's health concerns. *National campaign to restore abortion funding*, 8–9.

Americans with Disabilities Act of 1990. 42 U.S.C. 12101–12213 (Supp. II 1990).

Asch, A., and M. Fine. 1988. Introduction: Beyond Pedestals. In *Women with disabilities: Essays in psychology, culture, and politics*. Edited by M. Fine and A. Asch. Philadelphia: Temple University Press, 1–37.

Asch, A., and L. Sacks. 1983. Lives without, lives within: The autobiographies of blind women and men. *Journal of Visual Impairment and Blindness* 77(6):242–47.

Becker, G. 1980. *Growing old in silence*. Berkeley: University of California Press.

Berscheid, E., and E. Walster. 1972, March. Beauty and the beast. *Psychology Today* 42–46, 74.

Bonwich, E. 1985. Sex role attitudes and role reorganization in spinal cord injured women. In *Women and disability: The double handicap*. Edited by M. J. Deegan and N. A. Brooks. New Brunswick, N.J.: Transaction.

The Boston Women's Health Book Collective. 1998. *Our bodies, ourselves for the new century: A book by and for women*. New York: Touchstone.

Bowe, F. 1980. *Rehabilitating America*. New York: Harper and Row.
———. 1981. *Comeback: Six remarkable people who triumphed over disability*. New York: Harper and Row.
———. 1984. *Disabled women in America*. Washington, D.C.: President's Committee on Employment of the Handicapped.
Bradsher, J. 1996. *Disability among racial and ethnic groups: Abstract 10*. Disability Statistics Center. http://dsc.ucsf.edu/UCSF/pub.taf?_UserRef...BBB1739A&_function=search&recid=56&grow=1.
Brightman, A. J., ed. 1984. *Ordinary moments: The disabled experience*. Baltimore: University Park Press.
Broverman, I., S. Vogel, D. Broverman, F. Clarkson, and S. Rosenkrantz. 1972. Sex-role stereotypes: A current appraisal. *Journal of Social Issues* 28: 59–78.
Browne, S., D. Connors, and N. Stern, eds. 1985. *With the power of each breath*. Pittsburgh: Cleis Press.
Brownmiller, S. 1984. *Femininity*. New York: Simon and Schuster.
Campling, J., ed. 1981. *Images of ourselves: Disabled women talking*. Boston: Routledge and Kegan Paul.
Chodorow, N. J. 1978. *The reproduction of mothering*. Berkeley: University of California Press.
Coll, C., J. Surrey, and K. Weingarten, eds. 1998. *Mothering against the odds: Diverse voices of contemporary mothers*. New York: The Guilford Press.
Cox, S., ed. 1981. *Female psychology: The emerging self*. New York: St. Martin's Press.
Darling, R. B. 1979. *Families against society: A study of reactions to children with birth defects*. Beverly Hills: Sage.
Davis, E. 1961. Deviance disavowal: The management of strained interaction by the visibly handicapped. *Social Problems* 9:120–32.
———. 1963. *Passage through crisis: Polio victims and their families*. Bloomington: Bobbs-Merrill.
Deegan, M. I., and N. A. Brooks, eds. 1985. *Women and disability: The double handicap*. New Brunswick, N.J.: Transaction.
Dreidger, D., and Gray, S. 1992. *Imprinting our image: An International anthology of writings by women with disabilities*. Charlottetown, Prince Edward Island, Canada: Gynergy books.
Duffy, Y. 1981. *. . . All things are possible*. Ann Arbor, Mich.: A. J. Garvin Associates.
Eisenstein, H. 1983. *Contemporary feminist thought*. Boston: G. K. Hall.
Eisenstein, H., and A. Jardine, eds. 1985 (1981). *The future of difference*. New Brunswick, N.J.: Rutgers University Press.
Eisenstein Z. 1984. *Feminism and sexual equality: Crisis in liberal America*. New York: Monthly Review Press.
Fine, M., and A. Asch. 1981. Disabled women: Sexism without the pedestal. *Journal of Sociology and Social Welfare* 8(2):233–48.
Fine, M., and A. Asch, eds. 1988. *Women with disabilities: Essays in psychology, culture, and politics*. Philadelphia: Temple University Press.
Fisher, B., and R. Galler. 1988. Friendship and fairness: How disability affects friendship between women. In *Women with disabilities: Essays in psychol-

ogy, culture, and politics. Edited by M. Fine and A. Asch. Philadelphia: Temple University Press, 172–94.

Frank, G. 1981. *Venus on wheels: The life history of a congenital amputee.* Unpublished doctoral dissertation. Anthropology Department, University of California, Los Angeles.

Franklin, R. 1977. Impact of disability on the family structure. *Social Security Bulletin* 40:3–18.

Freeman, J., ed. 1984. *Women: A feminist perspective.* Palo Alto, Calif.: Mayfield.

Friedman, G. 1980. The mother-daughter bond. *Contemporary Psychoanalysis* 16(l):90–97.

Funk, R. 1987. Disability rights: From caste to class in the context of civil rights. In *Images of the disabled: Disabling images.* Edited by A. Gartner and T. Joe. New York: Praeger.

Galler, R. 1984. The myth of the perfect body. In *Pleasure and danger.* Edited by C. S. Vance. Boston: Routledge and Kegan Paul.

Gay Canada. *Dykes, Disability and Stuff.* http//www.gaycanada.com/womonspace/april.htm. Accessed 27 October 1999.

Gerhart, K., J. Koziol-McLain, S. Lowenstein, and G. Whiteneck. 1994. Quality of life following spinal cord injury: Knowledge and attitudes of emergency care providers. *Annals of Emergency Medicine* 23:807–812.

Gill, C. 1996a. Dating and relationship issues. In *Women with physical disabilities: Achieving and maintaining health and well-being.* Edited by D. Krotoski, M. Nosek, and M. Turk. Baltimore: Paul H. Brookes Publishing Co., 117–124.

———. 1996b, May/June. When is a woman not a woman? *Disability Rag.*

Gillespie, R., and A. Fink. 1974. The influence of sexism on the education of handicapped children. *Exceptional Children* 5:155–162.

Gilligan, C. 1982. *In a different voice: Psychological theory and women's development.* Cambridge, Mass.: Harvard University Press.

Gliedman, J., and W. Roth. 1980. *The unexpected minority: Handicapped children in America.* New York: Harcourt Brace Jovanovich.

Goffman, E. 1963. *Stigma: Notes on the management of spoiled identity.* Englewood Cliffs, N.J.: Prentice-Hall.

Grealy, L. 1994. *Autobiography of a Face.* Boston: Houghton Mifflin.

Haber, L., and J. McNeil. 1983. *Methodological questions in the estimation of disability prevalence.* Available from Population Division, Bureau of the Census. Washington, D.C.: Government Printing Office.

Hahn, H. 1983a, March–April. Paternalism and public policy. *Society*, 36–44.

———. 1983b, December. *"The good parts": Interpersonal relationships in the autobiographies of physically disabled persons.* Wenner-Gren Foundation Working Papers in Anthropology, 1–38.

———. 1987. Civil rights for disabled Americans: The foundation of a political agenda. In *Images of the disabled: Disabling images.* Edited by A. Gartner and T. Joe. New York: Praeger.

Hanigsberg, J., and S. Ruddick. 1999. *Mother troubles: Rethinking contemporary maternal dilemmas.* Boston: Beacon Press.

Hanna, W., and J. Rogovsky. 1986. Women and disability: Stigma and "the third factor." Unpublished paper, Department of Family and Community Development, College of Human Ecology, University of Maryland, College Park.

Hanna, W., and J. Rogovsky. 1993. Women with disabilities: two handicaps plus. In *Perspectives on disability*. Edited by M. Nagler. Palo Alto, Calif.: Health Markets Research, 109–121.

Hannaford, S. 1985. *Living outside inside: A disabled woman's experience: Towards a social and political perspective*. Berkeley: Canterbury Press.

Hansen, K., and I. Philipson, eds. 1990. *Women, class, and the feminist imagination: A socialist-feminist reader*. Philadelphia: Temple University Press.

Harris, A., and D. Wideman. 1988. The construction of gender and disability in early attachment. In *Women with disabilities: Essays in psychology, culture, and politics*. Edited by M. Fine and A. Asch. Philadelphia: Temple University Press, 115–138.

Hartmann, H. 1981. The unhappy marriage of Marxism and feminism: Towards a more progressive union. In *Women and revolution: A discussion of the unhappy marriage of Marxism and feminism*. Edited by L. Sargent. Boston: South End Press.

Heinrich, E., and L. Kriegel. 1961. *Experiments in survival*. New York: Association for the Aid of Crippled Children.

Heppner, C. 1992. *Seeds of disquiet: One deaf woman's experience*. Washington, D.C.: Gallaudet University Press.

Higgins, R. 1980. *Outsiders in a hearing world*. Beverly Hills: Sage.

Hillyer, B. 1993. *Feminism and disability*. Norman: University of Oklahoma Press.

Hobbs, N. 1975. *The futures of children: Categories, labels, and their consequences*. San Francisco: Jossey-Bass.

Hochschild, A. 1997. *Second shift*. New York: Avon Books.

Jacobson, D. 1999. *The question of David*. Creative Arts Book Co.

Jans, L., and S. Stoddard. 1999. *Chartbook on women and disability in the United States. An InfoUse Report*. Washington D.C.: U.S. Department of Education, NIDRR.

Johnson, M. 1987. Emotion and pride. *Disability Rag* 8(l):I, 4–6.

Jordan, J. (Ed.). 1997. *Women's growth in diversity: More writings from the Stone Center*. New York: The Guilford Press.

Jordan, J., A. Kaplan, J. B. Miller, I. Striver, and J. Surrey. 1991. *Women's growth in connection: Writings from the Stone Center*. New York: The Guilford Press.

Journal of Disability Policy Studies. (1997). 8(1, 2): entire issue.

Journal of Sociology and Social Welfare. 1981. Women and disability: The double handicap. 8(2). Entire issue.

Kaysen, S. 1993. *Girl, interrupted*. New York: Turtle Bay/Random House.

Keith, L. (Ed.). 1996. *What happened to you? Writing by disabled women*. New York: The New Press.

Kent, D. 1993. Being seen and heard: Women with disabilities speak out. *Feminist Collections*, 14, (4): 2–4.

———. 1994. A movement or a monolith? *Women's Review of Books*: 10–11.

———. 1996. A long way to go. *Women's Review of Books*, XIV, (2): 23.

———. 1999. Coming to terms. *Women's Review of Books*, XVI, (8): 10.

Kirchner, C. 1987. *Assessing the effects of vocational rehabilitation on disadvantaged persons: Theoretical perspectives and issues for research.* In Proceedings of the Annual Meeting of the Society for the Study of Chronic Illness, Impairment and Disability, 1984–1985. Salem, Ore.: Willamette University Press.

Klein, B. 1997. *Slow dance: A story of stroke, love, and disability.* Berkeley: Pagemill/Circulus Publishing.

Lakoff, R., and R. L. Scherr. 1984. *Face value: The politics of beauty.* Boston: Routledge and Kegan Paul.

LaPlante, M., J. Kennedy, S. Kaye, and B. Wenger. 1996. *Disability and employment: Abstract 11.* Disability Statistics Center. http://dsc.ucsf.edu/UCSF/pub.taf?_UserRef...BBB1891B&_function =search&recid=57&grow=1. Accessed 10/25/99.

Lonsdale, S. (1990). *Women and disability: The experience of physical disability among women.* New York: Henry Holt.

Lorde, A. 1980. *The cancer journals.* Argyle, N.Y.: Spinsters, Ink.

Luczak, R. 1993. *Eyes of desire: A deaf gay and lesbian reader.* Boston: Alyson Publications, Inc.

Mairs, N. 1997. *Waist-high in the world: A life among the non-disabled.* Boston: Beacon Press.

Matthews, G. E. 1983. *Voices from the shadows: Women with disabilities speak out.* Toronto: Women's Educational Press.

Matthews, J. 1992. *The Tiffany Callos story.* New York: Henry Holt.

McNeil, J. 1997. *Current population reports: Americans with disabilities 1994–1995.* Series P70–61. U.S. Department of Commerce; Bureau of the Census.

Miller, A. 1970. Role of physical attractiveness in impression formation. *Psychonomic Science* 19:241–243.

Miller, J. B. 1976. *Toward a new psychology of women.* Boston: Beacon.

———. 1987. *Toward a new psychology of women* (2nd ed.). Boston: Beacon Press.

Minow, M. 1990. *Making all the difference: Inclusion, exclusion, and American law.* Ithaca: Cornell University Press.

Morris, J. 1989. *Able lives: Women's experience of paralysis.* London: The Women's Press.

———. 1993. *Pride against prejudice: Transforming attitudes toward disability.* Philadelphia: New Society Publications.

Nagi, S. 1969. *Disability and rehabilitation.* Columbus: Ohio University Press.

National Organization on Disability. 1998. *Harris survey of Americans with disabilities.* HYPERLINK http://www.nod.org/press.html#poll. Accessed 29 August 1999.

The National Women's Health Information Center at hhtp://www.4woman.gov/wwd/. Accessed 27 October 1999.

Noble, B. 1995, March 5. At work: A level playing field, for just $121. *New York Times*, F21.

Nosek, M., C. Howlan, D. Rintala, M. Young, and G. Chanpong. 1997. *National study of women with physical disabilities: Final report.* Houston: Center for Research on Women with Disabilities. Baylor College of Medicine. http://www.bcm.tmc.edu/crowd/. Accessed 27 October 1999.

O'Toole, C. 1996. Disabled lesbians: Challenging monocultural constructs. In *Women with physical disabilities: Achieving and maintaining health and well-being.* Edited by D. Krotoski, M. Nosek, and M. Turk. Baltimore: Paul H. Brookes Publishing Co., 135–151.

Packer, J. 1983. Sex stereotyping in vocational counseling of blind/visually impaired persons: A national study of counselor choices. *Journal of Visual Impairment and Blindness* 77(6):261–68.

Panzarino, C. 1994. *The me in the mirror.* Seattle: Seal Press.

Person, E. S. 1982. Women working: Fears of failure, deviance, and success. *Journal of the American Academy of Psychoanalysis* 10(l):67–84.

Rapp, R. 1987. Chromosomes and communication: The discourse of genetic counseling. *Medical Anthropology Quarterly* (forthcoming).

Ray, C., and West, J. 1984. Social, sexual and personal implications of paraplegia. *Paraplegia* 22:75–86.

Rose, R. 1984, April 5. Hers. *New York Times* C2.

Roskies, E. 1972. *Abnormality and normality: The mothering of thalidomide children.* Ithaca, N.Y.: Cornell University Press.

Roth, W. 1981. *The handicapped speak.* Jefferson, N.C.: McFarland and Co.

Rousso, H. 1984, December. Fostering healthy self-esteem. *The Exceptional Parent,* 9–14.

———. 1988. Daughters with disabilities: Defective women or minority women? In *Women with disabilities: Essays in psychology, culture, and politics.* Edited by M. Fine and A. Asch. Philadelphia: Temple University Press, 139–171.

Ruddick, S. 1980. Maternal thinking. *Feminist Studies* 6(3):343–367.

———. 1989. *Maternal thinking: Toward a politics of peace.* Boston: Beacon Press.

Russel, M. 1998. *Beyond ramps: Disability at the end of the social contract.* Munroe, Maine: Common Courage Press.

Safilios-Rothschild, C. 1977, February. Discrimination against disabled women. *International Rehabilitation Review* 4.

Saigal, S., D. Feeny, P. Rosenbaum, W. Furlong, E. Burrows, B. Stoskopf. 1996. Self-perceived health status and health-related quality of life of extremely low-birth-weight infants at adolescence. *Journal of the American Medical Association* 276:453–459.

Sargent, L. 1981. *Women and revolution: A discussion of the unhappy marriage of Marxism and feminism.* Boston: South End Press.

Scotch, R. K. 1984. *From good will to civil rights: Transforming federal disability policy.* Philadelphia: Temple University Press.

Seinkowicz-Mercer, R., and S. Kaplan. 1989. *I raise my eyes to say yes.* New York: Houghton Mifflin.

Shakespeare, T. 1999. When is a man not a man? When he's disabled. In *Working with men for change.* Edited by J. Wild. University College London Press, 47–58.

Shakespeare, T., K. Gillespie-Sells, and D. Davies. 1996. *The sexual politics of disability: Untold desires*. New York: Cassell.

Shapiro, J. 1994. *No pity: People with disabilities forging a new civil rights movement*. New York: Times Books.

Siller, J., L. Ferguson, D. H. Vann, and B. Holland. 1976. *Structure of attitudes toward the physically disabled*. New York: New York University School of Education.

Snitow, A., C. E. Stansell, and S. Thompson. 1983. *Powers of desire: The politics of sexuality*. New York: Monthly Review Press.

Stewart, H., B. Percival, and E. Epperly, eds. 1992. *The more we get together*. Charlottetown, Prince Edward Island, Canada: Gynergy Books.

Stone, D. 1986, May. *Policy case: Selecting clients for rehabilitation*. Paper presented at the Hastings Center for Society, Ethics, and the Life Sciences. Hastings-on-Hudson, New York, May.

Titley R., and W. Viney. 1969. Expression of aggression toward the physically handicapped. *Perceptual and Motor Skills* 29:51–56.

Tucker, B. 1995. *The feel of silence*. Philadelphia: Temple University Press.

Unger, R. 1985. Personal appearance and social control. In *Women's world: A new scholarship*. Edited by M. Safire, M. Mednick, D. lzraeli, J. Bernard. New York: Praeger.

Unger, R., M. Hilderbrand, and T. Mador. 1982. Physical attractiveness and assumptions about social deviance: Some sex-by-sex comparison. *Personality and Social Psychology Bulletin* 8:293–301.

U.S. Census Bureau. 1990. Official 1990 U.S. Census Form Appendix E. *Facsimiles of respondent instructions and questionnaire pages*. http://www.census.gov/main/www/cen1990.html. Accessed 10/21/99.

U.S. Census Bureau. 1995. *Americans with disabilities 1994–1995*. Tables 2B, 3B, 4B, 5B, 6B. hhttp://www.census.gov/hhes/www/disable/sipp/disable9495.html. Accessed 21 October 1999.

———. 1999, March. *Current population survey: Disability data*. Tables 1, 2, 3. http//www.census.gov/hhes/www/disable/cps/. Accessed 22 October 1999.

U.S. Department of Education. 1987. *Ninth annual report to Congress on the implementation of the Education of the Handicapped Act*. Washington, D.C.: U.S. Department of Education.

———. 1998. Section II: *Genders as a factor in special education eligibility, services, and results*. Twentieth Annual Report to Congress on the Implementation of the Individuals with Disabilities Education Act.

Vash, C. 1982. Employment issues for women with disabilities. *Rehabilitation Literature* 43(7–8):198–207.

Wagner, M. 1992. *Being female—A secondary disability? Gender differences in the transition experiences of young people with disabilities*. Menlo Park, Calif.: SRI International.

Wates, M. 1997. *Disabled parents: Dispelling the myths*. Cambridge, U.K.: National Childbirth Trust Publishing.

Wates, M., ed. 1999. *Bigger than the sky: Disabled women talk about parenting*. London: The Women's Press.

Weinberg, N. 1976, September. The effect of physical disability on self-perception. *Rehabilitation Counseling Bulletin*, 15–20.

Wendell, S. 1996. *The rejected body: Feminist philosophical reflections on disability*. New York: Routledge.

West, J. 1996. *Implementing the Americans with Disabilities Act*. Blackwell Publishers.

Williams, D. 1992. *Nobody nowhere: The extraordinary autobiography of an autistic*. New York: Times Books.

Women and Disability Awareness Project. 1984. *Building community: A manual exploring issues of women and disability*. New York: Educational Equity Concepts.

Wright, B. A. 1960. *Physical disability: A psychological approach*. New York: Harper and Row.

———. 1983. *Physical disability: A psycho-social approach*. New York: Harper and Row.

CHAPTER 2

Won't You Know All of Me? Recognizing the Confluence of Disability, Gender, and Ethnicity

Eric Jolly

INTRODUCTION

It was a lot like hypnosis . . . my attention was focused, distractions were filtered out, and I felt acutely aware of the "sounds" and motions being generated by the person before me. I had never before seen music interpreted into sign language. I stood mesmerized as the artist before me wrestled the air, pushing out words with her whole body and creating an impact stronger than the beating pulse of speakers at a rock concert. It was startling how someone could seemingly take hold of the air, resisting its pressures at one moment and creating a flow that seemed to cause a ripple on her fingers the next. Witnessing that sign language performance by award-winning actor Phyllis Frelich opened a window for me that would later mold much of my view and appreciation for the power of art. Watching her interpret music through the eyes and heart of a different culture of experience allowed me to "feel" music for the first time. Even though I had not yet learned sign language, I began to understand the image of music in a way I still cannot translate into words. This image is visceral, affective, and intuitive. What Phyllis had given me was a new understanding of that which I had thought to be familiar.

The window she opened was not simply a window to another world and another culture; it was a looking glass through which I could revisit my world as well. I could never again watch my uncle stroke the air to illustrate his stories without connecting with a profoundly deeper, sometimes different, meaning than those simple motions revealed. It changed my level of experience for all kinds of performances. No modern dance, no ballet, no street corner mime would ever again be experienced as it had in the past. I had come to know what thoughts looked like and how you could see a heartbeat exit a body.

Once someone opened that window to an alternative understanding of "music," I could begin to understand the "feel" of jazz or the "weight" of a dirge. As I began to conceive of rhythm, tempo, and rhyme in ways I had not previously imagined, I learned to embrace other challenges to my preconceptions about how people experience their world.

Later, as I traveled, Phyllis's lesson would extend to my relationships with the many people I would encounter on my journeys. Whether it was the intense and personal way of relating to others in one community or the calm and collected mannerisms of another, each experience broadened my frame of reference. Every encounter allowed me to enrich my understanding of my own behaviors as a part of the diverse range of human interaction. Each new experience extended the view from the window that Phyllis had opened for me.

WINDOWS ON TEACHING

This is the gift teachers can both give to and receive from their students: the ability to understand how many worldviews can be expressed in a single encounter. In my encounter with Phyllis, I began to develop one more way of interpreting and experiencing my world. It added to the dimensions of diversity that I expressed and could recognize in others. Too often we speak of someone's "diversity" using the singular form of that word. The truth is, we all have an unending set of diversities that are a part of both our own behavior and our interpretation of others' behavior. At any time an individual might represent a view of disability, gender, race, ethnicity, age, sexual orientation, or another factor, as well as any unique combination thereof.

Before we can open this window on multiple worldviews for our students, we have to learn to appreciate it ourselves. Managing this expanded and often dynamic perspective of others and self is a challenge. It requires that we abandon any one-dimensional, single label of difference in favor of a more fluid system that allows a person to be many things at different times. A friend of mine once remarked how marginalized he felt whenever someone would turn to him during a conversation on cultural diversity and say, with all kind intention, "I don't think of you as African American." Although he didn't want to be thought of only as a black man, he didn't want that perspective and his own unique life experiences diminished to the point where it no longer had a place in his conversations. Moreover, he didn't consider race, disability status, sexual orientation, or the like as characteristics that were stigmatizing and hence needed to be overlooked. He would always be black, a man, and for the time being, middle aged and middle class.

Imagine a heterosexual couple spending the week in anticipation of a Friday night date. They might both enjoy the anticipation and preparation for an evening of flirtation, each concerned with how he or she would dress, hairstyle, grooming, and what they might do or talk about. Now, how validated or valued would either feel if the other were to turn and say, "I don't think of you as a male/female?" In the circumstances and customs of dating, whether in a homosexual or heterosexual couple, one's gender is an integral part of the relationship. It isn't the only part of us that we want considered during the evening, but it is an essential element of our social self, and we often put great care into how we present this part of ourselves.

What might be an essential element of who we are in one circumstance, such as dating or discussing cultural diversity, may have lesser bearing in another. We all shift constantly in presenting the many dimensions of ourselves. In the best of environments, we have the ability to express these many facets of our personality and experiences without being weighed down by that one characteristic that is, in a particular context, most unusual, rare, or noticeable. Unfortunately, in the presence of one clear or outstanding characteristic that contributes to a person's diversity, many other distinguishing characteristics will often go unnoticed. This can mean that in a classroom of mostly nondisabled students, the student who has a disability is viewed almost exclusively through that window. That is to say, we might overattribute that student's behavior, personality, mood, and learning style to issues of disability, when in fact ethnicity, gender, or other personal circumstances would better account for many of the differences they bring to their educational experience. Similarly, making an attribution solely on the basis of gender or ethnicity can also lead to misunderstandings.

It is important not only to recognize the many aspects of difference that make each individual unique but also the ways in which these differences can come together to affect one another. This can be an even more complex undertaking in the presence of a disability because a disability can sometimes change the way we operate on a number of levels, resulting in a style or characteristics that are often considered to be markers of racial or ethnic culture or gender identity. For example, it has been noted that persons who are deaf, when compared to people who do not have hearing impairments, use "touching" more in social circumstances. The same observation has been made in comparing persons from Latin cultures with people from the United States (Axtell, 1991). Thus, very different features and aspects of identity, like deafness and ethnicity, can have similar effects. When two such compounding factors are present, for example when someone is deaf and from a Latin culture, it becomes almost impossible to separate out their influence.

No one dimension of difference can be fully understood independent of another. The dimensions of diversity do not simply add on to each other; they often modify each other in unique and striking ways. This can be illustrated by how society frames a student's struggles with issues of gender and emerging sexuality. There are many varied preconceptions and expectations that center on issues of disability status and ethnicity. Historically, nondisabled students have been included in such social support activities as physical education, dance instruction, school dances, social etiquette classes, and so forth to facilitate "appropriate" social and sexual maturation. The cultural expectations for sexually maturing students with disabilities are often unclear or even discouraging of sensual or sexual expression. Developmental supports for students with disabilities have rarely focused on issues of sexual maturation, dating, and romantic interactions. This is a sharp contrast to the experience of some ethnic groups who are stereotyped as maturing more quickly or being more "demonstrative" during maturation. Sex education and social programs often include communications that are specifically tailored to the perceived needs of different ethnic groups but rarely tailored to the needs of disabled students. The roles of gender and sex are clearly changed by the windows of culture and disability and the merging of the two.

Be it gender, disability, ethnicity, sexual orientation, or some other factor, what defines us as unique individuals is ever-changing. Particular circumstances can call to the forefront any combination of factors, elevating the importance of some while minimizing the significance of others. As young people explore the many aspects of who they are and what they can bring to a range of circumstances, teachers will be challenged to recognize the whole of the student. If we are to enable students to grow into multidimensional adults, we must be able to support the expression of the many factors that are reflections of the complex identity all students have. We must see each aspect of identity yet also see beyond any one factor in order to recognize and support the expression of all the diversities a student brings into a learning environment.

Teaching the whole student means recognizing that, depending on context, issues of gender, disability, and racial or ethnic culture may or may not have a central role in a particular interaction. It also requires understanding that the gender or cultural issues brought forward by a student with a disability may be different, or differently expressed, than that of a nondisabled student. Teachers should assume that all aspects of the student come into play, and the challenging task is to recognize the different ways in which they are expressed.

There are recommendations that can help a teacher more effectively engage the whole student. Central to all of them is that educators recognize the fluid nature of a young person's developing expressions of self and the unique combination of diversities that each student brings to the classroom. Other suggestions include:

1. Don't be distracted by the most obvious dimension of difference. That is, in a room full of children with disabilities, one of whom belongs to an ethnic minority, it is quite common for that child's behaviors to be overattributed to issues of ethnicity, whereas if he or she were the only disabled child in an ethnically mixed classroom, those behaviors might be overattributed to issues of disability. The same risk of misattribution can occur around issues of gender. Try to understand each child on the same dimensions that are expressed by all children.

2. Don't ignore any aspect of a student's identity. Assess the adequacy of context for bringing forward all aspects of a student's identity. For example, issues of gender may seem less obviously in play or not as important in a single-sex classroom. This can lead to an error of omission, and important issues can often be overlooked. It can also mean overlooking the unique interplay of a set of identity issues. For example, there can exist issues around gender identity that have a different form and relevancy for disabled students than for nondisabled students (Rousso, chapter 15, this volume).

3. Identify students' assets and not simply their real or perceived deficits. All too often the label and description of a disability focus on the limiting conditions. Do not confuse the description of the disability with the description of the person. All students bring a set of skills and talents that allows them to explore and master their world. The characteristics of each student, individually and collectively, include many strengths that need nurturing and should be a focus in the educational process. Students with disabilities often have unique skill sets developed at home and in other learning situations that allow them to encounter the world in creative, efficient ways. While the experience of disability is often seen only as a source of deficits, it can entail many assets as well, such as a unique talent for communication, an alternative worldview, and experience in perseverance and creative response to physical challenges.

4. Let a focus on outcome define the means and not the other way around. A teacher's goal should be student learning. There can be

many ways in which a student will achieve a particular outcome. Teachers should examine the goal set of a particular activity. What skills are being developed? What is the purpose behind the mastery? Are there alternative routes or means to expression of these goals? What is the essential learning that is being pursued?

5. Focus beyond social integration. One parent of a child with a disability, in reflecting on her son's experience in school, noted that teachers and aides spend all their time working on his social integration into the classroom; she wants to know who thinks about what he's learning. Although social integration is often a first and important step to a child's education, it is not the sole purpose of a student's presence in school. Teachers need to consciously move beyond this first step and monitor what every child is actually learning.

6. Seek out and engage parents and guardians in meaningful ways. Recognize that parents bring multiple perspectives to understanding their child's world and to expressing their own views. They can often identify successful learning adventures and a broad range of learning styles that are a part of the student's history.

7. Actively learn about the life, needs, community, and communication style of every child and all aspects of her or his identity. For example, a teacher might:

   a. Learn how each child desires reinforcement. For some students a private congratulation or a positive note home brings more joy than any manner of public praise.

   b. Learn the hobbies, lifestyle, or interest of each pupil so that every student gets to be a star example at least once each year.

   c. Learn how each child "holds pause." How does a child delay a response to a question while he or she works to generate an answer? Some students do this by filling space with "umms and ahhs" while others might quietly shuffle their feet or look away. Assure that each of these is supported in the classroom.

   d. Create connections between the curriculum and the student's home life so that the curriculum is relevant and the parent or guardian's activities and work have a value that is recognized in everyday classroom examples.

   e. Learn to pronounce (or sign) the name of every student prior to the opening day of classes. Learn a few words of praise in the home language of every student. (Today one in eight Americans over the age of five speaks a language other than English at home).

CONCLUSION

As a teacher, you are placing the stepping stones before your students that define their possible paths in life. Your actions, words, and hopes for children can have powerful and lifelong impact in determining their future. Don't let such power be exercised nonchalantly or unintentionally. Superior teachers continue to develop an understanding of their students and their students' needs and thoughtfully address any of their own issues that can interfere with the mission of helping each child to achieve. It is essential for teachers to recognize the powerful role they play in giving students feedback throughout the time that these young people are developing their identities around issues of disability, gender, and culture.

As teachers we must be thoughtful of the many ways in which we are constantly transmitting values, expectations, and biases to all of our students; engaged in developing the whole student and recognizing all aspects of a child's life that influence identity and learning and communication styles; as concerned with what students are learning and how they are learning it as with issues of social development and acceptance; and flexible about the style and manner in which a student approaches a problem and attains subject mastery. We should expect learning that demonstrates high outcome standards for all students.

Recall that an equal demonstration of learning does not require an identical demonstration of manner or process. Equitable outcomes don't require sameness of treatment or process, they require attention to the path that best suits each child for success. Every day, teachers are laying out a path that gives direction to each student's life and provides mirrors to the sense of self that she or he is developing. If we can be thoughtful, self-aware, open to learning, engaged in whole student development, flexible to manner and style but focused on outcome, we will know and love the whole student.

REFERENCE

Axtell, R. E. 1991. *Gestures. The do's and taboos of body language around the world.* New York: John Wiley and Sons.

SECTION II

Gender Issues in the Education of All Students

CHAPTER 3

Gender Equity in Education: Change and Challenge

Katherine Hanson
and Susan J. Smith

Gender equity in education is now a global issue, and the education of girls and women is seen as critical to the social and economic well-being of democracies worldwide. The 1995 United Nations Fourth World Conference on Women issued a call "to ensure women's access to quality education and training for self-reliance at all levels and in all fields and sectors; remove gender disparities in national education programs and policies, and provide education and training to girls as well as boys, and women as well as men, on an equal basis." As Federico Mayor, director-general of UNESCO, notes, "Women's full participation in social and economic development at all levels is imperative for a world preparing to enter the third millennium" (UNESCO, 1998).

Since the passage of Title IX, girls and women have had more opportunities than previous generations. This progress occurred through varied events, including implementation of new laws, shifts in public perceptions of women's roles, alterations in teaching and learning, and changes in families and the workplace. Together they have created a level of overall educational and employment success for girls and women as a whole that places it ahead of many other countries, such as the following:

1. The high school graduation rate for females and males is 82 percent (U.S. Department of Commerce, 1998).

2. Girls and boys have similar scores on national mathematics achievement tests and often receive similar grades, particularly at the lower grade levels (National Science Foundation, 1998).

3. Girls have higher reading scores than boys do; and girls' overall math proficiency has improved since 1992 (National Science Foundation, 1998).

4. High school girls participating in athletics increased from 300,000 in 1971 to 2.4 million in 1996 (Women's Sports Foundation, 1997b).

5. In 1996, women were the majority (56 percent) of undergraduates on U.S. college campuses (National Center for Education Statistics, 1997b).

These successes disguise remaining barriers and inequities, particularly for specific groups of girls and women. There has been little research on educational outcomes focusing on gender and race, ethnicity, socioeconomic class, disability, or language. To achieve equitable outcomes, we must look beyond the general data to the particularities of access and outcomes for specific groups of girls and women and incorporate this into our efforts to improve educational outcomes for all students. We also must "leave behind our boys-only and girls-only assumptions and stereotypes. On any given measure of achievement or skill, we find greater similarity between the average score of girls as a group and the average score of boys as a group than we find when comparing among individual girls or among individual boys" (Bailey, 1996).

Researchers such as Lee (1997) note that "gender equity should be defined as the absence of gender differences in outcomes." She suggests that a lack of differences in outcomes—as in the recent national scores for mathematics achievement—indicate that education is working for all students. This is a critical outcome, as long as all individuals are performing at a high level. No difference in outcomes—when all students score poorly—is not equity. An examination of the research that shows discrepancies in outcomes can help us develop a better educational system, one that responds to the particular needs and strengths of gender, race, ethnicity, disability, and language proficiency. Gender-equitable education supports the teaching and learning of both girls and boys. It is as important for both girls and boys to learn about the contributions of women—from all groups and cultures—as it is to develop cooperative learning skills, or to learn about parenting. As Bailey (1996) reminds us, "Gender equity in education is more than putting girls on equal footing with boys—it's eliminating the barriers and stereotypes that limit the opportunities and choices of both sexes" (p. 75).

Amid the national clamor for high standards, educators are frantically developing benchmarks to measure our success in reaching these as yet ambiguous goals. These benchmarks take on new meaning when we look at how girls as a whole and then how specific groups of girls are doing in terms of school experience, completion, enrollments, coursetaking, degrees, and rewards for those degrees (income and careers). While there are a number of areas where all women and girls are doing well, the story is often much more complicated when we look at women and girls of color, girls with disabilities, and girls from poor backgrounds.

This chapter provides an overview of what is happening for girls in school, moving beyond the general findings to reveal those cultural and institutional barriers that prevent girls from dreaming big dreams and fulfilling them. It summarizes major research findings on gender bias and presents implications and recommendations for educators to ensure equitable education. It also highlights progress and remaining gaps on several key educational equity issues, including classroom climate, mathematics and science, athletics, career education, and participation in higher education. The chapter concludes with a look at women's progress in employment—a critical indicator of educational progress. Throughout this section the authors pay particular attention to specific groups of women and girls. Gender, race, ethnicity, language, disability, and sexual orientation are all factors of individual and group identity that enrich the human experience. It is when they are used to limit, define, or harass that they are problems. The authors point to how institutions may perpetuate bias and stereotyping rather than equity and excellence.

SCHOOL CLIMATE

While Title IX and other equity laws offer a legal framework for equitable education, discrimination and stereotypes remain, reflecting the ambivalence in our society about roles for females and males. Schools cannot, by themselves, change societal practices, perceptions, or expectations, but they can address these in the school community. They can also make a contribution to the development of a new generation the members of which view things differently. The climate of a school—its policies, practices, intergroup behaviors, curriculum, testing, expectations, and communications—foster school success or failure. Over time, the rules and expectations of school communities about gender, race, ethnicity, class, disability, merit, and conformity are formed. These rules are invisible, so they feel as normal as breathing. Unfortunately for some, the "air" is toxic. This "hidden curriculum" is not just the culture of the school itself, especially teachers' interactions and behaviors, but also includes the culture of the students—the peer culture with its own impact on student outcomes.

Over the past two decades, research has documented gender biases in the school climate. For example, boys demand more attention in schools, and when teachers attempt to provide equitable time for girls, boys begin to act out, to draw teacher attention back to them. Research also shows that some teachers encourage active learning in boys by encouraging them to think through their wrong answers, while barely acknowledging either the right or the wrong answers girls give; praise boys for problem solving and girls for neatness and verbal skills; and foster "boys vs. girls" competitions and perspectives that increase antagonism between girls and boys (AAUW, 1992; Sadker and Sadker, 1994; Bogart, 1992; Klein, 1985). These lessons are not lost on girls. As one girl says: "Teachers treat the guys differently than the girls. It's almost like they like the girls better, but they respect the guys more. I think maybe because we don't give them as many problems, they're glad we're there, but they seem to expect the guys to think better and be better at things like physics and computers. I don't know if they think guys are more intelligent, but they seem more interested in them when they say things, and they take the girls for granted" (Phillips, 1998, p. 56).

Research has shown that white male students receive most teacher attention, followed by minority males, white females, and minority females (Sadker and Sadker, 1994, p. 50). African American females are least likely to receive clear academic feedback (Phillips, 1998). Many teachers do not believe Latino students are capable of doing high-quality academic work and avoid contact with them more often than with other students (Ortiz, 1988). Schools and teachers are sources of stress for American Indian children; few Indian girls feel their teachers are interested in or listen to them (Bowker, 1993). Little effort is given to addressing the needs of girls with disabilities either in inclusive settings or in special education classrooms.

The messages about gender roles that students receive through their interactions with adults and in texts, magazines, and other materials reinforce stereotyped gender patterns of interaction. Both boys and girls think boys can do more, are viewed as better, have different expectations, and have different restrictions. Boys generally think of themselves as having a lot to enjoy just by being a boy, whereas girls struggle to find good things about being a girl and easily identify negative aspects. Although both boys and girls are satisfied with their gender and do not want to change, both feel that boys' lives are easier and more fun, while girls had more responsibilities and more to worry about (Riley et al., 1993).

Biased interactions in the classroom are supported by bias in textbooks. What students read and what they learn in their books too often perpetuate a second-class education for girls, while preventing boys from seeing females as fully competent people who have jobs and families. Textbooks, often seen by students as objective truth, may be training materials for gender bias (Koza, 1992; Bazler and Simonis, 1990; also see Shaffer and Shevitz, this volume).

The unconsciously gender-biased culture does affect girls—they may end up not liking school or learning. Recent research suggested girls in the United States lack self-esteem (Linn et al., 1992). However, rather than treat this as a problem with girls, it would be more effective to examine what the problem is with the classroom that leads some girls to employ survival strategies that silence themselves. Girls have different responses to the bias in the school climate, and these responses may indicate useful strategies for survival for different groups of girls, rather than lack of self-esteem (Linn et al., 1992). In fact, many girls do not have a lower sense of self as they grow older, but they do "pick their spots" and choose when to express their true opinions (AAUW, 1991; Erkut, 1996; Harter, 1997; Pastor, McCormick, and Fine, 1996; Rotheram-Borus et al., 1996; Swadener and Lubeck, 1995; Swadener, 1995; Linn et al., 1992; Ward, 1996; Leadbeater and Way, 1996; all cited in Phillips, 1998, pp. 6–14). Though they may tell their friends or others what they think, girls may not want to call attention to themselves or their opinions in class. The research indicates that "many girls learn to respond to gender bias by not responding, gritting their teeth, or pretending it's a joke. Other girls are taught to speak out and affirm their power. Either response can be turned on the girls; they are either 'suffering from lack of self-esteem' because they do not respond or they are 'acting inappropriately (not like a girl)'—a pattern that reappears in the workplace when women face similar taunts and put-downs" (Phillips, 1998).

Early studies did not disaggregate the data to determine if the lower self-esteem was true for all girls. The National Council for Research on Women reported that African American girls, unlike Latina and white girls "demonstrated high self-esteem in high school. However, while older black girls reported high levels of personal feelings of self-worth, they experienced less positive feelings toward their teachers and schoolwork than black elementary school girls. Hispanic girls, on the other hand, showed the largest differences in self-esteem across grade levels. Although elementary school Hispanic girls expressed higher self-esteem than other girls their age, Hispanic girls in high school expressed less confidence about their talents, abilities, physical appearance, and family relations than their counterparts in elementary or middle school" (Phillips, 1998, pp. 8–9).

Similarly, research finds that American Indian girls' self-esteem is eroded once they go to school, where they face a climate of humiliation in which teachers make judgments about them based on stereotyped racial traits (Bowker, 1993, p. 64). Collectively, girls may resist, critique, or accommodate to the oppressive situations in schools, and their silences and vocal responses reflect strategies to maintain a sense of dignity (Pastor, McCormick, and Fine, 1996). Understanding these differences is important because there is a strong link between self-confidence and academic outcomes.

"Liking" school is another factor with a strong link to academic outcomes. Over the years, girls' liking of school has been diminishing. In the annual survey conducted by the National Center for Education Statistics, both females and males say they like school less than seniors did ten and fifteen years ago; the numbers for girls have decreased more than the numbers for boys (University of Michigan, various years, cited in NCES, 2000).

Dropping Out

Reducing the high school dropout rate continues to be an important issue for girls, particularly girls of color. In 1996, the dropout rate for Latinas was 28.3 percent, almost triple the overall female rate of 10.9 percent (U.S. Department of Education, 1996). At 12.5 percent, in 1996, the dropout rate for African American girls was almost double the overall rate, while the rate for white girls, at 7.3 percent, was below the average rate. Estimates in 1991 placed the overall dropout rate of American Indians at 50 percent or above; girls were 54 to 60 percent of that figure (Chavers, 1991, pp. 28–29; cited in Bowker 1993, p. 8). Students receiving special education services are two and a half times more likely than other students to drop out between the eighth and tenth grades (Kaufman, Bradby, and Owings, 1992), and fewer students with disabilities graduate with a topflight diploma (NCES, 1999). Additionally, no formal data is available to track "dropping out" between middle school and high school so that the dropout rate for students, especially Hispanics may be even higher than the current statistics reflect.

Pregnancy and/or parenting are the leading reason girls give for dropping out of school: 43 percent of female dropouts cite marriage and/or pregnancy (U.S. Department of Education, 1992). However, some of the larger social barriers to staying in school apply equally to girls and boys, including low socioeconomic status, minority status, and low parental education levels. Specific factors that seem to influence more female than male dropouts include having a large number of siblings, their mother's educational level, low academic achievement, and low self-esteem (Earle and Roach, 1989). The very climate of the school, designed to prepare students for one kind of culture, may also be designed to push certain girls out, particularly if we look at early socialization experiences that teach girls to be less assertive, cognitive differences in the ways that many girls and boys learn, teacher interaction patterns that favor boys' response patterns and learning styles, and course selections that often do not prepare girls for higher-paying jobs and careers (Earle and Roach, 1989). American Indian girls identify an accumulation of "school factors" as the most prevalent reason for leaving school, whether or not they are having academic problems (Bowker, 1993, p. 245). As one student said: "I never felt good in school. I always felt like I wasn't good enough or that the teachers were doing me a favor because they were trying to teach me. As I got older, I realized that education for Indians meant nothing. There were no jobs, no opportunities. So why even try?" (Bowker, 1993, p. 109).

Research by psychologist Michelle Fine also challenges the conventional wisdom about dropouts. In her work with Latino and African American students in New York, she concludes that given the inadequacies of their educational environment, the dropouts may be healthier than those students who remain in school, stating that

> the dropout was an adolescent who scored as psychologically healthy. Critical of social and economic injustice, this student was willing to challenge an unfair grade and unwilling to conform mindlessly. In contrast, the student who remained in school was relatively depressed. Self-blaming, this student was more teacher-dependent, unwilling to challenge a misgrade, and endlessly willing to conform. . . . Dropouts could be reconceptualized as critics of educational and labor market arrangements. The act of dropping out could be recast as a strategy for taking control of lives fundamentally out of control. (Fine, 1991, p. 4)

Unfortunately, these acts of resistance have severe consequences. Eventually, they serve to help push women who drop out permanently off the ladder to economic self-sufficiency and real empowerment.

Clearly, the culture of the classroom and the larger school community continue to be a critical factor in creating equitable education and outcomes. Focusing on the culture of learning within the classroom may be the key to expanding options for girls—especially if this is done with a focus on cultural variance, which sees differences as legitimate and valued by all (Allen, 1981, pp. 26–40; cited in Pollard, 1992, pp. 1–7). Gender-fair interactions, combined with engaged teaching and challenging curriculum can reduce students' negative responses to school that lead to dropping out, tuning out, or violence. This new framework calls for a thorough examination of teacher preparation programs—to determine how they can more effectively infuse gender-fair multicultural pedagogy and practice into education. It also calls for professional development that goes beyond effective classroom practice or content. It also requires clear school policies and practices with a model of inclusive, challenging, and critical engagement for all students.

Gendered Violence

The school climate for girls and women is also marred by violence. Such behavior takes many forms, including teasing and bullying, sexual harassment, and dating violence behaviors often called "gendered violence." Violence, or the fear of it, affects all students. Research has shown that beginning in elementary school and in middle and high schools, verbal and hurtful "random acts of unkindness" are part of students' daily experience (Shakeshaft et al., 1997). Bullying—"teasing, taunting, threatening, hitting, and stealing that are initiated by one or more students against a victim"—and social exclusion most often take place in elementary school (Banks, 1997, p. 1). Bullying can be directed at both girls and boys, at anyone who is seen as different because of race, ethnicity, class, disability status, or physical appearance. Boys most typically engage in direct bullying, but girls who bully are more likely to do things such as spread rumors or enforce social isolation (Owleus, 1993; cited in Banks, 1997). Direct bullying seems to increase through elementary school, to peak in middle school, and to decline during high school. Many adults do not take teasing and bullying seriously, seeing it as a passing phase of childhood in which "boys will simply be boys."

Sexual harassment—discussed extensively in Linn and Rousso (this volume)—usually begins in middle school and continues throughout high school and into college and the workplace. While both males and females engage in or are victims of sexual harassment, it is primarily boys who initiate it (Froschl et al., 1998). Girls are the primary targets of sexual harassment, particularly unattractive or unstylish girls, physically mature girls, and boys not fitting the male stereotype (Froschl et al., 1998, p. 115). Peer sexual harassment is pervasive and often takes place in public places. Adults play a key role in perpetuating the harassment, and students want teachers to intervene. Most students believe that teachers see harassment but do not want to get involved (Shakeshaft, 1997, pp. 22–25; Banks, 1997, p. 2). Students also fear reporting incidents, so teachers seldom hear complaints, leading them to "mistakenly believe that the harassing climate is not troublesome to adolescents" (Shakeshaft et al., 1998). One research report found that one out of twelve youngsters who stay away from school does so because of fear (Stephens, 1996, p. 1); harassment keeps youth away from school, classes, activities.

One of the most overlooked aspects of sexual harassment is that directed at gay, lesbian, and bisexual students. However, there is growing documentation that these students are frequent targets for attack. For example, a Washington State Safe Schools Coalition study reported ninety-one incidents of harassment and violence over the past four years directed at students who either were or were thought to be gay or lesbian. The perpetrators ganged up on individuals—at a ratio of three to one—and in half the incidents, adults stood by in silence. As a result of gang rapes, physical assaults, harassment, ongoing verbal assaults, and intimidation, nine students dropped out of school and there were eight reported suicide attempts and one suicide (Reiss, 1997). The 1997 Massachusetts Youth Risk Behavior Survey Results found similar incidents for gay and lesbian youth.

There is even less public awareness of the sexual harassment issues of students with disabilities. According to the National Center for Injury Prevention and Control (1998), students with disabilities may be at greater risk than nondisabled students, not only because their disabilities may prevent them from protecting themselves, but also because they are seen as easy targets who will not be believed.

"Dating violence" is another form of gendered violence and often foreshadows "domestic violence" (Katz, 1998). In dating violence a person (1) repeatedly uses or threatens to use physical force against the other; (2) verbally attacks, demeans or humiliates the other to control her or him; and/or (3) forces or coerces the other to participate in sexual acts. Dating violence is not the same as getting angry or having a fight (Levy and Giggans, 1995, p. 5). Girls do not leave the effects of dating violence at the school door; they bring them into the classrooms, where they cannot concentrate on studies or where they sit in fear of violence after class. Surveys of high school and college students indicate that about 28 percent of students have experienced physical violence in a dating relationship (Sugarman and Hotaling, 1991). Studies of date rape indicate that 67 percent of young women reporting rape were assaulted in a dating situation (Ageton, 1983). In Massachusetts alone, last year more than 20 percent of high school girls surveyed reported experiencing dating violence (Massachusetts Department of Education, 1998). The *Christian Science Monitor* in 1996 reported that at least one in eight teenage relationships involved abuse and 15 percent of fourteen- to seventeen-year-old girls said their boyfriends tried to force them to have sex (Gardner, 1996).

Many teachers and parents do not recognize the signs of dating violence, leaving girls particularly vulnerable. While adolescent girls claim they are generally confident that they could assert their own preferences and stand up to others regarding sexual issues, this may be an illusion, leaving them in grave danger (Anderson, Reis, and Stephens, 1997). As Gardner (1996, p. 12) concludes, "Because teenagers don't know what the rules of dating relationships are yet and don't know what their own boundaries are, it's very easy for girls to get into relationships like that [battering] and very difficult to extricate themselves." As policy makers, administrators, educators, parents, and caregivers, adults need to reflect on their own biases to ensure that they are not inadvertently fostering an environment in which any child feels unheard or disrespected. Fear of physical or emotional harm cannot be a part of that environment. Focusing on a higher standard of respect for all students is essential to creating a safe and productive educational environment.

MATHEMATICS, SCIENCE, ENGINEERING, AND TECHNOLOGY

The transformation of the U.S. economy into the knowledge-based Information Age is underway—making mathematics, science, engineering, and technology critical to the future of American students. Women and girls have made remarkable progress in mathematics and science over the past few years—from elementary school, where girls and boys do equally well in tests and grades, to college, where young women are majoring in these fields at a higher rate than in the past. Women still have not reached parity with men in these fields, however. As females progress through school and into college and graduate school, despite their higher course grades, they score lower on standardized tests than males do and take fewer advanced courses in mathematics, science, and technology. Gender stereotypes about women's abilities in these fields are a persistent barrier. Even as some math and science gaps between boys and girls diminish overall, research indicates that a new gender gap is developing in the realm of technology, which may result in women being unprepared for opportunities in emerging industries such as computer science, biotechnology, and environmental science. And there are differences in opportunities and achievement among girls based on race, ethnicity, class, disability, and region.

Success in mathematics, science, and technology at the K–12 level prepares students for higher-level courses in these fields during high school and college. Generally, in the early elementary years, girls and boys do equally well in tests and grades in mathematics and science courses. Additionally, more girls are taking beginning algebra and geometry today than in 1990. Taking these courses by the ninth and tenth grades is seen as a major predictor of a student's continuing to college. High school course-taking has also increased. In 1994 among high school graduates who took math and science courses, a larger percentage of girls than boys took these courses in all subjects except calculus and physics (AAUW, 1998, p. 24). In college, young women are majoring in math and science fields at a higher rate (AAUW, 1992, p. 28). National data indicate that girls consistently earn grades equivalent to or higher than those of boys in all points of their academic careers (NCES, 1997).

Male and female students have similar proficiency in the National Assessment of Educational Progress (NAEP) mathematics assessment test at ages nine, thirteen, and seventeen. In 1992, 82 percent of males and 81 percent of females scored at or above 200 at age nine; 78 percent of both sexes scored at or above 250 at age thirteen; and 60 percent of males and 58 percent of females scored at or above 300 at age seventeen. Additionally, girls of all ages, races, and ethnicities outperformed or were equal performers to boys on the most recent NAEP measures of reading and writing. Boys outperformed girls in twelfth-grade history, fourth-grade mathematics, twelfth-grade science, and all grade levels of the geography assessments (NCES, 1997).

As females progress through school and into college, despite their frequently higher course grades, they score lower on standardized tests and take fewer advanced courses than males do (Sanders, Koch, and Urso, 1997, p. 1). The Third International Mathematics and Science Study (TIMMS), an achievement test given to fourth-, eighth-, and twelfth-grade students in forty-one nations from 1995 through 1996, revealed that a gender gap in these fields increases with age. Significant gender differences were also noted in the "special," more advanced mathematics survey, which measures achievement among students who have taken advanced mathematics classes (AAUW, 1996).

Although equal numbers of males and females enter college intending to be math majors, females compose 46 percent of those completing the undergraduate degree and 22 percent of those completing the Ph.D. degree (NCES, 1996). As Linn and Kessel (1996) conclude, "Gender and not grades or test scores predicts who switches out of mathematics. Based on their undergraduate grades in mathematics, women should predominate in mathematics careers, but the reverse is true." They also found that women are less confident about mathematics and that both males and females stereotype mathematics as a male domain.

Engineering continues to be one of the least popular fields for women. In 1994, women earned 16 percent of all baccalaureates in engineering (Linn and Kessel, 1996). That year, white women received 11.1 percent of undergraduate degrees in engineering, as did 1.4 percent of African American women, 0.7 percent of Latinas, 2 percent of Asian/Pacific Islander women, and 0.06 percent of American Indian women (NCES, 1995). In most science and engineering fields, women earned a higher proportion of bachelor's degrees in 1993 than they did in 1983. In computer science and economics, however, women's share of bachelor's degrees decreased since 1983 (National Science Foundation, 1996).

Although data by gender is not available, research suggests that girls and women with disabilities are underrepresented in science and engineering. (See Wahl, this volume, for a fuller discussion.) According to the National Science Foundation (NSF), "Students with physical disabilities make up 4% to 6% of the science students and 2% to 6% of the mathematics students in grades 1 through 12. Students with mental disabilities make up 2% to 9% of the science students and 1% to 5% of the mathematics students in grades 1 to 12. Students with mental disabilities are more likely to be included in regular science instruction than in mathematics instruction" (1996, p. xix). In college, students with disabilities are as likely to choose science and engineering majors as they are to choose other majors. Students with disabilities constituted 9 percent of first-year students with planned majors in science and engineering fields. Students with disabilities earned about 1 percent (329) of doctorates in science and engineering in 1993 (National Science Foundation, 1996, p. xix).

Computer science course enrollment, test scores, and computer-use figures indicate a disparity between boys and girls. Research indicates that girls are more likely to take lower-end computing classes (e.g., data entry or word processing), less likely to identify computer science as a possible college major, and less likely to use computers weekly (AAUW, 1998). Girls form only a small percentage of students in computer science and computer design classes, and the gender gap widens from eighth grade to eleventh grade (AAUW, 1998). Moreover, girls of all ethnicities consistently rate themselves significantly lower than boys on computer ability. Boys exhibit higher computer self-confidence and a more positive attitudes about computers than girls do. Teachers receive little or no training in how to use technology in an innovative, engaging, equitable environment (AAUW, 1998).

Since 1992, girls' test scores have climbed in every subject except computer science. Moreover, girls constitute only 17 percent of high school students taking the Advanced Placement computer science test (AAUW, 1998). Girls display what Turkle calls "computer reticence," in part because culture and stereotypes steer them away from machines (Hartigan, 1999). Computers and computer games are marketed almost exclusively to boys, and even those games purportedly for both sexes, such as elementary math software, reflect sexist attitudes: Only 12 percent of the characters in such games are female, and even then they are generally portrayed as either a mother or a princess (Hartigan, 1999). One study showed that more personal computers were purchased for homes with boys than for homes with girls. Thus, boys get more experience with computers and become more comfortable with them (Bloom, 1999).

At the high school, Silverman and Pritchard (1996) found that lack of knowledge of technological careers, failure to connect what students were doing in class with future careers, and lack of a sense of economic realities were particularly discouraging to girls because they had less information about technology from experiences outside school (p. 2). These researchers also found that only a few girls were willing to be "pathbreakers" and challenge stereotypes about nontraditional careers for women. Most girls could not picture themselves in technological jobs and were reluctant to be in classes where they were one of few girls (Silverman and Pritchard, 1996). Gurer found that girls in high school worry about the "nerd" effect and try to avoid the label of "computer geek" (Bloom, 1999).

Girls are attracted or fail to be attracted to mathematics and science not only because of their own aptitudes or interests but also because of their reaction to the attitudes of their teachers, parents, and peers (Vetter, 1996). Little evidence indicates that girls are born less inclined to mathematics or mechanics than boys, but strong evidence indicates that society believes this to be the case and encourages a division between boys and girls. A 1992 study by the AAUW found that preteen girls are self-confident and generally equal to boys in mathematics, but as many of them enter adolescence, their confidence diminishes (AAUW, 1992). Parents pass along their biases—unconscious or not—about appropriate female behavior. They accept the myth that sons, simply because of their sex, are more talented than their daughters in mechanics and mathematics (Vetter, 1996, p. 32). Efforts to provide K–12 teachers with an awareness of the problem and knowledge of effective strategies to increase girls' participation in math, science, and technology have resulted in progress, although much remains to be done (Vetter, 1996, p. 3). Sanders, Koch, and Urso (1997) found that 68 percent of teacher education instructors spend two hours or less per semester on gender equity (p. 94). As Sanders said, "When girls and women fail to persist in mathematics, science and technology to the extent they otherwise could, this is not a women's problem. It is a human problem" (p. 4).

ATHLETICS AND PHYSICAL EDUCATION

Perhaps the most visible affirmation of Title IX was the celebration of the 1999 U.S. women's soccer team victory. Every day similar celebrations are heard as parents, relatives, and friends watch eager girls speeding around playing fields across the country. For the latest generation of girls, sports and physical activity are fun; more than 75 percent of nine to twelve-year-old girls in one study gave that as their primary reason for participating in athletics (Women's Sport's Foundation, 1998). Participation of girls and women in interscholastic and intercollegiate athletics has skyrocketed since the early 1970s. In 1971, one in twenty-seven girls participated in high school athletics, compared with one in three in 1994. Girls account for some 37 percent of all high school athletes, while 63 percent are boys (National Federation of State High School Associations, 1996). And girls are supported in their involvement: most parents now feel that sports are equally important for boys and girls, and almost all feel that sports and physical fitness have real benefits for girls. However, at the current rate of increase, girls' participation will not be comparable with boys' until the year 2033 (Phillips, 1998, pp. 18–19).

Stereotypes about girls and athletics remain, and girls are aware that these stand in their way. In response to an online questionnaire on gender bias in school (A Girls' World Website, www.agirlsworld.com), Cassie, an eleven year old who attends sixth grade in a public school in Missouri, says, "Boys are treated way better than girls at our school. Boys have a *much* bigger gym." Kourtney, a twelve-year-old public school sixth grader from Idaho, says that at her school, "all the teachers say that the boys are bigger and stronger and better than the girls"; and ninth grader Shannon, from Delaware, reports, "The only thing I can think of that definitely *isn't* equal in schools is sports. It's glaringly obvious when half the sports available to play at my school don't offer them for girls. Where's the justice?"[1]

Poor girls, particularly girls of color, are also not participating in sports because they have no money for transportation, lessons, or equipment (Weiler, 1998). African American and white girls are equally likely to participate in sports, but white girls are three times as likely to be involved in sports through a private organization (Weiler, 1998). Most low-income girls of color have sports opportunities through schools, recreation departments, and other nonprofit agencies that limit their participation to "popular" sports: basketball and track and field. These sports are not always of primary interest to African American females, who, in one survey, reported negative attitudes toward track and field, preferring instead swimming, volleyball, tennis, gymnastics, badminton, and dance. However, limited resources, and lack of sports opportunities, have contributed to the overrepresentation of African American girls in track and field and basketball, thus "perpetuating racial stereotyping that they naturally excel at only certain sports" (Manley, 1997).

Girls with disabilities are least likely to have access to athletics and physical activities. It may be lack of opportunity, rather than choice, that limits physical activity in women with disabilities (Henderson and Bedoni, 1995). This can have severe effects: children with disabilities are almost three times as likely to be sedentary as their nondisabled peers (29 percent vs. 10 percent) (Longmuir and Bar-Or, 1994).

Girls derive as many benefits from athletic participation as boys.

Research shows that "girls who participated in athletics were more likely than their nonathletic peers to score well on achievement tests, to stay in high school, to attend college, and to make progress toward a bachelor's degree" (Women's Sports Foundation, 1997). Additionally, nearly 50 percent of female respondents from minority groups in a 1996 survey reported that "an athletic activity, such as playing basketball or baseball, swimming, or doing gymnastics, made them feel good about themselves" (Erkut, Fields, and Marx, 1997; cited in Weiler, 1998). Yet only about half of high school girls exercise vigorously, compared with about three-quarters of boys. While the percentage of girls and boys who exercise regularly declines considerably during high school, girls decline from 62 percent in ninth grade to 42 percent in twelfth, compared with a decline from 80 percent to 67 percent for boys (Kann et al., 1995; cited in Phillips, 1998).

Two opposing and alarming trends are also evident among adolescent females: "to become either dramatically more inactive or more involved in extreme dieting behaviors and extensive exercise"(Rhea, 1995; Sundgot-Borgen and Plaisted, 1995). At one extreme are girls who do not exercise at all. If a girl does not participate in sports by the time she is 10, there is only a 10% chance she will participate when she is 25 (Bunker, 1989, cited in Women's Sports Foundation, 1997a), causing problems for normal skeletal development but also leading to ongoing health problems including osteoporosis in women after menopause (Manley, 1997). At the other end of the spectrum, for girls and women who are active and also participate in competitive sports, body image and the need to outperform their peers can create new health problems such as "female athlete triad"—overtraining, disordered eating, and amennorhea (disruption in the menstrual cycle) (President's Council on Physical Fitness and Sports, 1997, cited in Phillips, 1998). The number of female athletes who demonstrate unhealthy attitudes and use unhealthy weight loss methods (e.g., excessive exercise) is higher than the number of clinically diagnosed eating disorders (Rhea, 1995; Sundgot-Borgen and Plaisted, 1995). Another serious health issue that affects both females and males in athletics is a greater risk of binge drinking (Zill, Nord, and Loomis, 1995).

CAREER DEVELOPMENT

Twenty-five years ago, girls and young women were routinely directed into traditionally female careers—teacher, nurse, secretary, waitress. Courses were explicitly labeled "male" or "female," and career guidance directed students to male jobs and to female jobs. In fact, career interest tests were color-coded pink and blue, and the results of these tests were interpreted based on the sex of the test taker (National Advisory Council on Women's Educational Programs, 1981). Before Title IX, few girls or women were even aware of the range of careers, much less the possibility that they might be an architect, lawyer, superintendent of schools, or member of Congress (Lester and Perry, 1995, p. 2). Today many more young women are exploring new fields, declaring new majors, and routinely choosing occupations that their mothers never considered.

Yet challenges remain. While courses and careers are no longer overtly labeled male or female, the majority of women are still concentrated in a few job categories that are not unlike those women occupied twenty-five years ago. Gender stereotypes about careers still limit girls' interest and participation in career options. Career development—learning about different jobs, choosing a field of study, and planning for work—is an important component in every student's life yet is often an overlooked aspect of girls' and women's education. Existing programs, including counseling and career awareness, usually begin in adolescence, thereby missing opportunities to reach elementary and middle-school girls before gender socialization and stereotyping become a stronger influence on career choice. Further, although girls and women of color have high academic and career aspirations, significant structural factors—including socioeconomic status, lack of culturally sensitive career development initiatives, and lack of access and opportunities—limit their career options.

Historically, research on career development was conducted on white males and then generalized to other groups, without taking into account the complexities of gender discrimination, sex stereotyping, economic status, or racism (Stitt-Gohdes, 1997). As these theories are tested with research on new populations, "a complex picture emerges, suggesting that career choice and development are influenced by multiple factors: personality (including vocational interests); how individuals perceive themselves and the world (self-concept, racial/cultural identity, world view); socialization; resources (financial, information, role models, social supports); experiences of sexism, racism, classism; and the salience of various life roles and identity" (Kerka, 1998, p.3). This has important implications for career development for women who are now moving into the workplace. For example, research indicates that while college women now have career expectations similar to those of males, they still perceive role conflicts and see family issues such as raising children and lacking affordable, quality child care as potential career barriers, concerns shared by few men (Luzzo, 1995). Conventional career development is not useful for many poor girls and women, who, struggling with immediate economic survival, must quickly find whatever work is available (Weiler, 1997). And teen mothers often face "low self-esteem, low aspirations, motivation, and expectations; unrealistic goals and ambitions; limited emotional resources for support and maintenance; and lack role models" (Ettinger, 1991).

Career development programs and classes that reduce stereotypes through exposure to a wider variety of work environments, role models in nontraditional occupations, mentors, classroom discussions about occupational stereotypes, and gender-fair interest assessments, when combined with curriculum innovations and changes in classroom practice, hold promise for continued improvement in women's career options (Klein, 1985). Career development for girls and women must integrate the needs and interests of the individual, her cultural background, and the historical, social, and economic experiences of her group and offer a range of options (Stitt-Gohdes, 1997, p. 3). This means, for example, addressing the findings that the "alienation of many Latinas from school stems from lack of role models and counseling, stereotypes in curricula, and low teacher expectations," as well as lower expectations that mothers may have for their daughters (Tinajero, Gonzalez, and Dick, 1993). Girls and young women with disabilities have additional career development needs. They face high unemployment rates and are often channeled into clerical, care, or service work, with race and ethnicity compounding the picture: more white women with disabilities are in clerical work, while more African American women with disabilities are in service work (Russo and Jansen, 1988). Few career development models address these multiple aspects of a girl's or woman's identity and experience, locking many women into low-end jobs or no job at all.

Some research shows differences in career aspirations among groups of women and girls. African American females' socialization is more gender equitable, which may make them consider nontraditional careers (Hackett and Byars, 1996). However, class and race bias, disillusionment about real job opportunities, internalized oppression, and continual discrimination can cause black women and girls to lower their expectations and efforts to make other choices (Stitt-Gohdes, 1997). Research has also found that while Latinas have one of the highest dropout rates in the country, they also have high occupational and educational aspirations (Arbona, 1990). Yet social class, parent education and occupation, and acculturation and discrimination all affect how students develop their career expectations, with structural factors, such as socioeconomic status, lack of opportunity, and for some, the mobility of living as migrant or seasonal working families, having even greater impact.

Career exploration usually begins in adolescence. While some feel this is a developmentally appropriate time to begin the process, vocational educators continue to find that by early adolescence, students have strongly defined gender-role expectations about work—stereotypes that could be addressed more effectively through career exploration in earlier grades. In fact, research has found that children begin to eliminate careers because they are the wrong "sextype" between the ages of six and eight (Stitt-Gohdes, 1997).

Most students, however, receive little career development. Studies of middle school students indicated that while the majority of both girls and boys planned to go to college, only a minority planned to take college-prep classes, and most had no career education (NCES, 1991; cited in Kerka, 1994). Campbell and others have shown that middle school is a key decision time for girls. It is here they will make their first set of decisions about whether or not to continue in math and science. Despite dreams for their future, most girls do not make the connection between "what they learn in school and future careers, and they often lack guidance in selecting courses that lay the groundwork for their high school and post–high school plans" (Kerka, 1998).

Career interest assessments are often used for career exploration. In the 1970s, these assessments were criticized because they used sexist language and had items biased toward men, resulting in scores that did not encourage girls to explore nontraditional occupations (Farmer, 1995, p. 2). In 1975, the National Institute for Education (NIE) issued guidelines for reducing gender bias in career interest assessments, and the most frequently used measures were revised to be more gender-fair (Farmer, 1995, p. 2). Over the past twenty years, "most interest measures have met the criteria established by the NIE to eliminate sexist language, to use the same form of the test for both sexes, to provide scores on all occupational scales for both sexes with an explanation of which norms were used to develop the scale, and to use items that equally reflected the experiences/activities familiar to both sexes" (Farmer, 1995, p. 2). Little research exists on whether girls from various groups respond differently to the assessments, how closely the measurements reflect the link between interests and occupations, or whether the measurements reflect assumptions about what is required in a job (Stitt-Gohdes, 1997).

It is evident from new theories of vocational choice and career development that no one set procedure or style exists for everyone. As Stitt-Gohdes (1997) says, "Clearly, vocational choice and career development are influenced by who we are and how we perceive ourselves fitting into the larger social and economic arena. This perception is influenced by one's self-concept as well as how one sextypes occupations. In addition, career choice is clearly influenced by gender, race, and class" (p. 17).

Vocational Education

Vocational education was originally created to train workers—particularly males—for the trades. Until recently, girls were routinely barred from shop, woodworking, and traditionally male vocational courses. Boys were not allowed into home economics. This traditional division of labor spilled over into the workplace, where "Help Wanted—Male" and "Help Wanted—Female" were the accepted job advertisement categories (U.S. Department of Labor 1998a, p. 13). This changed with the passage of Title IX, the Women's Educational Equity Act of 1974, and the 1976 amendments to the Vocational Equity Act of 1963, which called for sex equity within vocational education systems and funded a sex-equity coordinator in each state. In 1984, the Carl D. Perkins Vocational and Applied Technology Education Act mandated that funds be provided to eliminate sex-role stereotyping in vocational education and to increase enrollment in nontraditional careers. But in 1998, the Perkins Act was reauthorized only after lengthy "debate over gender equity provisions." As a result, Congress eliminated the sex-equity coordinator and integrated gender-equity responsibilities into state administration and state leadership. Since states often have eliminated equity positions when federal funds or mandates disappear, the future of equitable vocational education for girls and women is uncertain.

The current state of vocational education is murky at best. There is no comprehensive review of outcomes for girls and women in vocational education, and states lack consistency in reporting data. This has made it difficult to track information on girls and women in vocational education. Moreover, little or no data are available that integrate gender with race, ethnicity, or disability, so a comprehensive picture of the impact of vocational education on specific groups of girls is not available. Although the Perkins Act, School-to-Work Opportunities Act (STWOA), the Individuals with Disabilities Education Act (IDEA), and other legislation require students with disabilities to be included in vocational education, little data indicate how and with what success schools are integrating students with disabilities—especially disabled girls of color.

Much of the work in gender equity in vocational education addressed deeply held stereotypes about appropriate careers for males and females and pushed for the inclusion of women and girls in nontraditional arenas. These jobs in the skilled trades, crafts, engineering, and construction were opportunities for high-wage, flexible careers. This work preceded and then paralleled concerns surfacing about females' participation in mathematics and science. However, unlike nontraditional careers, the need for advanced mathematics is now often an accepted reality for girls, their teachers, their parents, and future employers. Thus, while female enrollment in vocational programs has increased over the years, gender stereotyping in enrollment patterns remains the norm. Fewer students now choose vocational education, with little shift in vocational education course enrollment between 1982 and 1994 (NCES, 1997). Males take more vocational education courses than females. Additionally, females continue to be found in significantly greater numbers in business and occupational home economics, a traditional track to clerical and service jobs with lower pay. Males continue to predominate in trade and industry programs that lead to apprenticeships and high paying work.

The challenge to counter prevailing societal stereotypes about males and females remains. Females and males still have different perceptions of their experience in vocational education and very different assumptions about their futures. For example, while students in one New England vocational and technical high school mostly agreed that their learning environment was equitable, only slightly more than half felt teachers treated males and females the same (Interview with D. Robbins, 3 September 1998). A majority of students believed that sexual harassment was an issue: 82 percent of females felt this way, compared with 55 percent of males. Students as a whole felt females should be in construction, but those who did not were mostly males. While less than half of all students believed there were certain jobs that only men should perform, well over half of males felt this way, compared to a small number of females. For example, only 24 percent of males felt they could work in nursing, child care, or clerical jobs, demonstrating that enormous societal pressure remains against males doing what are considered to be "female" jobs (Robin, 1992). While most females expected to have jobs and maybe families after graduating, almost all males expected they would have a job, marry, and have a wife who stayed home with children. Collectively, these responses seem to show that we have done a better job of broadening females' expectations than we have with male expectations. Unless such discrepancies are addressed, girls and boys will continue to grow up with conflicting expectations about their career options and family responsibilities.

Participation in Higher Education

The U.S. higher education system has one of the fullest participation rates in the world, with more than 14 million students enrolled in colleges and universities nationwide (NCES, 1998). Today women are the majority of students enrolled in both undergraduate and graduate institutions. Further, women as a group have surpassed men in degree attainment at the associate's, bachelor's, and master's levels. It is hard to imagine that only a few decades ago, many universities—particularly elite ones—denied women admission outright; those that admitted women had quotas or higher admissions standards for them (National Advisory Council on Women's Educational Programs, 1981, pp. 25–26). However, challenges remain. For example, progress among groups of women (African American, Latina, Asian American, Native American, and white) has been uneven; gaps among enrollment, retention, and degree completion need to be eliminated; and women of all races are still concentrated in fields of study dominated by women and leading to lower-paying jobs upon graduation. Some argue that the gains women have made in postsecondary education are tenuous, given the current climate of retrenchment on affirmative action in eligibility, admissions, financial aid, and scholarships (Fryre, 1996–97).

In the past ten years, college enrollments have grown by more than 16 percent, and the share of recent high school graduates who go on to college has increased from 57 percent to 62 percent. Moreover, the gap has begun to close for groups historically underrepresented in higher education, particularly women (NCES, 1998b, p. 5). According to the National Center for Education Statistics, from 1976 to 1996 women's enrollment in college grew to 8 million. In 1996 (the most recent data available), women were the majority (56 percent) of students in undergraduate institutions, compared with 48 percent in 1976. African American women accounted for 7 percent of the undergraduate student body in 1996, compared with 5.5 percent in 1976; Latinas were 5 percent in 1996, compared with 1.7 percent in 1976; Asian American women were 3 percent in 1996, compared with 0.8 percent in 1976; and American Indian women were 0.5 percent in 1996, compared with 0.3 percent in 1976. While white women composed about 40 percent of the student population in 1996, the same proportion as in 1976, they had a numerical increase from 3,688,300 to 4,840,200. Enrollment levels in higher education are expected to rise further between 1996 and 2008.

Participation of students with disabilities has also increased over the past two decades. In the 1995–1996 academic year, about 6 percent of undergraduates, half of them female, reported a disability (NCES, 1998b, p.9). About 81 percent of students with disabilities were white non-Hispanic, 8 percent Hispanic, 7 percent black non-Hispanic, 2 percent Asian/Pacific Islander, and 2 percent American Indian/Alaska Native (NCES, 1998b, p. 10). For women, visual impairment (55 percent), learning disability (54 percent), and other disability (53 percent) were the most reported categories of disability, while speech impairment (70 percent), hearing impairment (61 percent), and orthopedic impairment (50 percent) were most often cited for men.

A majority of the studies examining young adults with disabilities show that gender impacts their educational and employment outcomes. Findings consistently show that by the time they reach young adulthood, women are often at a disadvantage relative to males in basic skills, academic options and aspirations, vocational and career opportunities, and anticipated economic security (Lichtenstein, 1996; Doren and Benz, this volume). Only 16 percent of all women with disabilities are likely to have any college education, compared with 31 percent of nondisabled women and 28 percent of men with disabilities (Froschl. Rubin, and Sprung, 1999). For women with disabilities who do go on to college, little is known about their needs and how colleges and universities can meet them (WEEA Equity Resource Center, 1999). A 1991 study found that fewer women than men are served by campus offices for disability services, and almost no students of color of either sex are served. The study suggests that greater collaboration between these offices and organizations that serve women and students of color could result in greater use of disability services by these students (Educational Equity Concepts, 1993).

Between 1976 and 1996, the number of degrees awarded to women rose at all levels. As table 3.1 shows, at the bachelor's level women earned more than 50 percent of the 1.1 million degrees awarded in 1996. While African American, Latina, Asian American, and Native American women have gained some access during the past two decades, women of color are still underrepresented in higher education. About 24 percent of the U.S. population twenty-five years or older has four years or more of education; that figure is 29 percent for white males, and 24 percent for white females. It is 14 percent for African American women (12.5 percent for African American men) and 10 percent for Latinas (11 percent for Latinos) (NCES, 1998a). (Data are not available for American Indians.)

Women continue to be concentrated in fields that historically have been dominated by women. For example, in 1996 women earned 75 percent of education degrees, the same rate as in 1970. In fields such as engineering, where males are the majority, women have made a slow climb, from less than 1 percent in 1970 to 16 percent in 1996. The clustering of women in traditionally female occupations directly limits women's earning power upon graduation. Careers in traditionally male occupations frequently result in higher pay. For example, in 1996 engineers had median weekly earnings of $949; in contrast, elementary school teachers' median weekly earnings that year were $662, about 30 percent less (National Coalition for Women and Girls in Education, 1997).

Retention and degree completion are also important issues for women. In 1994, about three out of four women (367,058) who began their postsecondary education at a community college in 1989–1990 had not received a degree after five years: 80 percent (35,909) of African American women, 77 percent (36,438) of Latinas, 76 percent (13,835) of "other" women, and 73 percent (280,876) of white women (National Coalition for Women and Girls Education, 1997). Research suggests that this may be even more of an issue for women with disabilities. A 1994 survey of undergraduates who enrolled in postsecondary education for the first time in 1989–1990 indicates that students with disabilities were less likely than their nondisabled counterparts to have stayed enrolled or earned a postsecondary degree or credential within five years (53 percent, compared with 64 percent without disabilities) (NCES, 1999). In addition to any obstacles they may have faced related to their disability, these students also had other experiences or circumstances related to lower rates of degree attainment, including delaying postsecondary enrollment a year or more after high school, completing high school through an alternative program or receiving a GED (General Equivalency Degree), and having a dependent other than a spouse (NCES, 1999).

At the graduate level, women have also made significant gains. The percentage of women earning master's and Ph.D. degrees is increasing in fields where women have predominated, such as education and health sciences. In fact, in 1996 women earned more doctorates than men in education (62 percent) and health professions (57 percent) (NCES, 2000). The percentage of women earning first professional degrees has also increased dramatically. For example, in dentistry, women increased from less than 10 percent in 1970 to 36 percent in 1996; in medicine, women increased from less than 10 percent in 1970 to 41 percent in 1996; and in law, women increased from less than 10 percent in 1970 to 44 percent in 1996 (NCES, 2000). However, women still lag behind men in earning Ph.D.s and other professional degrees. In 1995–1996, despite the higher number of women receiving bachelor's degrees, women were awarded only 15,075 of the 33,195 Ph.D.s conferred that year (see table 3.1). There is a large disparity among women in obtaining Ph.D.s, with women of color receiving less than 7 percent of the total. In 1996, American Indian/Alaska native women earned 78 Ph.D.s (.02 percent); Latinas earned 483 (1.4 percent); African Americans earned 906 (2.7 percent); Asian American women earned 952 (2.7 percent); and white women earned 12,655 (38 percent) (U.S. Department of Education, 1998a).

EMPLOYMENT

Increased opportunities for employment is one of the most important educational outcomes. Equitable education allows all students to pre-

TABLE 3.1

Degrees Conferred by Institutions of Higher Education, by Racial/Ethnic Group and Sex of Student: Selected Years
(Percentage of Total Degrees Awarded)

	Associate's Degree		Bachelor's Degree		Master's Degree		Ph.D.		First Professional Degree	
	1976	1996	1976	1996	1976	1996	1976	1996	1976	1996
Women										
All women	194,110	328,905	419,118	625,302	145,355	208,844	7,591	15,075	11,886	31,453
White	164,054 (40.8%)	256,170 (47.1%)	369,527 (40.9%)	495,880 (44.0%)	126,851 (42.3%)	173,044 (48.3%)	6,819 (23.25)	12,655 (38.1%)	10,645 (16.8%)	23,724 (31.6%)
Black	17,829 (4.4%)	33,818 (6.2%)	33,489 (3.7%)	58,314 (5.1%)	13,256 (4.4%)	17,359 (4.8%)	487 (1.6%)	906 (2.7%)	776 (1.2%)	2,909 (3.8%)
Hispanic	7,531 (1.8%)	22,463 (4.1%)	8,425 (0.9%)	33,294 (2.9%)	2,803 (0.9%)	8,579 (2.3%)	139 (0.4%)	483 (1.4%)	183 (0.2%)	1,529 (2.0%)
Asian American	3,414 (0.8%)	12,887 (2.4%)	6,155 (0.6%)	33,729 (2.9%)	1,999 (0.6%)	8,788 (2.4%)	118 (0.4%)	953 (2.8%)	245 (0.3%)	3,084 (4.1%)
American Indian/ Alaska Native	1,282 (0.3%)	3,567 (0.6%)	1,522 (0.1%)	4,085 (0.3%)	446 (0.1%)	1,074 (0.3%)	28 (0.09%)	78 (0.2%)	37 (0.05%)	207 (0.2%)

(continued on next page)

TABLE 3.1 *(continued)*

	Associate's Degree		Bachelor's Degree		Master's Degree		Ph.D.		First Professional Degree	
	1976	1996	1976	1996	1976	1996	1976	1996	1976	1996
Men										
All men	205,517	214,605	483,068	500,190	153,903	148,866	21,788	18,120	51,336	43,575
White	178,236 (44.3%)	168,858 (31.0%)	438,161 (48.5%)	408,829 (36.3%)	139,210 (46.5%)	124,514 (34.8%)	20,032 (68.1%)	15,101 (45.5%)	47,777 (75.2%)	35,732 (47.6%)
Black	15,330 (3.8%)	17,854 (3.2%)	25,147 (2.7%)	32,852 (2.9%)	7,781 (2.6%)	8,442 (2.3%)	766 (2.6%)	730 (2.1%)	1,761 (2.7%)	2,107 (2.8%)
Hispanic	9,105 (2.2%)	15,700 (2.8%)	10,318 (1.1%)	24,994 (2.2%)	3,268 (1.0%)	5,833 (1.6%)	383 (1.3%)	516 (1.5%)	893 (1.4%)	1,947 (2.5%)
Asian American	3,630 (0.8%)	10,204 (1.8%)	7,683 (0.8%)	30,630 (2.7%)	3,123 (1.0%)	9,373 (2.6%)	540 (1.8%)	1,693 (5.1%)	776 (1.2%)	3,533 (4.7%)
American Indian/ Alaska Native	1,216 (0.3%)	1,989 (0.3%)	1,804 (0.2%)	2,885 (0.02%)	521 (0.2%)	704 (0.1%)	67 (0.2%)	80 (0.2%)	159 (0.2%)	256 (0.3%)
TOTAL	401,627	543,510	902,186	1,125,492	299,258	357,710	29,379	33,195	63,252	75,028

Source: U.S. Department of Education, *1998 Digest of Education Stratistics.*

Note: Annual totals do not include nonresident aliens.

pare for and pursue careers based on their interests and abilities without regard to gender. Given the dramatic increase in women's educational attainment over the past two decades, one would expect to see a corresponding increase in occupational distribution and earnings. Yet women continue to be concentrated in a small number of lower-paying occupations that are dominated by women. Additionally, women still earn less than men, whether it is in the same fields or in different ones. In fact, women and girls constitute the majority of those in poverty in the U.S. Increased education is a means for elevating women out of poverty and raising their earnings over those of other women. The investment of time and money for education should offer more than a route out of poverty for women, however. Women and men should attain the same level of benefits for their academic achievements.

Women have a large stake in the current and future job market. In 1996, there were 63 million (46 percent) women workers in the U.S. labor force, compared with 31 million (or 38 percent) in 1972. This included 51,325,000 white women, 7,689,000 African American women, 5,128,000 Latinas, and 2,125,000 Asian Pacific Islanders (data were unavailable for American Indians) (U.S. Department of Commerce, 1996; U.S. Department of Labor, 1997). At 60 percent, the participation rate of African American women was the highest of all groups; white women follow closely, with a rate of 59 percent. Women's labor force growth is expected to increase at a faster rate than men's—16.6 percent between 1994 and 2005 as compared with 8.5 percent for men, increasing women's share of the labor force from 46 to 48 percent. The workforce itself is expected to expand: between 1994 and 2005, employment is predicted to increase 14 percent, from 127 million to 145 million. These jobs are expected to have higher than average earnings, and many will require advanced levels of education and training (U.S. Department of Labor, 1998b).

Although women are entering the labor market in record numbers, most women continue to be segregated in lower-paying occupations that offer fewer benefits and training opportunities and less job security. More than half (59 percent) of all women workers are in sales, clerical, and service jobs (U.S. Department of Commerce, 1996; U.S. Department of Labor, 1997). Within these few broad occupational categories in which women are concentrated, further segregation also exists by race. For example, the occupations with the highest concentrations of African American women are nursing aides, cashiers, and secretaries; for Native American women it is welfare aides, childcare workers, and teacher's aides; and for white women it is administrative support workers, dental hygienists and assistants, and occupational therapists. The three occupations with the highest concentrations of white men are executive and managerial workers, airplane pilots, and sales engineers (U.S. Department of Commerce, 1993). Research suggests that occupational segregation also exists for women with disabilities. While disabled men are mostly employed in traditionally male occupations such as semiskilled or unskilled laborers, disabled women are mostly employed in traditionally female occupations such as service or clerical positions (National Information Center for Children and Youth with Handicaps, 1990).

Concentration in traditional occupations by women is associated with numerous drawbacks: lower wages, lower status, lower skill requirements, less flexible hours, fewer benefits, fewer training opportunities, and less job security. However, women in nontraditional occupations earn higher wages than women employed in traditionally female occupations. These nontraditional jobs (defined as those with less than 25 percent women workers) offer higher entry-level wages and a career ladder with pay between $20 and $30 per hour (Institute for Women in Trades, Technology, and Sciences website). For example, in 1994, women were less than 1 percent of auto mechanics (0.6 percent), carpenters (0.9 percent), and plumbers (0.7 percent) and only 1.1 percent of electricians and 3.5 percent of welders (National Partnership for Women and Families website).

Education elevates women out of poverty and increases their earnings over those of other women. However, overall, men with the same level of education earn more than women. In 1995, men with a bachelor's degree earned $46,111, while women earned $26,841. In fact, as

TABLE 3.2
Median Annual Earnings of Women and Men
for Full-Time, Year-Round Workers by Educational Level, 1995

		High School	*College (B.A.)*	*Postgraduate*
White	Women	$16,196	$26,916	$35,125
	Men	27,467	47,016	58,817
Black	Women	14,473	25,577	35,222
	Men	19,514	36,026	41,777
Hispanic	Women	14,989	25,338	33,390
	Men	20,882	35,109	38,539
All	Women	15,970	26,841	34,911
	Men	26,333	46,111	58,302

Source: Institute for Women's Policy Research, 1997.

the table below shows, that same year, men with a high school diploma earned only about $500 less than women with a bachelor's degree ($26,333 versus $26,841) (Spalter-Roth, Blurr, Hartmann, and Shaw, 1995). Pay disparities exist even when women and men are in the same occupations. According to the AFL-CIO, women lawyers' median weekly earnings are nearly $300 a week less than those of male attorneys; women secretaries receive $100 less than male clericals; and women elementary school teachers receive $70 less per week than men teachers (AFL-CIO website).

Women earn less than men in the same fields from the start. According to the National Center for Education Statistics, in 1993 women college graduates generally received lower starting salaries than those of men in their graduating class. For example, for those in social and behavioral sciences, men had a median starting salary about $2,800 more than women in their field. For business majors, men received $4,000 more than women. NCES also found that salary disparities persisted one year later among 1993 bachelor's degree recipients in the same occupations, even when controlled by age and occupation (two reasons often given for pay disparities). Overall among college graduates one year after graduation, men earned $4,000 more annually than women ($26,400 and $22,500, respectively) (NCES, 2000). In 1996 (the most recent year for which data are available), women overall were paid 74 cents for every dollar men received; the figure ranged from a low of 58 cents for Latinas to 80 cents for Asian American women (AFL-CIO, 1998).

In the United States, as in every other nation, the burden of poverty falls most heavily on women. Of the 22.7 million people in this country currently living in poverty, 14.1 million are female—4.5 million women and 9.6 million girls. Approximately one-third of families maintained by single women had an income below the poverty line. The proportion of female-headed households was higher for Latinas (51.6 percent) and African American women (49.9 percent) than for white women (29.2 percent) (Proctor, 1993). (Data were unavailable for American Indians.) Although the poverty rate for whites was lower than for any other racial/ethnic group, the majority of poor people in 1993 were white (66.8 percent). African Americans constituted 27.7 percent of those in poverty, Latinos were 20.7 percent, and Asian and Pacific Islanders were 2.9 percent (Proctor, 1993). Education offers a way out of poverty for these women and girls.

Degree completion is associated with increased employment and income potential (NCES, 2000). Overall, women with a college degree earned almost $11,000 more than women with a high school diploma ($26,841 versus $15,970). Additionally, the risk of living in poverty falls with higher levels of education. Out of all persons in the labor force for at least half of 1996 (the most recent year for which data are available), those with less than a high school diploma had a higher poverty rate (16.2 percent) than high school graduates (6.3 percent). Workers with an associate's or a four-year college degree reported the lowest poverty rates, 3.2 and 1.5 percent, respectively (U.S. Department of Labor, 1997, p. 2).

Gender equitable education would encourage women and girls to pursue careers in higher-paying occupations that have traditionally been occupied by males. Teaching males and females the value of work performed by women could also help efforts to raise wages in traditionally female occupations.

CONCLUSION

The United States has taken major strides toward achieving equity for women and girls. As shown in this chapter, this includes successes in several key areas, such as mathematics and science achievement, athletics, and participation in higher education are dramatic and inspiring. Without question, new educational opportunities have been open to more women than ever before. However, it is equally clear that much work remains to be done before the goal of educational equity is fulfilled. Several mechanisms are still in place that hinder progress for all women and girls. Educational and career choices are still limited by gender stereotypes. Lack of participation exists in nontraditional areas of study and careers. Sexual harassment and gender-based violence continue to grow. The wage gap is pervasive. Gender bias and discrimination in curricula, classroom practices, assessment, and polices still persist, but gender equity practices and principles are often considered to be add-ons in the professional education of school personnel.

The successes that we can point to now are the result of hard-won laws and polices and the enduring hard work, enterprising spirit, and positive actions of women and men across the country from all backgrounds and experiences. As this work continues, we must resist efforts to pit males and females against each other and remember that gender equity encourages increased options for both genders. Eliminating gender bias and stereotyping allows males and females to defy restrictions and pursue all their talents and interests. Early indicators suggest that both boys and girls benefit from nonstereotyped thinking, expanded methods of teaching and learning, opportunities to participate in a range of courses and careers, and habits of respecting and valuing others. Focusing our efforts in this direction will ensure future progress for all students.

NOTE

1. The following questions were posted on A Girls' World website (http://www.agirlsworld.com): Are girls and boys treated the same way in your school? If not, how are they treated differently? What are the biggest issues in your school when it comes to treating girls and boys equally, or fairly? Thirty-eight girls responded.

REFERENCES

American Association of University Women (AAUW). 1991. *Shortchanging girls, shortchanging America.* Washington, D.C.: Author.

——. 1992. *How schools shortchange girls: A study of major findings on girls and education.* Washington, D.C.: Author.

——. 1993. *Hostile hallways: The AAUW survey on sexual harassment in America's schools 7.* (Executive summary). Washington, D.C.: Author.

——. 1995. *Growing smart: What's working for girls in school.* Washington, D.C.: Author.

——. 1998a. *Gender gaps: Where schools still fail our children.* Washington D.C.: Author.

——. 1998b. *Tech check for schools.* Washington, D.C.: Author.

AFL-CIO. 1998. *Working women equal pay* 1. Washington, D.C.: Author.

——. *Equal pay by occupation.* (http://www.aflcio.org/women/eqp_occ.htm).

Ageton, S. 1983. *Sexual assault among adolescents.* Lexington, Mass.: Heath.

Allen, W. R. 1992, February. The social and economic status of black women in the United States. *Phylon* 42(1981):26–40.

Anderson, V., J. Reis, and Y. Stephens. 1997. Male and female adolescents' perceived interpersonal communication skills according to history of sexual coercion. *Adolescence* 32(126): 419–427.

Arbona, C. 1990. Career counseling research and Hispanics: A review of the literature. *Counseling Psychologist* 18(2):300–323.

Bailey, S. McGee. 1996, May. Shortchanging girls and boys. *Education Leadership* 75–79.

Banks, R. 1997, April. Bullying in schools. *Eric Digest*, April, 1997, 1. Campaign, Ill.: ERIC Clearinghouse on Elementary and Early Childhood Education.

Bazler J., and D. Simonis. 1990, December. Are women out of the picture? *Science Teacher* 57(9):24–26.

Bloom, N. 1999, March. Why do fewer women choose computing careers? *Boston Software News* 2(7).

Bogart, K. 1992. *Solutions that work: Identification and elimination of barriers to the participation of female and minority students in academic educational programs* (3 volumes). Washington, D.C.: National Education Association

Bowker, A. 1993. *Sisters in the blood: The education of women in native America.* Newton, Mass.: WEEA Resource Center/EDC, 245–264.

Bunker, L. 1989. Cited in *Women's Sports Facts*. 1997. Women's Sports Foundation. (http://www.lifetimetv.com/WoSport/stage/TOPISS/html/ women _ssports-facts.html).

Campbell, P. B., and J. Sanders. 1997. Uninformed by interested: Findings of a national survey on gender equity in preservice teacher education. *Journal of Teacher Education*. 48(1), 69–75.

Chavers, A. D. 1991. Indian education: Dealing with disaster. *Principal* 70(3):28–29. Cited in A. Bowker. 1993. *Sisters in the blood: The education of women in native America* 8. Newton, Mass.: WEEA Resource Center/EDC.

Earle, J., and V. Roach. 1989. *Female dropouts: A new perspective.* Newton, Mass.: Education Development Center, vii.

Educational Equity Concepts. 1993, April. *A report on women with disabilities in postsecondary education.* Issue Paper Number 1.

Erkut, S., J. P. Fields, and R. Marx. 1997. Diversity in girls' experiences: Feeling good about who you are. In *Urban girls: Resisting stereotypes, creating identities*. Edited by B. J. Ross Leadbeater and N. Way. New York: New York University Press; Cited in J. Weiler. 1998. The athletic experiences of ethnically diverse girls. *ERIC/CUE__Digest*, 131. (http://www.ed.gov/database/ERIC_Digests/ed416268.html).

Ettinger, J. 1991. Cited in Bettina A. Lankard. Career education for teen parents. *ERIC Digest* 148. Columbus, Ohio: ERIC Clearinghouse on Adult, Career, and Vocational Education, 1994.

Farmer, H. S. 1995, January. Gender differences in adolescent career exploration. *Eric Digest*, p. 2. Greensboro, NC: ERIC Clearinghouse on Counseling and Student Services.

Fine, M. 1991. *Framing dropouts: Notes on the politics of an urban public high school* 4. Albany: State University of New York Press.

Froschl, M., E. Rubin, and B. Sprung. 1999. *Connecting gender and disability.* Newton, Mass.: WEEA Equity Resource Center.

Froschl, M., B. Sprung, N. Mullin-Ridler, N. Stein, and N. Gropper. 1998. *Quit it ! A teacher's guide on teasing and bullying for use with students in grades K–3.* New York, N.Y.: Educational Equity Concepts; Wellesley, Mass.: Wellesley College Center for Research on Women; Washington, D.C.: National Education Association.

Fryre, J. 1996–97. Affirmative action: Understanding the past and present. In *The American woman.* Edited by C. Costello and B. Kivimal Kringold. New York: W. W. Norton, 33–43.

Futrell, M. H., and L. E. Powell. 1998. *Preventing violence in schools* (www://ericweb.tc.columbia.edu/monographs/uds107/preventing).

Gardner, M. 1996, March 11. Teaching teens to put a stop to dating violence. *Christian Science Monitor.*

A Girls' World website. (http://www.agirlsworld.com).

Hackett G., and A. M. Byars. 1996. Social cognitive theory and the career development of African American women. *Career Development Quarterly* 44(4):323–340.

Hartigan, R. 1999, April. Girls byte back. *Teacher Magazine* 6. (www.teacher-magazine.org/tm-/current/07/girls.h10).

Henderson, F., and R. Bedoni. 1995. *Research Quarterly for Exercise and Sport* 66:151–161. Cited on *SportsFacts: Women's Sports Foundation.*

Institute for Women in Trades, Technology, and Science. *School-to-work fact sheet.* (http:/www.serve.com/iwitts/html/stw-fact-sheet.htm).

Kann, L., C. W. Warren, W. A. Harris, J. L. Collins, B. I. Williams, J. G. Ross, and L. J. Kolbe. 1995. Youth Risk Behavior Surveillance—United States. Center for Disease Control Surveillance Summaries, MMWR45:SS-4; Cited in Phillips. 1998. *The Girls Report* 18.

Katz. 1998. More than a few good men: Strategies for inspiring boys and young men to be allies in anti-sexist education. *Working Paper Series.* Wellesley, Mass.: Wellesley College Center for Research on Women.

Kaufman, P., D. Bradby, and J. Owings. 1992. Characteristics of at-risk students. *NELS 88.* Washington, D.C.: NCES.

Kerka, S. 1998. Career development and gender, race, and class. *ERIC Digest* 199:3. Columbus, Ohio: ERIC Clearinghouse on Adult, Career, and Vocational Education.

Klein, S., ed. 1985. *Handbook for achieving sex equity through education.* Baltimore, Md.: Johns Hopkins University Press.

Koza, E. 1992, Summer. The boys in the band: Sexism and the construction of gender in middle school textbook illustrations. *Educational Foundations* 6(3):85–105.

Lee, V. E. 1997. Gender equity and the organization of schools. In *Gender, equity, and schooling: Policy and practice.* Edited by B. J. Bank and P. M. Hall. NewYork/London: Garland Publishing.

Lee, V. E., R. Croninger, E. Linn, and X. Chen. 1996. The culture of sexual harassment in secondary schools. *American Educational Research Journal.* Washington, D.C.: American Educational Research Association.

Lester, J. N., and N. S. Perry. 1995, January. Assessing career development with portfolios. *ERIC Digest 2.* ERIC Clearinghouse on Counseling and Student Services.

Levy, B., and P. Occhiuzzo Giggans. 1995. *What Parents Need to Know about Dating Violence 5.* Seattle, Wash.: Seal Press.

Lichtenstein, S. 1996, January. Gender differences in the education and employment of young adults. *Remedial and Special Education* 17(1):4–20.

Linn, M., and C. Kessel. 1996. Success in mathematics: Increasing talent and gender diversity among college majors. *Issues in Mathematics Education 6.*

Linn, E., N. C. Stein, J. Young, and S. Davis. 1992. Bitter lessons for all: Sexual harassment in schools. In *Sexuality and the curriculum.* Edited by J. Sears. New York: Teachers College Press.

Longmuir and Bar-Or. 1994. Pediatric exercise science 6:168–177. Cited on *SportsFacts: Women's Sports Foundation.*

Luzzo, A. 1995. Gender differences in college students' career maturity and perceived barriers in career development. *Journal of Counseling and Development* 73(3):319–322.

Manley, A. F. 1997. *Physical activity and health: A report of the surgeon general.* Washington, D.C.: Center for Disease Control. (http:/www.cdc.gov/nccdphp/sgr/ataglan.htm).

Massachusetts Department of Education. 1997. *Massachusetts youth risk behavior survey results.* Malden: Massachusetts Department of Education.

Mc Grew, S., M. L. Vanderwood, M. L. Thurlow, and J. E. Ysseldyke. 1995. *Why we can't say much about the status of students with disabilities during education reform.* Minneapolis, Minn.: National Center for Education Outcomes. (www.coled.umn.edu/NCEO/OnlinePubs/ Synthesis21.html).

National Advisory Council on Women's Educational Programs. 1981. *Title IX: The half full, half empty glass.* Washington, D.C.: U.S. Department of Education, 25–26.

National Center for Education Statistics (NCES). 1991. Survey of 23,000 eighth-graders; Wells and Georgia, U.S. study, 1991, and Indiana study. All cited in S. Kerka. 1994. Vocational education in the middle school. *ERIC Digest* 155. ERIC Clearinghouse on Adult, Career, and Vocational Education.

———. 1995. *The condition of education 1995.* Washington, D.C.: U.S. Department of Education, NCES (www.nces.ed.gov).

———. 1996. *The condition of education 1996.* Washington, D.C.: U.S. Department of Education, NCES.

———. 1997a. *Women in mathematics and science* 11. Washington, D.C.: U.S. Department of Education, NCES.

———. 1997b. *The condition of education 1997.* Washington, D.C.: U.S. Department of Education, NCES.

———. 1997c. High school and beyond: First follow-up survey; 1994 High school transcript study, table 137. *Education Digest.* Washington, D.C.: U.S. Department of Education, NCES.

———. 1998a. *Digest of Education Statistics*, tables 172:187–189. Washington, D.C.: U.S. Department of Education, NCES.

———. 1998b. *Reconceptualizing access in postsecondary education: Report of the policy panel on access.* NCES 98–283. Prepared for the Council of the National Postsecondary Education Cooperative, Subcommittee on the Policy Panel on Access, Washington, D.C.

———. 1999. *Students with disabilities in postsecondary education: A profile of preparation, participation, and outcomes.* Washington, D.C.: NCES, U.S. Department of Education.

———. 2000. *Trends in educational equity of women and girls.* Washington, D.C.: U.S. Department of Education, NCES.

National Center for Injury Prevention and Control. 1998. *Sexual violence against people with disabilities.* Atlanta, Ga.: Centers for Disease Control and Prevention.

National Coalition for Women and Girls in Education. 1997. *Title IX at 25: Report card on gender equity.* Washington, D.C.: National Women's Law Center.

National Federation of State High School Associations 1996. *The National Federation of State High School Associations Handbook, 1995–1996.* Kansas City, Mo.: National Federation of State High School Associations.

National Information Center for Children and Youth with Handicaps (NICHCY). 1990, October. Having a daughter with a disability: Is it different for girls? *News Digest* 14:4.

National Partnership for Women and Families web site. (*http://www.national-partnerships.org*).

National Science Foundation. 1998. *Women, minorities and persons with disabilities in science and engineering*. Arlington, Va.: Author.

Ortiz, F. I. 1988. Hispanic-American children's experiences in classrooms: A comparison between Hispanic and non-Hispanic children. In *Class, race, and gender in American education*. Edited by Lois Weis. Albany: State University of New York Press.

Owleus, D. 1993. Bullying at school: What we know and can do. Cambridge, Mass.: Blackwell, cited in R. Banks, Bullying in schools. *Eric Digest* 1. ERIC Clearinghouse on Elementary and Early Childhood Education.

Pastor, J, J. McCormick, and M. Fine. 1996. Makin' homes: An urban girl thing. *Urban girls: Resisting stereotypes, creating identities*. Edited by B. J. Ross Leadbeater and N. Way. New York: New York University Press.

Phillips, L. 1998. *The girls report: What we know and need to know about growing up female*. New York: National Council for Research on Women.

Pollard, D. 1992. Toward a pluralistic perspective on equity. *WEEA Digest* 1–7.

President's Council on Physical Fitness and Sports. 1997. *Physical activity and sport in the lives of girls: Physical and mental health dimensions from an interdisciplinary approach*. Minneapolis: The Center for Research on Girls and Women in Sport.

Proctor, B. D. 1993. *Poverty, income, and valuation of noncash benefits*. U. S. Census Bureau, based on Current Population Reports, series P60–188. Poverty and wealth statistics branch.

Reiss, B. 1997. *The Fourth Annual Safe Schools Report of the Anti-Violence Documentation Project from the Safe Schools Coalition of Washington*. Seattle, Wash.: Safe Schools Coalition.

Rhea, D. J. 1995. Risk and trigger factors for the development of eating disorders in female elite athletes. *Medicine and Science in Sports and Exercise* 26(4):414–419.

Riley, L., M. Baldus, M. Keyes, and B. Schuler. 1993. My worst nightmare: Wisconsin students' perceptions of being the other gender. Menomonie, Wisc.: Center for Vocational, Technical, and Adult Education, University of Wisconsin at Stout.

Robin, D. 1992, August. Gender equity in vocational education. *WEEA Digest: Gender Equity in Vocational Education* 1–2. Newton, Mass.: WEEA Resource Center/EDC.

Russo, N. F., and M. A. Jansen. 1988. Women, work, and disability: Opportunities and challenges. *Women with disabilities: Essays in psychology, culture, and politics*. Edited by M. Fine and A. Asch. Philadelphia: Temple University Press.

Sadker, M., and D. Sadker. 1994. *Failing at fairness: How America's schools cheat girls*. New York: C. Scribner's Sons.

Sanders, J., J. Koch, and J. Urso. 1997. *Gender equity right from the start*. Mahwah, N.J.: Lawrence Erlbaun Associates, Publishers.

Shakeshaft, C., L. Mandel, Y. M. Johnson, and A. Wenk. 1998, April. *Transitions into middle school: The harassing nature of adolescent culture*. Paper presented at the Annual Meeting of the American Educational Research Association, San Diego, Calif.

Shakeshaft, C, et al. 1997. Boys call me cow. *Educational Leadership* 55(2):22–25.

Silverman, S., and A. Pritchard. 1996. Building their future: Girls and technology education in Connecticut. *Journal of Technology Education* 7:2.

Spalter-Roth, R., B. Blurr, H. Hartmann, and L. Shaw. 1995. *Welfare that works: The working lives of AFDC recipients.* Washington, D.C.: Institute for Policy Research.

Stephens, R. D. 1996. The art of safe school planning. *The School Administrator* 2(53):1.

Stitt-Gohdes, W. L. 1997. *Career development: Issues of gender, race, and class.* Columbus, Ohio: ERIC Clearinghouse on Adult, Career, and Vocational Education.

Sugarman, D., and G. Hotaling. 1991. Dating violence: A review of contextual and risk factors. In *Dating violence: Young women in danger.* Edited by B. Levy. Seattle: Seal Press, 100–118.

Sundgot-Borgen, J., and V. Plaisted. 1995. Gender in sport. In T. Morris and J. Summers, eds. *Sport Psychology: Theory application and Issues.* New York: John Wiley and Sons, 535–574.

Tinajero, J. V., M. L. Gonzalez, and F. Dick. 1993. Raising career aspirations of Hispanic girls. Cited in S. Kerka. 1993. *"Gender equity in vocational education," trends and issues alert.* ERIC Clearinghouse on Adult, Career, and Vocational Education.

UNESCO. 1998. *Gender equality.* Paris: UNESCO Unit for the Promotion of the Status of Women and Gender Equality.

University of Michigan, Institute for Social Research. Various years. *Monitoring the future.* Cited in NCES, 2000. *Trends in educational equity of girls and women.* Washington, D.C.: U.S. Department of Education.

U. S. Department of Labor. 1996. *A profile of the working poor 2.* Report 918. Washington, D.C.: Author. Bureau of Labor Statistics.

U.S. Department of Commerce. 1993. Bureau of the Census.

———. 1996, March. *Current population survey.* Washington, D.C.: Author, Bureau of Census.

———. 1998, October. *Current population survey.* Washington, D.C.: Author, Bureau of Census.

U.S. Department of Education. 1992. *Dropout rates in the U.S.: 1988.* Cited in Office for Civil Rights, 1992, *Teenage Pregnancy and Parenthood Issues Under Title IX of the Education Amendments of 1972.* Washington, D.C.: Office for Civil Rights, 14.

———. September 12, 1996. Presidential Advisory Commission Calls for Action on Hispanic American Education. Press Release. (www.ed.gov/Press-Releases/ 09–1996/hiscom.html).

U.S. Department of Labor, Women's Bureau. 1997, January. *Employment and earnings.* Washington D.C.: Author, Bureau of Labor Statistics.

———. 1998a. *Equal pay: A thirty-five year perspective 13.* Washington, D.C.: Author, Bureau of Labor Statistics.

———. 1998b, January. *Facts on working women*. Washington D.C.: Author, Bureau of Labor Statistics.

Vetter, B. M. 1996. Myths and realties of women's progress in the sciences, mathematics, and engineering. In *The equity equation*. Edited by C. S. Davis, A. B. Ginorio, C. S. Hollenshead, Barbara B. Lazarus, and Paula M. Rayman and Associates. San Francisco: Jossey-Bass, 29–56.

Weiler, J. 1998. The athletic experiences of ethnically diverse girls. *ERIC/CUE Digest* 131. (http://www.ed.gov/database/ERIC_Digests/ed416268.html).

Weiler, J. 1997, August. Career development for African-American and Latina females. *ERIC Clearinghouse on Urban Education Digest*.

Women's Sports Foundation. 1997a. *Women's sports foundation report*. East Meadow, NY: Women's Sports Foundation. (http://www.lifetimetv.com/WoSport/stage/TOPISS/html/-women_ssportsfacts.html).

———. 1997b. *Gender equity report card. NCAA study*. National Federation of State High School Athletic Associations.

Zill, N., C. W. Nord, and L. S. Loomis. 1995. Adolescent time use risky behaviors and outcomes: An analysis of National data. Washington, D.C.: Westat, Inc. for the Office of the Assistant Secretary for Planning and Evaluation, USDHHS.

CHAPTER 4

Title IX:
What Does It Mean for Teachers?

Melissa Keyes

> No person shall, on the basis of sex, be excluded from participation in, be denied the benefits of, or be subjected to discrimination under any program or activity receiving Federal financial assistance.
>
> —20 U.S.C. §1681

On its face, Title IX is a fairly simple statute. When it was passed as an amendment to the Higher Education Act of 1972, however, only a handful of people understood the far-reaching effect it would have on K–12 and higher education. As a teacher in a small high school in Wisconsin in the early 1970s, I certainly was not aware of its impact. No one knew that it would become one of the most complex and difficult statutes to implement, a task that remains unfinished. Regulations explaining how schools and colleges would implement the law were not issued until 1975, and even then court cases and training by the Office of Education staff and civil rights attorneys were needed to clarify what it would mean for daily practice.

As I became aware of Title IX's requirements as a teacher, the topic interested me and I asked my principal if I could take over the job as the district's Title IX coordinator, which every district had to have. The vice principal who had held the job was leaving, and no one else wanted the assignment. It was added to my extracurricular duties for a "salary" of three hundred dollars per year. Learning about Title IX made me superficially aware of how boys and girls are treated differently in classrooms but did not have a major effect on how I was teaching or on the materials I used. That was 1977, and our state education agency, like many others, was beginning to realize (with much prodding by women's groups) that Title IX coordinators in local school districts, like myself, wanted and needed training. They hired specialists and applied for Title IV funding in 1979 (see subsequent section), then began offering conferences and workshops. In 1980, I left my teaching position to become a sex equity consultant with the state education agency. From 1980 to January 1996, I gained considerable knowledge as the Title IX regulations were interpreted. There was some leadership in the form of training materials and workshops from the U.S. Department of Education and one or two nongovernmental organizations, but no courses I could take. I attended many national workshops and learned from other sex equity consultants. I used my training to facilitate hundreds of workshops and conferences around my state, often talking with teachers, counselors, and administrators who had no idea of how to implement the new law.

Nearly three decades after Title IX became law, one cannot imagine excluding students from classes because of their gender. The general public is a strong and constant supporter of girls' and women's interscholastic and intercollegiate athletics, programs in which only a handful of females took part prior to 1975. Although Title IX does not regulate textbooks, learning materials have been scrutinized by publishers and local textbook adoption committees, and new texts are the results of efforts to eliminate the pervasive sex stereotyping and bias found in books used in schools and colleges. Career education teachers and counselors are more careful to assure students that all occupations are open to both females and males. Vocational teachers have worked to eliminate biased curriculum and to encourage both genders to elect courses that, in earlier generations, excluded students simply because of their sex. The most public forms of discrimination have been addressed, we hope, and attention has turned to more subtle forms of discrimination, those of bias, stereotyping, and harassment. Title IX has been used as the lever to focus attention and change in all these areas. In addition, we are just beginning to integrate and take into account all forms of discrimination, recognizing that when we say all boys and girls are protected from discrimination, that means boys and girls of all abilities, races, languages, and ethnicity. This chapter will highlight the implications of Title IX and its regulations for educators and show how the law might be used in conjunction with disability rights laws to ensure equity and nondiscrimination for all students who receive educational services in institutions that receive federal support.

Despite gains since the passage of Title IX, the law has not resulted in the level of sex equity in education that its sponsors envisioned. The context and history of the law are keys to understanding its limitations and will provide the rationale for interpreting the law in a new way.

HISTORY OF TITLE IX

Activities that brought about the passage of Title IX grew out of efforts by a variety of individuals and groups outside the government, task forces within the (then) Office of Education located within the Department of Health, Education, and Welfare (DHEW), and by activists interested in applying executive orders and employment law to education. What started as individual complaints against schools provided impetus for women's groups to take up the banner, so by the early 1970s sex equity had become a national policy issue. Those concerned about discrimination and inequities in education built on the awareness raised by feminist groups and the state Commissions on the Status of Women to lobby for data collection to be conducted by the federal government. Elliot Richardson, secretary of DHEW, established a group to examine discrimination against women, both as employees of the department and as potential clients for its health, education, and welfare programs and to recommend activities to end that discrimination (Fishel and Pottker 1977). Earlier, women in academic circles had utilized President Johnson's executive order prohibiting discrimination in federal contracts, insisting that colleges receiving research and development funds from the federal government must not discriminate against women. The Women's Equity Action League filed a class action complaint against hundreds of colleges and universities with contracts from the federal government, charging them with violating the executive order. Advocacy groups outside government were examining textbooks and collecting information on inequities in schools and colleges. The report *Dick and Jane as Victims*, illustrated the lack of female examples in children's texts and the stereotypic role models of both males and females in those books. Examples of inequity on college campuses included differences in professors' pay and status by gender, discriminatory hiring practices, and differences in athletic opportunities for women and men. Persons advocating for the elimination of sex discrimination in elementary and secondary schools were less organized at first and thus less obvious on the national level, but many women's groups, such as branches of the American Association of University Women (AAUW), chapters of the National Organization for Women (NOW), and the League of Women Voters (LWV) became interested in the issue in the early 1970s. NOW's Legal Defense and Education Fund provided valuable assistance and lobbying pressure.

The first hearings to be held by Congress on sex discrimination in education were called by Representative Edith Green (D-Oregon) in June and July of 1970. Green intended to include prohibitions against sex discrimination in the reauthorization of the Higher Education Act bill that year. While women's groups presented ample evidence of discrimination, schools and colleges did not attend, and the hearings were poorly attended by the committee's own members. The plan to include prohibitions went no further. In 1971, however, several senators, including Birch Bayh (D-Indiana), brought new versions of sex discrimination bills forward. Extensive lobbying resulted in changes by the Senate, the House, and the Conference Committee, which led to passage of a stand-alone bill, Title IX of the Education Amendments of 1972, not tied to other civil rights laws, that was signed into law by President Nixon in July 1972. The law languished in relative obscurity, however, until public awareness, and the regulations, caught up with the intent of the law.

Initially, most educators were unaware of the law's existence, officials in state education agencies ignored it, and federal education leaders did not issue information on its implementation. Hearings held throughout the country finally caught the attention of colleges, and groups such as the National Collegiate Athletic Association (NCAA), the American Football Coaches Association, members of Congress, and organizations of institutions of higher education opposed stringent regulations. Many women's groups spoke in favor of more detailed regulation, and several members of Congress supported regulation as well. Although the process of adopting regulations for Title IX was slow and difficult, compromise regulations were finally adopted in July 1975. The task force implementing the compromise regulations fell to the Office for Civil Rights (OCR) at the U.S. Department of Education. At least one OCR regional office declared at the time that it would not enforce the regulations that addressed intercollegiate athletics. Women's groups, therefore, went to court to force DHEW to enforce Title IX and provide training to OCR's representatives in every region of the country.

There was little infrastructure in schools, colleges, or state education agencies to explain the law and provide the technical knowledge to implement it. OCR personnel received inadequate training on how to implement the law, and as a result regional offices gave out conflicting information about Title IX (Fishel and Pottker, 1977). In 1978, Congress appropriated separate funding for technical assistance in what was called "sex desegregation," then desegregation on the basis of national origin in 1979. Funding for assistance in race, sex, and national origin was to be used to address compliance with Title IX (sex) and Title VI (race and national origin) by four entities. The largest of the four were the regional desegregation assistance centers (DACs), often located in universities, each of which provided services to several states or territories in ten regions of the United States. State education agencies (SEAs) could also apply for federal funding in all three areas (race, national origin, and sex), as could local school districts (local education agencies, or LEAs). A fourth group, the Title IV institutes, was funded as well. In the early 1980s, appropriations for LEAs and institutes were discontinued, leaving the SEAs and DACs to provide all technical assistance to schools and colleges for race, sex, and national origin. Regulations outlining the purposes and acceptable activities for each of the three areas were separate and often dissimilar, making it difficult to work together. SEAs competed against each other for federal grants, and educational institutions competed for the contracts to operate the DACs. Several DACs changed locations when universities within the same region were successful in subsequent funding cycles. The discretionary nature of the funding also meant that many states did not apply for funds at all or applied for funds in one or two areas rather than in all three. In those states that did not apply for federal funding, no one worked on Title IX or Title VI, unless the state itself funded staff (e.g., Florida).

Because of separate funding mechanisms and funding regulations, the three civil rights areas of race, national origin, and sex were frequently physically separated as well, often located in separate offices within the same state agency or university. National training meetings often separated the issues of sex, race, and national origin, and, in my experience, specialists working in those areas rarely met with colleagues working on issues of disability. As a result of this systematic "silencing" of the issues, ignorance of parallel civil rights issues, mistrust, competition, and even hostility emerged. It was often easy to focus on only one issue; for example, if facilities were made available to boys and girls, it appeared that the job was done without considering whether the facilities were accessible, and thus available, to students with disabilities of both genders. Some states made sincere and concerted efforts to link the programs, but these efforts were not widespread.

Another federal funding mechanism that helped schools and colleges meet the requirements of Title IX was vocational legislation that later became the Carl D. Perkins Vocational and Applied Technology Act. This required, starting in 1976, that each state set aside at least fifty thousand dollars to hire a sex equity consultant. The Perkins Act has funded efforts designed to provide single parents, displaced homemakers, and single pregnant women with marketable skills. It also provided funds for sex equity programs to eliminate sex bias and stereotyping in secondary and postsecondary vocational education. In some states, the vocational equity consultant frequently worked with the Title IV-funded sex equity consultant to provide technical assistance on implementation of Title IX.

People initially hired by the Title IV-funded agencies too often had little background or training in civil rights law, training techniques, or the provision of technical assistance. Many were classroom teachers, myself included, who were interested in the elimination of discrimination based on race, sex, or national origin and were self-taught about these issues. Few of us had any formal training in civil rights compliance because few such courses were available, especially for educators. As a result, the U.S. Department of Health, Education, and Welfare (later the Department of Education, established under President Carter) and its Office for Civil Rights hired specialists to design and provide "training of trainers" workshops throughout the country. Title IV funds provided resources for the new equity specialists to attend these workshops. In the workshops, participants learned how to apply the requirements of the Title IX regulations to practical situations in schools.

In 1979, Shirley McCune, then with the U.S. Office of Education and responsible for training equity trainers to help schools with Title IX, and Barb Landers, the Title IV-funded sex equity specialist with the California Department of Education, founded the National Coalition for Sex Equity in Education (NCSEE). At NCSEE's subsequent annual meetings, the growing field of sex equity developed, and sex equity professionals received and provided more training on how to implement Title IX.

As sex equity professionals worked with the Title IX statute and its regulations, they noticed several shortcomings. There is no definition of "discrimination," for example, or what "benefits" students should not be denied. The notions of stereotyping and bias are not mentioned in Title IX, though they do turn up in the later Vocational Education Acts. There were no provisions for ongoing monitoring or evaluation of compliance. School districts or institutions of postsecondary education who undertook efforts to comply with Title IX did so because of community pressure, commitment by a small group of employees, or because a complaint had been filed against them. As a result, compliance was often haphazard throughout the system, and many schools and colleges avoided compliance as long as possible. The groups that applied pressure from the community were often single-issue groups that did not take into account other civil rights areas; groups that applied pressure for schools to provide access for students with disabilities often did not talk about sex or race equity, and vice versa. Equity professionals also failed to make early connections to other civil rights laws that protected students. For many who worked in school districts dominated by students and teachers of European-American ancestry, notions of race were rarely taken into account. Sex-biased conditions experienced by both male and female students with disabilities were frequently ignored and misunderstood.

As the case law related to Title IX emerged, and as persons providing technical assistance became more sophisticated in their knowledge of the law, the study of sex equity came into its own. As in any field of study, gaps in understanding and training emerged. A significant gap grew, for example, between educators working for gender equity and educators working with students with disabilities. Because of the systemic separation of sex, race, and national origin, those areas often did not share their natural linkages. Other civil rights issues, such as religious freedom and acceptance of all sexual orientations, were not even considered during the first decade of Title IX implementation. The majority of equity professionals working on Title IX assistance were middle-class women of European origin. Consequently, the field of sex equity in education developed a reputation as being a field closed to issues of race, national origin, disability, class, and sexual orientation. For years, mainstream sex equity consultants did not focus much on boys' and men's issues either, since the initial reports of discrimination illuminated the many shortcomings in girls' education. Finally, by the 1990s, those who had urged that sex equity professionals address parallel civil rights issues began to be heard by the Department of Education and others. Shrinking resources became a force in helping people realize that gender is influenced by disability, race, national origin, ethnicity, religion, class, and sexual orientation, as are all these areas influenced by gender. In 1996, funding was eliminated for state education agency Title IV programs, but the Desegregation Assistance Centers continue to be funded through the U.S. Department of Education.

INTERSECTION OF TITLE IX WITH DISABILITY RIGHTS

Title IX is often regarded as a civil rights law that protects all girls and all boys, with the unstated assumption of homogeneity in each gender group. In reality, there are differences among students based on such factors as disability status, race, ethnicity, and socioeconomic status that may influence how different groups of boys and girls are treated. Title IX applies to students with disabilities, but to ensure equitable education for girls and young women with disabilities, who face double discrimination based on disability and gender, it is also necessary to consider the protections offered by disability rights laws, such as the Individuals with Disabilities Education Act (IDEA), Section 504 of the 1973 Rehabilitation Act, and the Americans with Disabilities Act (ADA). The presentation below of the various requirements of Title IX includes some discussion of disability equity issues as well.

Girls with disabilities must be able to access education programs equitably in comparison to both boys and nondisabled girls. For example, if shower and changing rooms are available to students in auto mechanics classes, they must be comparable for each sex and physically accessible. Elsewhere in this volume, Doren and Benz document how girls and young women with disabilities have more limited access to employment and other postsecondary opportunities. Public schools and colleges must provide equitable, accessible vocational and career training to all girls and boys. It is important that educators not fall back on comfortable gender or disability stereotypes when providing programs for girls and boys or men and women with disabilities studying in education institutions that receive federal funding.

TITLE IX REQUIREMENTS

The statute itself does not illustrate by example or define its requirements. To clarify the meaning of Title IX and assist schools and colleges in implementing its intent, the U.S. Department of Education issued regulations, some of which are explained below. Also included under each section are implications for teachers, case studies for review and response, and examples of how the law might apply to girls and boys with disabilities.

Policies and Procedures (§106.8 & 106.9)

Requirement   This part of the regulation stipulates that each school, college, or university that accepts federal funding (called the "recipient") must designate at least one employee to coordinate its efforts to comply with and carry out its responsibilities under Title IX, including investigation of any complaints that are filed against the school alleging that it does not comply with Title IX (§106.8 [a]). In most schools and colleges, that designated person's title is the "Title IX coordinator," and in most institutions, the Title IX coordinator duties are only a small part of the designated employee's duties. Further, a public school or college must notify all its students and employees of the name, office address, and telephone number of the Title IX coordinator. Recipients must also adopt and publish grievance procedures providing "prompt and equitable resolution of student and employee complaints regarding noncompliance" with Title IX (§106.8[b]).

Schools are also required to adopt and disseminate to specific groups (students, employees, applicants for employment, and all unions or professional organizations) their policy of nondiscrimination, stating that the school, college, or university does not discriminate on the basis of sex in the educational programs or activities that it operates and that it is required by Title IX not to discriminate in such a manner

(§106.9[a]). Recipients are further prohibited from using or distributing a publication that suggests, by illustration or text, that the institution treats applicants, students, or employees differently on the basis of sex.

Practice Institutions that receive federal financial assistance often post a notice that they do not discriminate on the basis of sex as required by Title IX and that questions concerning compliance or desire to file formal complaints may be directed to the Title IX coordinator, with information on how to contact that person. As required under §106.9(b), that statement is then published on each announcement, bulletin, catalog, or application form disseminated by the institution. Schools and colleges often combine this statement with requirements for other federal civil rights laws, such as statements that they do not discriminate on the basis of race, national origin, color, religion, or disability, in addition to sex. While the statement will be included in many school publications, it need not be on each piece of paper printed by the school, like programs for drama productions or graduation. The institution's policy of nondiscrimination indicates its intention not to discriminate but does not guarantee that the institution is free from discrimination in all areas at all times.

Schools should make policies prohibiting discrimination on the basis of sex available in Braille, in any language likely spoken by students, in large print, cassette, and computer disk. Accommodations should be provided, when needed, to enable the Title IX coordinator to communicate with all students. Policies should be written so they can be understood by all students, including students with cognitive disabilities. All students should receive an explanation of the policies that is consistent with their age and ability/disability status.

Policies and procedures stating the institution's intent and commitment to treat students and employees equitably serve as the foundation for all other requirements in the Title IX regulations. Actions of the school can be measured against its stated policy prohibiting discrimination. Investigations of complaints filed will usually begin with a request for the institution's policies and procedures for nondiscrimination. The policies and procedures function as roadmaps to ensure smooth resolutions of concerns and complaints.

Admissions (§106.15)

Institutions receiving federal financial assistance may not discriminate on the basis of sex in admission or recruitment. That means school districts may not offer "girls' schools" or "boys' schools." Detroit, Michigan, for example, wanted to open boys' and girls' academies but was prohibited from doing so by the OCR.

Education Programs and Activities (§106.31)

Requirement   This section of the regulations states that "no person shall, on the basis of sex, be excluded from participation in, be denied the benefits of, or be subjected to discrimination under any academic, extracurricular, research, occupational training, or other education program or activity operated by an educational institution which receives or benefits from Federal financial assistance." Further, this section specifically states that educational institutions receiving federal money may not, on the basis of sex

- treat one person differently from another in determining whether to provide aid, benefit, or service;
- provide different aid, benefits or services, or services in a different manner;
- deny any person such aid, benefit or service;
- subject any person to separate rules of behavior, sanctions, or other treatment;
- apply any rule concerning the domicile or residence of a student differently;
- aid or perpetuate discrimination against any person by providing significant assistance to any agency, organization, or person which discriminates on the basis of sex in providing any aid, benefit, or service to students or employees; or
- otherwise limit any person in the enjoyment of any right privilege, advantage, or opportunity.

This section requires that if scholarships, fellowships, or other awards established by foreign or domestic governments, wills, trusts, or similar legal instruments are restricted to members of one sex, the institution may continue to administer those restricted funds if it offers a similar opportunity for the members of the other sex. This section also addresses programs not operated, in whole or in part, by the educational institution, yet requires, facilitates, permits, or offers participation by students or employees. It requires that the school or college making such programs available to students or employees develop procedures to assure that the operator or sponsor of the external program does not discriminate. If discrimination occurs, the educational institution may not require, facilitate, or permit its students or employees to participate. An example of an external program might be a study program in another country that the student's school coordinates or collaborates with, which may be overtly or covertly discriminating by sex. The U.S.

educational institution is obligated to sever its relationship with the external program if the discrimination does not stop. Thus, for example, if high school seniors are enrolled in work-study placements in the community, the school cannot discriminate by gender.

In March 1997, the Office for Civil Rights, citing this section of the regulations among others, issued its "Sexual Harassment Guidance: Harassment of Students by School Employees, Other Students, or Third Parties." In the Introduction, OCR draws on Title IX regulations and relevant court cases to state that "Sexual Harassment of students is a form of prohibited sex discrimination under the circumstances described in the Guidance." The Guidance clarifies that Title IX may be used as the basis of prohibition of sexual harassment by adults against students, and subsequent court cases have clarified a school or college's vulnerability to liable suits in student-to-student harassment as well (*Davis v. Monroe County Board of Education*). Like other regulations, this protection against sexual harassment applies to all students, including students with disabilities who may face higher rates of sexual harassment than their nondisabled peers (see Linn and Rousso, this volume).

Practice The regulations do not define the meanings of "aid, benefit, or service," although it might be inferred that all programs and activities provided by a school are covered here. As a result, Title IX has been used in many cases alleging sexual harassment as a form of sex discrimination.

CASE STUDY 1

Can Title IX Be Used in This Case to Provide Relief for a Student?

A substitute teacher, seated at the front of the room, is showing a film in a darkened, middle school classroom. In the back of the room, two boys force a girl to perform oral sex. Later, the girl tells her guidance counselor. Nothing is done because, as the counselor later states, the girl "makes up things to get attention." The girl's mother comes to the school to complain, but the school insists that the girl has made up the story; officials state it is how she "acts out" with her disability. She must return to the classroom, where the boys taunt her and scare her.

What Could They Have Done?

Title IX could be used in this case. The mother could have asked for the school's complaint procedure to compel the school to address the issue formally. In the event upon which this case study was based, however, the mother was forced to hire an attorney to get the school to respond. The school should have taken preventative measures long before the incident happened, by having a complaint procedure the students understood and could use, teaching students appropriate behavior and consequences for not acting appropriately, and providing staff development for teachers and substitutes. In addition, all schools need to address equality between boys and girls, women and men so as not to perpetuate unequal power relationships. This can be done by developing and implementing an age appropriate curriculum that teaches students the effects of valuing and treating one sex as if they are inferior to the other. All students, including students with disabilities, must be taught how to protect themselves against harassment and discrimination and appropriate treatment of others.

Housing (§106.32)

This section of the regulations sets standards for sex-segregated housing, such as dormitories on campus or hotel rooms during travel for school-sponsored activities. Such separate housing must be comparable in quantity to the number of students of one sex and in quality and cost to that provided students of the other sex. Disability law notes that such housing should be accessible to both females and males with disabilities.

CASE STUDY 2

Anthony High School provides hotel rooms for coaches and members of the boys' basketball team, two athletes per room, when they travel to the state's capital for the state basketball tournament. When the girls' basketball team competes in their state tournament one week later, it stays in hotels paid for by the school, four girls per room. The school says it does not have enough money for the girls' tournament.

What Could They Have Done?

The school should fund the boys' and girls' sports more equitably to ensure equal treatment. If money is not budgeted for tournament expenses incurred by the girls' basketball team, the school must find a way to raise necessary funds. In some schools, the money from school vending machines is allocated for such unanticipated expenses. In this situation, the girls and their parents could file a complaint under Title IX.

Comparable Facilities (§106.33)

Requirement   This section states that while educational institutions receiving federal funds may provide separate facilities by gender for toilets, locker rooms, and showers, those facilities must be comparable.

Practice   Most schools were built before Title IX, so personnel had to adapt facilities to provide for girls' and women's athletics and to provide facilities for the gender integration of vocational education classes. Change was often slow, but some schools moved quickly as students and parents advocated for equal facilities. A group of female students at the University of Wisconsin-Madison "liberated" the Red Gym in the mid-1970s, which had for over a century been open only to men. The women stormed the gym and rushed the swimming pool, throwing off their clothes and jumping into the pool like the men, who had been allowed to swim naked. The action worked; the facility was soon adapted for use by both men and women. Unfortunately, it took many more years before the facility was remodeled to become accessible to college students with disabilities (personal communication, McBurney Disability Resource Center, University of Wisconsin-Madison, August 1997).

CASE STUDY 3

In 1980, a sex equity consultant at a state education agency received a petition signed by most students attending a small junior high school. There was no hair dryer in the boys' locker room that they could use after physical education classes or athletic practice. There were two such hair dryers installed in the girls' locker room. The students insisted this was a violation of Title IX, which they had learned about from an assistant principal. The consultant called the school, and new dryers were installed in the boys' locker room. The consultant did not mention that dryers should be accessible to all boys, including boys who use wheelchairs.

What Could They Have Done?

The school could have undertaken a review of its facilities to make sure that sections of the school building segregated by sex were comparable and made necessary changes. The consultant could also have suggested that in the review of facilities school officials make sure that facilities were accessible to all.

Access to Course Offerings (§106.43)

Requirement   The regulations state that a school may not carry out any educational program or activity separately on the basis of sex or require or refuse participation in any program or activity on the basis of sex. The regulation lists programs that must not be segregated as "health, physical education, industrial, business, vocational, technical, home economics, music, and adult education courses. " Several caveats are mentioned:

1. Students in physical education classes and activities may be grouped by ability as assessed by "objective standards of individual performance developed and applied without regard to sex." For example, students may be given grades in "basketball" based on numbers of baskets made, an objective standard.

2. Students may be separated by sex (it is not required) within physical education classes or activities during participation in wrestling, boxing, rugby, ice hockey, football, basketball, and other sorts of activities the major purpose of which involves bodily contact. Students must not be separated for the instructional part of the class, but if so desired, students may be separated by gender for the physical contact portion of the class.

3. Where use of a single standard of measuring skill or progress in a physical education class has an adverse effect on members of one sex, the school shall use appropriate standards that do not have such an effect. Asking all students in a weightlifting class to lift a certain amount to get a good grade, for example, may have an adverse effect on girls, whose upper body strength, in general, is not as well-developed as boys' upper body strength.

4. Teachers may separate girls and boys in elementary and secondary school during those portions of classes that deal exclusively with human sexuality. Students may not, however, be separated for an entire semester for instruction in "health," unless every single class discussed human sexuality.

5. Schools may separate students by "vocal range or quality" (but not sex) even if the result is a chorus or choruses of one or predominately one sex. Calling a choral group a "Boys' Glee club" or "Girls' Chorus" is inadmissible, though "Tenor Choir" is acceptable.

Practice   This section compelled education entities to integrate courses that had been traditionally separated by gender. Title IX specifically states that girls and boys must receive the same curriculum, although regulations allow for gender separation for discussion of human sexuality. Most schools, however, do not separate students for sex education classes.

Counseling and Use of Appraisal
and Counseling Materials (§106.36)

Requirement   The regulations state that a recipient of federal funds may not discriminate on the basis of sex in the counseling or guidance of students or applications for admission. The section addresses testing materials, which may not be different for students based on sex, unless such materials cover the same occupations and interest areas and their use is shown to be essential for eliminating sex bias. Schools and colleges must develop and use internal procedures to ensure that such materials do not discriminate. Further, where the use of a counseling test or other instrument results in a substantially disproportionate number of members of one sex in any course of study or classification, the school must take action to assure that such disproportion is not the result of discrimination in the instrument or its application. Where a class contains a substantially disproportionate number of individuals of one sex, the school must act to assure that the disproportion is not the result of discrimination by materials or counselors.

Practice   Although it took some time, and some areas (like recruitment materials from the military) were particularly problematic, at this point in time most materials are generally unbiased. Aptitude and interest tests have also been changed so that outcomes are not reported by gender, and suggestions for occupations are not made or ignored on the basis of sex. Counselors appear to be more aware of their actions that encourage students in course selection.

This regulation has considerable potential application to the education of students with disabilities. As discussed in the chapter by Doren and Benz (this volume), there are well-known differences in outcomes, including vocational outcomes, between males and females with disabilities. There is little evidence, however, as to what influences these outcomes. When thinking about students with disabilities, schools must ensure that courses and counseling materials are free of both gender and disability stereotyping and are accessible.

CASE STUDY 4

A school requires that all students complete an occupational interest survey. A girl who has been raised on a farm, loves farm work, and wants to continue working in agriculture receives the results of the interest survey. Where her interests lie with farming, the occupation blank lists "Not applicable," since she has indicated that she is female, and the occupation possibility based on her answer is agricultural agent.

What Could They Have Done?

The school's counseling department should be held accountable for using a biased test and using the test's results to encourage or discourage a student based on her sex. The school should use another, unbiased test for this purpose. Furthermore, the school is promoting actions that would be illegal in the workplace under another civil rights law, Title VII, which prohibits discrimination in the workplace.)

Financial Assistance (§106.37)

Requirement   This section stipulates that a recipient may not, on the basis of sex, marital, or parental status provide different amounts or types of financial assistance to students. This prohibits differences in solicitation, listing, approval, or application of rules of eligibility for financial assistance. It permits schools or colleges to administer scholarships, fellowships, or other forms of assistance that require awards to be made to members of a particular sex, provided that the overall effect of sex-restricted awards does not discriminate on the basis of sex. Athletic scholarships may be awarded on the basis of sex, provided that such awards be made in proportion to the number of students of each sex participating in interscholastic or intercollegiate athletics.

Practice   When athletic opportunities developed for women on college campuses, scholarships became available, though they are still sometimes smaller and less frequently available than those for males. A more difficult problem for high schools has been equalizing scholarships or grants provided for in wills or bequests.

CASE STUDY 5

A decade before the passage of Title IX, a wealthy alumnus of a high school left a trust fund to be used for scholarships for a "worthy boy" graduating from the school. The trust provided for one thousand dollars per year for four years for the boy to study at a posthigh school institution. The wife of the alumni is still alive and comes to the school annually to award the money, accompanied by the local newspaper's photographer, who ensures that the school and the recipient receive ample coverage in the local media. The widow is unwilling to change the terms of the trust to open the benefits to girls as well as boys.

What Could the School Do?

The school has an obligation to equalize the money or persuade the widow to open the trust to both sexes. If she is unwilling to do so, the school must raise an equal amount for girls. Another option is for the widow to continue to award the money to one sex but use another type of institution to make and publicize the award.

Employment Assistance to Students (§106.38)

Requirement This section requires that schools or colleges that hire students or help them find employment elsewhere make sure that no discrimination occurs in the hiring or notification of hiring opportunities. This means that the school may not provide names of students or provide any assistance to agencies, organizations, or individuals that discriminate on the basis of sex when employing students.

Practice In some places, community members might call a school asking counselors to post a notice asking for "a boy to mow lawns." This section prohibits a school from posting such a notice, unless the caller agrees that the notice ask for "a student to mow lawns." No one may hire or advertise for only one gender.

Health and Insurance Benefits and Services (§106.39)

Requirement If a recipient of federal funds provides a medical, hospital, accident, or life insurance benefit, service, policy, or plan to any of its students, it may not discriminate on the basis of sex in any of those. A college may provide a benefit, service, policy, or plan that is used by different proportion of students of one sex than of the other, including family planning services. In addition, if a school provides full coverage health services, it must also provide gynecological care.

Practice Sometimes secondary schools provide physical examinations for students taking part in athletics during the school year. When this is the case, the school must make examinations available to both male and female athletes. Colleges often offer a health benefit plan for student purchase or use; in these cases, the services must be available to and comparable for both sexes.

Marital or Parental Status (§106.40)

Requirement This section prohibits a school or college from discriminating on the basis of sex in applying any rule concerning a student's actual or potential parental, family, or marital status. The school must treat pregnancy, childbirth, false pregnancy, termination of pregnancy, and recovery therefrom in the same manner and under the same policies as any other temporary disability with respect to any medical or hospital benefit, service, plan, or policy with respect to students admitted to any educational program or activity.

Practice Schools may not suspend students for pregnancy or any related condition. Students may not be disciplined or prohibited from participating in any school program because of pregnancy. If a female student participates in athletics, she may participate as long as she and her doctor think it is safe for her to do so.

Athletics (§106.41)

Requirement   No one may, on the basis of sex, be excluded from participation in, be denied the benefits of, be treated differently from another person or otherwise be discriminated against in any interscholastic, intercollegiate, club, or intramural athletics offered by an educational institution receiving federal funds. This section allows for separate male and female teams, provided they are comparable and supported according to the needs of the program and the interests of the students.

Students with disabilities must be afforded an equal opportunity to participate in extracurricular activities, including sports. The steps, if any, the school must take to permit a disabled student to participate in a sport will depend on the specific facts of each case, including the nature of the disability and the particular sport. The school should take steps to provide a student with a disability an opportunity to the maximum extent appropriate to the needs and abilities of the student. The student may not be denied the opportunity to try out for a team, or be excluded from a team, because of disability. However, decisions regarding the selection of team members, position played, level of participation, and playing time all involve the exercise of judgment and a great deal of discretion by the coach. As always, spectator facilities must be accessible to everyone.

Textbooks and Curricular Materials (§106.42)

Under this section, Title IX specifically excludes textbooks from regulation. It states that Title IX does not require or prohibit the use of particular textbooks or curricular materials. In practice, equity professionals often work with educators to help them voluntarily assess textbooks prior to adoption, with sex equity as only one criterion. Criteria should include all equity issues (sex, race, disability, etc.), as well as such factors as "readability," "relationship to school standards," and "attractiveness to students."

Employment (§106.51–106.60)

This section prohibits discrimination on the basis of sex in any aspect of employment.

SEX AS A BONA-FIDE OCCUPATIONAL QUALIFICATION (§106.61)

Requirement   If a school or college uses sex as a reason to hire or provide benefits to a person, it must show that is a legitimate reason for that employment action. Sex/gender may be used, however, in relation to employment in a locker room or toilet facility used only by members of one sex.

Practice   Schools and colleges had to be careful initially that they were not hiring a physical education teacher of a particular sex because a small portion of that teacher's duties might be locker room supervision. Locker room supervision had to be assigned to aides or to other teachers of the same sex as those being supervised.

A CALL FOR INTEGRATION AND INCLUSION

All students are protected from discrimination on the basis of sex by Title IX, but we have been limited in our vision of who "all" students might be. While this chapter has begun the discussion of the intersection of gender and disability under Title IX, we must continue that discussion and include disability, race, ethnicity, national origin, sexual orientation, and other civil rights issues when we talk about sex equity.

REFERENCES

Fishel, A., and J. Pottker. 1977. *National politics and sex discrimination in education*. Toronto, D.C.: Heath.

Title IX of the Education Amendments. 1972. Volume 20, Sections 1681–1688 (197).

CHAPTER 5

She Bakes and He Builds:
Gender Bias in the Curriculum

Susan Shaffer
and Linda Shevitz

Curriculum should function both as window and mirror. Education should enable a student to look through window frames to
see the realities of others and into mirrors to see her or his own
reality.

—Emily Style

CURRICULUM: AN OVERVIEW

Curriculum profoundly affects the way our schools meet their promise
of success for all children. It can be defined as what students should
know and do (content), how information is taught (instruction), how
learning is measured (assessment), how the educational system is organized (context), and what is used to teach skills, values, and content
(instructional materials), even extracurricular activities, displayed
images, and the nature of field trips, school events, or assemblies. All are
part of the curriculum of school districts or individual schools.

All aspects of the curriculum, including the "evaded" curriculum,
that which is not taught, can contain gender and other forms of bias that
impede the learning and educational opportunities of all students. This
chapter will examine the extent, nature and impact of gender bias in the
curriculum and will provide a set of strategies and tools to counter such
bias. Other forms of bias, including disability bias, will be addressed to
some degree. Our definition of "curriculum" will be purposefully limited to instructional materials. When evaluating curricular materials for
bias, it is important to look at the wide range of instructional resources

in schools. These include textbooks, supplementary reading materials, reference books, assessments, newspapers, periodicals, pamphlets, audio and video tapes, transparencies, artifacts, maps and globes, music and art, manipulative objects, learning games, visual displays, computer software, Internet sites, television and film.

The selection of instructional materials in planning curriculum is critical, given that much of students' classroom time is spent interacting with these materials. To promote academic achievement and success for all students, it is necessary to be sensitive to the often subtle gender, disability, racial, ethnic, age, economic, and sexual orientation biases in curriculum content. Although the main function of textbooks and other instructional materials is to convey specific information, textbooks also provide children with role models, aspirations, and moral values. Thus, at the same time a child is learning history, music, mathematics, or science, he or she is also learning standards for how women, men, girls, and boys should act, how individuals with disabilities and other diverse groups should and should not behave, and options open to members of each group.

Despite the importance of curriculum content, recent studies of educational reform have failed to examine the equity content of instructional materials (AAUW, 1995). Surveys conducted in the 1970s and early 1980s identified race and gender biases at all grade levels and in all subject areas (Weitzman and Rizzo, 1974; Burns, Cohen, and Williams, 1981; Scott, Foresman, and Co., 1972). The pattern of omitting contributions of girls, women, and persons of color was clear. Girls and women were portrayed less often than males in text and illustrations, and female activities were generally reduced to homemaking, grooming, following males passively, and being protected or rescued by males. In contrast, boys and men were portrayed as active, independent, creative, and possessing leadership capabilities. Basically, boys acted, and girls watched; boys built, and girls baked.

Today, texts are less sexist and racist than those of the 1970s. Reviewers have noted an increased emphasis on women and persons of color from the early 1990s through the mid-1990s (Reese, 1994; Beyer, 1996). Still, research reports that while text publishers have included more representations of women, the quality of content is lacking, and stereotypical images are still reinforced (Chapman, 1997). While much of the gender bias in curriculum relates to females, sex role stereotyping of males also occurs in the media, in textbooks, in computer software, and in other materials. While boys and men are often portrayed positively in leadership roles and in a wide range of activities and careers, they are also portrayed negatively—as violent and overly aggressive or as proficient only in traditional male areas, such as athletics. Although there is a growing number of young children's books that depict boys in nurturing ways (Sadker and Sadker, 1994), males are generally not depicted in sensitive or caring roles. Males of color and males with disabilities are also underrepresented in most texts.

With the dramatic increase in use of electronic media in schools, bias has also been documented in computer materials intended for classroom use. In a study of mathematics software, Hodes (1996) found that of all characters identifiable by gender, only 12 percent of those depicted were female. Also, most female characters were mothers or princesses and had passive roles, while males held active occupations, such as factory workers, shopkeepers, mountain climbers, and equipment operators. In addition, advertisements and promotions for computer software and computer usage are often targeted at males. The lack of positive and realistic images of females in computer software and games, the stereotypical portrayal of males, and the unequal expectations for males versus females in the use of computer technology have implications for curriculum development.

When evaluating software, educators should consider not only gender equity issues but also whether the software is available in more than one language or in alternative formats for students with disabilities and whether the software accommodates different learning styles and varying ability levels.

FORMS OF BIAS IN INSTRUCTIONAL MATERIALS

Six general forms of gender bias in instructional materials have been identified (Sadker and Sadker, 1982). These forms of bias, which can also be applied to race, disability, socioeconomic status, and other diversity factors are listed below. Each form is described in greater detail later in this chapter.

1. Exclusion/Invisibility: The omission or underrepresentation of females and the contributions of women.

2. Stereotyping: The assigning of traditional or rigid roles to girls and women and/or to boys and men.

3. Imbalance/Selectivity: The presentation of only one interpretation of an issue, event, or situation.

4. Unreality: The unrealistic portrayal of history and life experience, often with an avoidance of controversial topics.

5. Fragmentation/Isolation: The separation of issues or contributions related to women from the main body of the text; the portrayal of women in isolation from other groups.

6. Linguistic Bias: The use of language in a noninclusive way or in a way that reinforces stereotypes.

Research on Bias in Instructional Material

Research conducted in the 1980s indicated that 90 percent of learning time was spent using educational materials, which include textbooks, library books, audiovisual materials, and other supplementary items (Scott and Schau, 1985). In the 1990s, with the increasing use of electronic media in schools, this large percentage of time interacting with materials has continued to expand. Children internalize the images that these materials present. They learn who is beautiful, who is important, what is good, what to strive for, what opportunities are available, and who is expected to achieve in school. Researchers continue to find gender bias in textbooks, which are still the basic source of information for students. A 1994 study reported that social studies texts have become less gender biased over the years, but found that there are still major concerns—absence of discussion in texts of analysis of gender perspectives about historical events; lack of integration of women's history into texts; limited acknowledgment of women's economic contributions; lack of exploring the family as a historical institution; omissions of women's issues in historical contexts; and an overemphasis on physical appearance of women in print and illustrations (Reese, 1994). After reviewing three editions of a widely used high school biology text, Bianchini (1993) found that more women are depicted in the most recent edition but that the text projected science as a domain better suited for males than for females. An analysis of illustrations in middle school music textbooks (Koza, 1994) found that females are underrepresented and stereotyped. A study of the seven most commonly taught novels in high school English classes reported that women characters are usually vehicles for male protagonists to achieve their goals, rather than central figures pursuing their own goals (Connell, 1994).

The National Council for Research on Women (Phillips, 1998) reports that school curriculum materials still focus on the accomplishments of white European and American men and fail to acknowledge important contributions by women and men of color. Although sexism has decreased in school texts, examples of omission, tokenism, and gender stereotyping still occur frequently in textbook references to women and girls (AAUW, 1992). Studies of commonly used science, math, English, and social studies texts found that only 31 percent of textbook illustrations included females and that the percentage of females shown decreased as the grade level increased. The same pattern held for illustrations of persons of color. While persons of color were represented in 33 percent of the illustrations in first-grade textbooks, they were depicted in only 26 percent of books at the sixth-grade level. By the sixth grade, only 15 percent of the illustrations in mathematics books and 8 percent in science books displayed persons of color. Women of color were even less visible in these texts, appearing only half as often as men of color and making up only 7 percent of all females in textbooks. Persons with disabilities remained virtually invisible, and few adults presented were persons with disabilities (Sadker and Sadker, 1994).

Research Bias in Special Education Curricular Materials

Studies and surveys in the 1970s and early 1980s found instances of gender bias and sex role stereotyping in curriculum materials designed for special education students (Kratovil and Bailey, 1986). Since the late 1980s, with the inclusion of students with disabilities into regular education settings, many schools are adapting general curricular materials for use with disabled students, rather than working with materials specifically designed for special education. Disabled students participate in the general curricula, so they are exposed to the same forms of bias experienced by all students.

The authors of this chapter reviewed samples of career development texts for special education students published between 1992 and 1997 and found examples of gender bias. The general texts reviewed used gender fair language (referring to both she and he), had roughly equal representations of females and males, showed ethnic diversity, and depicted both males and females in supervisory roles. However, males held a wider range of careers and were shown in more active roles. In one text, the men held thirty-six different careers, while the women held only twenty. Only one of the texts discussed the changing demographics in the United States workforce, which encompasses increasingly larger percentages of women and people of color year after year. Only one text pictured individuals with disabilities and discussed the equity provisions of the Americans with Disabilities Act.

Four specialized texts related to career planning for individuals with disabilities were also reviewed. Only one of the books, which was written specifically for women with disabilities, mentioned gender issues in the workplace. The one book that contained illustrations depicted ethnically diverse females and males with a range of disabilities and in a wide array of careers. A campus access guide for students with disabilities preparing for the workplace made no reference to gender issues. We also reviewed five textbooks used in special education introduction courses at colleges and universities. In general, there was little discussion of curricular resources, with no mention of curriculum bias in any of the textbooks.

IMPACT OF CURRICULUM MATERIALS

Research and classroom applications suggest that students achieve better and retain information and concepts longer when their school experiences are relevant to their life experiences (Greenberg and Shaffer, 1990). Students should recognize something of their own lives in their instructional materials, as well as to see beyond themselves to the possibilities available in the future, without regard to gender, disability, race, ethnicity, sexual orientation, or economic background. When materials reflect students' backgrounds and include persons or groups similar to them, a positive climate for learning can be achieved. By presenting positive role models from diverse backgrounds and characteristics and conveying accurate and balanced information, materials help students gain an understanding of the roles and capabilities of their ancestors, peers, and themselves.

Curriculum Materials Affect Student Learning

Attitudes and Expectations for Oneself and Others   How students perceive their own self-worth—as mitigated by factors such as race, gender, economic class, cultural heritage—is shaped by the significant people in their lives and from messages present in their environment. Their perceptions are influenced by curriculum materials in which women, persons of color, and individuals with disabilities continue to be absent from the content, and where discussions of history, government, society, and valued ways of life only cover certain groups of people. These omissions affect the perceptions of young people, who are taught to believe that only certain roles in society are appropriate. As female and male roles change in society, many of the instructional materials used in schools do not keep pace. The identification of bias and the creative use of biased material also help students gain a high regard for others. Such instructional content and activities can help students acquire an appreciation of cultural differences and develop respect for both females and males of diverse groups and backgrounds. Such perceptions can increase student goals and success in school and in the society.

Self-esteem   Research has demonstrated that children need positive role models to develop self-esteem. When females and persons with disabilities are omitted from textbooks, a "hidden" curriculum is created, one teaching children that females and persons with disabilities are less important and less significant in our society.

Academic Achievement   Research shows that gender-biased achievement tests affect scores. On average, female students perform better on items with female references than items with male references. As such references are underrepresented in standardized exam questions, they reflect gender bias (AAUW, 1992).

Career Aspirations   Many young children view the world of work as being divided between work men do and work women do, divided again between work people of color do and work white people do, and divided still further by work for nondisabled people and that for individuals with disabilities. This identity development continues through adolescence. Persons with disabilities are rarely pictured in texts working in a career. Special education materials developed for teaching basic skills and career preparation contain sex-role stereotyping messages, which convey different expectations for lifestyle and occupational choices (Greenberg and Shaffer, 1990).

Today, men and women work in a variety of careers and share roles and activities that were formerly exclusive to one gender or the other, a change not reflected in many textbooks. Recent statistics show that one in six families in the United States is headed by a single parent, and one in every seventeen children lives in a single-parent household. Only 7 percent of American families fit the stereotyped view of a father working and a mother at home with two children, yet they are more likely to be represented in textbooks than other family structures. Both boys and girls will work, and they will work with diverse people. More than 80 percent of the new entries into the United States workforce will be women, persons of color, and immigrants (U.S. Department of Labor, 1998).

IDENTIFYING BIAS IN CURRICULAR MATERIAL

The activities and checklists included in this section can be used to assist students, parents, and educators to identify biased and unbiased materials. Instructional materials should be reviewed and analyzed for the different types of bias discussed in this chapter. The areas of inquiry should also include plot, characterizations, illustrations, the author's background and perspective, and the illustrator's background and perspective. Copyright dates should be noted to reference the historical time periods in which the biases appeared in publications. Schools and districts should survey their entire collection of media center materials, classroom resources, textbook selections, and library holdings. The composition of school committees that evaluate and select instructional materials should also be assessed to assure that individuals from diverse backgrounds and perspectives are represented. These committees should be given guidelines for assessing bias and determining the extent to which materials are available in alternative formats for students with disabilities.

Identifying Forms of Bias

A comprehensive means of evaluating curricular materials is to use the six forms of bias listed above. This framework was originally developed by McCune and Matthews, formerly of the Council of Chief State School Officers Equity Resource Center, and adapted by Sadker and Sadker (1982). These forms of bias correspond to the following concerns: frequency of representation of individuals/groups; role portrayals of individuals/groups; range of perspectives shown; accuracy of the content, setting, and placement of the content; and use of language.

Exclusion/Invisibility   This form of bias is indicated by the omission of one gender or of particular ethnic or racial groups, individuals with disabilities, older persons, and other groups who are appropriate to the context. In some cases, people from diverse socioeconomic backgrounds or geographic regions are excluded. Omissions of this sort are often found in social studies and science texts, but occur in all subjects. Surveys by the authors of this chapter of texts being used in high schools reveal that invisibility is still a problem. In one high school American history text reviewed, the numbers of pages discussing individual women or women's history, as compared with the total pages in the book, was 85 out of 1,126. In another book, the representation was 25 out of 695 pages. The two books combined allotted only 13 pages to the history of the women's rights movement (from the 1848 women's rights convention through the twentieth century).

A review of three high school literature texts published since 1990 found that ratios of male to female authors represented were ninety-six to fifty-one; fifty-four to twenty-one; and eighty-six to twenty-eight. The ratio of male to female authors was equitable in only one specialized text focusing on multicultural perspectives. In a study of widely used history textbooks published in 1990 and 1991, researchers found that the book illustrations depicted four to five times more male than female figures, and less than 3 percent of the name listings in the index referred to women (Sadker and Sadker, 1994).

A comparison of high school chemistry texts published in the 1970s with similar texts published in 1990 found that only two of the seven books published in 1990 contained greater and more substantive representations of women than the earlier texts (Bazler and Simonis, 1990). A study of five science textbooks (Bazler and Simonis, 1990) reported that the proportion of the drawings representing males ranged from two-thirds to three-fourths of the total and that not one book pictured a female scientist. As part of a classroom exercise, high school students were asked to name twenty famous U.S. women from the past or present in a five-minute time period. On average, they could only name four or five women (Sadker and Sadker, 1994).

Invisibility of people with disabilities is also common. Researchers point out that feminist anthologies, including those that address race and ethnicity, typically exclude people with disabilities (Fine and Asch, 1988). This invisibility can impact a student's aspirations and expectations for the future. A female student with a disability commented, "In my childhood, I wanted to grow up to be able-bodied . . . or, I wanted to be a boy . . . boys could grow up to be important, even if they were disabled. There was Franklin Roosevelt, Beethoven . . . and male athletes . . . but there was no one I could be, except maybe Helen Keller" (O'Toole, 1979).

Stereotyping   In this form of bias, groups or members of those groups are portrayed in narrowly defined ways, ignoring the wide range of interests and abilities represented within the group. Stereotyping may occur in numerous areas, such as physical appearance, personality characteristics, leadership or dependency roles, intellectual ability, creativity, variety of activities and competencies, career options, domestic roles, social activities, authority or power, athletic skill. Stereotyping may be particularly pervasive in the way male and female characters are portrayed, each having limited but differing descriptions. Women are still depicted more often than males in traditional roles and occupations. Women with disabilities are often depicted as inactive, sedentary, and alone rather than as parents, part of a family, and employed in a variety of occupations.

A review of two high school health education textbooks by the authors of this chapter found that sex-role stereotypes were prevalent: Females were pictured in discussions of nutrition, childcare, psychological aspects of love and caring, and personal care related to physical appearance. By contrast, males were pictured in discussions of competition, violence, stress, and mental disorders. Only one male was depicted in a nurturing role. When individuals were pictured holding jobs, women were shown as nurses and mothers, while men were shown as welders, fishers, athletes, doctors, farmers, police officers, broadcasters, and architects.

Imbalance/Selectivity   Textbooks can perpetuate bias by presenting only one interpretation of an issue, situation, or historical event. Imbalanced accounts limit students' knowledge of the varied perspectives that may apply to a particular situation or period in history. One example is discussing the suffrage movement exclusively from a white, middle-class, prosuffrage female perspective, rather than examining the tensions between white and black women in the suffrage movement period, analyzing the differences among suffragists, men's groups, and women of different political backgrounds. Another example is the view that women were given the right to vote, which ignores the fact that women struggled for more than seven decades to win the right to vote. Another common example of imbalance is that references to immigration discuss hardships faced by immigrants without noting these individuals' and groups' contributions to society. By presenting unbalanced information, textbooks distort reality and limit other possible interpretations. Consequently, students acquire a narrow and skewed understanding of the contributions, struggles, and participation of groups in our society, particularly of women, people of color, and individuals with disabilities.

Unreality   Textbooks frequently present an unrealistic portrayal of history and contemporary life experience. Controversial topics are glossed over, and discussion of discrimination and prejudice are avoided. For example, few if any career education materials inform readers of the discrimination people face in the workplace because of race, gender, disability, ethnicity, or sexual orientation. This denies students knowledge of barriers they may face in the world of work and the broader society, as well as information they need to recognize, understand, and use toward solving complex problems in society, which includes overt and subtle forms of discrimination on the basis of factors such as race, gender, disability, ethnicity, or sexual orientation.

Fragmentation/Isolation   This form of bias is exhibited in two ways. In the first instance, content about women and minorities is either marginalized or accorded a separate status among curricular materials instead of being fully infused into the curriculum (Phillips, 1998). For example, courses might add units on women's issues, instead of incorporating the subject matter into the mainstream content. Also, discussions of women and minority issues may be relegated to separate units or chapters in books, with subtitles such as "Women in the Civil War" or "Careers for Individuals with Disabilities." The contributions of women and minorities to history and society may also only be addressed during designated times of the year, such as Women's History Month or Black History Month. Yet another manifestation of this form of bias is the inclusion of a separate box at the side of a textbook page to describe the contributions of a certain group (for example, "The Achievements of Ten Distinguished Black Americans," rather than integrating this content into the main narrative of the text).

    In a second form of isolation, members of a particular group—distinguishable by race, gender, language, culture, and disability status—are shown in instructional materials interacting only with, or primarily with, members of their own group. This isolates the group members from being shown as fully integrated members of society. Both types of fragmentation/isolation bias convey that the roles and experiences of certain groups are peripheral to the dominant culture or less valued as important aspects of history.

Linguistic Bias   Language is a strong vehicle for conveying bias and attitudes about particular groups. This bias may be obvious, such as using the generic *he* to refer to both males and females or using terms such as *forefathers* rather than *ancestors*. It may also be subtle, shown through treatment in the adjectives used to describe groups or group members, or in titles of units (e.g., use of words such as *savage* or *uncivilized* to describe certain groups). Because language has biases based on many societal and cultural, as well as gender, issues, language can be a strong deterrent to the fair treatment of certain groups. Today, sexism and ableism are still found in many forms of language, including sign language. When using language of any type, it is important to eliminate biases based on disability, gender, race, national origin, or age. Below is a discussion of terms that are biased against women and persons with disabilities and nonbiased alternatives to these terms.

Nonsexist Language

Pharases such as *manning the space shuttle, using manpower,* or *doing a man-sized job* illustrate the language of a male-centered culture. Such language does not adequately serve our changing society. Language is changing, with new words being created that can help change our culture or society. According to the American Heritage *Book of English Usage*, some of the most notable changes that have taken place in the English language over the last thirty years have been driven by the desire to avoid, if not banish, sexism in the language (Miller, Swift, and Maggio, 1997). Below are suggestions for increasing equity and clarity in the use of language:

1. Pronouns: The masculine pronoun *he* fails to represent the female half of the human species. Suggested alternatives: use the plural *they, he/she, she and he,* or *her and him.*

2. Gender-specific words and job titles that seem to denote only males when females are also represented in the category: E.g., *forefathers, mankind, congressman, mailman, policeman.* Suggested alternatives: *ancestors, humankind, member of Congress, mail carrier, police officer.*

3. Feminine suffixes: Most nouns in English that reference the performer of an action can be used for a person of either sex. Feminine gender suffixes such as *ess* often imply that the feminine gender is a substandard variation of the masculine, and the suffix *ette* is a diminutive term—e.g., *hostess, actress, poetess, usherette.* Suggested alternatives: *host, actor, poet, usher.*

Nonbiased Language Related to Disability

Many terms referring to people with disabilities can be offensive to individuals and to groups. Many disability advocates prefer people-first language, with the disability mentioned second because it is only one of many characteristics used to define the person. Using alternate terms conveys the appropriate image of whole, vital, varied individuals who have disabilities as one part of who they are. Educators should also avoid language that reinforces negative stereotypes, such as *"suffers from cerebral palsy"* or *"confined to a wheelchair."* Because language is constantly evolving, educators should keep informed of changes in language that counter stereotypes and present positive images related to gender, disability, race, or ethnicity.

Strategies to Address Bias

In general, to provide gender equitable curriculum, educators need to be aware of forms of bias that still exist in all types of instructional materials. Students can be taught to become skilled evaluators of curriculum, and school curriculum review committees can be given guidance in ways to identify and select appropriate classroom materials. Teachers can creatively use biased materials found in their schools in positive ways by encouraging students to examine the materials critically as part of a broader discussion on bias and its effects on various groups and individuals. Students and educators can be activists by conveying to publishers their support of equitable materials and their criticism of biased materials. Researchers who have studied exemplary curricular practices for students with disabilities stress that the educational content must reflect real-world contexts, that current technology must be integrated into the curriculum, and that access to role models with disabilities must be provided (Kochhar and West, 1996).

To address biases and stereotypes, concerned teachers can analyze texts critically and bring supplemental materials into the classroom to expose students to multiple perspectives on topics and issues. Several publishers, including Macmillan, Harper and Row, McGraw Hill, and Holt, Rinehart, and Winston, have published specific guidelines for identifying nonsexist materials.

New gender-fair supplementary materials that have been developed in recent years focus particularly on expanding options and expectations for females. These include teen magazines such as *New Moon* and *Hues*, which portray positive images of girls and women from a variety of cultural backgrounds. Prompted by the focus on global issues at the Fourth World Conference on Women held in Beijing in 1995, organizations such as the Wellesley Center for Research on Women and the Women of Color Resource Center are developing curricula that address bias and discrimination issues in other countries. Also, several anthologies and collections of essays on women with disabilities have been published (e.g., *Disabled, Female and Proud*, by Rousso, 1988; *With Wings*, by Saxon and Howe, 1987). A growing number of classroom literature anthologies are including more works by women and people of color. Because of continued lack of visibility and limited portrayals of women's contributions in textbooks, it is still necessary to explore the use of supplementary materials. A comprehensive single source of supplementary multicultural women's history materials—across grade levels and subject areas—is the National Women's History Project. This organization's catalog lists many annotated resources, including print, video, display, and computer materials related to contributions of women in social studies, literature, the arts, and mathematics and science.

Students can develop analytical and critical thinking skills by analyzing biased materials. Materials can be examined for the six forms of bias described in this chapter, and students can discuss issues and develop alternative materials or projects that (1) incorporate contrasting and differing points of view, (2) include additional information that provides balance and demonstrates nonstereotyped realities, (3) identify the forms of bias contained in materials and point out why they limit student knowledge and perceived life options, and (4) redesign materials so that they are fair, inclusive, and representative of all groups in society.

Strategies for Dealing with Biased Language

1. Point out that the use of gender-biased words such as *mankind* or *policeman* limits visions of an inclusive world. Ask students to consider nonbiased alternatives.

2. Point out inconsistencies in language usage, such as describing the energetic leader when referring to a man but the beautiful leader when referring to a woman, reporting about the athletic (male) basketball player but the cute (female) basketball player, or doctor (male) and female doctor. Ask students to revise the statements.

3. Ask students to discuss the effects that sex-biased language may have on students' views of themselves and of possibilities related to their careers and life choices.

Strategies for Dealing with Roles and Representation

1. Call attention to instances where males or females are portrayed only in traditional career roles, such as women only as mothers, sec-

retaries, nurses, or teachers, or males shown in leadership or supervisory positions. Discuss the new role of women in the workforce and why some career choices are not open to them (or others because of race or disability). Discuss males in nontraditional roles, such as nurses or daycare providers. Have students view texts or periodicals and record male and female roles portrayed.

2. Look at the social roles of individuals in materials related to leadership, risk-taking, assertiveness, and so on. Have students read biographies of individuals, both women and men, who broke barriers or stereotypes.

3. Call attention to texts that isolate the contributions of one group into separate chapters or sidebars. Ask students how this information could be integrated into the main narrative of the textbook.

4. Call attention to texts in which females, people from diverse ethnic groups, and people with disabilities are underrepresented. Look at the table of contents, index, and illustrations. Have students identify others representing greater diversity who might be included in the book, including authors represented in literature anthologies and art and music books.

Strategies Related to Perspectives

1. Point out when only one perspective, for example the military/governmental perspective, of events and historical periods is represented in texts. Note how such a perspective focuses almost exclusively on the contributions of European American males, who have historically been in power positions. Discuss how history is shaped through communities, as well as through political leadership. Provide alternative sources, such as oral histories, journals, and original source documents to supplement traditional history texts. Utilize multicultural organizations to identify multicultural women's history resources.

2. Have students note copyright dates and investigate authors' backgrounds to examine why books convey certain perspectives and interpretations of events. Does the book reflect the conventional thinking and role stereotyping at the time it was written or published? (For example, in an older science text, students may see no mention of female astronauts or of astronauts of color.) Bring in more contemporary resources or gather information from reliable sources on the Internet to provide more accurate updated information.

3. Ask students to write a companion piece to an event in a text that offers a different perspective from that of the text. (For example, in a discussion of ancient Roman male senators, write about the role of women in Rome at that time.)

4. Discuss why observances such as Women's History Month or African American History Month were originated. How were these observances motivated by biases found in instructional materials?

Biased materials can serve as a learning tool for students to understand the roots and prevalence of forms of curricular bias, as well as to identify actions that can be taken to create more inclusive, gender-fair instructional materials. Students can analyze curricula and write letters detailing concerns about biased materials to editors of textbooks and/or commend publishers for exemplary publications.

CONCLUSION

Progress has been made in addressing the various forms of bias in school curricula, from invisibility to stereotyping to linguistic issues, but much remains to be improved. For students who face multiple biases, curricular materials and programs have an especially strong impact. What students study in school and the materials that guide their learning play important roles in developing their expectations for themselves, in shaping their view of others, in enabling them to become productive citizens, and in empowering them to lead successful and rewarding lives. While curricular materials have begun to move beyond the stereotypical images of she bakes and he builds, educators must continue to work to ensure that curricular materials remain truly gender-fair and inclusive.

REFERENCES

American Association of University Women (AAUW). 1992. *How schools short-change girls: A study of major findings on girls and education.* Washington, D.C.: American Association of University Women Educational Foundation (AAUW).

———. 1995. *Growing smart: What's working for girls in school.* Washington, D.C.: American Association of University Women Educational Foundation (AAUW).

———. 1998. *Gender gaps: Where schools still fail our children.* Washington D.C.: American Association of University Women Educational Foundation.

Bazler, J. A., and D. A. Simonis. 1990. Are women out of the picture? *Science Teacher* 57(9).

130   SUSAN SHAFFER AND LINDA SHEVITZ

Beyer, Christine E. 1996. Gender representations in illustrations, text, and topic area in sexuality education curricula. *Journal of School Health* 66.

Bianchini, J. 1993. *The high school biology textbook: A changing mosaic of gender, science, and purpose.* Paper presented at the American Educational Research Association Annual Meeting, Atlanta, April.

Burns, J. F. L. Cohen and S. Williams. 1981. *Evaluation of curriculum materials for sexism in language arts, social studies and counseling.* Indianapolis: Great Lakes Desegregation Assistance Center.

Chapman, Anne 1997. *A great balancing act: Equitable education for girls and boys.* Washington, D.C.: National Association of Independent Schools.

Connell, H. H. 1994, November. *Reading gender bias in the high school canon novels.* Paper presented at the Annual Meeting of the National Council of Teachers of English, Orlando.

Corporation for Public Broadcasting. 1998. *Report on study of school uses of television and video.* Washington, D.C.: Author.

Fine, M., and A. Asch. 1988. *Women with disabilities: Essays in psychology, culture, and politics.* Philadelphia: Temple University Press.

Greenberg, J. M., and S. M. Shaffer. 1990. *Gender and disability: A manual for educational training.* College Park: University of Maryland Vocational Technical Assistance Project.

Harris, L., and Associates. 1998. *Survey on disability and the workforce.* Washington, D.C.: National Organization on Disability.

Hodes, C. L. 1996. Gender representation in mathematics software. *Journal of Educational Systems* 24(1).

Kochhar, C. A., and L. L. West. 1996. *Handbook for successful inclusion.* Maryland: Aspen Publications.

Kolb, F., and R. Rose. 1991. *The equitable school continuum.* Andover, Mass.: The Network.

Koza, J. E. 1994, Summer. Females in middle school music textbooks: An analysis of illustrations. *Journal of Research in Music Education* 42(2).

Kratovil, J., and S. Bailey. 1986, Autumn. Sex equity and disabled students. *Theory into Practice* 25(4).

Miller, C., K. Swift and R. Maggio. 1997, September-October. Liberating language. *Ms. Magazine.*

O'Toole, M. L. 1979. Disabled women: The case of the missing role model. *Independent Magazine* 2.

Phillips, L. 1998. *The girls report: What we know and need to know about growing up female.* New York: National Council for Research on Women.

Reese, L. 1994, Winter. Gender equity and texts. *Social Studies Review.*

Rosser, S. V. 1993. Female friendly science: Including women in curricular content and pedagogy in science. *Journal of General Education* 42(3).

Rousso, H., with S. D'Malley, and M. Severance. 1988. *Disabled, female, and proud.* Boston: Exceptional Parent Press.

Sadker, M., and D..Sadker. 1994. *Failing at fairness: How America' s schools cheat girls.* New York: C. Scribner's Sons.

———. 1992. *Sex equity handbook for schools.* New York: Longman.

Saxon, M., and F. Howe, eds. 1987. *With wings: An anthology of literature by, for and about women with disabilities.* New York: The Feminist Press.

Scott, K., and C. G. Schau. 1985. Sex equity and sex bias in instructional materials. In *Handbook for achieving sex equity through education.* Edited by S. Klein. Baltimore: Johns Hopkins University Press.

Scott, Foresman, and Company. 1972. *Improving the image of women in textbooks.* Sexism in Textbooks Committee. Glenview, Ill.: Author.

Style, E. (1988). Curriculum as window and mirror. In *Gender balancing the school curriculum.* New Jersey: Oak Knoll School.

U.S. Department of Labor. 1998. *Twenty Facts on women workers.* Washington, D.C.: Government Printing Office.

Weitzman, L., and D. Rizzo. 1974. *Biased textbooks.* Washington, D.C.: National Foundation for the Improvement of Education.

CHAPTER 6

Can She Really Do Science?
Gender Disparities in
Math and Science Education

Ellen Wahl

INTRODUCTION

Math and science have been called "critical filters" (Sells, 1978; Beane, 1985). If students don't pursue these subjects through high school, they are screened out of most college majors and many jobs that pay well. Knowledge of math and science—and the methods and processes inherent in these disciplines—is increasingly fundamental to being an informed citizen in a technological society and participating in decisions that affect the everyday health and welfare of the populace. It is essential knowledge, but knowledge that has been denied to large segments of our society based on race, class, gender, and disability.

Girls with disabilities are among those least likely to have access to math and science experiences. Of the barriers that have limited their participation, the most persistent has been disbelief that girls who were disabled could actually do science and math. The title of this chapter is a challenge to recognize and reject these negative attitudes and to draw on the growing list of positive practices demonstrating that girls of all colors, backgrounds, and abilities can not only do science, but have a great deal to contribute to its practice and knowledge.

THE PROBLEM

Historically, math and science were the province of an elite few. Only a small percentage of students were expected to go beyond general math and

133

science in the middle grades, and the technical needs of our country were seen as being well served by the existing supply of scientists and engineers. That changed in the post–World War II era, with the rapid increase in industrial and scientific development. Still, it wasn't until the 1970s and 1980s that concern about the "pipeline" supply translated into action about the untapped talents of women, minorities, and people with disabilities. From there, it became clear that scientific literacy and an adequate flow of scientists were important to maintaining the health of science and society.

The National Science Foundation (NSF) considers women, minorities, and disabled people "underrepresented" in the scientific and technical workforce compared to their numbers in the population, and to the percentages of white males in science, mathematics, and engineering. For the past thirty years there has been a growing awareness that females and minority males have been denied opportunity in these critical fields, and there has been attention focused to narrow the gender and race gaps in participation and achievement.

For disabled people, ensuring the right to a free, appropriate public education became the law only twenty-five years ago, and exclusion from math and science was one among many educational opportunity concerns. Although there is literature on providing science education for students with disabilities that predates the federal law (Keller, 1994), there has been relatively little specific focus on girls with disabilities in science and math.

Math and science education reform efforts have gained momentum in response to declining achievement and concern about increasing gaps between groups. Unlike the elitism of the 1950s, the reform effort's rallying cry has been science and math for "all students," and it is accompanied by standards for what students "should know and be able to do" (NCTM, 1989; NRC, 1996; AAAS, 1990). The standards are intended to raise achievement and the overall quality of math and science education. The reform effort is further supported by NSF initiatives that transform state and local systems of education so that all students achieve. Equity of outcome, not simply equal opportunity, is the intent. Participation and success in math and science should not be predictable by demographic factors such as race, class, gender, or disability (Kreinberg, 1997). That intent has not yet been realized. The next section discusses how girls with disabilities are faring.

THE RESEARCH BASE

It is important to note that the available information is fragmented and incomplete. Studies tend to focus on girls versus boys, minority versus white, or disabled versus nondisabled. Very rarely are these combined to give us a picture of what the situation is for girls with disabilities from a range of ethnic and racial backgrounds. With this caveat, the following is a selective review of the literature.

Data about Participation

Taking the sequential science and math courses (physics, biology, chemistry; geometry, algebra, trigonometry, calculus) is the first critical filter for staying in the math/science track. When examined by gender alone, the gap in course-taking between girls and boys without disabilities now appears to be closing (although very few girls *or* boys are enrolling in the highest level math courses) (Campbell, 1997, pp. 62–63). But minority students are not enrolling in the high level courses in the same percentages as their white counterparts. And although the percentages of black, Hispanic, and American Indian students taking basic and advanced mathematics courses doubled between 1982 and 1994, black and Hispanic students are far more likely than white and Asian students to be enrolled in remedial math courses (NSF, 1999, p. xv).

Students with disabilities take fewer academic courses than their nondisabled peers. Their science credits are usually earned in remedial classes, and their math credits are earned in special education or remedial classes, indicating "that they are not likely to be prepared for advanced coursework in these subjects" (NCEO, 1992, p. 5). "Very few special education students were enrolled in advanced math courses, such as geometry, trigonometry, or calculus (Wagner, 1993, pp. 4–8). Students with disabilities from poor and minority backgrounds were less likely than their more affluent, white counterparts to be enrolled in courses such as advanced mathematics "that are considered part of the path to postsecondary education" (Wagner, 1993, p. S–13*)*. Within this dismal picture of course-taking for students with disabilities, there do not appear to be gender differences (p. S–12): neither girls nor boys with disabilities have access to the essential courses in math and science.

At higher education, the participation of women in the physical sciences, mathematics, and engineering "still lags significantly behind that of white men and Asians" (NSF, 1999, p. 39). "Women received a minority of science and engineering doctorates in all fields except psychology" (NSF, 1999, p. xiv). Minority women appear to be faring better than their male counterparts in higher education, but blacks, American Indians, and Hispanics continue to be underrepresented in graduate science and engineering programs (NSF, 1999, p. xiv).

Few disabled students attend higher education. Figures from 1991 put the estimate at 15 percent, including 9 percent vocational/trade schools, 3.5 percent two-year colleges, and 1.4 percent four-year colleges (Butler-Nalin and Wagner, 1991, pp. 9–3). Thus, it is no surprise that disabled persons earned only 329 science and engineering doctorates in 1993, just over 1 percent of the 25,184 total such degrees awarded (NSF, 1996). Data are not broken down by gender.

With regard to the workforce, the disparities in participation between groups remain striking, as noted in NSF figures (NSF, 1999, p. 3). From the standpoint of gender gaps:

- Women are 51.1 percent of the population, but only 22.4 percent of the science and engineering workforce.
- Men are 48.9 percent of the population, and 77.6 percent of the science and engineering workforce.

With respect to race and ethnicity:

- Blacks are 12 percent of the population but only 3.4 percent of the science and engineering workforce.
- Hispanics are 10.4 percent of the population but only 2.8 percent of the science and engineering workforce.
- American Indians are .7 percent of the population but only .2 percent of the science and engineering workforce.
- Asians are 3.4 percent of the population and 9.7 percent of the science and engineering workforce.
- Whites are 73.5 percent of the population and 83.8 percent of the science and engineering workforce.

And on the disability divide:

- Disabled people are 20.6 percent of the population but only 4.9 percent of the science and engineering workforce.
- Nondisabled persons are 79.4 percent of the population and 95.1 percent of the science and engineering workforce.

It is worth noting that most scientists who are disabled became so after their K–12 educational experience. "The proportion of scientists and engineers with disabilities increases with age. More than half have become disabled at age 35 or later. Only 7% had been disabled since birth, and only one-fourth had been disabled before the age of 20" (NSF 1996, p. 84). Egelston-Dodd (1994), noting this fact, concluded that lack of participation in the scientific workforce was not due to a lack of ability or interest of disabled students but rather inadequate science preparation in schools (p. iv).

Data about Achievement

Gender differences in both math and science achievement have been declining, but the gap between ethnic/racial groups continues to be significant. By 1996, for example, there were no notable differences in average math scores for males and females in the eighth and twelfth grades, though scores for fourth-grade boys were slightly higher than for fourth-grade girls (NSF, 1999, p. 1). But white students scored twenty-five points higher than Hispanic students on the 1996 National Assessment of Educational Progress (NAEP) and thirty-one points higher than black students, only a slight narrowing of the gap between 1992 and 1996 (NSF, 1999, p. 2). Gender gaps within minority groups, however, continue to be a problem, with African American boys outscoring girls on both math and physical science measures, although African American girls outscored African American boys in natural science.

We know relatively little about the achievement of students with disabilities on the basis of the above measures. Prior to 1995, half or more of all students with disabilities were excluded from the NAEP and could be excused from state and local standardized testing with relative ease. New requirements in federal law and increased use of accommodations have reduced this exclusion to some degree, but data are still limited. Analysis of existing data is further complicated because (a) achievement and participation vary significantly according to type of disability but data are usually collected and reported without distinctions, and (b) inclusion of additional students and improved testing of students with disabilities who have in the past been assessed under standard conditions complicates the interpretation of trend results.

What is clear from all this inconclusive information is that girls with disabilities are underrepresented in the math/science track all the way through the pipeline and that attempts to engage and assess their efforts are still in the nascent stage. The following section attempts to shed light on what contributes to this situation.

Factors Influencing Participation and Achievement

Attitudes While we acknowledge the progress of the past twenty-five years concerning popular beliefs about the abilities and rights of girls, women, and people with disabilities, the battle is far from over. Stereotyped expectations continue to limit opportunities and reinforce the view that math and science are not appropriate pursuits for girls.

The myth that girls lack a "math gene" persists, despite the specious research on which it is based (Bailey et al., 1992, p. 51; Campbell, Kibler, and Campbell-Kibler, 1991, pp. 8–10). There is no evidence that girls are born less inclined to mathematics or mechanics than boys, but there is strong evidence that society believes this to be the case and encourages a division between boys and girls. Classroom attitudes of teachers, books written for children, and subtle but constant parental and societal pressures persuade children that boys are better at science, engineering, and mathematics than are girls and that girls are better with words than are boys (Vetter, 1996, p. 30).

In an important early study, Fennema and Sherman (1977) found that girls' confidence in their ability to do mathematics dropped before any decline in achievement, leading researchers and program developers to focus on girls' attitudes about math and science, as well as the societal influences that were discouraging them from participation. Guidance counselors, parents, and other adults contributed to girls' opting out of science, believing these courses to be "too difficult for females and/or unnecessary for their future" (Clewell, Anderson, and Thorpe, p. 9, citing Casserly, 1975; Haven, 1972; Luchins, 1976).

Girls with disabilities face double discrimination. They are hit with the bias that girls can't do math and science and that people with disabilities can't do math and science. This is compounded by a perception that somehow their disability makes them weak, needy, incompetent, or dependent, which often translates into protecting them from challenging work and learning. "Misconceptions can limit job opportunities," notes the NSF report on the situation of women, minorities, and disabled people in science and engineering (1999, p. 117). "Young people can be discouraged by parents, teachers, and others from pursuing careers in science." One working chemist stated that "Nobody wanted me to be a chemist . . . everyone thought it was crazy for a kid, almost blind, to major in chemistry. I had to fight my parents, the school, teachers, guidance counselors, and the state vocational rehabilitation agency (NSF, 1999, p. 117).

Experience   When work on gender equity started in the 1970s, it was clear that girls had fewer chances than boys to engage in meaningful hands-on experiences with science and technology. They were also less likely to have played sports, built with blocks, or manipulated the moveable transportation toys that can provide an experiential foundation for understanding the laws of nature and physics. "Males more frequently have early extracurricular experiences that develop mechanical inquisitiveness and skills," while girls' activities are more often stationary, "stimulating little interest in understanding natural laws that govern the physical world . . . [or] that build spatial and physical concepts (Clewell, Anderson, and Thorpe, 1992, p. 10). For disabled girls, these experiential opportunities continue to be less available, both because of a lack of afterschool and educational programs they can access (Educational Equity Concepts, 1994) and because the reform movements in science and mathematics where the pedagogy of inquiry and hands-on exploration now dominates have not included students with disabilities (Center for Children and Technology, 1999).

Exposure It was also clear in the 1970s that girls and young women had limited knowledge of the range of careers in math and science and of the essential role that math and science education plays in preparing girls for these lucrative careers. With the underrepresentation of women and especially women with disabilities in the science, math, and engineering workforce, there were few mentors and role models to provide connections, networks, and inspiration. A good deal of effort has since gone into this area for girls, and students with disabilities have benefited from the twenty-five years of work done by the American Association for the Advancement of Science in identifying and helping to connect scientists with disabilities to young people (Stern and Summers, 1995). Still, the lack of mentors is one of the key barriers to participation and engagement in science for girls with disabilities (Summers, 1994, p. 46).

Classroom Climate and Teaching Strategies Numerous studies have focused on the unresponsive or downright "hostile climate" for girls and women in math and science classrooms, from the precollege level through graduate school and into the workplace (Hall and Sandler, 1982; Sadker and Sadker, 1993). The emphasis on speed and competition over understanding and cooperative learning has often been raised as an obstacle to girls' engagement with math and science (Rowe, 1972); for people with disabilities, the issue of time is particularly problematic. It may take persons with disabilities a longer amount of time to accomplish a given task. If academic success is determined by time-related criteria, as it often is in mathematics classes especially, students may be penalized regardless of whether the time-related criteria is relevant to the student's acquisition of knowledge and skills. In research at one university, all study participants reported that they had to deal with time-related problems, including "problems of pace; speed of learning, comprehension, and recall; temporal disruptions in physical and mental functions; time-related educational needs; and time expended in coping with difficulties raised by their disabilities" (NSF, 1999, p. 46).

Tracking and Lack of Access to High-Quality Curricula Even though there is widespread agreement that preparation in math, science, and technology is critical, most educational systems continue to separate students by perceived ability in ways that deny some students access to rigorous content and high expectations for learning. The practice of assigning students to classes based on perceptions of their ability influences the quality of education students receive depending on whether they are assigned to high- or low-track classes. Students in higher track classes learn "much more" than otherwise comparable students in lower track classes. "The results are strongest in mathematics but are present in science as well" (Campbell and Steinbrueck, 1996, p. iv). There is strong evidence that students who are poor and minority are more likely to be assigned to lower track classes than white middle-class students (Wahl, 1997); the effects of gender are less clear, although there are anecdotal reports about the highest track math and science being predominantly male.

With regard to students with disabilities, there are significant differences between disability groups. Visually impaired students were most likely to take advanced mathematics courses and be on a college prep track (Wagner, 1993, p. S–10), followed by students with speech impairments (Wagner, 1993, p. S–8), while students with learning disabilities were enrolled in academic courses that were rarely at the college prep level. Students with physical disabilities were spread throughout the range (Wagner, 1993, p. S–10), while students with mental retardation were the least likely to be assigned to grade-level programs (Wagner, 1993, p. S–9). Students with emotional disabilities were likely to be assigned to regular education, grade-level programs and more likely than students with learning disabilities to emphasize academic courses over vocational training, but they had the lowest grade point average and the highest rates of course failure and grade retention of any category of disability (Wagner, 1993, p. S–7).

Finally, students with disabilities have limited access to standards-based math and science curricula and pedagogy and are often confined to remediation and drill and practice approaches that do little to advance their understanding of basic concepts. Because even standards-based approaches assume progression, students who have trouble with one set of ideas as a result of their disability are often kept from moving on, caught in what one parent (a science educator) called "calculation purgatory":

> My daughter could not grasp basic addition or subtraction for several years. Nor could she understand that a higher number represented more of, or a greater amount of something, than a smaller number. No matter how many M&M piles we worked with, or how many number lines we posted around the house, she simply couldn't get it. The school's reaction was to continue to push these concepts until she was

able to memorize some simple addition. She could not progress to other topics, and was behind other students. This continued until 4th grade, when her new teacher decided to put calculations aside and start her on fractions. I thought she was crazy. However, my daughter grasped the concept of fractions in one day, more quickly than the entire class. You see, while my daughter is considered speech impaired, she is uniquely talented visually. She embraced the "pie" diagrams of fractions, and immediately began comparing fractions successfully. She has since begun studying basic geometry concepts and loves it! Interestingly, her success with these topics has led to greater success and confidence in computation. (Kahn, 1999)

THE ASSET APPROACH

The preceding story exemplifies how a focus on assets rather than deficits can be the key that unlocks learning and achievement. Too often we focus on what a group of people is lacking rather than what they have to offer. Most efforts start with what students can't do or don't do because of their disabilities and figure out how we can compensate for what's wrong. Girls with disabilities are usually not seen as bringing something positive to the learning and doing of science and mathematics. Yet having a disability gives one a different view of the physical world, which can be a distinct advantage in providing alternative ways of exploring, analyzing, and drawing conclusions from data and experience.

Temple Grandin, a scientist who is autistic, developed more humane and effective methods for handling livestock. Facilities she has designed are located in the United States, Canada, Europe, Mexico, Australia, and New Zealand. In North America, almost half of all cattle are handled in a center track restrainer system that she designed for meat plants. As a child, she says, "My reaction to being touched was like a wild horse flinching and pulling away" (Grandin, 1996). She discovered that a holding device, based on a the "squeeze" machine she invented for herself, in which pressure is applied gradually, so the animal is enveloped, worked to tame wild horses and calm livestock. "Thinking in language and words is alien to me. "I think totally in pictures," says Grandin. "Drafting elaborate drawings of steel and concrete livestock stockyards and equipment is easy. I can visualize a video of the finished equipment in my imagination. I can run test simulations in my imagination of how the systems would work with different size cattle." For Grandin, her visual capacity has been "a great asset" and enabled her to become internationally recognized as a livestock equipment designer (Grandin, 1996).

Geeret Vermeij is a geologist who made a major breakthrough in evolutionary theory about the role of predators in determining how and why species change. He noted, "Being blind, I have a different perspective. There's a big difference between how you see things and how you feel them." Warren Allmon, director of the Paleontological Research Institute, concurred: "Gary focused on the shape of things. He recognized patterns. It's something that maybe the rest of us didn't take time to notice" (Wahl, 1997, pp. 7–8).

Using your life's experience to enable you to think "outside the box" and to see things others don't see can make a real contribution to science. Jane Goodall's approach to living with and observing apes in their natural habitat transformed the field of primatology, and Barbara McClintock's practice of "listening to the corn" enabled her to discover the transposable elements of DNA. How much did these alternative approaches derive from these scientists' experiences as women in this society and in the world of science? It's hard to say, but it is clear that they, along with Grandin and Vermeij, received enough support along the way to pursue their interests and make use of their talents.

As educators, we need to figure out how we can cultivate that engagement and provide the kind of support that will enable girls with disabilities to persist in science and math. A great deal has to do with helping girls to see that it IS possible for them to do it, which means offering examples, models, and comrades. "If we don't stop to make them aware, the possibilities don't occur to them," observed Ellen Rubin, disability coordinator and science educator at Educational Equity Concepts. "In my teaching at the School for the Blind, at some point I noticed that the kids weren't aware that I too was blind, until I started talking about it and focusing on it. It's a difficult issue to get that concept across—their automatic reaction is to assume that I can't be blind because I'm the teacher" (Rubin, May, 1999, personal communication).

My daughter Laura is nineteen and loves science. She has Down syndrome and learned to read in her early teens. Fascinated by the human body, interested in weather and planets and machines, and facile in her use of computers, Laura loves science. She was always able to operate the VCR and construct the complicated LEGO machines that eluded both her parents. Her formal education has provided relatively little in the way of hands-on science, but she has been lucky enough to have an afterschool program led by a skilled hands-on science educator.

Laura has not been so fortunate with regard to mathematics, however. Consigned to the "coin purgatory" noted above, Laura's curriculum has been incessantly focused around learning the "daily living skills" of identifying how much coins are worth. But her understanding of one-to-one correspondence is very limited—a five-dollar bill is no more to her than a one-dollar bill because it is only one piece of paper. Identifying patterns and sorting and categorizing, activities she did in early intervention programs when she was a preschooler, were never continued in her regular schooling, and Laura has no concept of even and odd. Is it because it's beyond her capacity? I think not. Four years ago Laura began to study the violin, something she had always wanted to do. She is passionate about the instrument and works hard, independently and without frustration or opposition, not her usual mode of learning. She reads music, decodes abstract symbols, and keeps strings of relationships in her head (pun intended). The skills are not dissimilar to those needed for understanding basic mathematics. My contention is that we as educators simply haven't figured out what the right path is that will help Laura to tap her mathematical talent.

PROGRAMS AND STRATEGIES FOR CHANGE

The past thirty years have seen the development of programs, strategies, and systemic efforts to counter the negative influences identified above and positively support girls' achievement and participation. Programs and interventions developed in the late 1970s and early 1980s contained one or more of the following elements:

Inquiry and hands-on exploration: promoting questioning, curiosity, joy, discovery, and invention as core to the learning of math and science.

Career development and exposure: providing mentors, role models, and career development strategies that expanded girls' ideas about jobs and helped them stay in the science track.

Attention to course taking: working with girls, educators, guidance counselors, parents, and schools to educate them about course-taking issues and help them to change the pattern of dropping out of these courses.

Countering negative attitudes and stereotypes: changing perceptions that girls as well as boys can excel in math and science, and that girls with disabilities can participate fully and effectively in these subjects.

Staff development to support teachers' and informal educators' capacity and awareness about the problem and about methods for engaging girls in math and science: making connections and helping girls to make connections to the science-rich resources in their communities and lives, from science museums to scientific and technical businesses and industry to practicing scientists.

The Lawrence Hall of Science's EQUALS program, led by Nancy Kreinberg, was a groundbreaking effort in the 1970s that continues to be a powerful influence today. Initially focused on training teachers, EQUALS was the first to identify cooperative learning as a strategy more likely to engage girls than the competitive individualistic achievement model of most classrooms. EQUALS workshops often began with activities to raise awareness about the problem, and their "Startling Statements" exercises (which contained surprising—or maybe not so surprising—information about women's often unrecognized achievements as well as their experiences of discrimination and underrepresentation in mathematics) woke up thousands of teachers, parents, advocates, and girls to the unfair situation in math education. EQUALS' hands-on activities became a model for the field, as they posed challenging math problems that required sharing of knowledge and valuing of alternative and multiple approaches to problem solving. And they made math fun. EQUALS' Family Math and Family Science Programs are immensely popular with parents, schools, and afterschool programs, based on the same principles of making math accessible, relevant, and something that everyone does and can do.

All roads led to EQUALS in 1984 when I got involved in the development of Operation SMART, an afterschool program to encourage girls' participation in science, math, and relevant technology at Girls Incorporated. SMART was one of a growing number of such programs focused on girls and young women, which increasingly addressed the whole cycle of development, from the preschool years through workforce participation.

Programs in math and science education for students with disabilities appeared somewhat later, but aside from Project Gold, a University of Minnesota program for girls in grades four through eight, most have focused on both girls and boys. The Program for Persons with Disabilities at the National Science Foundation and the Department of Education's Office of Special Education Programs are among the primary funders and catalysts for these activities. The Do-It Program (*Disabilities, Opportunities, Internetworking and Technology*) at the University of Washington was one of the first efforts, and like EQUALS, has had a profound influence on the field. It is a comprehensive program of academic and social support for students with disabilities to enable them to enter and succeed in college. The Biotechnology Works! project at the University of Southern Maine provides students with opportunities to study immunology and genetics in a rigorous summer program, while projects such as the Easter Seals Access Science project, a collaboration with AAAS and Playtime Is Science for Students with Disabilities of Educational Equity Concepts concentrate on making the hands-on and exploration experience more accessible to students with moderate to severe disabilities, through modification of tools and approaches. On the formal education side, curricula developed at the Lawrence Hall of Science—Full Option Science System and SAVI-SELPH—were among the earliest and most successful efforts to involve students with disabilities in high quality, hands-on science education. Interestingly, those curricula have themselves become "mainstreamed"; they are now used in regular classrooms and recommended as consistent with the standards; little mention is made of their origins in special education.

This kind of mainstreaming moves closer to including "all students." While special programs and curricula can help to identify exemplary practices and can produce powerful outcomes for the girls who participate, they don't automatically change the practices, policies, or values of the education system or work world at large.

That realization led many of us who were in the program development business to design strategies aimed at larger scale change. The Collaboration for Equity, a partnership of the American Association for the Advancement of Science, Education Development Center, Campbell-Kibler Associates, Nancy Kreinberg, Beatriz Chu Clewell, and Girls Incorporated, was intended to make equity a driving force in the efforts to reform math and science education and to make the case for the inextricable link between equity and excellence. We had been concerned that attention to improving quality had to concentrate on reducing the gaps at the same time because an education system in which only a portion of students achieve, and where outcomes can be predicted on the basis of group membership, cannot be defined as "excellent." Our efforts have been fairly successful (see NSF, 1998b; and the AAAS website for information), but one thing is clear: despite increased attention to race, gender, and income, students with disabilities are still last on the list. Backed by amendments to the Individuals with Disabilities Act (1996) and efforts at the state level for full inclusion of students with disabilities in high quality education, it is a fertile time for creating strategies to support the advancement of girls with disabilities in science and math. There is a great deal that can be done.

TAKING ACTION

Technology Can Help

Assistive technology has made it possible for people with disabilities to participate more fully in many arenas, including science education and the practice of science. A wide range of tools has been developed: adjustable work stations, alternative input devices to voice recognition, Braille printers and readers, communications boards, and captioning for television and other visual media, to name just a few.

Assistive technology has another benefit. It has become a model for thinking about design that works for lots of different people (inclusive or universal design), instead of a mythical "norm." Curb cuts make it easier not just for people who use wheelchairs but also for joggers and walkers and delivery people and parents with strollers; airbags designed for people of all sizes actually protect rather than endanger children and short people; appliances with rubber grips are easier for people with arthritis to hold and safer for children and everyone else to use. Inclusive design assumes that people come in different shapes and sizes and have different needs and preferences. It assumes that the purpose of design and technology is to serve the person, not the other way around. It is a useful way to think not just about design but also about education.

In addition to technology that has been specifically designed for people with disabilities, new technologies support more independent and individualized learning, faster and easier communication that can help to decrease isolation and foster connections, and pacing that can be more easily controlled by the student. It is important to insure that the tools and technology used in the classroom are accessible, which may mean having a number of different formats and versions of the materials being used and checking that software and World Wide Web sites can be viewed, heard, and manipulated by students with different abilities.

Accommodations Can Help

A primary strategy for including people with disabilities is to modify existing activities and develop "accommodations." The term refers to the obligation, within reason, to make it possible for persons with disabilities to participate in employment and education. Providing accommodations in math/science education may mean making the classroom and lab environment physically accessible or making the scientific tools of investigation more easily manipulated—by enlarging them, redesigning them, or simulating them with computer technology. It may mean modifying the test or extending the time requirement. Resistance to providing accommodations is usually based on concerns that the accommodations will provide some kind of unfair advantage (NSF, 1999, p. 45). Yet we can challenge these misconceptions if we assume that making learning available to all is the *responsibility* of our learning institutions and that the measure of success is the degree to which high quality outcomes are attained by the vast majority of students. The job is to support students on the path to such learning and achievement.

We Can Help

The first step is to shift our attitudes and think of girls with disabilities as strong and powerful rather than weak and needy. What is lacking are the supports and systems to nurture rather than squelch those strengths. Girls with disabilities have strengths that come from their talents, from their unique perspective as persons with disabilities, and from their social and political experiences of being female and disabled in this society. That includes the courage and awareness that comes from resisting low expectations and countering historical discrimination. Becoming an aggressive learner and doer of science requires a determination that is not incompatible with the skills acquired in self-advocacy. Six basic principles underlie all other strategies:

1. *Assume interest.* "If I hadn't been so talkative or insistent about trying to participate in everything," said Laureen Summers, a science educator with cerebral palsy, "my ability to learn might never have been noticed at all!" (Summers, 1994, p. 46). Even if girls don't ask, it doesn't mean they're not interested. In research conducted about girls' participation in science and math, girls would not necessarily seek out the experience, but once presented with it, they engaged with enthusiasm and persistence (Frederick and Nicholson, 1986).

2. *Assume talent.* With the suggestion that there are many kinds of intelligence, it is clear that people excel in different ways (Sternberg, 1990; Gardner, 1993). Discard preconceived notions about who can do math and science. Give credit for approaching problems from various perspectives and for generating alternative strategies.

3. *Assume participation.* The rhetoric of the reform and standards movements talks about "all students." The phrase remains rhetorical unless every student is engaged. Don't protect girls because you're worried it might be too hard for them or rush to rescue them from making mistakes or taking risks. Create an environment that makes it comfortable for everyone to take part.

4. *Assume "all students" includes everyone but that "all students" are not the same.* Each child needs something different to learn and achieve, and as educators we need to figure out what that is.

5. *Make it accessible.* Accessibility applies to the social as well as the physical organization. Make it easy for girls with disabilities to get in and use space, and provide materials and tools in accessible formats and designs. Numerous resources are available (e.g., EASI, Equal Access to Software and Information; CAST, Center for Applied Special Technology; the Alliance for Technology Access; and NCAM, the WBGO National Center for Accessible Media). Talk with each student about what she needs and prefers in the way of support and accommodation. Give the message through the accessible environment and the atmosphere you create that girls with disabilities are expected and welcomed.

6. *Educate yourself.* Learn all you can about human development and contextualize your understanding of the particular disabilities of students with whom you work within the range of human development. You *can* choose to make modifications based on the needs of the students with disabilities. Or you might decide to rethink the way you approach the problem for all students. If the assignment involves observation, for example, you could ask just a blind student to come up with other ways to observe. But it would promote all students' science skills to challenge the class to come up with as many different ways to "observe" something as they can, and have them record data gathered through these different methods, comparing their results and reflecting on the process.

The following strategies are ways to put these principles into practice:

Strategy 1. Encourage girls to question, explore, and challenge.
Inquiry is fundamental to good science and good science education. It is a means of both motivating and engaging girls and necessary to achieving high quality outcomes in math and science because it lays the groundwork for serious and deep investigation. Encourage girls to ask questions, identify questions worth pursuing, and persist in the investigation; to take intellectual risks; to make mistakes and try it again in the quest for understanding; to get messy; to persist even in the face of demands from others for attention and service. Support girls to resist traditional socialization that values being neat, getting the right answer, and being compliant and unquestioning. Help girls—and boys—to challenge constraining stereotypes about who can do math and science and who can be a scientist.

Strategy 2. Keep girls in the science track—and change the tracks.
Make sure girls with disabilities are enrolled in the most advanced sequence of math and science courses possible and have the support

to succeed. Consider eliminating tracking and segregation from math and science education. Clearly, these suggestions require much more than what a single teacher can accomplish alone, but it is essential that educators, individually and collectively, speak out and become a force for change in schools, districts, and states. There are numerous resources available now about both inclusion and detracking that can help (e.g., Oakes, 1990; Wheelock, 1992).

Strategy 3. Include girls—and all students with disabilities—in assessments of progress, and rethink the assessments. All assessments, from the classroom level to the international test, must include disabled students and results analyzed in ways that provide information about how different groups of students are doing. Current assessments, especially traditional multiple-choice paper and pencil tests, are a poor measure of what students with disabilities (and often students without disabilities) know and are able to do. Hands-on science and reformed mathematics also do not lend themselves well to traditional measures, so the burden is on the assessment community to devise better ways to determine what students are actually able to do. At the classroom level, a variety of strategies to assess progress have been developed—discussions, hands-on activities and observations, using drawing and visual representation—that educators can draw on.

Strategy 4. Rethink teaching and classroom organization. Different people learn in different ways, and many people learn best when taught using more than one approach. Use multiple methods and formats to ensure accessibility: large print, captioning, audio tape, computer disk versions, speech readable format, Braille, closed captioning, hands-on materials. You want girls to use all the senses they have available to them in exploring science—touch, sound, sight, smell—and to invent new ways to explore. Innovations using assistive technology in such areas as visual tactile simulation give blind students a visceral sense of two- and three-dimensional graphs and shapes on the computer and offer sighted students another way to conceptualize space.

Similarly, make it clear that there are multiple ways of solving problems. Traditional approaches to math and science have sometimes implied that there is only one correct approach to an answer. Reformed math/science education emphasizes children developing and explaining their own strategies, proposing their own research designs, and inventing their own problem-solving algorithms. While there are more and less efficient ways of solving problems and methodological conventions that insure rigor, it may be useful to discuss these choices explicitly—when it is important to have an efficient or an elegant proof, when it might be more important to have an inventive and novel approach, and when what matters most is whether there is deep understanding of the core concept.

Become conversant with a variety of teaching methods. Within the special education literature, there is increasing research about instructional techniques that help students break down tasks into component parts, organize their thinking, draw out the main concepts and big ideas, and learn how to learn (U.S. Department of Education, 1997, p. III–60). Such methods can help students without disabilities as well.

Don't make time an issue when it is not central to the math or science concept. It is true that students with disabilities may need extra time. It is just as likely that other students need extra time as well, yet most classrooms, especially math classrooms, credit the quickest and the first. It is not a matter of slowing a whole group down but of structuring the learning process so that each student can proceed at his or her "right" pace.

Develop cooperative relationships for teaching and planning among specialists and teachers. A promising approach is collaborative teaching, bringing together the expertise of special education teachers with that of science and math educators. Use cooperative learning and peer tutoring, and tap students' talents to share what they know with each other (U.S. Department of Education, 1997, p. III–68).

Strategy 5. Create networks and connections. Decreasing the isolation of girls with disabilities, showing them that there are others like them who have been successful in math and science, and providing them with networks for support can go a long way toward helping girls with disabilities persist in science. Connect girls to mentors, role models, and each other around the experience of math and science. Expose them to careers and real life applications of math and science through field trips, partnerships with industry, internships, and opportunities to engage in serious research and exploration.

CONCLUSION

Girls with disabilities, like all other students in the United States public education system, are entitled to a high quality education. They have a right to the skills and knowledge that will prepare them for the challenges of the twenty-first century. Math and science are clearly essential to that preparation. Access is a prerequisite, but it is not enough. The focus must be on achievement with accountability for outcomes shared by all. In order for girls with disabilities to achieve those outcomes, pedagogy, curricula, environment, and tools must be available that allow them to develop and demonstrate their full range of talents. The educational system and the public must back teachers up with the resources and policies that enable this to happen.

This is not just about the achievement of individual students. It is about creating communities of learners and norms of mutual support and exchange among us all, between girls and boys, adults and youth, persons with and without disabilities of all races, classes, and backgrounds. The goal is to create classrooms, schools, organizations, and communities where all are welcomed, valued for who they are and what they bring, and supported to succeed. That is the responsibility of us all, as educators, as citizens, and as human beings.

REFERENCES

American Association for the Advancement of Science. 1990. *Science for all Americans: Project 2061.* Washington D.C.: AAAS.

Bailey, S., L. Burbidge, P. B. Campbell, B. Jackson, F. Marx, and P. McIntosh. 1992. *The AAUW report: How schools shortchange girls.* Washington, D.C.: AAUW Educational Foundation.

Beane, DeAnna Banks. 1985 (Reprinted in 1988). *Mathematics and science: Critical filters for the future of minority students.* Washington, D.C.: The Mid-Atlantic Equity Center, the American University.

Butler-Nalin, P., and M. Wagner. 1991. Enrollment in postsecondary schools. In *Youth with disabilities: How are they doing? The first comprehensive report from the national longitudinal transition study of special education students.* Menlo Park, Calif.: SRI International, ch. 9.

Campbell, P. 1997. Utility is not enough. In *Thoughts and deeds. Equity in mathematics and science education.* Edited by N. Kreinberg and E. Wahl. Washington D.C.: Collaboration for Equity, the American Association for the Advancement of Science.

Campbell, P., T. Kibler, and K. Campbell-Kibler. 1991. Taking the SAT at twelve: One family's view of talent search. *College Prep* 7:8–10.

Campbell, P., and K. Steinbrueck. 1996. *Striving for gender equity.* Washington, D.C.: Collaboration for Equity, American Association for the Advancement of Science.

Casserly, P. 1975. *An assessment of factors affecting female participation in advanced placement programs in math, chemistry, and physics.* Unpublished manuscript. Princeton, N.J.: Educational Testing Service.

Center for Children and Technology. 1999, May 14. A response to the 1998 discussion draft of the NCTM principles and standards for school mathematics center for children and technology. In *Promoting assets and access project: Reframing the standards to include all students.*

Clewell, B., B. Anderson, M. Thorpe. 1992. *Breaking the barriers.* New York: Jossey-Bass.

Educational Equity Concepts. 1994. *Crafting an agenda for citywide mainstreaming.* New York: Educational Equity Concepts. Alliance for Mainstreaming Youth with Disabilities. Unpublished report.

Egelston-Dodd, J., ed. 1994. *A futures agenda: Proceedings of a working conference on science for persons with disabilities.* Cedar Falls: University of Northern Iowa.

Fennema, E., J. Sherman. 1977. Sex-related differences in math achievement, spatial visualization and affective factors. *American Educational Research Journal* 14:51–71.

Frederick. J. D., and H. J. Nicholson. 1986. *The explorer's pass: A report on case studies of girls and math, science, and technology.* Indianapolis: Girls Incorporated.

Gardner, H. 1993. *Multiple Intelligences: The Theory in Practice.* New York: Basic Books.

Grandin, T. 1996. *My experiences with visual thinking, sensory problems and communication difficulties.* Internet, http://www.autism.org//temple/visual.html.

Hall, R., and B. Sandler. 1982. *The classroom climate: A chilly one for women?* Washington, D.C.: Project on the Status and Education of Women. Association of American Colleges.

Haven, E. 1972. *Factors associated with the selection of advanced mathematics courses by girls in high school.* Princeton, N.J.: Educational Testing Service.

Kahn, S. 1999. Comments on chapter 2 of the NCTM Standards 2000 discussion draft. Personal communication.

Keller, E. 1994. Motor/orthpedically-impaired students in science. In *A futures agenda: Proceedings of a working conference on science for persons with disabilities.* Edited by J. Egelston-Dodd. Cedar Falls: University of Northern Iowa.

Kreinberg, N. 1997. How much time do we have? In *Thoughts and deeds: Equity in mathematics and science education.* Edited by N. Kreinberg and E. Wahl. Washington, D.C.: American Association for the Advancement of Science, 11–16.

Luchins, E.H. 1976, February. *Women mathematicians: A contemporary appraisal.* Paper presented at the annual meeting of the American Association for the Advancement of Science, Boston.

National Center on Educational Outcome (NCEO). 1992. *Including students with disabilities in national and state data collection programs.* Minneapolis, Minn.: National Center on Educational Outcomes.

NCTM National Council of Teachers of Mathematics. 1989. Curriculum and Evaluation Standards for School Mathematics. Reston, Va.: NCTM.

NRC National Research Council. 1996. *National science education standards.* Washington, D.C.: National Academy Press.

National Science Foundation (NSF). 1996. *Women, minorities, and persons with disabilities in science and engineering.* Arlington, Va.: National Science Foundation.

———. 1998a. *Science and engineering indicators.* Arlington, Va.: National Science Foundation. National Science Board

———. 1998b. *Infusing equity in systemic reform: An implementation scheme.* Arlington, Va.: National Science Foundation.

———. 1999. *Women, minorities, and persons with disabilities in science and engineering.* Arlington, Va.: National Science Foundation.

Oakes, J. 1990. *Multiplying inequalities: The effect of race, social class, and tracking on opportunities to learn mathematics and science.* Santa Monica, Calif.: Rand Corporation.

Rowe, M. B. 1972, April. *Wait-time and rewards as instructional variables: Their influences on language, logic, and fate control.* Chicago: Paper presented at the National Association for Research in Science Teaching.

Sadker, M., and D. Sadker. 1994. *Failing at fairness: How America's schools cheat girls.* New York: C. Scribner's Sons.

Sells, Lucy W. 1978, February. The forum: Mathematics—a critical filter. *The Science Teacher* 45(2):28–29.

Stern, V., and L. Summers. 1995. *Resource Directory of Scientists and Engineers with Disabilities.* Washington, D.C.: AAAS.

Sternberg, R. 1990. *Metaphors of Mind: Conceptions of the Nature of Intelligence.* Cambridge and New York: Cambridge University Press.

Summers, L. 1994. Response to Ed Keller's presentation: 'Motor/Orthpedically-impaired students in science.' In *A futures agenda: Proceedings of a working conference on science for persons with disabilities.* Edited by J. Egleston-Dodd. Cedar Falls, Iowa: University of Northern Iowa, 45–47.

U.S. Department of Education. 1996. *Eighteenth annual report to Congress on the implementation of the Individuals with Disabilities Education Act, Appendix A.* Washington, D.C.: Author.

———. 1997. *Nineteenth annual report to Congress on the implementation of the Individuals with Disabilities Education Act.* Washington, D.C.: Author.

Vetter, B. 1996. Myths and realities of women's progress in the sciences, mathematics, and engineering. In *The equity equation: Fostering the advancement of women in the sciences, mathematics, and engineering.* Edited by C. Davis, A. Ginorio, C. Hollenshead, B. Lazarus, and P. Rayman. San Francisco: Jossey-Bass, 29–56.

Wagner, M. 1993. *The secondary school programs of students with disabilities.* Menlo Park, Calif.: SRI International.

Wahl, E. 1997. *The case for equity and excellence in science and math education.* Washington, D.C.: American Association for the Advancement of Science.

Wheelock, A. 1992. *Crossing the tracks: How untracking can save America's Schools.* New York: The New Press.

CHAPTER 7

Squeaky Wheels versus Invisibility: Gender Bias in Teacher-Student Interactions

Dolores A. Grayson

For more than twenty-five years, research and practice have repeatedly shown that teacher attention in classrooms is directly, positively correlated with student achievement (Grayson and Martin, 1984; 1990; 1997). During that time, my colleagues and I have compiled an extensive literature review of and examined research in this area and, while working with educators across this and other countries, have conducted training for and obtained feedback from more than fifty thousand teachers during presentations and site visitations.

We have focused our efforts on combining investigations of the problems in teacher-student interactions with identification of research-based solutions that ensure excellence in education for all students. Since 1976, a major portion of my work has been to encourage and train teachers to use effective teaching strategies to counter educational inequity for all students, particularly students in underserved populations. This includes fostering positive and supportive interactions between teachers and students, interactions that communicate the educators' high expectations for students.

This chapter describes the ways in which teachers' interactions with students differ based on the gender, ethnicity, and racial characteristics of students. The combined effects of socioeconomic class, gender, race, ethnicity, culture, disability status, and personality types are examined as to their influence on teacher perceptions and expectations and with regard to how these perceptions and expectations are manifested through the teacher's interactions in the classroom. As indicated earlier, the chapter includes strategies to help teachers assess their own interactions and encourages them to make needed changes to how they interact with students in order to eliminate bias. Finally, but perhaps most important, the chapter is enriched by the accumulated voices and responses of teachers who have shared their stories and experiences with us.

Dear Teacher . . .

The nature of the teaching profession is such that we have frequent opportunities to communicate with our students, their parents, and our colleagues. It is not uncommon for a student to include a note on a written assignment or for a parent to send a message to the teacher. Usually these communications request permission to do something; offer an excuse for an absence, lack of participation, or missed assignment; or make an appeal for some special consideration. Over the last three years, we have asked teachers with whom we've worked to write a "Dear Teacher . . ." note to express a message related to a critical incident with a teacher from their past. When teachers reflect on their own educational experiences, it is easy for most to recall some person or situation that left an impression on them. These messages are overwhelmingly (85 percent to 90 percent) positive, though a small portion of the teachers who recall negative experiences are especially vitriolic and speak volumes about the impact of teacher behavior and attitudes on students (Grayson 1998), as illustrated in the following:

- I made it in spite of all of the prejudiced things that you said about me. (Grade unknown)
- I felt very humiliated when you told me to sweep the floor. When I said "No," you said, "What would your mother say?" You knew she was deceased! (Grade unknown)
- I remember being the shy kid in the back of the room. I wish you had taught handwriting differently than putting our names on the board as being either in jail or on parole or free. I spent the year "on parole" and felt very frustrated that no matter how hard I tried, I could not improve. (Second grade)
- I wish you hadn't made a negative example of me in math. It took me years to overcome my fears and regain my self-confidence. (Fourth grade)
- Thank you for retiring. I knew you were ready when you told me I shouldn't take your math class because I wasn't "college material." (High school)

- Because you told me to not bother with college, I was determined to prove you wrong. I completed college in three years and became a teacher. (High school)
- Why did you make me stand up in front of the class and read my list of wrongly spelled words to the whole class? It was the most embarrassing day of my young life. (Grade unknown)

However, most of the teachers' responses are positive. Approximately a third of these express appreciation for assistance in a specific academic area, such as the following examples: Dear Teacher, Thank you for . . .

- encouraging me and showing high expectations for me in English class! I enjoyed your oral reading, even though we were seniors. (High school)
- opening my eyes to the world of art, architecture and ideas for being a strong woman of principle and for being a role model. (High school)
- inspiring a life-long love of history. (Middle school)
- opening the doors to reading and enriching my life. (Elementary school)
- forcing me to read *The New York Times* every day. (High school)
- being so excited about biology and influencing me to teach science. (High school)
- making us laugh in U.S. history. Believing in us and not doubting that we could accomplish our dreams. (High school)
- letting me know that I was smart in math and language arts. (Middle school)
- bringing *Julius Caesar* to life, making it interesting and enjoying your teaching. (High school)

The remaining two-thirds of the positive responses deal more with the affective and reinforce the importance of supportive feedback and its influence on feelings of worth, importance, and perceived capability. A few of the hundreds of responses are demonstrated in the following examples: Dear Teacher, Thank you for . . .

- preparing me to be an educator. You continued to set high expectations for the group, and we continued to reach them. (High school)
- helping me see my strengths and for mentoring me. (High school)
- the support and motivation you gave. I still draw on the support I received from you. (High school)

- letting me know that I could go to college. You saved my life. (High school)
- believing in me, encouraging me, dreaming with me, and modeling professionalism for me. (Grade unknown)
- your decency and kindness. (High school)
- challenging me without discouraging me. Allowing me to take risks and helping me to develop my philosophical orientation. (High school)
- showing me that being poor didn't mean that I couldn't set goals and attain them. (High school)
- telling me I could and believing in me. (Elementary school)
- showing me that an African American woman could be intelligent, powerful, affluent, and respected in a time when that wasn't prevalent. (Grade unknown)

PERCEPTIONS, EXPECTATIONS, BEHAVIORS, AND ACHIEVEMENT

These responses illustrate the importance of significant adults in students' lives and the impact their actions and words have. Our research on classroom interaction patterns has generally agreed with the prevalent finding in educational research that teacher's beliefs about and expectations of students impact student achievement and students' perceptions about their capacity to achieve. This has been an accepted fact among educational researchers for over thirty years, since the landmark work on the Pygmalion effects (e.g., self-fulfilling prophecy) in the classroom (Rosenthal and Jacobson, 1968). In classroom settings, teachers' perceptions and expectations for students dictate how they (teachers) will act and what they will say to students, and these perceived expectations and behaviors are directly related to student achievement. Any attempts to explore or assess the influence of gender, race, ethnicity, socioeconomic class, disability status, language dominance, or other student characteristics on achievement must consider their effects on teacher perceptions and expectations.

DIFFERENTIAL TREATMENT

A persistent dilemma in education has been how to prevent students from being dealt out or dealing themselves out of the learning cycle, resulting in a lack of achievement, participation, and eventual exit from school. While not suggesting that this problem is rooted solely in the classroom, this section focuses on areas of differential treatment of female and male students from diverse backgrounds within the instructional domain.

Teacher-Student Interaction and Attention

One of the measurable ways we, as teachers, manifest our expectations for others is through our attention and to whom we give it. On the one hand, research has shown that teachers communicate high expectations for students by providing their undivided attention. On the other hand, students for whom teachers have low expectations may receive little or no attention. When discussing teacher-student interactions and attention, it is important to examine traditional patterns related to frequency distribution of attention, as well as the quality of the attention.

In the 1970s and 1980s, research reported that males had more contacts with teachers, but a higher portion of the female contacts were positive (Good, Sikes, and Brophy, 1973; Good and Brophy, 1978; 1987). Although most teachers believe they treat girls and boys the same, this is not so. Both female and male teachers have been found to interact more with boys and provide boys with more approval, disapproval, and opportunities to respond. Boys receive more teacher messages dealing with keeping order, misbehaving, and interpreting class rules and receive, on average, two and a half times as many disapproving comments as girls.

In the 1990s, a report released by the American Association of University Women (AAUW) found that girls still received less teacher attention than boys, engaged in less complex, less challenging interactions with their teachers than did boys, and received less constructive feedback than did male peers (AAUW, 1991). These compiled results reflected what many gender studies had been reporting for years.

Remembering that studies and practice have shown that attention correlates with achievement, one persistent finding in our work is particularly troubling. That is, our own research, and that of others, suggests that in a typical classroom in the United States, one, two, or three students occupy a minimum of 25 percent of a teacher's instructional time by calling out, raising their hands, or demanding attention in some assertive way. More often than not, these students are Caucasian and male, their dominant language is English, they are perceived to be nondisabled, and they come from an upper-middle socioeconomic background. These students represent no more than 13 percent to 15 percent of the total population but have been the target of most educational attention and utilized as the standard or mythical norm (Grayson and Martin, 1984; 1990; 1997).

Conversely, in a majority of classrooms, a minimum of 25 percent of students receive no instructional contact from the teacher. This appears to be the case whether the teacher is female or male. There has been a great deal written about those on the receiving end of most of the attention, but very little written about the students who are in the more invisible category. Clearly, the evidence indicates that the squeaky wheel still gets the oil in most classrooms. This is especially true when the teacher is functioning in a 'reactive mode' and the student is permitted to be the stimulus that drives the teacher's behavior. Only when teachers become more proactive and take the initiative to draw students into instructional activity with them and other classmates do we see the patterns of disproportionate attention decrease. The invisible group increases in classrooms where students have disabilities, are older (secondary and postsecondary), come from cultural conditions that discourage calling attention to oneself (e.g. indigenous populations), speak a language other than English, or tend to be shy (Grayson, 1992; Grayson and Martin, 1997). Teachers need to examine their perceptions and expectations and take the initiative and responsibility for their actions, reactions, and interactions with students. Similarly, following a three-year study of gender disparities in teacher-student interaction, Myra and David Sadker concluded: "Teaching should be an intentional and active process rather than one that is passive and reactive in nature. When teachers become aware of differences in the way they interact with male and female students and when they receive appropriate resources and training, they can become more equitable in their response patterns" (Sadker and Sadker, 1984).

Anecdotal information we have gathered from educators during a fifteen-year retrospective evaluation of our work included several observations that illustrate this same issue:

- In (my) typically large classes, the most disruptive, the most vocal, the seekers of constant attention repeatedly get (my attention). During my training, awareness of all individuals and their participation in an equitable manner was emphasized. So the little voice within me constantly reminds me not to overlook anybody. I look for the forgotten and transparent ones and bring positive attention to them through teacher-student and student-student dynamics. After training [in gender equity], I paid more attention to giving response opportunities to quieter members of various groups. I have found that not only does this provide a greater variety of experiences and responses, but [it] affords everyone with opportunities for self-expression and sharing.

- In a math class, there is a female student who is very quiet. Realizing that I do not talk with her very much, I decided to see what she was doing. She was lost, but as I probed, listened, and spent time with her, understanding came. She got very excited and became more involved with subsequent activities.

• I find myself speaking and acknowledging my students' performance more, and they like it! I find more students wanting to do their work. I compared my grade book for this past semester (since the training) to the previous semester (before the training). More students are turning in completed assignments, and my typing classes have more As and Bs than my previous classes. I like it!

• I became aware of how inequitable I was to male and female students in my class. I thought I was pretty equitable, but I found out that I was biased. I found out that I was favoring the males in my class. I'm telling you, this was a big wake-up call for me! I have improved myself as a teacher and provide more opportunities for all my students.

These examples are from high school teachers teaching students from diverse racial and ethnic backgrounds, many of whom have learning disabilities and come from homes below the poverty level (Grayson, 1998).

Grouping and Organization

Classroom organization refers to physical environment and social structure. The teacher usually decides how to cluster students and products. Seating patterns, work groups, recreational activities, classroom chores, team compositions, and peer interactions reflect how teachers expect students to work and play together. Students throughout elementary school voluntarily group themselves by gender. This preference for playing and working with students of the same sex is a powerful tool for (and a result of) sex role socialization. Classroom management and instructional groupings based on gender reinforce the separation of the sexes so that females and males are segregated both in the classroom and at play. In the United States, the 1964 Civil Rights Act, Title VI and Title IX of the 1972 Educational Amendments, and the 1988 Civil Rights Restoration Act prohibit classroom grouping based on gender and race. Nevertheless, in 1984 the Sadkers reported that "one out of every three classrooms was segregated by sex," and in 1997 the participants in our teacher clusters reported that students continue to self-segregate by gender, race, ethnicity, and other characteristics (Grayson and Martin, 1997).

Recently, studies have revisited the perceived advantages of sex-segregated instructional settings, and a few trends are emerging. First, most of the studies are targeting the curriculum content areas of math and science. Second, often the studies are conducted with student populations from the middle school level. In most instances, teachers behave and organize classes differently for male and female students, even when the content being taught is the same. Finally, the perceived advantages are almost always in favor of female students. In 1998 while reviewing the research, we found no studies available in the Educational Resources Information Clearinghouse (ERIC) on single-sex classes in language arts or social studies. There is a need for a study on single-sex classes where teachers have knowledge of gender- (and race-) sensitive behaviors and utilize the same effective equitable instructional strategies and materials with all students, which is what our work with teachers has attempted to accomplish in co-instructional settings (Grayson and Martin, 1998).

A recent study by the AAUW Educational Foundation, released on 12 March 1998, challenges the idea that single-sex education is better for girls than co-education. Titled *Separated by Sex: A Critical Look at Single-Sex Education for Girls*, the study found that qualities of a good education foster student achievement, regardless of whether boys and girls learn separately or together. Some of the study's findings were:

1. When elements of a quality education are present, girls and boys succeed. These elements include small classes and schools, equitable teaching practices, and focused academic curriculum.

2. Some kinds of single-sex programs produce positive results for some students, including a preference for math and science among girls. While girls' achievement has improved in some single-sex schools, there is no significant improvement in girls' achievement in single-sex classes.

3. There is no evidence in general that single-sex education works or is better for girls than coeducation.

4. Single-sex classes in particular disrupt the coeducational public school environment.

Among positive aspects of single-sex programs discussed in the report are an increase in girls' risk-taking and a gain in girls' confidence from academic competence. However, researchers debate whether these benefits derive from factors unique to single-sex programs or factors that promote good education, as mentioned above. Often overlooked in these discussions is the disruption of the sex ratio in coeducational classes in public schools from which the experimental single-sex classes are drawn (AAUW, 1998). When teachers group students by gender, race, ethnicity, social groups, or perceived ability, they seldom realize they are (1) missing chances for students to learn about skills and interests of other students; (2) contributing to barriers that prevent females and males with differing abilities from diverse backgrounds from learning to work and play together; and 3) reinforcing behavior patterns to perpetuate stereotyping in and out of schools. The AAUW report is one more piece of evidence that simplistic approaches are not effective and do not endure. Ongoing teacher education that includes equity as a criterion of success in both co-instructional and single-sex settings is the key.

Classroom Management/Discipline

Research has found that males receive more criticism and punishment than females (AAUW, 1998). This both reflects and reinforces the stereotype of females as docile and males as aggressive. According to studies spanning the 1970s and 1980s, even when males and females misbehave equally, males are more likely to get harsher reprimands (Sadker and Sadker, 1982; Serbin et al., 1973). Responses from our teacher clusters agree with these findings (Grayson and Martin, 1984; 1990; 1997; Grayson, 1985; 1987; 1998). Most educators know that males receive more punishment, referrals, suspensions and expulsions than females and that African American, Latino American and low socioeconomic European American males are the major recipients, far exceeding their representation in the population. Many of these students have been identified as having learning disabilities and attention disorders. Traditional sex role characteristics and expectations for some males lead them to believe that acting out, aggression, rebellious and risk-taking behavior, harassing others and bullying is all part of "being a man." Although the research reveals mixed findings, the following trends are discernible:

- more males than females are referred to school authorities;
- teachers tend to notice more disruptive behavior from males when it occurs—and sometimes when it does not occur;
- males receive more severe disciplinary action than females;
- students from diverse racial and ethnic backgrounds are most harshly treated, especially African Americans and males from indigenous populations, especially when measured by school suspension records or other discipline referrals (Grayson and Martin, 1984; 1988; 1990; 1997).

Evaluation of Performance

Another way teachers treat students differently is related to assessing the value and worth of student performance. Considerable evidence suggests that teacher-held stereotypes of females as being good with words and males as being good with numbers affect how teachers evaluate student learning and what students actually learn. Studies document that schools respond to students of varying race, class, and gender status in systematically different ways. These reinforce differential performances and evaluations in classrooms. Many school policies regarding grading and testing have influenced groups negatively. The most frequently used standardized testing models have been proven to favor middle- and upper-class white students and males over females (Grayson and Martin, 1988; 1990). Traditional forms of ability grouping and other forms of tracking have fallen along class, race, and gender lines, yet educators continue to sort, screen, and attempt to predict success utilizing similar instrumentation (Grayson and Martin, 1990; 1997). All of this influences the manner in which people are evaluated. Three major patterns of disparity have emerged as teachers assess performance.

First, males are given feedback related to the task, content, or thought process. Too often, females are given feedback related to the appearance of their work, appearance being a dominant influence in many aspects of girls' lives. Second, "effort" statements are used more frequently with males than with females. (I.e., "Carlos, if you tried harder in this class, you could do it.") With females, the emphasis is often limited to whether they have exerted any effort. (I.e., "Maria, you had trouble with this homework, didn't you? Well, you tried!") Males are sent the message that they have the ability, but are not using it. Females are sent the message that they don't have to work because they don't have the ability. The message is that less is expected and accepted.

Third, there is a differential pattern to which students are told to "read back through" an assignment or "work through" a problem themselves (males) and those students for whom the teacher is willing to do the work, explain in detail, or demonstrate (females). This is typically through subtle interactions such as finishing sentences or taking pencils (or other objects) out of a student's hand and doing the task for her. Obviously, this can have a very negative effect on one's perception of one's capabilities (Grayson and Martin, 1984; 1990; 1997).

SUGGESTED STRATEGIES FOR SELF-ASSESSMENT

Introduction and Rationale

Professional development research contains many assumptions regarding effective intervention with teachers. For example, we have learned that recognizing and changing deep-seated attitudes and stereotypes is difficult. When asked to complete self-evaluation surveys on gender bias in classroom settings prior to training, teachers tend to perceive and rate themselves as being gender-fair with their students (Grayson and Martin, 1990; 1997). When asked to watch a videotape of classroom interactions, teachers miss basic indicators of gender bias (Sadker, 1999). Bailey, Scantlebury, and Letts (1997) refer to unrealistic perceptions and this state of oblivion regarding gender bias as "gender blindness." Following presentations or classes that include information to increase their basic knowledge, combined with suggested action steps for peer observation and analysis, teachers are amazed at the differences in their earlier perceptions and the reality of what is happening in their classroom, much of which is subtle or unintended. Peer observation components that provide opportunities for partnering and teamwork permit teachers to reinforce each other in the change process by providing immediate, specific feedback. Research indicates that teachers learn best from observing in their colleagues' classrooms and from being observed by their peers. The process appears to be most effective when limited to a few techniques, focusing on proven effective teaching strategies related to increasing student achievement. It is less threatening when the teacher to be observed prepares the seating chart/recording sheet for the observer in advance, is aware when the class will be observed, and retains the recorded information following the observation.

The purpose of the following strategies for peer observation and self-assessment is to provide participants with an opportunity to learn from their own teaching experience and to examine the impact of their own behavior on classroom disparity. It is a discovery process that provides teachers with an opportunity to apply their own professional judgment in self-analysis of their classroom interactions on learning.

Numerous studies discuss the impact of classroom interactions on student achievement. While virtually all interactions between students, teachers, and administrators are important, there is general agreement among researchers that the interaction patterns that most influence student achievement are those between teacher and student (Brophy and Good, 1970; Fennema and Peterson, 1986; Flanders, 1964; Grayson and Martin, 1984; 1990; 1997; Good and Brophy, 1978; 1987). This section examines categories of behaviors or actions in which teachers might treat students differently and provides suggestions for teacher assessment in each category.

As discussed earlier, when observing in classrooms or supervising teachers about equity concerns related to interaction, it is important to address issues of both quantity and quality. Of the following categories, the first two provide information on frequency distribution patterns in classrooms. The remaining address the quality of the interaction patterns in classrooms. These have been identified as positive, supportive, motivational interactions used by teachers on a consistent basis with students from whom they expect the most. Guidelines for recording observations of the behaviors are included below.

Categories of Self-Assessment

Response Opportunities   A teacher provides a response opportunity by giving a student a chance to act in relation to an instruction. Response opportunities include asking students to answer questions, contribute to discussions, state opinions, write on the board, or present to the class. Most teachers do not consciously treat students differently, yet differential treatment often occurs. In subtle ways teachers communicate that some students are more valued than others. Students are less apt to learn from someone who doesn't like them or doesn't expect them to learn. Students who are asked easy questions don't have a chance to develop problem-solving or inductive-thinking skills or to express opinions. When they are asked questions to which there is only one right answer and they miss, they feel embarrassed. Expressing opinions is fun and provides an entry into a discussion, encouraging task participation. These consequences are compounded by the reactions of other students, who notice which students receive specific assignments or certain types of attention from the teacher.

Recording Response Opportunities   An observer records a response opportunity when the teacher does the following: asks a student to answer a question; accepts a student's answer to a question; calls on a student to perform in some other way before the class or small group (i.e., the student is asked to read aloud, work a problem on the board, give a report, express an opinion, demonstrate a lab experiment, sing, or recite a poem). If the response opportunity is directed toward a small group or the entire class, a collective response may be recorded. Record one mark for each response opportunity, not for each comment or question in a continuous interaction.

Acknowledgment of Response/Feedback   Communication theory emphasizes the importance of feedback in modifying our behavior so that the consequences of that behavior more closely match our intentions. Teachers spend only limited time analyzing the impact of the feedback they provide. The most frequent form of feedback is simple acceptance. Research findings generally agree that more often than not, male students receive more feedback than female students (Grayson and Martin, 1984; 1990; 1997).

Recording Acknowledgment of Response/Feedback   The observer should record feedback when the teacher affirms, praises, corrects, criticizes, or rejects a student's response. The key aspect of feedback is that students realize they have been heard or observed by the teacher. The intent of such feedback is to suggest positive directions or corrections. Record only feedback that relates to the instructional task.

Wait Time   The time elapsing between offering and terminating a response opportunity is called "wait time" (Rowe, 1969; 1986). The length of time students need to respond tends to be longest when the teacher asks questions that require the student to interpret or reorganize the facts or to form an opinion. The average time a teacher waits for a student to respond to a question is about 2.6 seconds. Teachers wait an average of 5 seconds if a correct response is anticipated but cut the wait time to less than 1 second if the student's answer is expected to be incorrect. During one of our pilot studies, this interaction was identified by teachers as having the most impact on the quality of responses and increasing the participation of previously invisible female students, students with disabilities, and students with English as a second language (Grayson and Martin, 1984; 1990; 1997).

Recording Wait Time   Wait time should be recorded each time a student is asked by the teacher or classmates and provided with time (two to three seconds) to think about a response. The teacher waits three to five seconds before ending a response opportunity by asking another student the question or providing additional information. This should be three to five seconds of uninterrupted silence, so students can consider their answer.

Physical Closeness   Teachers often organize classrooms to determine where students will be seated, and some students may be unconsciously kept at a distance. Other times, when students have been given the chance to choose where they sit, they may consciously "deal" themselves in or out of classroom participation based on their choice. Physical closeness means that the student and teacher engage in classroom activities physically near one another at least for a period of time. In most classrooms, favored locations can be easily spotted. These are the work locations of students who get the most attention. In a classroom where students move between work stations, the favored location may shift frequently. Several observation studies have examined room arrangement and teacher mobility and their impact on achievement, especially science and math, and on classroom management.

A teacher can remedy the uneven distribution of physical closeness by moving about the room to be near each student for a portion of the class period. If the classroom environment makes this impossible, the teacher can move the students or suggest that they move. A combination of teacher and student movement in a variety of groupings appears to be the most effective way to ensure that all students benefit from physical proximity to the teacher, according to reports from our teacher participants and field tests (Grayson and Martin, 1984; 1990; 1997).

Recording Physical Closeness   When a teacher stands or sits within an arm's reach, in a stationary position, physical closeness should be recorded for each student. Nothing is recorded if the teacher simply walks past a student. If a student approaches the teacher and stands within an arm's reach, physical closeness is recorded. If the teacher remains near one or more students during an entire observation period, physical closeness is recorded only once for each student. If the teacher leaves those students and later returns, physical closeness is recorded again. In other words, the initiation of the physical closeness is recorded, not the duration.

Touching   Discussions, responses, and studies pertaining to touch indicate a variety of attitudes toward this form of student-teacher interaction. Many people are averse to being touched, for a variety of reasons. Some regard contact as a physical attack and respond quickly and harshly. Others are afraid to touch because of potential consequences. Rules and regulations in many schools forbid physical contact between teacher and student. Both parties are sensitized to their personal rights that they do not want violated. However, touch is an important means of communicating success and providing reinforcement, and such interactions between teachers and the students is in no way sexual or abusive. Research indicates that teachers are most apt to position themselves physically close to and to touch students they perceive as fast learners. Who the teacher touches may also depend on the student's age and the gender and ethnicity of both teacher and student (Grayson and Martin, 1984; 1990; 1997).

Recording Touching   Touching is recorded when the teacher's hand contacts the student, usually on the student's arm or hand, in a way that expresses helpfulness, encouragement, or regard. Touching is not recorded if the teacher touches the student with a pencil, ruler or other object, even if it is a friendly gesture.

Reproof   Reproof is a verbal or nonverbal indication that a student's behavior is unacceptable. Providing firm but calm communications of inappropriate behavior in an unemotional and respectful manner is more effective than engaging in angry outbursts. To avoid inequitable responses to inappropriate behavior, focus on the behavior and not on the person. Consistency is the key to improvement (Grayson and Martin 1984; 1990; 1997).

Recording Reproof   Reproof is recorded when the teacher calmly, unemotionally, and respectfully attempts to interrupt, stop, or change problem behavior. The student may or may not change the behavior. If the teacher later repeats the same request, a second reproof is recorded. Reproof may be nonverbal.

Probing   If a student cannot answer a question, the teacher may supply the answer, call on another student, or stay with the student who could not answer, probing for a response. Probing may involve rephrasing the question, providing clues, providing additional information, suggesting an appropriate thought process for getting to the answer, or reminding the student of related information already known. Probing is a powerful teaching tool. When probing elicits an acceptable response, the student feels successful. Teachers are less inclined to encourage females to risk or expand a response. If the teacher always accepts a student's "I don't know" or non-response without probing, that student learns to avoid risking a response (Grayson and Martin, 1984; 1990; 1997).

Recording Probing   The observer records probing when the instructor provides assistance to a student. There is no mark for the original question. If a series of probing techniques is used with one student on one original question, only record one probing mark for the collective series. When the instructor leaves the student, returns, asks a question, and assists the student, an additional mark is recorded.

Listening   Listening is a powerful way of relating to another person. We all have a need to be heard, to hold someone's attention. Yet research reveals a number of insights about listening patterns in traditional classrooms and about teachers as listeners. In fact, teachers do most of the talking and very little listening. In the United States and in many cultures around the world, females are taught to be listeners, and males are encouraged to speak. Consequently, females generally have more difficulty than males getting attention when they wish to say something and may begin to believe that what they say is unimportant. Another consequence of typical listening patterns in school and society is that males do not develop effective listening skills, which in turn impacts their capacity to engage in successful interpersonal relationships (Grayson and Martin 1984; 1990; 1997).

Recording Listening   Listening is recorded when the teacher's attention to a student's question, response, comment, and so forth, is apparent. Attentiveness may be indicated by the instructor's expression, gestures, or verbal response. Any indication that the instructor is obviously listening is recorded.

Higher-Level Questioning   Often teachers ask students questions requiring only that the student recall something from a reading assignment or previous instruction. This type of question is often useful and appropriate, but the questions that promote learning and challenge students to think are those that require students to engage in more complex mental processes than simple recall. For example, a higher level question might require the student to (1) recall related facts from several sources, (2) express an opinion and give reasons, (3) summarize what the class has learned in an instructional unit, (4) predict the consequences of certain actions, and (5) organize information in a new way.

Studies generally suggest that males have more opportunities to respond to higher level questions. The student who is asked to answer a question or perform in some other way is usually in a more compelling learning situation than a student who is merely listening. A student who is asked to answer a higher level question is in an even more educationally beneficial situation. If, as such, a teacher falls into the habit of asking simple recall questions of some students and higher level questions of only select students, an inequitable situation exists where some students receive a lower quality of instruction than others. For example, students with learning disabilities are the least likely to receive higher level questions in a general education classroom. However, repeated reports and observations indicate that these students respond more successfully to questions eliciting an opinion, example, or their thoughts on how something happened, rather than to simple recall questions requiring memorized, verbatim responses. It appears that students who may most need higher order skills development are least likely to have such learning opportunities (Grayson and Martin 1984; 1990; 1997).

Recording Higher-Level Questions   The observer records a higher level question when the teacher asks any question that requires a more complex thought process to answer than does a question requiring only simple recall. Additional probing and everything that the teacher says to help the student understand the original question is recorded as one question only. If a teacher poses a higher level question to the entire class, then begins to call on students, a mark is tallied for each student provided with an opportunity to respond.

Analytical Feedback   Analytical feedback refers to providing a reason for acceptance, praise, rejection, or correction. Providing analytical feedback means explaining to a student why his or her response was satisfactory or unsatisfactory. When providing the opportunity for students to answer more higher level questions, there are more chances for analytical feedback. A student's responses to higher level questions offer more opportunities to explain the strengths and weaknesses of the response than simple recall questions. For example, the instructor might (1) explain where the student's thinking process went astray, (2) point out a false assumption, (3) explain that the wrong process was used, (4) praise the student's use of multiple sources, (5) praise the student's use of color in a painting, or (6) point out that the student has solved a problem by transferring knowledge acquired in a different situation. Whether the student's performance is satisfactory or not, the instructor's feedback can assist the learning process if it is positive and informative. Sarcasm or denigrating criticism hinders the learning process.

Research informs us that, in general, males are told that their lack of success is linked to a lack of effort, while females receive messages that their lack of success is due to a lack of ability. The implications of such interactions on a student's approach to school tasks and his or her willingness to take on such tasks is significant. How long will a female keep trying if she thinks she simply can't do something? One consequence of believing that failure is insurmountable is that students acquire a sense that they have no control over the factors that cause failure, leading to declining performance.

Recording Analytical Feedback   The observer records analytical feedback each time a teacher explains in a supportive way why a student's performance was or was not acceptable. When recording, listen for the reason "why," for the spoken or implied "because." The feedback must be helpful to the learning process.

SUMMARY

This chapter has described how teachers interact differently with female and male students from diverse racial and ethnic backgrounds, depending on their perceived expectations for the student. It includes research based strategies which may be used to help teachers reflect and assess their own interactions and encourage them to make needed changes in the ways they relate to students in order to eliminate bias.

The chapter summarizes work done in classrooms throughout the United States over a twenty year period and would not have been possible without the collective voices and responses of all of the teachers and other professional educators who have shared their classrooms, stories, experiences and students with us. Most teachers know that some students can learn. Good teachers know that all students can learn . . . and how to help them. If students are not learning in the way we're teaching, we must teach them in the ways they can learn.

REFERENCES

American Association of University Women (AAUW). 1991. *Shortchanging girls, shortchanging America*. Washington, D.C.: American Association of University Women Foundation.

———. 1998. *Separated by sex: A critical look at single-sex education for girls*. Washington, D.C.: American Association of University Women Foundation.

Bailey, B. L., K. Scantlebury, and W. J. Letts. 1997. It's not my style: Using disclaimers to ignore issues in science. *Journal of Teacher Education* 48(1):29–35.

Brophy, J. and T. Good. 1970. Teachers' communications of differential expectations for children's classroom performance: Some behavioral data. *Journal of Educational Psychology* 61: 356–374.

Campbell, P. B. *Girls, boys and educational excellence*. Paper presented at the annual meeting of the American Educational Research Association (AERA). New Orleans, April 1984.

Fennema, E., and Penelope L. Peterson. 1986. Teacher-student interactions and sex-related differences in learning mathematics. *Teaching and Teacher Education* 2(3):19–42.

Flanders, N. A. 1964. Interaction model of critical teaching behaviors. In *An analysis and projection of research in teacher education*. Edited by F. R. Cyphert and E. Spaights, 97–218. Columbus: College of Education, Ohio State University.

Good, T. L., and J. E. Brophy. 1978; 1987. *Looking in classrooms* (2nd & 4th editions). New York: Harper & Row, Publishers.

Good, T. L., J. N. Sikes, and J. E. Brophy. 1973. Effects of teacher sex and student sex on classroom interaction. *Journal of Educational Psychology* 65(1):74–87.

Grayson, D. A. 1985. *Implementing the GESA teacher training program*. Paper presented at the AERA annual meeting, Chicago, Ill. Available from ERIC.

———. 1987. *Evaluating the impact of the GESA program*. Paper presented at the AERA annual meeting. Washington, D.C. Available from ERIC.

———. 1992. *Classroom and site-based leadership development: Increasing achievement and participation for all students with an emphasis on underserved populations*. Paper presented at the AERA annual meeting. San Francisco, Calif. Available from ERIC.

———. 1998. *Generating expectations for student achievement: A fifteen year retrospective of an equitable approach to excellence in teaching*. Paper presented at the AERA annual meeting. San Diego, Calif. Available from ERIC.

———. 1999. Dear teacher. *GREAT Newsletter*. Available from GrayMill, 22821 Cove View, St., Canyon Lake, Calif. 92587.

Grayson, D. A., and M. D. Martin. 1984; 1990. *Gender/ethnic expectations for student achievement: Teacher handbook*. Canyon Lake, Calif.: GrayMill, 22821 Cove View, St., Canyon Lake, Calif. 92587.

———. 1988a. *Gender/ethnic expectations for student achievement: Facilitators handbook*. Canyon Lake, Calif.: GrayMill, 22821 Cove View, St., Canyon Lake, Calif. 92587, 1988.

———. 1988b. *Generating expectations for student achievement: Participant booklet.* Canyon Lake, Calif.: GrayMill, 22821 Cove View, St., Canyon Lake, Calif. 92587, 1998.

———. 1997. *Generating expectations for student achievement: Teacher handbook.* Canyon Lake, Calif.: GrayMill, 22821 Cove View, St., Canyon Lake, Calif. 92587.

Rosenthal, R., and L. Jacobson. 1968. *Pygmalion in the classroom: Teacher expectations and pupil's intellectual development.* New York: Holt, Rinehart, and Winston 1968.

Rowe, M. B. 1969. Science, silence and sanctions. *Science and Children* 6:11–13.

———. 1986, January–February. Wait time: Slowing down may be a way of speeding up! *Journal of Teacher Education*:43–50.

Sadker, D. 1999. Gender equity: Still knocking at the classroom door. *Educational Leadership* 56(7):22.

Sadker, D., and M. Sadker. 1982. *Sex equity handbook for schools.* New York: Longman, Inc.

———. 1984, April 27. *Teacher reactions to classroom responses of male and female students.* Paper presented at the American Educational Research Association Annual Meeting, New Orleans.

———. 1985, March. Sexism in the schoolroom of the eighties. *Psychology Today,* 54–57.

Serbin, L. et al. 1973. A comparison of teacher response to the pre-academic and problem behavior of boys and girls. *Child Development* 44.

SAMPLE CURRICULUM RATING FORM

Analyzing Texts, Workbooks, Curriculum Guides, Audio-Visual Materials and Supplementary Materials for Equity

Title of Work _____   Copyright Date _____

Author _____   Today's Date _____

Publisher _____   Evaluator _____

	Page #	Good	Fair	Poor	N/A
1. Avoids stereotyping behaviors, activities, life patterns, patterns, personality traits.	—	—	—	—	—
2. Illustrates people in non-stereotyped roles.	—	—	—	—	—
3. Conforms to non-biased language guidelines. (e.g., McGraw Hill)	—	—	—	—	—
4. Includes contributions of females and males of diverse cultures.	—	—	—	—	—
5. Includes factual and historical information pertaining to males and females of diverse cultures.	—	—	—	—	—
6. Gives adequate, up-to-date attention to social issues and problems affecting all women. (e.g., pay parity, child care, etc.)	—	—	—	—	—
7. Gives balanced treatment of social as well as military/political history or issues.	—	—	—	—	—
8. Describes a wide variety of career options for all females and males.	—	—	—	—	—

(continued on next page)

SAMPLE CURRICULUM RATING FORM (*continued*)

Generally, how would you rate this material for fairness?

Outstanding ____   Good ____   Fair ____   Poor ____

Write comments on the back.

GESA SELF-EVALUATION

(Suggested instrument for pre/post assessment)

Directions: Below is a list of 28 statements about situations that occur in a typical classroom. Please use the scale provided after each statement to rate how you usually handle that situation. Circle the number that best describes your behavior.

Circle 1 if you Strongly Disagree that the statement describes your behavior.
Circle 2 if you Disagree that the statement describes your behavior.
Circle 3 if you Neither Agree nor Disagree that the statement describes your behavior.
Circle 4 if you Agree with the statement that describes your behavior.
Circle 5 if you Strongly Agree that the statement describes your behavior.
An NA (not applicable) option has been provided just in case a statement involves a situation that you're never exposed to.

Begin by entering your social security number: SS# _____ - ____ - _____ .
We will use this only as an ID number when data from these forms are entered and analyzed, but the number will never be used in conjunction with your name or the names of any other teachers who complete this form.

1. I use examples in my teaching showing both women and men of diverse backgrounds with a wide range of feelings, interests, and career choices.

Strongly Disagree	Disagree	Neither Agree nor Disagree	Agree	Strongly Agree	
1	2	3	4	5	NA

2. I display and use accurate factual knowledge about the current economic and legal status of women.

Strongly Disagree	Disagree	Neither Agree nor Disagree	Agree	Strongly Agree	
1	2	3	4	5	NA

(continued on next page)

GESA SELF-EVALUATION *(continued)*

3. I supplement inadequate treatment of any group in classroom materials by adding information or by discussing the inaccurate portrayal of people's roles.

Strongly Disagree	Disagree	Neither Agree nor Disagree	Agree	Strongly Agree	NA
1	2	3	4	5	

4. I take the idea of equity seriously; for example, I avoid putting down men or women, or joking about their abilities, roles, race or ethnic backgrounds.

Strongly Disagree	Disagree	Neither Agree nor Disagree	Agree	Strongly Agree	NA
1	2	3	4	5	

5. I use non-biased language; for example, I avoid referring to all doctors or lawyers as "he," or all nurses or secretaries as "she."

Strongly Disagree	Disagree	Neither Agree nor Disagree	Agree	Strongly Agree	NA
1	2	3	4	5	

6. I avoid generalizations that refer to stereotyping; for example, "you throw like a girl," "you think like a man," "all Asians are good in math," "all Blacks are lazy," etc.

Strongly Disagree	Disagree	Neither Agree nor Disagree	Agree	Strongly Agree	NA
1	2	3	4	5	

(continued on next page)

GESA SELF-EVALUATION *(continued)*

7. I avoid comparison of students based on gender; for example, I would not say, "female students are working harder than males."

Strongly Disagree 1	Disagree 2	Neither Agree nor Disagree 3	Agree 4	Strongly Agree 5	NA

8. I give equitable attention to all males and females; I do not show preference for any one group

Strongly Disagree 1	Disagree 2	Neither Agree nor Disagree 3	Agree 4	Strongly Agree 5	NA

9. I address all inappropriate behavior with a calm, respectful regardless of the gender, race, ethnicity or socioeconomic class of the student.

Strongly Disagree 1	Disagree 2	Neither Agree nor Disagree 3	Agree 4	Strongly Agree 5	NA

10. I reinforce student expression of values without regard to their gender, race or ethnicity, so that all students can express assertiveness, gentleness and empathy.

Strongly Disagree 1	Disagree 2	Neither Agree nor Disagree 3	Agree 4	Strongly Agree 5	NA

(continued on next page)

GESA SELF-EVALUATION *(continued)*

11. I help students explore all vocational interests, not only those traditionally associated with their gender.

Strongly Disagree	Disagree	Neither Agree nor Disagree	Agree	Strongly Agree	NA
1	2	3	4	5	

12. I act as a model of non-biased behavior by performing activities traditionally done by the other gender; that is, if female, I don't always expect males to lift boxes; if male, I don't always expect females to perform clerical duties.

Strongly Disagree	Disagree	Neither Agree nor Disagree	Agree	Strongly Agree	NA
1	2	3	4	5	

13. My grading patterns do not favor any students, but reflect individual accomplishments.

Strongly Disagree	Disagree	Neither Agree nor Disagree	Agree	Strongly Agree	NA
1	2	3	4	5	

14. I expect comparable academic performance from all students; that is, all females are not assumed to be better in verbal skills and males superior in math and science.

Strongly Disagree	Disagree	Neither Agree nor Disagree	Agree	Strongly Agree	NA
1	2	3	4	5	

(continued on next page)

GESA SELF-EVALUATION *(continued)*

15. I recognize that students may have interests not traditionally associated with their gender; I do not expect females always to have typically feminine interests and males typically masculine interests.

Strongly Disagree	Disagree	Neither Agree nor Disagree	Agree	Strongly Agree	
1	2	3	4	5	NA

16. I expect the same behavior from all students, for example; I do not expect chivalrous behavior only from males or require neatness only from females.

Strongly Disagree	Disagree	Neither Agree nor Disagree	Agree	Strongly Agree	
1	2	3	4	5	NA

17. I allow students, within the limits of classroom rules, to express emotions without regard to gender; for example, I do not expect females always to cry and males always to get angry.

Strongly Disagree	Disagree	Neither Agree nor Disagree	Agree	Strongly Agree	
1	2	3	4	5	NA

18. I encourage all students to treat each other as equals; for example, I encourage them to include others from diverse backgrounds and both genders in all activities.

Strongly Disagree	Disagree	Neither Agree nor Disagree	Agree	Strongly Agree	
1	2	3	4	5	NA

(continued on next page)

GESA SELF-EVALUATION (*continued*)

19. All visual materials in my classroom are non-biased, showing men and women in a variety of roles which reflect the many interests of all females and males.

Strongly Disagree	Disagree	Neither Agree nor Disagree	Agree	Strongly Agree	NA
1	2	3	4	5	

20. When the treatment of either women or men is inadequate in a textbook, I make supplementary material available to students; for example, reference books about significant women in history, or family living books that explain the role of a father.

Strongly Disagree	Disagree	Neither Agree nor Disagree	Agree	Strongly Agree	NA
1	2	3	4	5	

21. I avoid dividing or grouping students on the basis of gender/ race/ ethnicity. For example, I take measures to have mixed grouping in lunch lines, in seating, or for academic or physical competition.

Strongly Disagree	Disagree	Neither Agree nor Disagree	Agree	Strongly Agree	NA
1	2	3	4	5	

22. A recommend all classroom activities to both males and females; for example, I would suggest both females and males try cooKing or a woodworking project as optional activities.

Strongly Disagree	Disagree	Neither Agree nor Disagree	Agree	Strongly Agree	NA
1	2	3	4	5	

(*continued on next page*)

GESA SELF-EVALUATION (continued)

23. I assign classroom chores and duties without regard to gender; for example, both females and males carry chairs, run AV equipment, take notes during classroom meetings, and water plants.

Strongly Disagree 1	Disagree 2	Neither Agree nor Disagree 3	Agree 4	Strongly Agree 5	NA

24. I work to make all school facilities, equipment and clubs equally available to all students.

Strongly Disagree 1	Disagree 2	Neither Agree nor Disagree 3	Agree 4	Strongly Agree 5	NA

25. I give equitable attention to the co-curricular achievements of males and females; for example, I acknowledge the athletic achievements of both.

Strongly Disagree 1	Disagree 2	Neither Agree nor Disagree 3	Agree 4	Strongly Agree 5	NA

26. I suggest that both females and males work on service projects.

Strongly Disagree 1	Disagree 2	Neither Agree nor Disagree 3	Agree 4	Strongly Agree 5	NA

(continued on next page)

GESA SELF-EVALUATION *(continued)*

27. I encourage both males and females to participate in all co-curricular activities; for example, athletics, cheerleading, clubs, stage crew.

Strongly Disagree 1	Disagree 2	Neither Agree nor Disagree 3	Agree 4	Strongly Agree 5	NA

28. I encourage both females and males to participate in a variety of roles within co-curricular activities; for example, committee head, hospitality committee, secretary, treasurer, president, etc.

Strongly Disagree 1	Disagree 2	Neither Agree nor Disagree 3	Agree 4	Strongly Agree 5	NA

(Validated by Dr. C. Malloy—UNC, Chapel Hill)
Adapted from GESA Teacher Handbook, Grayson, D., & M. Martin, GrayMill, Canyon Lake, CA.
Permission to duplicate with citation from: Grayson, D. A., and M. D. Martin, *Generating Expectations for Student Achievement—Teacher Handbook*. GrayMill, 22821 Cove View St., Canyon Lake, CA 92587 (909) 246-2106.

CHAPTER 8

Stopping Sexual Harassment in Schools

Eleanor Linn and Harilyn Rousso

QUESTION: Will you tell us how you liked attending school in the 6th grade at South Kortright?

EVE: I hated it. Never wanted to go. I would come home every day and cry and tell my parents I never wanted to go. Because . . . (tears, comforting from others, a drink of water) I was being called these horrible names, such as when that boy called me an ugly dog-faced bitch and all my girlfriends were being called names. And the guys were pushing us and pulling our hair and snapping our bras. And my teacher, he wouldn't do anything about it. Neither would my principal. (Eve was in ninth grade when she gave this testimony. She is white and nondisabled.)

—*Eve Bruneau v. South Kortright Central School District* 94-CV-864, 32–33

CAROL (in a group discussion of girls with disabilities): A boy came over to me, in back of me—I didn't know he was there—and was actually trying to undo my bra. I was extremely worried. He was trying to take advantage of me because I couldn't see him. I was scared to do anything. They could hurt you. Finally, I don't know how, but I got up enough courage and I took my cane and smacked the kid right in the shins. And he let go of my bra strap before he could undo it. (Carol was thirteen years old and attended an inclusive middle school when she gave this interview. She is white and is blind.)

—Rousso, 1994–95

SUSAN (in an interview): I was once on a van with a driver. . . . He would drive the girls home and he'd take me home last. [One day] instead of driving me home, he drove me to a deserted lot. He asked if he could have a kiss . . . I said "If you don't take me home, I'll kick you." He called me a whole bunch of names and then he took me home. . . . One of my friends got raped by this person. Finally . . . [the school] fired him (Susan was nineteen when interviewed. She is Latina and has cerebral palsy).

—Rousso, 1994–95

Sexual harassment in and around school is distressingly common. It occurs in classrooms, in hallways, on the way to and from school. It happens to students with and without disabilities, across gender, racial, ethnic, socioeconomic, and sexual orientation lines. Sexual harassment causes students to drop out, change career plans, lose friends, and feel emotional anguish. It sends a bitter message to everyone about the dangers of school life and makes clear that injustice really does happen. It implicitly teaches young people that some students can get away with appalling behavior without serious repercussions and causes the school community to doubt the power of the very adults who are supposed to administer fairness. Where sexual harassment occurs, it creates a climate of alienation, hostility, and mistrust, the very opposite of what is needed for learning. Sexual harassment prevents students from receiving the care that they need and respect that they deserve.

While sexual harassment is pervasive and its consequences highly disruptive and destructive to all students, girls and young women face some specific issues around the extent, nature, and effects of the problem. From what we know, girls with disabilities share the specific issues of their nondisabled female peers and face some unique challenges as well. This chapter provides an overview of sexual harassment in schools, highlighting some of the issues that girls in general, and girls with disabilities in particular, confront.

We note at the outset that there is almost no research on sexual harassment and students with disabilities. Sexual harassment has been a largely invisible problem for these students. To enhance visibility, we highlight the available facts, draw some tentative conclusions, and show readers the well-documented need for action.

DEFINITIONS

Sexual harassment is unwanted sexual attention including an array of behaviors from sexual comments to rape. It interrupts a person's ability to perform her/his usual activities and often heightens feelings of vulnerability. In school, sexual harassment of students, whether perpetrated by adults or other students, interferes with learning. It has been defined in legal terms as a violation of a student's equal right to protection and a form of sex discrimination. Schools and their employees may be held liable for monetary damages if they fail to respond to known sexual harassment. It is illegal not only under federal law, Title IX, but also under many state and local statutes. Sexual harassment in school has parallels to sexual harassment in the workplace, where it is also defined as a form of sex discrimination because of typical power inequities and gender differences between the perpetrator, often a male supervisor or employer, and the target, most likely a female employee. In the workplace and school, sexual harassment has more to do with power than sexual desire.

The U. S. Department of Education, Office for Civil Rights outlines two forms of sexual harassment:

1. quid pro quo sexual harassment in which "a school employee explicitly or implicitly conditions a student's participation in an education program or activity or bases an educational decision on the student's submission to unwelcome sexual advances, requests for sexual favors, or other verbal, nonverbal, or physical conduct of a sexual nature . . . whether or not the student resists and suffers the threatened harm or submits and thus avoid the threatened harm";

2. hostile environment sexual harassment "in which the sexual harassing conduct (which can include unwelcome sexual advances, requests for sexual favors, and other verbal, nonverbal, or physical conduct of a sexual nature) by an employee, by another students, or by a third party that is sufficiently severe, persistent, or pervasive to limit a student's ability to participate in or benefit from an education program or activity, or to create a hostile or abusive educational environment." (U.S. Department of Education, OCR, 1997)

The hostile environment form of sexual harassment is the far more common one in schools, so educators need to know how to recognize, resolve, and ultimately prevent it. Definitions are important when dealing with sexual harassment. Unlike other antisocial activities, such as theft or assault, the public is not in agreement about what constitutes sexual harassment. When a person describes a circumstance of harassment, she/he is likely to be told, "That isn't sexual harassment; it's just 'bad taste' or 'immature behavior'. By using a euphemism instead of the harsher term *sexual harassment,* the listener trivializes the severity of the perpetrator's antisocial behavior and denies the speaker's justifiable outrage. Even if intended to comfort, such a response intensifies the teller's feelings of vulnerability. "Here is someone else who is not willing to help," is the underlying message.

One of the best ways to help people understand the definition of sexual harassment is to give examples. Some examples include being called a sexually offensive name, being touched in a private part of your body, being stalked, being forced to make a sexual gesture or do something sexual, having your clothes pulled down or off, or being called "lesbian" or "gay" in a taunting manner, no matter what your sexual orientation. Student policies and handbooks, professional development materials, and student curricula need to provide a range of examples of unwanted sexual attention that will not be tolerated. Various aspects of the curriculum, including literature, writing projects, and work skills and social skills programs provide opportunities to introduce the concepts of wanted and unwanted sexual attention.

Some sexually harassing behaviors constitute child sexual abuse. Definitions of child sexual abuse vary by state, are generally administered by Child Protective Service agencies, and focus more on child sexual abuse within the family than in educational institutions. Sexual harassment can also be a form of hate crime. This is a continuum of intimidation, violence, and sexual abuse against people based on a particular characteristic such as gender, race, ethnicity, sexual orientation, or disability status. Hate crimes often combine sexual offensiveness with other forms of violent behavior to further demean and frighten the target and other people who have the same particular characteristic, as well. Most types of hate crimes are illegal. They are punished more severely than comparable acts with no prejudicial component. We mention child sexual abuse and hate crimes here because we refer to them in later sections addressing sexual harassment and students with disabilities.

PREVALENCE OF SEXUAL HARASSMENT IN SCHOOLS

Sexual harassment is a widespread phenomenon. A dozen research studies over the past six years, using different survey methodologies, have found similar results (Stein, 1999). A majority of high school students report having experienced sexual harassment. The most methodologically rigorous of the studies was the 1993 AAUW/Harris Poll titled Hostile Hallways (AAUW, 1993). This study used a scientifically drawn random sample that can be generalized to all U.S. public schools with students in grades eight through eleven. In this study, 85 percent of the girls and 76 percent of the boys reported that they had been sexually harassed in school. Examining the data more closely, Linn and colleagues (Lee et al., 1996) found that the likelihood of a student being sexually harassed did not depend on a student's grade point average, socioeconomic status, race, or ethnicity. Two factors were by far the largest predictors of the likelihood of a student's being harassed. The first was gender. Girls were harassed far more frequently than boys. They experienced more types of sexual harassment and especially more physical forms of sexual harassment. They also experienced more severe sexual harassment, such as harassment from teachers and other adults in authority. Girls reported being more upset by incidents of harassment and experienced more serious consequences than boys. They had more trouble eating and sleeping and a greater likelihood of withdrawing from school and social activities.

The other predictive factor was having friends who were sexually harassed. This finding is important because it indicates that harassment occurs in certain environments and not in others. It shows that in some places a large portion of students, particularly girls, is harassed, while in other places sexual harassment is relatively unheard of. The bad news is that there are schools and programs in which sexual harassment is rampant. The good news is that we can change these environments if we work to change how people behave in such places.

The most common forms of sexual harassment for both boys and girls are sexually offensive comments, gestures, and looks; closely followed by acts of unwanted sexual touching, grabbing, and pinching. More girls were subjected to all of the fourteen types of sexually harassing behavior mentioned in the survey, with one exception. More boys reported being called "gay/lesbian" and they reported being more upset about it than girls.

In a study of high school students in New Jersey (Trigg and Wittenstrom, 1996), 97 percent of girls and 70 percent of boys reported being sexually harassed in school, while in a statewide study in Connecticut, 92 percent of girls and 57 percent of boys reported they had been sexually harassed (Permanent Commission on the Status of Women, 1995). Stein's survey of young women through *Seventeen* magazine (1993), though not a scientific sample, yielded similar results. Eighty-nine percent of young women reported being sexually harassed in school, with gestures, looks, comments, and jokes being the most prevalent form of harassment.

Estimates of Prevalence for Students with Disabilities

Unfortunately, none of the studies examined disability as a factor, nor have there been separate studies of sexual harassment of students with disabilities. Sexual harassment has not gained recognition as a problem for this group, and no prevalence of sexual harassment of students with disabilities has been determined. Rousso, in a pilot study of sexual harassment and students with disabilities conducted in several high schools in New York, found that "there was insufficient information . . . to determine whether girls with disabilities face higher or lower rates of sexual harassment at school than their nondisabled peers. However, a majority of adults and young people interviewed expressed the opinion that girls with disabilities are more vulnerable to harassment than girls without disabilities" (1996, p. 4). She encountered numerous examples of sexual harassment from racially and ethnically diverse young people with a broad range of disabilities: mobility, sensory, learning, intellectual, and emotional disabilities. Many situations involved students with multiple disabilities, "suggesting that having more than one disability may increase the risk of sexual harassment" (p. 2).

As in the studies of nondisabled students, most examples involved females as targets, males as perpetrators. However, a high number of boys with disabilities were also reported as targets of sexual harassment, most frequently by nondisabled males (both peers and adults). This preliminary finding suggests that boys and young men with disabilities may experience far more sexual harassment at school than nondisabled boys. Unwanted touching and offensive comments were the most commonly mentioned forms of sexual harassment for both girls and boys with disabilities, as they are for both nondisabled girls and boys.

A 1994 study conducted by the chancellor of New York City Public Schools and the special commissioner of investigation substantiated sexual abuse cases within the school system, including special education programs, from February 1991 to September 1994 (Joint Commission). The study was limited to cases involving employees as perpetrators and students as targets of the abuse; student-to-student abuse was not considered. Sexual abuse was defined as criminal activity, such as rape, sodomy, or improper touching, and sexual relations between an employee and a student regardless of the student's age. One key finding was that cases involving the sexual abuse of children enrolled in special education programs were overrepresented: "Although the special education students represent only seven per cent of the public school population, they comprise fourteen percent of student victims in sexual abuse cases substantiated by the SCI" (pp. 20–21). Unfortunately, this study did not provide a breakdown of cases by gender.

Still another method to estimate the prevalence of sexual harassment of students with disabilities is to extrapolate from the literature on child sexual abuse and disabled children, as well as the small body of research on sexual abuse and women with disabilities.[1] According to Petersilia (1998), children with disabilities are almost twice as likely to be sexually abused as nondisabled children. Similarly, Crosse, Kaye, and

Ratnofsky (1993) reported that the incidence of child maltreatment for disabled children is 1.7 times the maltreatment rate for nondisabled children. Moreover, they found that children with disabilities are more likely to be maltreated by a person who is not a relative than nondisabled children (pp. 3–19). Neither study offered a breakdown of the location of the abuse, so we do not know what proportion of the abuse happens at home, at school, or in residential settings. Sobsey, in his review of the literature on sexual abuse of adults with disabilities, estimated that depending on whether the definition used is broad or narrow, and whether the focus is on single or multiple incidents, the abuse rates of disabled adults may be between 1.5 and 5 times the rate of nondisabled adults (1994, p. 69). His analysis of several studies of disabled people who have experienced abuse suggested that the abuse is often severe, for example involving penetration, and chronic, involving repeated incidents. In these studies, the sites of abuse were most frequently the place of residence; school was also mentioned as a common site in some research, but this designation included day and residential schools.

Although not all studies of sexual abuse of children and adults with disabilities provide a gender breakdown, many that did reported higher rates of abuse for females than for males. Some also found that disabled men and boys are at greater risk for abuse than nondisabled males (Sobsey, 1994). Two studies reported that a majority of disabled women experienced violent sexual abuse at some point in their lives (Stimpson and Best, 1991; Doucette, 1986). Doucette found that almost 50 percent of disabled women had been sexually abused as children, compared to 34 percent of nondisabled women. Waxman Fiduccia (1998), summarizing several studies, reported that women with disabilities are assaulted, raped, and abused at a rate more than two times greater than nondisabled women. The Center for Research on Women with Disabilities (Nosek et al., 1997), in contrast, found that the same percentage (62 percent) of women with physical disabilities and nondisabled women experienced emotional, physical, or sexual abuse, but noted that disabled women experienced abuse for longer time periods.

The research findings on school sexual harassment, child abuse, and sexual abuse of people with disabilities suggest that students with disabilities of both genders may experience higher rates of sexual harassment that their nondisabled peers and that young women with disabilities may experience higher rates than young men with disabilities. Clearly, there is a need for more research focused on this issue. Ideally, all further major studies of sexual harassment in school would include students with disabilities in the sample.

WHO ARE THE PERPETRATORS?

Not all studies of sexual harassment asked students who had harassed them or if they had harassed anyone themselves, and explanations of the motivation for harassing are hazier still. The AAUW/Harris Poll (1993) found that 86 percent of girls who had been sexually harassed and 71 percent of boys were harassed by another student. *Seventeen* magazine (Stein, 1993) reported that 96 percent of students in their study who were sexually harassed were harassed by peers. Although school employees do harass and abuse students (about 18 percent of the sexual harassment comes from school personnel according to the AAUW study), the primary problem is students harassing students.

Among girls, the most frequent source of sexual harassment is a boy acting alone. The second most frequent source is a group of boys. For boys, the most frequent source of harassment is a girl acting alone. The second most frequent source is a group of girls. Twenty-five percent of boys who were harassed were harassed by another boy. Ten percent of girls who were harassed were harassed by another girl (AAUW, 1993).

Linn and her colleagues' reanalysis of the AAUW data showed some disturbing results (Lee et al., 1996). Sexual harassment was not being perpetrated by a few disturbed individuals. Sixty-two percent of all boys and 54 percent of girls admitted to sexually harassing other students. The AAUW data did not adequately explain why students would do this. Bennett and Fineran's (1998) study of a single large Midwestern urban high school offers a possible explanation. Of 342 students surveyed, 84 percent experienced sexual harassment and 75 percent admitted to harassing someone. Sixty percent of the reported harassment was perpetrated by a schoolmate whom the student knew casually, 25 percent by students in dating or exdating relationships, and 15 percent by a schoolmate whom the student did not know. Dating and exdating relationships that involve violence may account for a part of the sexual harassment in schools. This finding is corroborated by Molidor and Tolman's study of violence in teenage dating relationships (1998), in which half of the students who reported they were in violent dating relationships also reported that the violence had erupted at least once in school.

Another explanation for some sexual harassment in schools is retaliation. When Fineran asked a focus group of girls why girls harass boys, they almost unanimously replied, "Because they did it first" (Fineran, telephone interview, March 1999). They erroneously believed that retaliation would stop harassment, rather than escalate it. Students who helped pilot the booklet *Tune in to Your Rights* (Morris et al., 1985) had similarly misinformed views about the efficacy of retaliation. When asked how to respond to sexual harassment, many students recommended retaliation. It is important, then, to help students understand that retaliation only perpetuates the problem and is likely to get the retaliator into trouble.

A third explanation of sexual harassment is that the environment in many schools promotes a sense of male entitlement and greater male procedural power. Using a hypothesis of male structural power drawn from Archer (1994), Fineran and Bennett administered a heterosexual relationship scale (HRS) that quantifies sex role power beliefs. They found that students (both male and female) who sexually harassed other students had higher male role power beliefs than students who did not. Considering that sexual harassment is concentrated in certain environments, we may infer that schools with high levels of sexual harassment have many individuals who believe strongly that men should dominate women. Attitudes about the value of women and the intrinsic rights of women and girls may have an influence on whether or not students harass others. In addition, given that sexist attitudes continue to pervade our society, it is no surprise that sexual harassment in schools is so widespread and that it targets young women somewhat more often, with more severe consequences.

Perpetrators of Sexual Harassment of Students with Disabilities

Unlike the studies of nondisabled students in which peer sexual harassment was far more common than adult to student sexual harassment, Rousso's pilot study of students with disabilities found almost as many examples of adult perpetrators as peers (1996). The adults were most frequently paraprofessionals, health aides, or van drivers. Students with disabilities have far more contact with adults in these roles than students without disabilities. Sobsey, in a related finding, reported that disability service providers are one of the major types of perpetrators of sexual abuse of people with disabilities (1994, p. 75). Rousso's preliminary findings, Sobsey's review, and the results of the Joint Commission study (1994) in New York City showing disproportionately high rates of employee-to-student sexual abuse for students with disabilities point to the need for schools to develop better methods to screen, train, and supervise employees who assist students with disabilities. In fact, this was one of the major recommendations of the Joint Commission study. Rousso also found that peer sexual harassment was more common in inclusive schools (i.e., schools serving both disabled and nondisabled students) than in schools serving only students with disabilities. The peer perpetrators were most often nondisabled boys who harassed girls with disabilities. This profile and the infrequency of peer sexual harassment in schools serving only students with disabilities call into question the commonly held assumption that boys in special education, particularly boys identified as having emotional disabilities, are a major source of sexual harassment.[2]

THE HARM OF SEXUAL HARASSMENT

We live in a culture that dismisses harm caused by sexual harassment. Too often, people blame the target, claiming she brought the pain upon herself, when instead we should blame the perpetrator. When Linn and some colleagues wrote their book for teenagers about sexual harassment, they found that no matter how they described a fictional situation, some students in their pilot group wanted to blame the target (Morris et al., 1985). She sounded too rich, so they changed her circumstances. Then students claimed that she dressed provocatively. When they changed the description of her clothes, she was accused of being too nerdish. Finally, the authors decided they could never have a totally sympathetic target, realizing that blaming the target, at least when she is female, is a central part of the problem of sexual harassment.

People who have been targets of sexual harassment react in different ways, depending on the circumstances of the event, previous experiences, personality, and other contributing factors. Some people feel confused. They may know that they can no longer rely on someone they previously trusted. And there may be confusion around whether or not to report the incident. Sometimes people feel intensely vulnerable, fearing that the perpetrator will strike again; this is not unfounded, since perpetrators often repeat and escalate their vile behavior or harass someone else. Some targets feel guilty and search for what they could have done to prevent the situation, even if they do not actually blame themselves for having caused the sexual harassment. Helping a target decide on a better strategy for the future may help her regain a sense of control after an experience that was frighteningly out of control. Some people react with anger, which can be empowering but may also cause further trouble, especially if they retaliate and later get in trouble or feel ashamed of what they did. Other students may feel so overwhelmed by harassment that they are unable to act on their feelings at all.

It can be difficult to document the long-term effects of sexual harassment on a student's goals, decisions, achievements, and well-being. Major life decisions in adolescence tend to be multiply determined. Regardless of what we know about the long-term impact, it seems clear that sexual harassment causes students pain that can impede learning, and at worst can jeopardize their lives. Many educators are familiar with situations in which sexual harassment contributed to a student's death, by suicide or homicide. The despair of sexual harassment can perhaps best be described by a participant in the *Seventeen* magazine survey who wrote, "It breaks your soul and brings you down" (Stein, 1993).

TARGETS FIGHT BACK

Only 13 percent of the young women in the *Seventeen* survey who reported being sexually harassed said they did nothing (Stein, 1993). Sixty-five percent said that they told the harasser to stop. Forty percent said that they walked away from the harasser, and 35 percent said that they resisted with physical force. Most young women are not passive in the face of such treatment. Three-quarters of the *Seventeen* survey participants (76 percent) spoke to someone about the incident later. Sixty-six percent told a friend, 18 percent told a parent, another 18 percent told a teacher or administrator, and 2 percent told a counselor or psychologist. Similarly, Rousso (1996) found that when girls with disabilities are harassed, they are far more likely to take action, such as tell someone, than be silent.

Unfortunately, when girls with and without disabilities seek the help of others, they often encounter further pain. They may be accused of provoking the harasser through their dress or behavior, or of initiating the incident themselves. In addition to challenges to credibility that all girls face, for girls with disabilities, stereotypes about their sexuality and disability-related limitations may further derail their efforts to report. For example, because the motivation for sexual harassment is often mistakenly believed to be sexual desire rather than power, school officials may discredit the reports of girls whom they view as undesirable and asexual. "When I tried to report how the boy had backed me into the dark corner and tried to rape me, the counselor said, 'Who would want to rape you? Are you sure you didn't make this up?' I immediately shut up. It was hopeless" (seventeen-year-old African American girl with a mobility disability, Rousso, 1994–95).

Other girls find their credibility called into question because it is assumed that the nature of their disability, particularly if they have an emotional or cognitive disability, makes them incompetent reporters. "She [the teacher] told me I was always imagining things, but I better stop it because this time I went too far. I know I have 'problems,' but I didn't imagine that boy's hand on my ass" (fifteen-year-old white girl with an emotional disability, Rousso, 1994–95).

In addition to stereotypes, disability-related limitations may impede reporting. For example, girls with communication or intellectual disabilities may have difficulty reporting the details of the incident in a way that is understood. Girls who are blind may have difficulty identifying the harasser or difficulty convincing officials that they can identify the harasser through nonvisual clues. In addition, a young woman may be reluctant to report a person who fulfills a disability-related need, such as communication, physical assistance, or transportation, fearing she may have to do without their help or may face retribution. As one student stated, "How will I manage in the bathroom if my aide is fired?" (Rousso, 1996).

RESPONDING TO A COMPLAINT OF HARASSMENT

Educators need to listen to students who have been the target of sexual harassment, respect their feelings, help them express how they feel, and help them decide how they can regain control over their lives. The ridicule they experience trying to report sexual harassment is often more hurtful than the harassment.

Adults' reactions of indifference may actually be expressions of their own pain, shock, or helplessness. Many of us, as students or employees, have been targets, perpetrators, or observers of harassment and know firsthand the distress that such experiences evoke. Our own feelings can build empathy or become a barrier. Awareness of our reactions is crucial to our ability to help students who face harassment. No teacher should blame a student, dismiss a student's feeling, or fail to report an alleged incident of sexual harassment.

Understanding the Issues for Girls with Disabilities

Being responsive to the sexual harassment complaints and concerns of students means understanding their issues. Earlier we noted some ways that gender may affect sexual harassment. Now we consider the role of gender and disability. While girls and young women with disabilities share many of the same experiences with sexual harassment as their nondisabled counterparts, they also face some unique, often complex issues.

Part of the complexity stems from the extent and nature of disability-related limitations themselves. Girls (and boys) with certain disabilities may find it more difficult to detect or fully understand the harassing nature of perpetrators' behaviors, to defend themselves against perpetrators, or to report incidents of sexual harassment. However, we believe that these disability-related limitations are far less problematic than the attitudinal barriers that youth with disabilities, particularly girls, face in school, at home, and in the community. Too often, this negative environment gives license to perpetrators, deprives girls with disabilities of skills and opportunities they need to recognize and address sexual harassment, and undermines the ability of some educators to respond appropriately to incidents of sexual harassment when they occur.

Research conducted over the past several decades suggests that the attitudes of nondisabled people toward people with disabilities are predominantly negative (Asch and Rousso, 1985). While there has been considerably less gender-specific research, there is some indication that disabled women, devalued by both disability status and gender, face more negative attitudes than disabled men (Hanna and Rogovsky, 1991). Typical stereotypes are that women with disabilities are sick, helpless, incompetent, unable to nurture, and asexual. Underlying these stereotypes is a host of conscious and unconscious factors that influence nondisabled people. These include lack of adequate contact with women with disabilities and the projection of anxieties about perfection, loss, weakness, and nurturance (Asch and Rousso, 1985; Fine and Asch, 1988).

It is now understood that negative attitudes form the basis of discriminatory policies and practices against people with disabilities in education, employment, and community programs. This connection is clearly articulated in the text of the Americans with Disabilities Act (PL 101–336, sec. 2). There is also a growing understanding that women with disabilities face double discrimination. For example, they are less likely to find partners and more likely be unemployed and earn less when they are employed compared to disabled men and nondisabled women (See Asch, with Rousso, and Jefferies, this volume). However, there is far less public recognition that negative attitudes and stereotypes underlie diverse acts of violence directed against people with disabilities that Waxman and others classify as "hate crimes" (Waxman, 1991; Hershey, 1998). Research shows disability to be a predisposing factor toward violence, not because of disability per se, but because of social and cultural beliefs toward disability. Some forms that hate crimes against people with disabilities have taken include widespread murder and medical experimentation by the Nazis during the Holocaust, involuntary confinement and sterilization, denial of needed treatment and medication, and physical and sexual assault (Waxman, 1991). Waxman further suggests that sexual abuse against disabled women, disturbingly pervasive, is a hybrid form of hate crime, blending misogyny with antidisability hatred. It is only recently that the legal system has begun to consider the sociopolitical aspect of such crimes instead of focusing on the limitations of disabled individuals as the basis for violence. Hence there is a growing movement to include disabled people and women in hate crimes and violence against women legislation.

The same attitudes that provoke hate crimes in society also provoke disability harassment at school. The limited research available suggests that disability harassment is widespread. Faibisch (1995) described the hostile psychological, social, and educational climate facing adolescents with physical disabilities in mainstream settings. Using an in-depth clinical interview approach with a small group of students, she noted repeated experiences that left students feeling intimidated, personally violated, denigrated, and under attack. "It was not so much that they were simply being picked on or bullied, but there is a problem in the structures and mores of their greater social environment. The respondents conveyed a picture of a socially dangerous environment which seems to have allowed individuals to get away with this type of abuse." (pp. 2–3)

Rousso (1996), in her pilot sexual harassment study, heard repeated stories from disabled young people of being teased, stared at, cornered, hit, and ostracized by peers and sometimes by adults as the result of their disability status and/or because of their placement in special education classes. The discussion of disability harassment often emerged unsolicited and with great passion. At least in that study, it was rare to find any young person who did not have a story of disability harassment to tell.

We believe a school climate that tolerates disability harassment may foster the sexual harassment of students with disabilities as well. To the extent that perpetrators of sexual harassment seek out targets with less power and status, students with disabilities, relegated to second class citizenship, may be perceived as easy targets. And girls with disabilities, often assumed to be physically weak and politically powerless, may seem particularly easy. As one young woman stated, "They think I'm easy because I'm deaf and I'm pretty. Who would know or care? I have fooled them, though. I can fight back and I will tell on them." (Rousso, 1994–95).

Negative attitudes toward women with disabilities not only contribute to a harassing environment but may also deprive girls with disabilities of the opportunities and information they need to fight harassment. Adolescence is a time of budding social and sexual feelings. Many parents have conflicting feelings and concerns about their child's sexual development. This may be particularly true for parents of daughters, who often perceive their daughter as sexually vulnerable and hence in danger of sexual assault and/or adolescent pregnancy. In response to such fears, parents may ill-advisedly seek to limit a girls' surroundings (for example, by setting overly strict curfews), her friendships, and her aspirations, while at the same time restricting the sex education that she receives at home to only the negative and dangerous aspects of sexuality.

For parents of children with disabilities, particularly daughters, the conflicts around sexuality may be intensified. Concerns about sexual vulnerability may be magnified not only by their daughter's concrete limitations, which may hinder her ability to flee or fight off a sexual attack, but also by an exaggerated sense of their daughter's fragility. These concerns about safety combined with stereotypes about her sexuality and capacity for independence may lead to parental decisions to keep young women with disabilities sheltered at home. For example, to the extent that parents assume that their daughter is asexual or perpetually childlike, they may overlook her developing social and sexual interests and her need for peer contact. Or they may assume that even if she is sexual, she is sexually undesirable and unlikely to be chosen as a date or mate; hence they may wish to protect her from the rejection they are convinced she will face (Rousso, 1988).

As a result, parents may greatly restrict their disabled daughters' social opportunities outside of school, keeping the family as the center of her world precisely at the time in her life when her peer group of girls and boys needs to be taking center stage. Attitudinal, architectural, and transportation barriers in the community support the parental impulse to keep a disabled daughter at home, further limiting her access to typical places where young people congregate. Wagner's research confirms that girls with disabilities are less likely to participate in nonschool activities outside the home than their male peers (1992). Some negative consequences of social isolation are that many disabled girls do not have opportunities to learn appropriate ways of interacting, to know when and how to say "yes" or "no" to social overtures, and to distinguish friendly or flirtatious behaviors from abusive ones. After all, no one is born socially sophisticated. Young people learn social skills through opportunities to practice them in different social settings.

Because of limited social opportunities, some young women with disabilities may become overly eager for any type of social encounter, especially those involving young men, even when the contact is abusive. Traditional definitions of womanhood focus on a woman's ability to catch and keep a man. Recent expansion of gender roles not withstanding, for many adolescent girls, disabled and nondisabled, heterosexual encounters that include flirting, dating, kissing, and sexual involvement remain important sources of their identity as women (Malmquist 1985, p. 68). Research (Rousso, 1988) shows that because of more limited opportunities rather than lack of interest, girls with disabilities tend to

have their first date, first kiss, and so forth much later than their nondisabled peers. These delays cause some girls to doubt their identity as
women. In the face of these doubts, any male attention, even abusive
attention, can feel better than no attention at all. In one distressing
example, a young woman with a mobility disability was extremely
reluctant to report a van driver who attempted to rape her because "at
least he saw me as a real woman" (Rousso, 1994–95).

Myths about sexuality may also contribute to the inadequacy of sex
education for girls with disabilities, both at home and at school. While
many parents may avoid talking about sex with their children because
of their own discomfort, there is even less incentive to do so when there
is presumed to be no need. As one woman reflected, "They [her parents]
simply did not think sexuality was going to be part of my repertoire"
(Rousso, 1988, p. 151). In one study, Rousso (1988) found that while
women with physical and sensory disabilities received about the same
amount of information from their mothers on the biological aspects of
sexuality as their nondisabled counterparts, they were less likely to have
talked about the social aspects of sexuality, such as dating, marriage,
and children. Mother-daughter conversations on sexual matters help
young women to become more aware of their own sexuality and make
responsible choices (Fox, 1980).

Schools similarly fail to provide adequate information on sexuality.
Research conducted over the past twenty years suggests that school sex
education programs for students with disabilities are limited (Dickman,
1975; Frith, Mitchell, and Lindsey, 1981; Brantlinger, 1992, all
reported in May and Kundert, 1996). Brantlinger, for example, found
that only a third of the programs for students with mild disabilities that
he surveyed offered comprehensive sex education or family life planning. We found no information on gender differences in access or content of sex education. In this area, most likely neither gender fares very
well.

May and Kundert (1996) suggest that a factor is the lack of adequate teacher preparation in sex education. In their study of special education teacher preparation programs, only 59 percent reported that
prospective teachers took course work in sex education, the same proportion of prospective teachers as had been documented in a study ten
years earlier (May, 1980, cited in May and Kundert, 1996). While there
are many reasons for this, we believe that educators may fail to recognize that students with disabilities have the same sexual desires, needs,
and issues as their nondisabled counterparts. Although there is some
indication that most students do not get the sex education they need
(AAUW, 1992), the consequences of inadequate sex education may be
more severe for students with disabilities. Young people with disabili-

ties, particularly girls, have less access to informal sources of sexual education, such as peers, casual observation, written materials, and the media, than their nondisabled peers (NICHCY, 1992).

In addition, some young people with disabilities face difficult issues around bodily touching that makes sex education all the more important. Depending on the nature of the disability, disabled youth may need the help of others for daily physical care, such as toileting, bathing, or dressing. The need for such intimate physical care at a time of rapid bodily change and heightened sexual feeling can cause adolescents with disabilities to feel confused and anxious. Many young women in Rousso's study (1996) noted difficulty distinguishing between appropriate and inappropriate touching. Types of touching by caregivers or aides that felt fine when they were younger now made them feel uneasy. Silenced by uncertainty, some young women allowed harassing behavior to continue unchallenged, leading to increasing distress. Sex education classes should be a place where disabled young people receive the information and support they need to direct their own physical care and sort through "good" and "bad" touching, done in the name of caretaking (NICHCY, 1992; Rousso, 1996).

WHAT CAN WE DO TO HELP?

We all have responsibilities to stop sexual harassment. Our main goals should be to support targets of sexual harassment, to stop perpetrators, and to be willing to intervene in situations that we observe. Most important, we need to change the larger educational environment in our schools so that sexual harassment is less likely to occur. In addition, we want to make sure that policies and programs about sexual harassment include students with disabilities and address their issues.

When we see or hear sexual harassment, we should:

1. Inform the perpetrator that this form of aggressive and hurtful behavior must stop.

2. Offer comfort and understanding to the target.

3. Offer informational support to the target about how to get further help and/or how to make a complaint.

4. Allow the target to make her/his own decision about next steps, unless the situation poses a direct threat to the person's safety and must be reported by law. (In such a case, inform the target of your need to report.)

5. Recognize an emergency and get help.

To provide long-range support and assistance, a school should do the following:

1. Widely publicize the name of the school's Title IX coordinator. That person should be trained to handle sex equity complaints, including problems of sexual harassment. The training must include information on particular sexual harassment issues facing students with disabilities.

2. Develop a school policy on sexual harassment that is easy to read and widely distributed. The policy needs to include a definition, examples, procedures for how to report complaints, and possible sanctions for perpetrators of sexual harassment. It should state clearly that sexual harassment affects all students, including disabled students. It should also insure confidentiality of complaints whenever possible and have a statement that retaliation will be punished more severely than initial incidents of harassment.

3. Help administrators, teachers, parents, and students understand the policy on sexual harassment. Make sure the policy and related information are available in accessible formats, such as on computer disk, audiotape, Braille, and large print. Provide workshops and class lessons on a regular basis. Particularly for parents of disabled students, educational sessions should make the link between appropriate social opportunities and sex education on the one hand and young people's preparedness to deal with sexual harassment on the other hand.

4. Ensure that sex education is part of the curriculum of all students, including students with disabilities.

5. Enforce the school policy on sexual harassment actively. See that there are complete and thorough investigations of all complaints of sexual harassment. Make sure that the procedures for filing a complaint are accessible to students with disabilities. Follow up on questionable situations to ensure that no further harassment or retaliation has occurred.

6. Screen, train, and supervise service-level employees, especially those who deal with bodily care or provide other assistance to young adolescents with disabilities.

7. Expect respectful behavior from everyone in the school community. There should be zero tolerance for sexual or any other form of harassment.

8. Look for patterns of problem situations in your school that seem likely to breed harassment (for example the school bus, playground, times of day). Work toward eliminating the source of the problem.

9. Refer out any students who you think need nonjudgmental therapeutic help to deal with their harassing behaviors. A classroom cannot be a place where harmful behaviors toward others are tolerated.

Sexual harassment is a problem for all students. As educators, we must commit ourselves to stopping sexual harassment so that young people with and without disabilities can have the supportive learning environment they need and deserve. Our awareness and our actions can make a difference.

NOTES

1. Several references for this section come from an unpublished paper, *Disabled Women and Violence*, 1998, developed by Barbara Waxman Fiduccia to support the inclusion of disabled women in upcoming federal violence against women legislation. We would like to thank her for developing this review, some of which has been incorporated into B. Waxman Fiduccia and L. Wolfe, 1999, *Women and Girls with Disabilities: Defining the Issues: An Overview*, Washington, D.C.: Center for Women Policy Studies and Women and Philanthropy.

2. For a set of guidelines on disciplining students with disabilities who perpetrate sexual harassment to ensure compliance with IDEA and Section 504 of 1973 Rehabilitation Act, see V. Williams and D. Brake, 1998, *Do the Right Thing: Understanding, Addressing and Preventing Sexual Harassment in School*, Washington, D.C.: National Women's Law Center, 36–37.

REFERENCES

American Association of University Women (AAUW). 1993. *Hostile hallways: The AAUW survey on sexual harassment in America's schools.* Washington D.C.: American Association of University Women Foundation.

Asch, A., and H. Rousso. 1985. Therapists with disabilities: Theoretical and clinical issues. *Psychiatry* 48:1–12.

Bennett, L., and S. Fineran. 1998. Sexual and severe physical violence among high school students: Power beliefs, gender and relationships. *American Journal of Orthopsychiatry* 68(4):645–652.

Brantlinger, E. 1992. Sexuality education in the secondary special education curriculum: Teachers' perceptions and concerns. *Teacher Education and Special Education* 15:32–40.

Eve Bruneau v. South Kortright Central School District 94-CV-864, transcript of proceedings held in U.S. District Court, Northern District of New York, 5 November 1996, 32–33.

Crosse, S., E. Kaye, and A. Ratnofsky. 1993. *A report on the maltreatment of children with disabilities.* Washington, D.C.: National Center on Child Abuse and Neglect, Administration on Child, Youth, and Families, Administration for Children and Families, U.S. Department of Health.

Dickman, I. 1975, December. *Sex education for disabled persons.* Public Affairs Pamphlet No. 531.

Doucette, J. 1986. *Violent acts against disabled women.* Toronto, Ontario: DAWN (DisAbled Women's Network) Canada.

Faibisch L. 1995. *Adolescents with physical disabilities cope with and resist insensitivity, harassment and discrimination.* Paper presented at the annual meeting of the American Psychological Association, New York City.

Fine M., and A. Asch. 1988. Introduction: Beyond pedestals. In *Women with disabilities: Essays in psychology, politics and culture.* Edited by M. Fine and A. Asch. Philadelphia: Temple University Press, 1–37.

Finkelhor, D. 1994. The international epidemiology of child sexual abuse. *Child Abuse and Neglect* 18(5):409–417.

Fox, G. I. 1980. The mother-daughter relationship as a sexual socialization structure: A research review. *Family Relations* 29:21–28.

Frith, G., J. Mitchell, and J. Lindsey. 1981. Sex education: The neglected dimension on the secondary level individualized plans. *The Clearing House* 54:197–199.

Hanna, W. J., and E. Rogovsky. 1991. Women with disabilities: Two handicaps plus. *Disability, Handicap and Society* 6(1):49–63.

Hershey, L. 1998, October. Prejudice and hate violence must be confronted. *Crip commentary: Laura Hershey's web column.* HYPERLINK: http://ourworld.compuserve.com/homepages/LauraHershey.

Joint Commission of the Chancellor and the Special Commissioner for the Prevention of Child Sexual Abuse. 1994. Final Report of the Joint Commission of the Chancellor and the Special Commissioner for the Prevention of Child Sexual Abuse. New York: Author.

Lee, V., R. Croninger, E. Linn, and X. Chen. 1996. The culture of sexual harassment in secondary schools. *American Educational Research Journal* 33(2):383–417.

Malmquist, C. P. 1985. *Handbook of adolescence.* New York: Aronson.

May, D. 1980. Survey of sex education coursework in special education programs. *The Journal of Special Education* 14:107–112.

May, D., and D. Kundert. 1996. Are special educators prepared to meet the sex education needs of their students: A progress report. *Journal of Special Education* 29:433–441.

Molidor, C., and R. Tolman. 1998. Gender and contextual factors in adolescent dating violence. *Violence against Women* 4(2):180–194.

Morris, B., J. Terpstra, B. Croninger, and E. Linn. 1985. *Tune into your rights. A guide for teenagers about turning off sexual harassment.* Ann Arbor: University of Michigan, Programs for Educational Opportunity.

NICHCY. 1992 *Sexuality education for children and youth with disabilities.* NICHCY News Digest (ND17).

Nosek, M., C. Howlan, D. Rintala, M. Young, and G. Chanpong. 1997. *National study of women with physical disabilities: Final report.* Houston: Center for Research On Women with Disabilities. Baylor College of Medicine.

Permanent Commission on the Status of Women. *In our own backyard: Sexual harassment in Connecticut's public high schools.* Hartford Conn.: Author, 1995.

Petersilia, J. 1998. Report by the California Senate Public Safety Committee hearings on persons with developmental disabilities in the criminal justice system. Irvine, Calif.: Author.

Rousso, H. 1988. Daughters with disabilities: Defective women or minority women? In *Women with disabilities: Essays in psychology, politics and culture.* Edited by M. Fine and A. Asch. Philadelphia: Temple University Press, 139–171.

———. 1994–1995. *Girls with disabilities and sexual harassment at school: Transcripts.* Unpublished paper.

———. 1996. *Girls with disabilities and sexual harassment at school: Summary of the pilot study.* Unpublished paper.

Sobsey, D. 1994. *Violence and abuse in the lives of people with disabilities. The end of silent acceptance?* Baltimore: Paul H. Brookes.

Stein, N. 1993. *Secrets in public: Sexual harassment in public (and private) school, working paper no. 256.* Wellesley, Mass.: Wellesley College Center for Research on Women.

Stein, N. 1999. *Classrooms and courtrooms: Facing sexual harassment in K–12 schools.* New York: Teachers College Press.

Stein, N., and D. Cappello, D. *Gender violence/Gender justice: An interdisciplinary teaching guide for teachers of English, literature, social studies, psychology, health, peer counseling and family and consumer sciences* (grades 7–12). Wellesley, Mass.: Wellesley Center for Research on Women.

Stimpson, L., and M. C. Best. 1991. *Courage above all: Sexual assault against women with disabilities.* Toronto, Ontario: DAWN (DisAbled Women's Network) Canada.

Trigg, M., and K. Wittenstrom. 1996. That's the way the world goes: Sexual harassment and New Jersey teenagers. *Initiatives* 57(2):55–65.

United States Department of Education. Office for Civil Rights. *Sexual harassment guidance: Harassment of students by school employees, other students, or third parties.* Federal Register 62:49, 13 March 1997. Available on-line HYPERLINK http://www.ed.gov/offices/OCR/sexhar01.html.

Wagner, M. 1992. *Being female: A secondary disability? Gender differences in the transition experiences of young people with disabilities.* Menlo Park, Calif.: SRI International.

Waxman, B.F. 1991. Hatred: The unacknowledged dimension in violence against disabled people. *Sexuality and Disability* 9(3):185–199.

Waxman Fiduccia, B. F. 1998. *Disabled women and violence fact sheet.* Unpublished position paper developed for the National Task Force on Violence against Women of the National Organization for Women (N.O.W.) Legal Defense and Education Fund, Washington, D.C.

CHAPTER 9

Schools Fail Boys Too: Exposing the Con of Traditional Masculinity

Craig Flood

INTRODUCTION: THE POWER OF OUR STORIES

The reaction of some gender equity advocates to the increasing attention paid to the ways schools also fail boys is, quite justifiably, often skeptical given that most of the history of our society has placed the lens on males. These have been the stories of power, control, and domination and have articulated a view of masculinity upon which a patriarchy is nourished and allowed to thrive. However, just as the women's movement directed its efforts at unraveling the negative effects of a patriarchal view of women's roles in that system, the new focus on the lives of boys and men takes a critical look at the damage such views have done to males in our culture.

One of the results of the women's movement has been a recognition of the importance of examining, and learning from, the inner lives of girls and women to provide opportunities for conversations that open a window into the experiences that guide them in their development. The voices of girls and women have given us stories of their inner lives. Taking these stories to be a history equally deserving of our attention has transformed our understanding of the psychological development of women. In schools, this has provided the opportunity for us to create the supports necessary to enable girls, according to Harvard psychologist Carol Gilligan, to develop healthy resistance to the patriarchal role expectations that limited their opportunities.

THE "CON" OF TRADITIONAL MASCULINITY:
REVEALING THE SECRET

In direct contrast to this recognition of the value of looking inward to learn about how we develop as humans, the centuries old attention to males in our culture yields a deliberately external view that attempts to keep men disconnected from their inner selves. It is the outside world of accomplishments, objectivity, control, and mastery that has drawn men's focus. The overwhelming value placed on that view has prevented us from listening to the stories of men's subjective and inner lives.

For years, I have been fascinated with the "con game" (i.e., the confidence game), and the sleight of hand that makes it effective. The first goal of a good con artist is to gain the target's confidence that his particular "view" of a situation deserves our attention. Once that confidence is gained and the target's attention "misdirected," the con is set and the "bad bill of goods" is sold. The target has been "used" to further the agenda of the con artist; the target's interests are ignored. Similarly, our patriarchal view of masculinity and the value it places on external sources of self-worth and satisfaction for men represents a con game. For thousands of years, it has served to misdirect men's attention anywhere and everywhere but on their inner lives.

The result of this con has been not only the perpetuation and wholesale valuing of an objective and detached perspective of the world but, also most critically, a profound loss of the power and true magic that men's inner lives can provide in helping them grow and develop as healthy individuals living in a relational world. Additionally, to reinforce that narrow perspective, it has been woven into the fabric of our theories of healthy psychological development. It is these theories, the canon of traditional psychology, that have finally been challenged as a result of our advocacy for healthier perspectives on girls' and women's development.

As institutions that represent the patriarchal system out of which those views evolved, schools continue to reflect them. In doing so, schools fail girls and boys in similar ways. It is time we direct some of our attention inward and listen to the stories our boys tell. If we do so, we will learn, as we have from girls, that there is more than one way of looking at our world and of defining masculinity, and the con will be revealed.

Brandon's Story

I begin with a story of my son, Brandon, who, at age four, had kissed my neighbor Ken, who had watched my three children one evening. Several days later, Ken expressed his concern about the kiss. He shared the feeling that if I weren't careful about Brandon's behavior toward other males, he might become gay. My response, after careful thought, was that the kiss reflected qualities I loved most in Brandon, the importance of relationships in his life and his need to express that with the tenderness and care that a kiss represents for a four-year-old boy.

Ken's homophobic reaction, though clearly an issue that frames the male experience, was not my primary concern. I understood the roots of such a perspective and the myths that support it for males in our culture. Primarily, the incident clarified the challenge for me as Brandon's father, the challenge of helping him maintain those essential human qualities as he grew up with the messages attached to rigid male stereotypes. I wondered how was I going to provide Brandon access to those qualities when they were going to be continually questioned and under attack as he moved toward manhood. Most important, what supports or tools could I provide him that would enable him to sustain a healthy sense of self as he grew?

The use of the term *access* is a deliberate attempt to draw a parallel with the use of access as it has been applied to other issues of educational equity, whether related to gender or to disability status. For girls and women, the passage of Title IX focused attention on access to economic self-sufficiency and to the male dominated cultural institutions of school and work. The Americans with Disabilities Act and Individuals with Disabilities Education Act expanded the definition of access to include educational and economic opportunity, as well as physical access. While qualitatively different and not easily legislated, the issue of access for boys and men also speaks to the limiting nature of stereotyping, gender or otherwise. Furthermore, drawing the parallel helps to identify important issues we need to address in boys' lives and chart a course that facilitates boys' entrance to a world that increasingly requires males to develop the healthy interpersonal skills.

At age thirteen, Brandon's story continues. As he entered adolescence, I helped him deal with the pain of losing his best friend, Jason, who found it necessary to cut Brandon out of his life at school. Brandon was not, in Jason's words, "cool" enough to be a part of the group of boys with whom Jason was connected in school. In turn, it was not "cool" for Jason to continue his association with Brandon at school. The primary way Jason chose to sever the ties was to humiliate and shame Brandon in front of these other boys. Though confusing to Brandon, Jason still showed a need to interact with Brandon back in the confines of the neighborhood when he was removed from the pressure to "fit in" as a member of the group. Though not an uncommon experience for boys, it reflects our growing understanding of the theme of dis-

connection in many boys' and men's lives. And, for males, this disconnection is often marked by a willingness to sacrifice the intimacy of relationship over the social status of being perceived as a "man."

Relationships continue to be important to Brandon, and the decision that his "friend" made was a confusing and painful one for him to
understand. Such scenarios play out every day in the lives of boys and,
in stereotypical fashion, serve to chart their traditional course toward
manhood. Brandon has been clear about how it has hurt him, but he is
also able to openly discuss the problem with me, to understand the situation and make decisions that help him move beyond the loss of friendship. Brandon's story frames the goal of this chapter. It exposes the lure
of the con of masculinity for Ken and Jason. Ken and Jason have already
bought into the con. Using Brandon's story as the backdrop for our
work as gender equity advocates, the goal of this chapter is twofold.
First, it will examine our cultural definitions of masculinity and their
link to old and emerging theories of psychological development. Second,
it will expose the impact of the con of traditional masculinity on boys'
lives in school and share strategies and models that provide boys with
alternative definitions of masculinity.

TRADITIONAL DEFINITIONS OF MASCULINITY
AND PSYCHOLOGICAL DEVELOPMENT

Historical Roots

Our traditional definitions of masculinity are rooted in the politics and
social science of the early twentieth century. Our collective sense of the
masculine and feminine roles that have defined much of this century was
informed primarily by the themes of world domination promoted by the
"Bully Politics" of Theodore Roosevelt in the early 1900s. Roosevelt's
tough-minded views of the political sphere and what constituted a "real
man" helped shape the mutually exclusive perceptions of masculinity
that are in question here; real men were tough, not tender. At the same
time, the psychological theories of essentialism espoused by psychologist
G. Stanley Hall reinforced distinct and separate views of the masculine
and feminine spheres. Hall's theories of adolescent development supported the notion that boys and girls had distinct and separate educational needs. He advocated for an educational system that made boys
more masculine and that minimized the influence of girls and women,
clearly leading to tenderminded males.

It was the view of Roosevelt, Hall, and others that the "tender"
male was the primary threat to America's emerging status as a dominant
world power. Schools, accordingly, were viewed as the training ground

for tough-minded men and were under attack for the "feminine" influence of increasing numbers of women teachers. Add to this mix our society's growing interest in the development of behavioral science and the overwhelming value placed on an objectivist, scientifically detached view of psychological development, and what emerged were hybrid views of masculinity and femininity; part science and part political and educational agenda.

With the advent of standardized intelligence testing and other forms of psychometric testing, the psychological community designed ways to understand how well males "measured up" to the standards of masculinity established in the early twentieth century. From within the context of modern science came the development of the Male Sex Role Identity (MSRI) model of masculinity. This was advanced by the academic psychology community of the mid-1930s as a scientific attempt to create a scale that measured an individual's ranking on a "hypothetical continuum ranging from masculine to feminine" (Pleck, 1983, p. 7). Well into the 1960s this psychological prescription for traditional masculinity and femininity "overwhelmingly dominated both scientific and popular conceptualizations of sex roles and their inherent problems" (Kimmel, 1995, p. 286).

As suggested earlier, and reported in David and Brannon's anthology on the male experience, *The Forty-Nine Percent Majority* (1976), it wasn't until feminists in the early 1970s questioned their predefined sex roles that men's consciousness of the concept of a male sex role and its concomitant set of problems emerged. While not simply the mirror image of the women's sex roles, the dualism that marked the mutually exclusive definition of male roles was quite evident. David and Brannon identified four central themes of a male sex role:

- *No Sissy Stuff:* The stigma of all stereotyped feminine characteristics and qualities, including openness and vulnerability
- *The Big Wheel:* Success, status, and the need to be looked up to
- *The Sturdy Oak:* A manly air of toughness, confidence and self-reliance
- *Give 'Em Hell:* The aura of aggression, violence, and daring. (p. 12)

These generalized themes resonate for most males in our culture; they represent the con. When considered in isolation, they are qualities we would like to see in all males and females, like confidence and success. However, their power is in the collective message for males; you are either a man or you are perceived as a woman, with the latter to be avoided at all costs. These injunctions for masculinity underscore the need for males to be independent of others, to be invulnerable (and "cut off" emotionally), and to forge a sense of self in relation to, as opposed to in relation with, others. Further, the idea that males derive a sense of who they are from a need to be looked up to further reflects the competitive, hierarchical, and controlling nature of a patriarchal worldview. "No sissy stuff," is the behavioral caveat to end all caveats for males, and it functions to seal the relational fate for those boys and men who use it as a personal credo to guide their behavior.

For the purposes of understanding how these views of gender impact individuals and shape other forms of bias in schools and society, it is critical to know that the prescription for masculinity that David and Brannon synthesized is primarily designed to serve in the best interests of high achieving and affluent white males in our culture. Most specifically, sociologist Erving Goffman (1963) wrote, "In an important sense there is only one complete unblushing male in America: a young, married, white, urban, northern, heterosexual, Protestant, father, of college education, fully employed, of good complexion, weight, and a recent record in sports. . . . Any male who fails to qualify in any one of these ways is likely to view himself—during moments at least—as unworthy, incomplete and inferior" (p. 128). Goffman's description of "true" masculinity provides a template for the filtering system that fuels our patriarchal positions of privilege, power, and authority. Systemically, there is very little room at the top of the hierarchy, and such a view of masculinity effectively filters out most of the men in our culture from access to those positions. Though exaggerated to make his point, this view grew out of a time of strong patriarchal influence in our history. In such a system privilege and power is only afforded to a few males. Paradoxically, this take on masculinity provided a standard that encouraged men of all backgrounds to relentlessly pursue an ideal that is virtually unattainable. It represents a powerfully alluring "bill of goods."

Sex Role Strain: The Con as Myth

These views of masculinity were embedded in the MSRI scale in an attempt to compare men's performance with the standard. The scale developers posited that "the failure of men to achieve sex role identity is a major problem in our culture, one obvious expression of which was male homosexuality" (Kimmel, 1995, p. 286). At the same time Brannon and others were framing their concept of the male sex role, psychologist Joseph Pleck challenged the validity of the MSRI and flipped the theory around, suggesting, as Kimmel discusses, that the model "creates role demands that are so internally contradictory that no one could possibly live up to them" (Kimmel, 1995, p. 286). Pleck (1983) showed that correlations between the prescribed masculine behaviors tapped on the MSRI were weak. In contrast to the implicit role demands of the scale, Pleck suggests an alternative model, Male Sex-Role Strain. Using Pleck's critique, Kimmel states that the MSRI model "placed tension, contradiction, and anxiety squarely on the center of men's efforts to demonstrate manhood. Psychology was thus not going to be the liberator of men but instead cast as the conduit for those very contradictory and confusing messages that kept us all in constant turmoil. It wasn't men as much as it was the prescription for masculinity that caused the crisis of masculinity and contributed to the oppression of women and minorities" (p. 286).

Psychologically based and presumably scientific, these views of manhood have prevailed throughout the twentieth century in America and have placed pressure on males to accept the con (or myth, according to Pleck) and conform to the prescription for masculinity. That pressure carried with it the weight of a "scientific" view of psychological development, a view that is central to the persistence of theories that have supported the perpetuation of a patriarchal and hierarchical view of the world. Sex-Role Strain, as Pleck saw it, was the result of males trying to fit into the MSRI model.

Men and Boys with Disabilities

These critiques raise questions about the impact of such rigid and unyielding prescriptions for masculinity on the development of males. However, they have not considered the potential impact and psychological burden of such standards on men and boys with disabilities. If these views of masculinity aim for standards that most nondisabled males struggle to attain, what about males who have physical or intellectual limitations that serve as barriers to accessing traditional notions of masculinity? If we are to consider the weight that traditional masculinity carries in the experience of all males, this and related questions must be addressed.

This text identifies the double jeopardy that girls and women with disabilities face in accessing educational and economic opportunities. Within the context of that critique we find the questions raised about the myth of the "perfect body" imposed on females. In a parallel sense, throughout this chapter the reader is encouraged to be conscious of the contradictions that traditional masculinity poses to the reality of most men's lives and, furthermore, the double jeopardy men with disabilities may face in trying to achieve a "myth of masculinity" that places so much emphasis on physical ability, independence, and invulnerability.

Theoretical Prescriptions for Male Development

The themes that support gender-based disconnection and separation are central to prevailing theories of psychological development implied in our educational system. Most theories of male development have focused on the development of self in isolation from others. The theories of Freud and neo-Freudians, such as Erikson, have all placed overwhelming value on an individual's separation from others, with a particular emphasis on males. This is also evident in Kohlberg's theories of moral development. Identity, according to Freud, and individuation, according to Erikson, are only achieved before intimacy or "real" connections with others. These views of male psychological development have valued the achievement of a separate and individuated self. In a critique of these theories, Bergman stated, "'Self' is based on separation from others and self-other-differentiation, self-versus-other, which may then become self-over-other" (Bergman, 1991, p. 2). Most important here is the central tenet of Freud's theory of healthy male development, the need for a boy to separate from his mother. Also based on Freud's view, Bergman further states, "A male's identification with father comes through competition, fear, and renunciation, not through the wish to connect. It sets the stage for hierarchy, that is, patriarchy, for dominance, entitlement, ownership of women and men's fear of men" (p. 2).

Expanding the view by placing some importance on others in self-development, the theories of self-psychologists, such as Kohut, remain unidirectional in that they focus only on what others contribute to the development of an independent and still separate self. There seems to be minimal attention to the individual's development with others.

In the past twenty years, these models of psychological development have been more closely examined for their relevance and presumed universality. Like Bergman, psychologists and researchers have questioned whether these views actually describe "normal" development for males and females in our culture. Just as Pleck did with the MSRI, many now suggest that such theories more accurately reflect patriarchal and hierarchical paradigms to the extent that they ignore or devalue the role of relationship and connection in the process of healthy psychological development. Most important, there is increasing evidence that these expectations for male development do more to explain the psychological toll or strain on males than they do in charting a "normal" course of development. From such critiques of long-accepted theories, patriarchy's hold on psychology and the traditional concept of masculinity has been exposed, the con revealed.

Relational Psychology: Boys' Developmental Crisis

In her landmark study, *In a Different Voice* (1982), and subsequent research conducted during the 1980s and 1990s, Carol Gilligan and colleagues identified a developmental crisis for girls as they moved into adolescence. In order to preserve the relational world central to girls' development and self-identity, girls "silenced" themselves and were less assertive and deferent in situations that were critical to their sense of self and well-being. According to Gilligan, this crisis results from adolescent girls "hitting the wall of Western culture" (Prose, 1990, p. 40), namely, the patriarchal expectations that support female subjugation. This research encouraged Gilligan and others to wonder whether boys faced a similar developmental crisis. Gilligan discussed the asymmetry she had observed between girls and boys in a 1997 *New York Times* interview (Norman, 1997, p. 50): "Girls are more at risk psychologically in adolescence, whereas boys are more at risk . . . in early childhood, when cultural norms pressure them to separate from their mothers." Wondering if this is boys' crisis in relationship, she further comments on the inherent vulnerability she observes in boys, suggesting a tender creature "hiding behind the psychic shield of masculinity." Finally, echoing the question I posed about Brandon in the story that opened this chapter, Gilligan asks, "How do we keep alive parts of our sons that we think are valuable for them but are also at risk when their masculinity is questioned?"

Gilligan's "psychic shield" is William Pollack's "mask of masculinity." Examining the ways boys try to understand what it means to be a man in today's society, Pollack draws on Brannon's four themes of the male sex role. Identifying these rules/roles as the Boy Code, he defines them as "four injunctions" to which all boys must conform on their path to manhood (Pollack, 1998, pp. 23–25). And just as Pleck identified the strain that men experienced in their efforts to conform, Pollack used the metaphor of a mask that boys feel they must wear to project the image of traditional masculinity while trying to express their emotions to conform with changing gender roles.

Pollack's studies rejected the notions of boys' inherent aggressive tendencies and confirmed boys' empathic and emotive qualities. However, boys learn early that it is in their interest to disconnect from those tendencies. Unlike the silent and disempowered voices of girls, Pollack's study reveals voices that appear strong and confident yet mask underlying feelings of role confusion and anxiety. Pollack suggests that "the psyches of boys are both consciously and unconsciously split, and that is literally driving them crazy" (Doten, 1998).

Pollack suggests that boys experience two developmental crisis points. The first comes in early childhood when, in the name of normal development, the Boy Code encourages boys to separate from their mothers, the individual who likely represents the source of their deepest relational bond. This separation from his Mother is inextricably tied to a boy's growing awareness of the expectations that he should hide his emotions and be a "big boy" or a "little man." The second crisis for boys comes during adolescence. Paralleling that of girls, the disconnection for boys manifests itself in depression and lowered self-esteem resulting from the pressure to conform to the unyielding standards that come into full play during adolescence, sex role strain.

In a sense, boys appear to be hitting the other side of the proverbial "wall" as do girls, and schools and the larger society do not appear ready for the challenge this presents. Barney Brawer, an expert on boys' development, suggests that, "an enormous crisis of men and boys is happening before our eyes without our seeing it. There's been an extraordinary shift in the plate tectonics of gender; everything we ever thought is open for examination" (Rosenfeld, 1998). Though the myths remain, the wall is developing fissures, and schools must begin to alter their own "walls" to better prepare boys to negotiate a world in which the traditional tools of masculinity have become obsolete.

The concern Ken expressed to me about Brandon's kiss and my questioning what parts of Brandon might be lost if that concern had been taken seriously or simply left unchecked go to the heart of what happens to boys as they accept the con or assume the mask. Ken knew that "to be a man" Brandon had best get rid of, or at least hide, that emotionally expressive side. As we have seen, to be a man means to not be a woman; it means to disavow all that we identify as feminine, exemplified in the separation from mother and the qualities she represents. Ken had learned that his road to manhood was marked by this loss. As Terrance Real describes, "Masculine identity development turns out to be not a process of development at all but rather a process of elimination, a successive unfolding of loss" (1997, p. 130). In his clinical work with boys and men, Real sees this loss as the basis for the widening spectrum of depression he has observed in males.

BOYS' EXPERIENCES IN SCHOOL

The Price Boys Pay for Accepting the Con

Consider the following and their possible links to the pressure on boys to conform to the masculine standard:

1. From elementary school through high school, boys receive lower report card grades than do girls.

2. By middle school boys are far more likely to be grade repeaters and dropouts (Sadker and Sadker, 1994, p. 221).

3. Boys lag behind girls in reading and writing proficiency at all educational levels (Pollack, 1998, p. 21).

4. Boys' misbehavior results in more frequent penalties, including corporal punishment.

5. Boys comprise 71 percent of all students who receive school suspensions (Sadker and Sadker, 1994, p. 221).

6. The majority of students identified for special education are boys. They represent 71 percent of students with learning disabilities and 80 percent of students with emotional and behavioral disorders (Sadker and Sadker, 1994, p. 221).

7. Boys are four times more likely to be referred to a school psychologist (Kindlon and Thompson, 1999).

8. Boys are nine times more likely to suffer from hyperactivity and higher levels of academic stress (Sadker and Sadker, 1994, p. 221).

9. It is estimated that one in six boys ages five to twelve is diagnosed with attention deficit disorder (ADD) (Diller, 1998).

10. When they attempt suicide, boys succeed in killing themselves seven times more often than girls (Ryan, 1998).

11. Though still proportionately lower than rates for white males, the suicide rate for African American males has increased 165 percent over the last twelve years (Pollack, 1998, p. 332).

12. Gay youths account for up to 30 percent of all suicides (Pollack, 1998, p. 210).

13. The death rate from firearms use among boys ages fifteen to nineteen more than doubled from 1985 to 1994, now representing its highest level ever of 49.2 deaths per 100,000 (Pollack, 1998, p. 209).

These statistics about boys' lives, many of which have been well documented for some time, reflect many boys' experiences. Other areas, such as the experiences of boys with disabilities other than those related to learning or emotional problems, have received little attention. With regard to all of these issues, there has been virtually no public outcry. This is a dynamic of our patriarchal system and emerges from a collective unconsciousness and, for some, an unwillingness to recognize the gender linkages to problems for boys in our schools.

KEY AREAS OF CONCERN FOR
BOYS IN SCHOOLS: THE CON EXPOSED

Gender equity advocates have critically examined the socialization process for girls and openly questioned and challenged the structures and messages that serve as barriers to girls' access to expanded roles and opportunities. We need to do the same for boys. The discussion that follows is intended to locate and name the narrow and confining definition of masculinity critiqued here as a common theme in each of the key areas of concern identified. As we have learned from our work with girls and women, developing such consciousness is a critical step in any process to redefine and expand our notions of gender roles. Our goal is to foster an acknowledgment that there is no singular definition of masculinity, expanded or otherwise, that functions for all males. Rather we need to promote the notion of multiple definitions, of masculinities as some see it, that are fluid and accessible for all boys and men as they negotiate their way through school and society. Such a perspective will enable educators to create school environments that are beneficial to girls and boys alike.

Following a consideration of the impact of homophobia on all males, this section explores the impact of traditional masculinity on specific subgroups of males, namely, gay and minority males and males with disabilities. Next, the discussion focuses on aspects of the school or educational experiences of boys, including developmental differences, elementary school, reading and writing skills, special education, school violence, and athletics. While not intended to be comprehensive, collectively the areas discussed provide passage to the identification of the strategies designed to assist boys in resisting the con of traditional masculinity.

Homophobia: The Box

Homophobia is an overwhelming power in motivating boys and men to accept the con. It is the social device responsible for shaming boys into the confining "box" of a singular and unyielding definition of masculinity. There likely isn't a boy in school who is not aware of the policing effect that homophobia has in keeping boys within the bounds of traditional masculinity. Though undeniably powerful in its direct impact on gays and lesbians, the policing effects of homophobia extend far beyond the narrow perspective that defines it as simply a fear of homosexuality. As Kimmel explains in *The Politics of Manhood*, "I take homophobia—this generalized fear of other men, in addition to its limited fears of homosexuality and homosexuals—to be one of the animating conditions of manhood" (1997, p. 370). Homophobia functions to maintain boys' separateness from each other because the walls of this box are impermeable. Pollack refers to it as "gender straightjacketing," and for boys it is the omnipresent fear that if they risk to step outside the box with a gesture of tenderness or empathy, they will be branded a "fairy, a wuss, . . . a fag" or "perceived as feminine or homosexual" (1998, p. 6). For adolescent boys, Thompson (1999) noted, "homophobia is a force stronger than gravity."

Homophobia finds its way into virtually every aspect of boys' experiences in school—social, recreational, and even academic. In some schools, to be academically successful opens up the potential of being branded with the telltale epithets, being labeled as a "brain" and, subsequently, labeled with other "brains" as "fairies" or in some sense like girls. When such views are perpetuated and imposed through peer group pressure, they cause some males to consciously downplay and minimize their academic achievement to fit into the group.

Most tragically, for boys who are homosexual, the effects of homophobia can be quite literally deadly. Gay youths account for up to 30 percent of all teenage suicides, and nearly one-third of gay youths reported that they had attempted suicide at least once (Pollack, 1998, p. 209). Homophobia feeds our culture's myths about homosexuality and plays a key role in the increasing numbers of antigay and lesbian hate crimes in schools. By reinforcing the rigid boundaries of masculinity, homophobia serves to keep boys who are gay "in the closet" and reluctant to seek the support of understanding adults, especially men, in the school community. Though still largely the exception, it is such support from peers, parents, teachers, and others that encourages gay males to take the risk to step out of the box and reveal male identities contradictory to traditional views of masculinity. In our efforts to expand the notion of masculinity, we may gain insight from those males who have had the courage to redefine the male roles for themselves, and it is critical to include their voices and perspectives in redefining masculinity.

Minority Males: Pushed to the Margins

Education and child advocates in minority communities recognize the pressure placed on young males in their communities to conform to expected male roles in that culture. For example, advocates note that black males are more likely than others to grow up in homes without a father present. Developmentally, the disconnections discussed here may come sooner for many of these boys if there are fewer adult male role models to provide guidance and serve as role models. My work with the

Men Helping Boys with Difficult Choices project (CASDA, 1996) offers insight into this dilemma. A participating urban middle school identified a group of boys with whom they chose to work in this project. As part of the program they developed at their school, each boy was asked to identify a significant adult male in their life and invite him to the evening program to kick off the project. Four of the African American boys participating were unable to identify anyone outside of the counselors and teachers from the school coordinating the project. Though seemingly insignificant, the coordinators of this project saw this as a reflection of a critical concern for this group of males.

Statistics also help to clarify related issues for minority males. In the introduction to *Beating the Odds: Raising Academically Successful African American Males* (Hrabowski, Maton, and Greif, 1998), Freeman Hrabowski, president of the University of Maryland, Baltimore County, cites the disproportionately lower academic performance of African American males in our schools. Accepting the fact that many minority students try not to be viewed as "smart" in school, he points out that "it is especially the case among many African American males that they do not want to be viewed as 'nerds' or as too excited about academic achievement" (1998, p. ix). Black males drop out of school at twice the rate of girls and three times that of whites in schools, citing dislike of school, poor grades, and suspension or expulsion as the reasons. Another reason, Hrabowski suggests, is the pressure to be "cool" over being successful in school (p. 12). This is the Boy Code and the lure of the con with an extra twist that only accelerates disconnection from school and, ultimately, society for far too many African American males. The recognition of these problems within the African American community has spawned interest in exploring the controversial concept of schools or programs for African American males in cities throughout the United States.

Geoffrey Canada, president of Rheedlen Centers for Children and Families in New York City, has worked extensively with minority males, directly assisting them in negotiating the confusing and contradictory messages about masculinity they face every day in their schools and communities. In his book, *Reaching Up for Manhood: Transforming the Lives of Boys in America* (1998), Canada writes:

> Our beliefs about maleness, the mythology that surrounds being male, has led many boys to ruin. The image of male as strong is mixed with the image of male as violent. Male as virile gets confused with male as promiscuous. Male as adventurous equals male as reckless. Male as intelligent often gets mixed with male as arrogant, racist and sexist. If we look around and see too many men in jail, on drugs, abandoning their families, acting without compassion or even violently, we as a

society must shoulder the responsibility for change. Boys find themselves pulled and tugged by forces beyond their control as they make the confusing and sometimes perilous trip to manhood. (p. xiii)

The perspectives these programs and child advocates illuminate are the complex intersection of race, class, and masculinity. The advocacy reflected in the work and viewpoints documented in the books cited extend well beyond a simple "call to action" and identification of concerns. While acknowledging the challenge of these concerns, they also provide hope with both strategies and encouraging results all connected to the goal of expanding opportunities and the concept of manhood and masculinity for the boys in their communities.

Males with Disabilities: Finding the "Man"

In his essay "When Is a Man Not a Man? When He's Disabled," Shakespeare explores the literature regarding disability and gender "looking for the disabled man" (1999, p. 47). He reports that while there is a growing body of literature examining the lives and experiences of disabled women, "the disabled man is largely absent as a subject of research" (p. 49). In general, our understanding of gender and disability as intersecting variables in the lives of both disabled men and women is just starting to benefit from inquiry within the educational community.

As suggested earlier, for males with disabilities, being disabled appears to run counter to the narrow definition of masculinity that is the subject of this critique, which rigidly values independence, autonomy, invulnerability, and strength. Further, in direct contradiction to this view of masculinity, having a disability has been viewed as "synonymous with being dependent, childlike, and helpless—an image fundamentally challenging all that is embodied in the ideal male" (Asch and Fine, 1988, p. 3). The title and content of Shakespeare's essay suggests that for many males with a disability, gender is rendered invisible when viewed within the narrow boundaries of traditional masculinity; thus, these males are often seen as simply disabled and, therefore, not male. Shakespeare suggested that "masculinity as an ideological and psychological process is connected to prejudice against disabled people in general." His theory rests on the assumption that male identity is constructed "in opposition to women, nature, children, black people, and gay men." As has been discussed previously, upholding this identity relies on disconnection from, and "superiority to, the 'other'" (Shakespeare, 1999, p. 52). Perceived, viewed, and treated as the other, males with disabilities may well be filtered out through such exclusion and may, on a more personal level, face their own particular confusion in attempting to conform to the masculine role.

How do men and boys with disabilities reconcile the conflict between masculinity and disability? What impact does it have on the educational experience of boys with disabilities? We know about the stigmatization that occurs when one is identified as disabled and/or placed in special education programs. Knowing that, a key question deserving of further inquiry is how do these boys struggle with the intersection of their disability and traditional notions of masculinity? How might the stigma of disability impact how they view their "maleness"?

While there is little research to answer these questions, the men interviewed by Shakespeare provide some direction. One man, Nigel, describes his confusion: "I get mixed messages. As a disabled person I am told to be meek and mild, childlike. Yet as a man I am meant to be masterful, a leader, get angry" (p. 54). Another man, Zebedee, corroborates this perception: "The stereotype of a man is of a strong person, a person who is able, and can take command. Now because of the number of friends who actually accept that I am dominant and able, I do tend to take control in situations like that, but in a lot of society I am treated as this rather wimpish person who can't make their own decisions. Unfortunately this means that I am unable to put over to some people the fact that I am male" (p. 54).

Shakespeare suggests that the "complexities and contradictions . . . endemic to disabled masculinity" (p. 56) are, in many ways, similar to those of nondisabled males. He posits that disabled males and nondisabled males may be able to learn and gain insight from each other in their efforts to negotiate and define themselves as men. In his conclusion, Shakespeare offers a challenge that clearly resonates with the objective of this chapter:

> It is vital not to buy into the screen myths and models of masculinity, which are unapplicable to the majority of men, let alone disabled men. It is time to redefine masculinity in less oppressive, more open, more acceptable ways, which draw on the lived experiences of men and the potentiality of men for change and self improvement. The models for such masculinity may well prove to exist on the margins, in the lives of disabled men, gay men, "new men" and others who have had the foresight and courage to reject hegemonic masculinity. It is my belief that this process will involve not only redefinitions of gender relations, but will also have significant implications for the concept of disability itself. (pp. 57–58)

As with race, gender and disability intersect with their own set of complexities. In schools it is critical to understand these intersections, in this instance, those particular to boys with disabilities and their struggle with the con of traditional masculinity. As Shakespeare suggests, it would be beneficial for them to have opportunities to discuss their struggles within the larger context of the contradictions other groups of nondisabled boys face in their attempts to define themselves as males. Such strategies provide the connections and community needed to move toward a conceptualization of masculinities.

Developmental Differences: Nature and Nurture

Developmental differences between boys and girls have been long established. A recent study showed that, in infancy, boys are more emotionally expressive, while girls are more reflective; boy babies tend to cry when unhappy, and girls suck their thumbs (Kantrowitz and Kalb, 1998). Some differences are particularly relevant as boys and girls start school. Boys lag behind girls in fine motor skills and expressive language development and, on average, begin to read later than girls. Boys enter school with generally better gross motor and visual spatial skills. Boys are also more active, needing to move about and expend energy at regular intervals.

Discussions of such difference frequently degenerate into nature/nurture arguments. The more accurate explanation is that nature and nurture interact in the developmental experience of girls and boys. While it is important to examine biological answers to these questions, schools clearly have enough information with which to create environments that match both genders' instructional needs yet which are also structured to nurture the skills that may require further development in either gender.

"On average, boys are physically more restless and more impulsive. We need to acknowledge boys' physical needs, and meet them," says Thompson (1999). Boys are too often asked to check their higher levels of energy and exuberance at the door when entering the school building. Though a "boys will be boys" attitude is allowed to exist to explain their higher levels of activity, there are only minimal attempts to integrate physical activity into the elementary curriculum beyond kindergarten, recess, and gym. If the school environment doesn't make the accommodations, Thompson adds, "we humiliate them and get them mad, or interpret their activity as willful aggression, and so begins the fulfillment of a prophesy where we try to punish and control boys more harshly than girls, and they come to resent it and dislike it and dislike authority and react back against it" (Goldberg, 1998, p. 1).

Boys' Early School Experiences: Developing Emotional Illiteracy

For most boys the socialization process that encourages them to separate and move toward independence begins early. When boys enter elementary school, they are clearly aware of the Boy Code and its expectations. In *Raising Cain: Protecting the Emotional Life of Boys*, Kindlon and Thompson described the process boys experience in elementary school as socializing them "away from their inner lives" and from their feelings and emotions. During this period boys begin to lose their emotional expressiveness. Thompson (1999) noted that a key to our understanding of this process lies in the fact that at age six and seven boys have as wide a range of emotions as girls. However, by the time they are teenagers, the "leading edge" of their emotional expression is anger. Third grade seems to be critical. It sets the attitude for many boys, and, as Thompson explained, "boys get pissed at school; they take their souls out of school. They turn off and underachieve."

Another indicator of the process of steering boys away from their emotions is found in the influence of gender role expectations on discipline patterns in schools. Throughout their school experience, boys are disciplined differently than girls. For girls, discipline more frequently takes the form of reasoning and connection; girls are encouraged to be reflective and connect with their feelings. For boys, according to Thompson, the intent of discipline is primarily to control their boy behavior, to "name, blame and shame."

Boys' disconnection from emotions is the centerpiece for the educational challenge that Thompson and Kindlon (1999) describe, resulting in what they term "emotional illiteracy," the inability to read and understand emotions. Consequently, boys have difficulty learning the prosocial skills vital to relationships and participation as an emotionally healthy member of any community. This illiteracy often manifests itself in what appears to be a "careless disregard for the feelings of others." Though often shocked by the ferocity of boys' anger, our cultural expectations for boys cause many adults to "excuse this behavior as harmless 'immaturity,' as if maturity will arrive someday—like puberty—to transform a boy's emotional life" (p. 5).

Much of *Raising Cain* focuses on the need to assist boys to develop emotional literacy. Goleman, in *Emotional Intelligence* (1995), theorizes that 'emotional intelligences' can be learned, nurtured and strengthened and, provides the skills that lead to successful lives and relationships. As Thompson and Kindlon described:

> Boys need an emotional vocabulary that expands their ability to express themselves in ways other than anger or aggression. They need to experience empathy at . . . school and be encouraged to use it if they are to develop conscience. . . . They need close, supportive relationships to protect them from becoming victims of their turbulent, disowned emotions. A boy needs male modeling of a rich emotional life. He needs to learn emotional literacy as much from a father and other men as from his mother and other women, because he must create a life and language for himself that speak with male identity. A boy must see and believe that emotions belong in the life of a man. (p. 7)

Elementary School Environment

Elementary schools continue to be primarily female-influenced environments. The majority of teachers at this level are women. At a time when boys, as many developmental psychologists agree, are pushed to separate from females, specifically their mothers, we need to consciously examine the role that this environment might play in that process. If the injunction says, no sissy stuff, and that translates into boys' progressive rejection of all we identify as feminine, such as emotions, is there an inherent conflict for boys in this environment?

It is critical that this perspective on elementary schools and boys' development not be interpreted as locating blame with women, either as teachers, mothers, or other significant adult females in their lives. Blame must be squarely focused on the injunctions that serve to disconnect boys from anything related to the "feminine" so early in their development. Most important here is the need for educators to be conscious of how the dynamic of no sissy stuff is played out in the early school experiences of boys. If there is a conflict, how might the environment of elementary schools be modified to interrupt the negative effects of this dynamic?

In examining this particular issue, critics often suggest that the gender equity agenda for boys is one that pathologizes boys' behavior and, in turn, the solutions promoted focus on the "feminization of boys." What is really at play here is the inability of these critics to move beyond the link between such essentially human qualities as emotional expressiveness and traditional notions of femininity. Ignoring the effects of socialization on boys, they back their claims with unsubstantiated theories of boys' innate "hardwiring" for particular behaviors. The result is a confusing and convoluted argument aimed more at maintaining the status quo than truly advancing our understanding of boys' development. *Raising Cain* offers insights relevant to this debate. In particular, Kindlon and Thompson (1999) provide a detailed analysis and refute of the "boy biology" and "testosterone" theories so frequently used by critics (pp. 11–14).

With these new insights into the developmental experience of boys and our understanding of the importance of emotional literacy, are elementary schools prepared to meet the needs of boys as they are being described in the literature that is emerging? Our awareness of this crisis raises many other questions previously unexamined about boys in schools. Some of the work with girls has focused on, as Gilligan and her colleagues have described it, helping girls maintain "healthy resistance" to the messages and expectations for girls that have contributed to the silencing observed. If boys are experiencing their own emotional silencing, the disconnection from self and others, the elementary school must be the place where they learn to know they do not have to succumb to the lure of the con. This is an example of the healthy resistance we must teach our boys.

Reading and Writing Skills: The Other Critical Filter

With the focus on boys' higher levels of participation and achievement in the areas of mathematics and science, the gender gap between girls and boys with respect to reading and writing skills has received little attention. Pollack (1998) cites a study of thirty years of educational achievement surveys. The results showed that in the areas of reading and writing, particularly "comprehension, perceptual speed, or word association, boys outnumbered girls at the bottom of the scales by a margin of 2 to 1, and many fewer boys than girls scored in the top 10% of the groups" (p. 234). That same study and a report from the U.S. Department of Education cite a similar gap between girls and boys in writing proficiency. The results of the National Assessment of Educational Progress 1998 Reading Report Card for the Nation and States indicated that in all forty-three participating states and at all three grades tested (fourth, eighth, and twelfth), "female students had higher average reading scale scores than their male peers, and the percentage of females attaining each of the reading achievement levels exceeded that of males" (Donahue et al., 1999, p. 2).

Mathematics and science have been a focus in the education of girls and women because proficiency in these areas is linked with increased self-confidence and self-efficacy and significantly expands opportunities for economic self-sufficiency. Similarly, reading and writing are critical filters to successful school experiences and beyond. Schools need to consciously identify and examine the links between gender and boys' potential deficits in these critical academic skills in the ways similar to those explored with girls in math and science.

Special Education: Dealing Boys Out Not In

As suggested earlier, the arena of special education presents a complex set of issues with respect to its intersection with the variable of gender. In theory, special education services ensure access to education for students identified with special needs. In practice, too often the stigma of labeling students with special needs and disabilities continues to be a barrier for many students. Girls and boys with special educational needs both face a double jeopardy that is confounded by the gender roles proscribed by our culture. As the previously cited statistics show, boys are overwhelmingly represented in special education programs throughout the country. Boys are six times more likely to be diagnosed with learning disabilities. There is increasing speculation that the standards we have established for learning disabilities provide so much latitude that it allows boys with behavioral problems to be identified to get them help or move them out of the classroom. Kavale noted that "the system has shaped the definition rather than the other way around" (Rosenfeld, 1998, p. A1). This focus on the intersection of behavior and learning disabilities may also have a limiting effect on disabled girls who are underrepresented in special education services (see Wehmeyer and Schwartz, this volume).

Among the reasons for the high numbers of boys identified with academic, social, and emotional problems are the themes of dominance, control, and detachment embedded in traditional definitions of masculinity. My experience clearly indicates that the Boy Code plays a role in the behaviors that led youth into these programs. These boys represent the filtering system of the Boy Code at work. They have been disconnected from themselves, from others, and, in some cases, from the mainstream of society. Curiously, while boys often exceeded 80 percent of the population in the programs with which I was involved, I do not recall any link to or discussion of gender as an issue in our work.

Gender Links to Violence in Schools

"Gender-based violence includes sexual harassment, dating violence, rape, battering and abuse, male-on-male violence, violence in the home, homophobic violence, and violence in gay and lesbian relationships. It is not only physical violence, but also the oft overlooked psychological abuse that includes verbal abuse, manipulation, threats, and economic control" (WEEA Publishing Center, 1995, p. 4). During the past two decades, educators have seen connections between violence and gender in society and schools. In the AAUW report *Hostile Hallways* (1993), an overwhelming number of students, male and female, reported being sexually harassed. While it is easy to blame males as they are more often perpetrators, this is unfair to most males who are not violent. It is more accurate to suggest that a common element in these acts of violence is their cultural link to a hegemonic view of masculinity with its emphasis on power and control over others.

Further exacerbating the problem is the love-hate relationship we appear to have with violence in our culture with males clearly playing a central role. Our love is evident in the violent, interactive computer games filled with graphic images of blood and body parts. Overwhelmingly popular, these games are marketed primarily to young males. The hate side is exemplified in the national outrage following the spate of school yard shootings in Colorado, Arkansas, Kentucky, Oregon, and other states in 1998 and 1999, some of which were deliberately directed at girls. Yet, even as tragic as those shootings were, there has been a virtual absence of commentary on their obvious links to gender. The shooters were not, as some headlines read, "Children with Guns!" They were all boys. Despite that glaring fact, the public, including the president, wanted to examine these acts to "see if there were some common elements that might explain such violence" (Johnson, 1998, p. 1).

Again, while boys may be a common element in these and other acts of violence, it is not boys that are to be blamed as the sole causal variable. In his book, *Lost Boys: Why Our Sons Turn Violent and How We Can Save Them*, Garbarino examines factors that contribute to boys' and young men's increasing vulnerability to committing violence. One issue examined is the narrow definition of masculinity, including pressure on boys to suppress emotions and be powerful, that may contribute to the choice of violence as the only alternative to resolving conflicts. Ultimately, we must ask how we provide boys with other definitions of masculinity that encourage resilience and resistance to messages that are linked to violence in school and beyond.

Athletics: Out of Bounds

Undoubtedly, competitive sports can have positive effects for student athletes. Girls' increased participation in sports since the inception of Title IX has yielded results that reach beyond the satisfaction of competition, such as a recent report released by the Women's Sports Foundation linking teen pregnancy prevention with girls' participation in sports (Women's Sports Foundation, 1998). While there are certainly benefits for males who participate, there is a downside to athletics that can be linked to the perpetuation of the Boy Code's prescribed masculine role.

At the high school level, athletic programs can become highly selective filtering systems excluding many boys. Competition begins before games are even played, namely, for the few slots on teams. In such systems athletic participation becomes limited to exclusive groups of students. When compounded by traditional masculine values, athletics can perpetuate many of the negative aspects of an exclusionary system. If athletics is highly valued within the school community, such exclusionary practices can become sources of conflict among groups of students. In particular, boys who do not participate in athletics and who are not seen as members of its exclusive club may be viewed and treated as outcasts. Finally, these practices appear to have obvious implications for boys with physical disabilities and their inclusion within the school community.

Additionally, news sources report many stories involving male athletes at any level who have been accused or arrested for acts of violence or sexual assault. Messner and Sabo (1994), both former collegiate athletes, underline this darker side of athletics in their book, *Sex, Violence and Power in Sports: Rethinking Masculinity*. With statistics and their own personal insights, they dissect the culture of male athletics. The negative force that sports can play in the lives of boys and men reinforces a view of traditional masculinity that breeds violence and homophobia and increases the likelihood that male athletes will be involved in sexual assault and rape. They write in the introduction to the book: "Too much of the athletic experience is distorted or muted by sexism, homophobia and aggressive domination thinly disguised as 'healthy competition'" (1994, p. 8).

As an illustration, a recent Associated Press story (1999) reported a Wisconsin school district basketball coach who, as part of a rebounding drill with his junior varsity team, had the boy who rebounded last wear women's panties to the next practice. The "panty drill," as it was called, was used to motivate the development of rebounding skills and not to humiliate, the coach explained. Further, if a boy wore the panties three days in a row, he was threatened with having to wear a matching bra. In response to parents' protests, the superintendent explained that coaches "were trying to loosen the kids up. They never meant any harm by it."

Addressing the Other Issues of Access for Boys

This chapter sought to identify another issue of access in our efforts to achieve gender equity in schools, namely, boys' access to those human qualities that keep them connected with themselves, with others, and to the educational and social communities within which they are developing their identities. The areas of concern associated with themes of disconnection in boys' and men's lives have been located in our patriarchal and narrow views of masculinity, views reflected in our schools. In these ways schools are also failing boys.

In our efforts to provide the access that boys so desperately need, we must consciously develop strategies that have the twofold purpose of addressing the systemic roots of the problem and focusing on the particular needs of the students involved. For boys, this means they need adults to serve as role models who are willing to challenge the traditional views and stereotypes as they are reflected in the institution, while also providing the tools and support mechanisms that allow boys access in strengthening their healthy resistance. The next section offers ten strategies aimed at helping boys resist the con of traditional masculinity.

TEN STRATEGIES TO PROMOTE
BOYS' HEALTHY RESISTANCE OF THE CON

Based on literature reviewed in this chapter and programs to provide healthy alternatives to traditional masculinity discussed below, I suggest the following strategies to assist educators to help boys.

Create Mutually Empowering School Environments

Bergman and Surrey (1992) have been working with males and females to assist them to create school environments to resist the divisive nature of traditional views of masculine-feminine relationships. Through the use of facilitated gender dialogues, their work focuses on the development of strategies that are mutually empowering for both genders. Such work can be beneficial to help educators break down walls to healthy development and construct environments that encourage perspective taking and respect. The kinds of conversations and dialogues advocated in this strategy also provide students and educators with the opportunity to consider the intersection of gender with multiple variables identified in this chapter and text, such as race and disability.

From a pedagogical and curriculum development perspective, the book *A Great Balancing Act: Equitable Education for Girls and Boys*, published by the National Association of Independent Schools, is an excellent resource for educators. Research based and mindful of the gender-related differences that influence the education of girls and boys, it is designed to assist educators in developing learning environments and instructional strategies deliberately directed at overcoming the negative impact of stereotyping.

Time for discussion is critical for any change process. In many schools, dialogue about gender rarely moves beyond the faculty lounge or single workshop. Adapting a model she developed for female faculty in her work with Carol Gilligan, Judith Dorney and I (Dorney and Flood, 1997) worked in a retreat setting with men and women educators to examine the impact of gender on the curriculum. Follow-up interviews showed these retreats to have a profound impact on many of the participants. In particular, for the men involved, they proved to be a rare opportunity to openly examine the impact of gender on males and place that understanding within the context of the school setting where males and females are required to learn and work together.

Connect Men to the Work of Gender Equity

Men are not the problem; it is systemic. Despite over twenty-five years of gender equity efforts, advocacy for the issues in schools is sadly lacking the participation of men. Men need to see their place in this work. Work with boys in schools has indicated the benefit of men's direct involvement in addressing gender bias and helping boys learn alternatives to the traditional masculine role in our culture. Boys need to see men as visible and vocal advocates of gender equity. Since men continue to hold the primary positions of leadership in schools, it is particularly important that they be encouraged to use those roles to promote healthy alternatives for boys.

In *I Don't Want to Talk about It*, Real discusses the fluid capacity that males have for developing a range of strengths and characteristics for healthy human development (1997, p. 132). Boys require models for that in their lives. In talking about fathers and other significant adult males, Real indicates that boys hunger for other models of masculinity. They need men "who have themselves emerged from the gauntlet of their own socialization with some degree of emotional intactness" (p. 132). Such role models would seem particularly relevant when programs are working with boys with disabilities and boys from other diverse backgrounds. Katz's working paper *More Than a Few Good Men: Strategies for Inspiring Boys and Young Men to Be Allies in Anti-Sexist Education* (1998), is an excellent resource.

Take an Active Stand against Homophobia

Homophobia has a negative impact on everyone in a school community, particularly gay and lesbian students. As we have seen, homophobic pressure plays a critical role in maintaining the rigidity of traditional male roles for boys. Adult males within the school community, particular administrators and counselors, need to take an active role to help boys understand this connection and to work with them to erase the shaming effect homophobia can have in the development of heterosexual males and gay and lesbian students.

Actively Listen to Boys

Provide opportunities for boys to talk (and write) about their lives beginning at an early age and in as many ways possible. We have learned a great deal about alternatives to prescribed roles by listening to the voices of girls. Pollack's work in *Real Boys* is, in part, based on his *Listening to Boys' Voices* project. Listening and voice should not be confined to simply verbal expression. Writing, art, physical activity, and other forms of expression can provide opportunities for understanding the inner lives of boys. The integration of such strategies into the curriculum can assist boys to develop the habit of expression while also allowing them to experience the value of being listened to by caring adults in the school environment.

Build in Physical Activity for Boys and Girls

Boys enjoy and benefit from chances for structured physical activities, particularly in the early grades. Consciously build such activity into the curriculum beyond free play or gym. Approaches such as project-based learning and experiential problem solving allow for moving about the environment and build in time for active reflection about what was learned and how it was learned. Engaging boys and girls in these active processes is beneficial in creating empowering learning environments grounded in respect and perspective taking.

Disaggregate School Testing and
Special Education Data by Gender

Many excellent programs for girls in mathematics and science have resulted from the disaggregation of test data, allowing schools to identify and isolate areas of need based on gender. We know from national statistics that boys are at risk in the areas of reading and writing; these would be areas to pay particular attention to at all levels. These data would also be useful to understand links between gender and special education services.

Teach Men's History

While the history we teach has primarily focused on men's contributions, little of that history has taken a critical look at the development and construction of gender roles or the inner lives of men. Likewise, in developing boys' voices, it is important to connect boys with the lives and voices of men from diverse backgrounds, including men with disabilities whose lives and experiences are rarely included in the curriculum. Boys of all backgrounds can learn a great deal about alternatives to traditional definitions of masculinity by understanding their developmental link to our past and how men of particular times in our history were feeling about their roles and lives. Rotundo's *American Manhood* (1993) and two of Kimmel's books, *Manhood in America* (1995) and *Against the Tide: Profeminist in American History, 1776–1990* (Kimmel and Mosmiller, 1997) offer engaging histories from these perspectives.

Identify the Links between Gender and Violence

There is ample evidence of the link between violence and the dynamics of power and control in our traditional definitions of masculinity. School officials, particularly men in positions of leadership, need to take a more proactive role in interrupting these connections. At the elementary level two particularly valuable resources for this are *Quit It*

(Froschl, Sprung, and Mullin-Rindler, 1998) and *Bullyproof* (Sjostrom and Stein, 1996). Both of these books are teacher guides to address teasing and bullying. At the secondary level, *Gender Violence/Gender Justice* (Stein and Cappello, 1999) explores connections between gender and violence with students in language arts and social science classes.

Play up the Positives of Athletics

Rather than perpetuating masculine stereotypes, competitive athletics needs to be the source of positive school experiences for boys and girls. Recognizing the benefits of active participation in sports and as a counter to the exclusivity that can develop in competitive athletics, many schools are opening up their programs to larger numbers of students. Often the most visible representatives of a school community, male athletes should be encouraged to reflect positive attributes and take an active stand in confronting gender-biased attitudes and behaviors. Many effective bias prevention programs in schools have used male athletes in leadership and mentoring roles with peers and younger males. One example of this and of the gender and violence strategy is the Mentors in Violence Prevention (MVP) program. Developed by Jackson Katz, this program utilizes athletes and focuses on the development of positive bystander behavior in encouraging athletes to stand up against gender-based bias and violence.

Educate Parents about Gender Roles and Boys

The critical role parents play in the life experiences of boys is obvious. Based on our understanding of the research, mothers need to be encouraged to maintain the connections they have with their sons, particularly in the elementary years. As Terrence Real (1997) indicated, fathers need encouragement to provide healthy alternatives to masculinity. Schools can be the conveyors of this information and provide opportunities to discuss it with parents.

FINAL THOUGHTS: THE STORY CONTINUES

Brandon entered high school this year. He is doing well academically and socially. Most important, he appears to be negotiating his world with a wonderful balance of confidence, courage, and compassion. Though not without its bumps, I feel his success is, in part, the result of sustained connections with his mother and myself. He continues to be encouraged to maintain a view of his inner life, while also setting his sights on what we hope will be a future of expanded opportunities for him as he moves toward manhood.

Ken, I am likewise pleased to report, is the father of a wonderful eight-year-old son, Eric, who seems on a course similar to Brandon. One evening when Eric was four, Ken and I revisited his comments about the kiss, in a deeply thoughtful conversation that lasted until dawn. The time was marked by equal amounts of honesty and intimacy, a quality we don't often associate with men's relationships. But it allowed us to wrestle with our own understanding of the con of masculinity. As with this chapter, we emerged with more questions than answers. But amidst that, most evident was a commitment to continue our dialogue and to assist each other in resisting the lure of those binding messages for ourselves and for the well-being of our sons. As our relationship continues, we are clearly able to attest to the change that happens when men have the courage to resist the con and remain connected to their hearts.

REFERENCES

American Association of University Women (AAUW). 1993. *Hostile hallways: The AAUW survey of sexual harassment in America's Schools.* Washington, D.C.: American Association of University Women Educational Foundation.

Asch, A., and M. Fine. 1988. Introduction: Beyond pedestals. In *Women with disabilities: Essays in psychology, culture and politics.* Edited by M. Fine and A. Asch. Philadelphia: Temple University Press.

Associated Press. 1999, February 25. Parents protest putting players in women's undies. America on Line news website.

Bergman, S. J. 1991. *Men's psychological development: A relational perspective.* Wellesley, Mass.: Stone Center, Wellesley College (Working Paper).

Bergman, S. J., and J. Surrey. 1992. *The woman-man relationship: Impasses and possibilities.* Wellesley, Mass.: Stone Center, Wellesley College (Paper Order No. 55).

Canada, G. 1998. *Reaching up for manhood: Transforming the lives of boys in America.* Boston: Beacon Press.

Capital Area School Development Association (CASDA). 1996, September. *Men helping boys with difficult choices: Final report.* Albany, N.Y.: Capital Area School Development Association.

Chapman, A. 1997. *A great balancing act: Equitable education for girls and boys.* National Association of Independent Schools.

Combs, M. 1998, July 26. What about boys? *Boston Sunday Globe,* 2.

David, D. S., and R. Brannon, eds. 1976. *The forty-nine percent majority: The male sex role.* Reading, Mass.: Addison-Wesley Publishing Co.

Diller, L. H. 1998, November 12. Pills for kids sound alarm bells in suburbs. *USA Today.*

Donahue, P. L., K. E. Voelki, J. R. Campbell, and J. Mazzeo. 1999, March. NAEP 1998 Reading report card for the nation and states: Executive summary. In *The nation's report card: National assessment of educational progress.*

Dorney, J., and C. P. Flood. 1997. Breaking gender silences in the curriculum: A retreat intervention with middle school educators. *Education Action Research* 5(2).

Doten, P. 1998, July 20. Without guidance, boys will be troubled boys. *Boston Globe*.

Froschl, M., B. Sprung, and N. Mullin-Rindler. 1998. *Quit it! A teacher's guide on teasing and bullying for use with students in grades K–3*. Wellesley, Mass.: Wellesley College Center for Research on Women and New York: Educational Equity Concepts.

Garbarino, J. 1999. *Lost boys: Why our sons turn violent and how we can save them*. New York: The Free Press.

Gilligan, C. 1982. *In a different voice*. Cambridge, Mass.: Harvard University Press.

Goffman, Erving. 1963. *Stigma: Notes on the manuscript of spoiled identity*. Englewood Cliffs, N.J.: Prentice Hall.

Goldberg, C. 1998, April 23. Growing move to address a cultural threat to boys. *New York Times*, 1.

Goleman, D. 1995. *Emotional intelligence: Why it can matter more than IQ*. New York: Bantam Books.

Gurien, Michael. 1996. *The wonder of boys: What parents, mentors and educators can do to shape boys into exceptional men*. New York: Jeremy P. Tarcher/Putnam Books.

Hanson, M. 1997. *Options: Making connections in today's world*. Williams, Calif.: Connections Leadership Project.

Hill, D. 1999, April. Mob squad. *Teacher magazine*, 29–32.

Hrabowski, F., K. I. Maton, and G. L. Greif. 1998. *Beating the odds: Raising academically successful African American males*. New York: Oxford University Press.

Johnson, A. G. 1998, April 22. The common element. *Feminista*, 1.

Johnson, M., and C. Gipson. 1997. *Visions program: Career guidance and life management for African American males*. Williams, Calif.: Connections Leadership Project.

Kantrowitz, B., and C. Kalb. 1998, May 11. Boys will be boys. *Newsweek*.

Katz, J. 1994. *Mentors in Violence Prevention playbook: High school*. Boston, Mass.: Northeastern University, Center for the Study of Sport in Society.

———. 1998. *More than a few good men: Strategies for inspiring boys and young men to be allies in anti-sexist education*. Wellesley, Mass.: Wellesley College, the Center for Research on Women (Working Paper Series, No. 291).

Kimmel, M. 1995. *Manhood in America: A cultural history*. New York: The Free Press.

———. 1997. *The politics of manhood: Profeminist response to mythopic men's movement*. Philadelphia: Temple University Press.

Kimmel, M., and T. Mosmiller. 1997. *Against the tide: Profeminist men in the United States, 1776–1990, a documentary history*. Boston: Beacon Press.

Kindlon, D., and M. Thompson. 1999. *Raising Cain: Protecting the emotional life of boys*. New York: Ballantine Books.

Messner, M., and D. Sabo. 1994. *Sex, violence and power in sports: Rethinking masculinity.* Freedom, Calif.: The Crossing Press.

Norman, M. 1997, November 9. From Carol Gilligan's chair. *New York Times Magazine,* 50.

Pleck, J. H. 1983. *The myth of masculinity.* Cambridge, Mass.: The MIT Press.

Pollack, W. 1998. *Real boys: Rescuing our sons from the myths of boyhood.* New York: Random House.

Prose, F. 1990, January 7. Confident at eleven, confused at sixteen. *New York Times Magazine,* 22–25, 37–40, 45.

Real, T. 1997. *I don't want to talk about it: Overcoming the secret legacy of male depression.* New York: Scribner.

Reveles, F. 1998. *Encuentros: Hombre a hombre.* Williams, Calif.: Connections Leadership Project.

Rosenfeld, M. 1998, March 26. Little boys blue: Reexamining the plight of young males. *Washington Post,* A1.

Rotundo, E. A. 1993. *American manhood: Transformations in masculinity from the revolution to the modern era.* New York: Basic Books.

Ryan, J. 1998, March 22. Boys to men. *San Francisco Chronicle,* 1.

Sadker, M., and D. Sadker. 1994. *Failing at fairness: How America's schools cheat girls.* New York: Macmillan.

Shakespeare, T. 1999. When is a man not a man? When he's disabled. In *Working with men for change.* Edited by J. Wild. University College of London Press, 47–58.

Sjostrom, L., and N. Stein. 1996. Bullyproof: A teacher's guide on teasing and bullying. Wellesley, Mass.: Wellesley College Center for Research on Women.

Stein, N., and D. Cappello. 1999. *Gender violence/gender justice.* Wellesley, Mass.: Wellesley College Center for Research on Women.

WEEA Publishing Center. 1995. *Gender stereotypes: The links to violence.* Newton, Mass.: WEEA Publishing Center.

Women's Sports Foundation. 1998. *The Women's Sports Foundation Report: Sport and teen pregnancy: Executive summary.*

CHAPTER 10

Teaching as Though Both Genders Count: Guidelines for Designing Nonsexist Inclusive Curricula

Theresa Mickey McCormick

I'm either an emblem of people's fear or an object of their admiration. Well, it's not either/or—the two interpenetrate considerably. Often the admiration is a distancing technique. If you admire me and think I'm an inspiration, then you don't have to acknowledge my humanness. And if I'm not human in the way you are, then you can't become me.

—Nancy Mairs, 1997

How can educators plan their classroom instruction and structure the formal curriculum so that students are immersed in the attitudes, knowledge, and skills of unbiased education? What are some of the problems and issues related to gender, race, and class for students receiving special education services? What can teachers do to address these issues and transform the curriculum so that it is nonsexist and inclusive?

Throughout this chapter, these questions are examined in a variety of ways. The primary focus is on guidelines for designing curricula that are inclusive of both genders, as well as diverse racial, ethnic, socioeconomic, and ability/disability groups. One underlying premise in this chapter is that disability is a social, political, and civil rights issue rather than a physical or medical issue. Another basic and unifying premise is that disability, gender, and race are social constructs that are interrelated. Social constructs are ideas and assumptions that people believe about "others" or "outsiders" who are different from themselves. The dominant or majority group's social constructs about others and what is "normal" are then imposed on the larger society through media and education institutions. Human relations are socially defined by the dominant group who, "through the structure of language required in schools" (Grant and Sachs, 1995, p. 94), label and define people (e.g., at-risk, slow learner). For example, McGuinness (1985) contends that dominant societal values determine what is labeled "deviant," noting that students are "learning disabled" only in skills that society values as important to the culture (e.g., reading, writing, math); while, for example, they are not labeled "learning disabled" if they have poor mechanical or athletic skills.

MULTICULTURAL AND FEMINIST PEDAGOGY— RATIONALES AND DEFINITIONS: POINTS OF CONCURRENCE AND POINTS OF DIVERGENCE

What is the rationale for multicultural and feminist pedagogy? We need multicultural and feminist pedagogies in schools because of the failure of traditional school curriculum to reflect the diversity and values of our multicultural population. The population of the United States and thus school populations become more diverse daily; yet school curricula still reflect the dominant white male, able-bodied value and knowledge system.

Multicultural education is a reform movement concerned with social justice and transformation in schools and in society. It was designed to acknowledge, affirm, and celebrate diversity and to address and help eradicate prejudices and discrimination based on students' sex, race, disability status, language, class, or religion. Ableism, racism, sexism, heterosexism, and ageism unfortunately are still evident in education. The "isms" are socially constructed beliefs about groups of people that the majority of people in a given culture have, in effect, agreed on. For example, in the United States, a proportion of people (both male and female) believe in the superiority of straight, white, able-bodied males as the ideal against which all citizens are to be measured.

Cultural pluralism is the philosophic basis for education that is multicultural, nonsexist, and inclusive of all people with their many differences. Cultural pluralism is a characterization of U.S. society as a common culture with ethnic and cultural microcultural groups. It views our society as a "salad bowl" or as a mosaic of many parts that hold together, rather than as a "melting pot." The "melting pot" idea is inaccurate since it envisions all people from diverse backgrounds and abilities melting into one new group known as "American." This so-called melting or total assimilation of all immigrants and other diverse groups has not happened in the United States because many groups retain their language, religion, and significant portions of their culture. Also, some groups, notably Native Americans and African Americans have not been allowed into the melting pot because of exclusion and slavery—oppressions based on the notion that they were less than fully human. It is important to note that many of these groups did not want to assimilate.

Feminism is a belief that women should have political, legal, and social rights equal to those of men and have educational and economic parity with men. It is also the social movement to obtain these rights. Feminists, whether male or female, advocate women's equal rights and status with men. Feminist theorists posit that knowledge is socially constructed, that it is both objective and subjective, and that its subjective elements should be made clear (Code, 1991). Feminists challenge the basic goals and assumptions of our male-as-norm (male-centric) education system and curriculum. Feminism has a direct relation to classroom practice. Feminist pedagogies actively engage students in the education process by drawing on their own experiences and by encouraging reflection on the meaning of their experiences for concepts in a course or field of study. This engagement and reflection enables students to make decisions regarding their life and goals.

The histories of multicultural and feminist pedagogy are linked with the civil rights movement of the 1950s and1960s, in which African Americans and other people of color demanded equal opportunity for educational and economic achievement, and what might be called the "contemporary women's movement" (McCormick, 1994, p. 13) of the 1960s and 1970s, when women joined the push for equity. Both of these movements and their resulting pedagogies promote social action to bring about social justice, fairness, cultural balance, inclusion, and educational equity for all students. These pedagogies involve students in social activism to transform the curriculum and the schools to reflect the concerns, contributions, viewpoints, values, and beliefs of diverse groups.

In practice, the relationship between multicultural and feminist pedagogies is one of debate and lack of clarity. Multicultural pedagogy, in practice, usually focuses on race and ethnicity awareness and activism to eradicate racism, while feminist pedagogy typically focuses on gender and educational transformation of the system so that it is free of sexism. In recent years, multicultural education authors have begun to include gender and class in their analyses of inequality in education.

A CONTINUUM: FROM A DEFICIT MODEL
TO A DIFFERENCE MODEL

We frequently find two different orientations to curriculum and instruction for students who are seen as different from the cultural norm by virtue of race, ethnicity, disability, or other factors: a deficit model and a difference model. In between these two, I position a "sameness" model or equal opportunity model. In the deficit model, the assumption is that the "outsiders" (i.e., females, students of color, gay males and lesbians, or students with disabilities) are deficient and have to mold themselves to fit into the traditional (male-as-norm) system of education. The danger is that by "fitting in" and adapting to the traditional "norm" in schools, these students run the very big risk of denying or losing their own cultural identity.

The deficit model denies opportunities to marginalized students to take courses or participate in programs in the curriculum that are defined along strict gender or ability lines. In this, and other ways, women, people of color, and people with disabilities are devalued and disempowered. Sleeter and Grant noted: "Those educators who subscribe to the *deficiency orientation* see prevailing standards for 'American culture' and 'normal' human development as universally correct, and they trace failures to achieve those standards to supposed deficiencies in children's home environments and/or children's physiological and mental endowments" (1994, 44).

In the sameness view (equality model) of curriculum and instruction, there is an emphasis on equality between diverse groups in education. The philosophy, curricula, and programs emphasize sameness for all students and assimilation into the mainstream curriculum. This politically liberal view of education grew out of the civil rights and women's rights movements, which pushed for equal opportunity in employment and educational and legal equality; later on, the disability rights movement developed similar aims, focusing, for example, on equal protection and due process in education. The goal of the model is described in terms of equal access, participation, and outcomes. It adapts the traditional curriculum to the needs of people/students with disabilities, white women, and people of color, but does not change its basic structures.

In the sameness model, revisions in curriculum included adding on courses about women or ethnic groups; including contributions of excluded groups, such as people with disabilities; critiquing and revising teaching materials and texts to eliminate disability, race, and sex stereotypes; and changing restrictive or exclusionary policies. Proponents of this approach believe that the main purpose of education is assimilation. That is, diverse students are to be assimilated into the standard school curricula after equity adjustments have taken place. Described by Sleeter and Grant as the human capital theory of education, they posit: "The goal of this approach is that students become equipped with the cognitive skills, concepts, information, language, and values required by American society in order to hold a job and function within the society's existing institutions and culture. . . . According to this approach, modifications are made in schooling to facilitate these students' academic achievement and their transition to the mainstream culture that White, middle-class children are learning" (1994, p. 42). The downside of the sameness model is that when people assimilate into another culture, they lose their own, in large measure, and usually their "difference" is viewed negatively or at best as a hindrance to "fitting in." For example, when people with disabilities are assimilated into the mainstream culture, they are at risk of losing the art, humor, language, history, symbols, and worldview that bind them together in their disability culture.

In the difference model, the educator's goal is still to enable the student who differs from the cultural norm to assimilate into the mainstream culture; however, the student's "difference" is not viewed negatively, rather it is treated as a strength. In this model, the curriculum content includes, affirms, and values the richness and variety that differentiate the student's culture. In my earlier work on early childhood education, I argue:

> The classifications "disadvantaged" or "deficient" are no longer appropriate to use for culturally different children whose behavior does not meet the expectations of the middle-class teacher. Rather, their cultural/ethnic difference is the more appropriate dimension to be considered. Children must be perceived according to their particular learning style, with their achievement being measured on more than one continuum. The general consensus of the research is that there are different, not deficient or deviant, learning styles; that there is no one way of knowing and processing information; that differences reflect diverse sociocultural antecedents. (McCormick, 1990, p. 113)

Educators who adhere to the *difference orientation*, according to Sleeter and Grant, "see prevailing standards as relative to the demands of a particular culture and hold that different cultural contexts produce equally healthy but different patterns of normal development. Individuals can learn to function productively in mainstream culture as well as in their own community culture" (1994, p. 44).

Philosophically more aligned with the difference model is the field of disability studies that has developed in the last twenty years. According to Linton (1998), disability studies focuses on "an organized critique on the constricted, inadequate, and inaccurate conceptualizations of disability that have dominated academic inquiry" (2). Linton posits that the main contributions of disability studies are its challenge to the view of disability as a medical category and its critique of the whole curriculum as inadequate in relation to the study of disability. Cassuto (1999) describes disability studies as an interdisciplinary grassroots movement "that focuses not only on disability, but also on how disability illuminates society and culture" (p. A60).

Disability studies, like the work done in multicultural studies, feminist studies, ethnic studies, and queer studies challenges the idea that "biology is destiny." Davis and Linton (1995) state, " Disability studies, like these other "new" discourses, challenges the assumption that biology, or any physical or psychological variation, destines people to their social status" (p. 2). Considering these tenets, disability studies is complementary with the nonsexist inclusive curriculum model that I develop in the following discussion.

NONSEXIST INCLUSIVE CURRICULUM MODEL

I propose a curriculum model that is transformative—one that includes some of the best concepts of the equality ("sameness") and difference models but goes much further in restructuring the whole of education. It is not an assimilationist model, but rather based on the idea of cultural pluralism. Cultural pluralism is the philosophic basis for education that is nonsexist and multicultural (McCormick, 1994, p. 89).

The model proposed here is gender balanced and inclusive of all races, cultures, socioeconomic classes, and people from all ability/disability groups—one that affirms their lives and experiences. It addresses social issues involving sexism, ableism, racism, classism, and heterosexism. That is, the model recognizes the oppression that results from discrimination based on a person' s sex/gender, disability, race, class, or sexual orientation. It takes account of the connection between power and prejudice to produce the "ism" or oppression of marginalized groups. It incorporates principles of equity (i.e., social justice, fairness, equal opportunity, access, participation) rather than expectations of quantitative equality.

The goal is to transform the education system to reflect the perspectives, values, and contributions of diverse groups; but this chapter focuses on the formal curriculum relative to this transformative perspective on education. This is not a "Band-Aid" approach to curriculum transformation; rather, a different orientation toward the education process. The nonsexist inclusive model supports the continuation of equality efforts (e.g., hiring more people with disabilities, white women, and people of color and infusing the curriculum with equity content) but goes beyond other curriculum models to challenge, critically examine, and promote change of the basic assumptions, curriculum, and structure of masculinist education. This curriculum model fits the "experientialist" orientation that, according to Schubert, is rooted in ideas of John Dewey and is integrative of diverse ideas and groups. Just as multicultural and feminist pedagogy reflects, affirms, and celebrates students' lived experience, Schubert says the "experientialist" orientation to curriculum is concerned with "everyday dilemmas . . . [that] relate to today's increased consciousness of persons who are oppressed or silenced because of race, class, gender, health, age, place" (1993, p. 84). Thus, in a multicultural feminist model of education, the students' experiences become grist for the mill of knowledge construction and making meaning of that knowledge as well as the "received" knowledge from past generations.

The nonsexist inclusive curriculum model is based on feminist pedagogies that incorporate the multiple voices of women, their experiences, concerns, and ethics (Noddings 1992; 1990; Gilligan 1982); methodologies (Bloom 1998); and ways of knowing (Belenky et al., 1986). Conceptually, it draws on the work of Darling-Hammond (1990) Laird (1988) Martin (1984) and Warren (1989). Additionally, it draws on recent theoretical works on critical multiculturalism (Kanpol and McLaren, 1995; Grant and Sachs, 1995) and black feminist thought (Collins, 1990; 1998) and on important scholarship on disability studies (Cassuto, 1999; Davis and Linton, 1995; Gill, 1995).

I contend that in any curriculum transformation project a foundation of feminist, disability, and critical multicultural studies is crucial. Elaborating on feminist pedagogy, K. Warren explains: "[It] encourages cooperative learning, classroom interactions that are free of gender biases, critical thinking in the classroom, . . . use of examples that grow out of the student's own experiences, recognition of different "learning styles" and "thinking styles" . . . appreciation of diversity and life experiences, and legitimate use of human emotion and experience" (1989, p. 50).

Feminists, disability studies scholars, and critical multiculturalists are engaged in a debate about power relations among different groups (gender, disability, ethnic, cultural, or sexual identity groups) in education and how to disrupt the structural inequities in institutions that maintain and reinforce social and economic inequity. Another dimension of feminist thought, disability studies, and critical multiculturalism is to understand and question the relation between knowledge and power. Grant and Sachs contend: "Knowledge and power are inseparable to the extent that forms of power are situated, constituted, and distributed within knowledge. For multicultural education this is significant because it provides the opportunity to further examine which discourses deny access to institutional structures that the dominant groups take for granted. These discourses may well be imbedded within both overt and hidden curricula, the *structure of language* [italics added] required in schools, or the commonsense knowledge that people use in their everyday interactions inside and outside of schools" (1995, p. 94). Simi Linton (1998) explores the use and structure of language in psychology that are opposed to the basic ideas in disability studies. For example, she states that "psychology is responsible for the formulations and research conventions that cement the ideas of 'normal,' 'deviant,' 'abnormal,' and 'pathology' in place" (p. 6).

From my earliest experience working in the public schools as a multicultural coordinator, I was concerned with power and the social construction of knowledge and their relation to the *structure of language* used to describe students of color, poor students, and students with disabilities. I, along with other multicultural educators, critiqued the use of the terms *disadvantaged* and *culturally deprived* that were commonly used to describe students in our schools. Then, in the 1980s, when I became a professor, to my dismay, the term *at-risk* took hold in academia and in school policies and practices as a way to label poor students, students of color, and people/students with disabilities.

The term or label *at-risk* is problematic because it places emphasis on the students; it implies that something is wrong with them, not with the school system or programs. This approach avoids examining the institutional patterns and policies that help keep alive the label *at-risk*. I support Grant and Sachs' conclusions that critical multicultural education helps "all students have a knowledge of the apparatus, formal and informal, structures and discourses that oppress them" (1995, p. 97) and increasingly "advocate the importance of teaching students how to take charge of their life circumstances" (1995, p. 101).

Multicultural, disability, and feminist studies are not just theoretical but also have direct meaning for classroom practice. Educators need to use these theories and related pedagogy as guides for creating schools that are free of bias and injustice. They can serve as guides for promoting social activism in students to confront biases and foster equity and social justice in school and throughout life.

In the following section, I build on the concepts of multicultural, disability, and feminist studies to delineate the model for nonsexist inclusive curriculum. These theoretical perspectives provide the foundation for classroom practices that are nonsexist and inclusive. They are the launching site for a curriculum that addresses the learning needs of a diverse student body. First I describe the characteristics of the model.

CHARACTERISTICS OF THE
NONSEXIST INCLUSIVE CURRICULUM MODEL

1. Intersection of the concepts of gender balance and inclusion with disability, race, ethnicity, and social class.

2. Incorporation of a reconceptualization of knowledge that shifts from a male-centric perspective to one that is more holistic and includes both females and males. Recognition that knowledge is created within the social and political context of a culture. Recognition that concepts such as gender, disability, and race are products of a society's beliefs and values, are sources of potential discrimination, and have an interactive effect.

3. Incorporation of a variety of instructional strategies that attend to the learning styles, needs, and interests of both genders, culturally diverse students, and students with disabilities. Includes problem-solving and inquiry strategies that encourage student growth in decision making regarding social issues.

4. Incorporates experientialist and interdisciplinary perspectives on curriculum development and feminist, disability, and critical multicultural theory and pedagogies.

GUIDELINES FOR DEVELOPING A
NONSEXIST INCLUSIVE CURRICULUM

Key goals of a curriculum for education that is nonsexist and inclusive are to enable students to understand social issues, such as sexism, racism, classism, heterosexism, and ableism and how they interrelate; to make decisions about these deep-rooted problems; and to take individual and/or group social action to help extinguish them. As the structure and content of the curriculum are transformed to reflect the wide range of human diversity, students are more likely to sense and understand the experiences of others.

The following guidelines for transforming the traditional curriculum are given to illustrate how equity content may be embedded in the structure of different curricular areas. Rigidly following these guidelines is not recommended; for doing so would not guarantee a successful inclusive and nonsexist curriculum. Teachers are the key players in this process of curriculum change. As you begin the process of curriculum transformation, use the following guidelines to get started. Move toward the goal of students taking charge of defining their own purposes then developing plans for action research that guide their decision making and social action.

These guidelines are based on interdisciplinary concepts that provide a framework for understanding a curriculum that is nonsexist and inclusive. These concepts are basic to the form and content of the model. From them, four goals are developed, and appropriate student objectives are devised in relation to each goal.

These key concepts are based on the theoretical works of educators, such as Banks (1997); Gollnick and Chinn (1998); my own research (1982; 1984; 1994); and classic works by others in related fields (e.g., Allport, 1954; Gordon, 1964). Teachers need to use a conceptual framework for nonsexist inclusive curriculum development and implementation (1) to ensure a coherent integration of attitudes, knowledge, and skills throughout the curriculum, and (2) to avoid a fragmented or "add-on" approach. The concepts are defined below.

Cultural Democracy: The relationship between the ideals of U.S. democracy and the historical and social realities of our pluralistic society.

Cultural/Gender Adaptation: The ability to retain one's own gender/ethnic identity while successfully participating in the mainstream culture.

Cultural/Gender Awareness: Consciousness of cultural and gender similarities and differences, cognizant of one's own culture and gender and that of others.

Cultural/Gender Literacy: Knowledge of history, contributions, and perspectives of different cultural/racial groups, ability/disability groups, and both sexes.

Cultural Pluralism: A characterization of U.S. society as a universal (common) culture with ethnic and cultural subgroups. A view of society as a "salad bowl" rather than a "melting pot." The philosophic basis for education that is nonsexist and multicultural.

Cultural Relativism: Recognition of the worth and role of both genders, diverse cultural, racial, ability/disability groups, with no inference of superiority of one group over another.

Disability: A socially derived definition of people based on their physical, sensory, emotional, and cognitive characteristics that may be a source of discrimination and is characterized by dimensions of a shared culture such as humor, art, and language.

Gender Sensibility: Receptiveness and responsiveness to the values, beliefs, and perspectives of each gender.

Individual and Institutional Bias: Inequalities created by institutions (e.g., schools, courts) and individuals that result in discrimination against a subgroup. The institutional type is usually a result of long-established practices and policies, whereas individual bias is typically rooted in low self-esteem and ignorance.

Selfhood: A concept of self-identity derived from early socialization and influenced by one's multiple sources of identity (i.e., gender, disability, ethnic group, or social class).

Social Action: Participation in activities to help solve the problems of inequality. Implementation of strategies to help eliminate intergroup conflict.

GOALS, OBJECTIVES, AND KEY CONCEPTS OF NONSEXIST INCLUSIVE CURRICULUM

These broad goals address the desired learning outcomes for students educated for successful living in our diverse nation and world. Attending to three learning domains (affective, cognitive, psychomotor), the goals address the need for understanding self and others, recognizing human diversity and its impact on values, attitudes, and behaviors, including the dynamics of discrimination, and developing the skills for problem solving and decision making needed for the new millennium. Making connections between the key concepts, the goals, and student objectives is most important, and the following provides an illustration.

Goal 1. To Understand Self and Others as
Cultural Beings Acting within a Cultural Context.

Objectives

1. Identifies self and others as members of several groups by virtue of sex, race, culture, disability status, or social class.
2. Chooses and uses a variety of interaction and learning styles as tools for self-actualization and effective interpersonal and intergroup relations.
3. Understands that the sexes are both alike and different, that disabled and nondisabled people are alike and different; distinguishes between the similarities that define people as human and the differences that make them unique.
4. Uses a nonsexist, multicultural knowledge base to understand individuals, groups, and events.
5. Demonstrates understanding that cultural, gender, and ability differences do not imply deficiencies.
6. Analyzes own feelings and behaviors toward people of different gender, sexual orientation, or disability status.

Goal 2. To Understand How Group Membership
Helps Determine Values, Attitudes, and Behaviors

Objectives

1. Compares the positive and negative experiences of females and males of different backgrounds and recognizes similarities and differences between and within genders, individuals with and without disabilities and across disability groups, and other cultural groups.
2. Recognizes how different experiences can influence males and females, cultural groups and disabled and nondisabled people to view events, trends, and innovations from various perspectives.
3. Identifies current and historical perspectives of gender, disability, and other cultural groups on issues, events, situations, and developments.
4. Traces specific influences of gender, disability, and culture on verbal and nonverbal interaction styles.
5. Predicts the effects of trends, events, and innovations on gender and cultural groups.
6. Demonstrates open-mindedness about the roles, rights, and responsibilities of persons regardless of gender, sexual orientation, race, disability status, or class.

Goal 3. To Understand the Dynamics of
Discrimination, Bias, Prejudice, and Stereotyping

Objectives

1. Differentiates between individual and institutional sexism, racism, classism, and ableism and knows how inequity is institutionalized.
2. Identifies how prejudice, discrimination, bias, and stereotyping impede interpersonal and intergroup relations.
3. Identifies how prejudice, discrimination, bias, and stereotyping impact aspirations and achievement of individuals and groups.
4. Detects beliefs and actions based on prejudice and bias in self, others, and institutions.
5. Tests cultural/gender information and generalizations for accuracy and uses accurate information as clues for understanding individual and group behaviors and perspectives.
6. Interacts without overgeneralizing (stereotyping) or overcompensating (patronizing).
7. Understands that no individual or group is inherently superior or inferior because of sex, race, disability status, culture, or class.

Goal 4. To Demonstrate Skills for Effective Social Action and Interaction between Gender, Racial, Disability Status, and Other Cultural Groups

Objectives

1. Identifies, describes, or predicts the impact of historical and current events, trends, and innovations on different groups.

2. Considers sex equity and multicultural dimensions in problem solving and decision making.

3. Reconciles points of view in conflicts arising within and between sex, race, ethnic, class, and ability/disability groups.

4. Confronts individual and institutional bias, prejudice, and discrimination in school and community.

5. Identifies, describes, and practices basic civil rights and responsibilities as defined by the Constitution and legislation.

6. Extends own intergroup experiences and understandings.

7. Resolves interpersonal and intergroup conflicts across sex, racial, and disability cultures.

8. Resists impact of stereotypes on self and others in expanding career and economic horizons.

9. Demonstrates respect for physical, sensory, emotional, cognitive, and cultural differences by modeling nonsexist culturally sensitive language and interaction patterns.

STRATEGIES FOR TRANSFORMING CURRICULUM AND INSTRUCTION

Some teacher strategies for achieving the goals and objectives are given below. Listed first are the curriculum strategies (numbers 1–7); listed second are the instructional strategies (numbers 8–14). Special attention should be paid to these for they address the kinds of teacher behaviors that are required for transforming education from the current mainstream model to a nonsexist inclusive model.

1. Infuse each subject area of the curriculum with nonsexist multicultural content including the contributions and perspectives of both genders, people of color, and people/students with disabilities.

2. Review and supplement textbooks, workbooks, computer software, supplementary materials, and media used in all classes and school activities for accurate, balanced, and specific representation of both sexes, people of color, people with disabilities.

3. Provide access to all courses, programs, and activities for students regardless of their race, sex, class status, or disability status.

4. Assure participation in courses, programs, and activities that are desired by male and female students, students of color, students who are poor, or students who are disabled.

5. Include the accurate cultural origins of music, art, games, dances, inventions, discoveries, and literature when they are infused into the curriculum or introduced in a class or in an extracurricular activity.

6. Interact with curriculum committee members and supervisors, administrators, counselors, school board members, parents, and other teachers about the goals and content of nonsexist inclusive curriculum.

7. Check yourself and other faculty members and administrators for familiarity with and requirements of Title IX, Title VI of the Civil Rights Act, Section 504 of the Rehabilitation Act of 1973, the Americans with Disabilities Act, and The Individuals with Disabilities Education Act (IDEA).

8. Vary instructional strategies to meet the needs of both sexes and of different cultural and ability/disability groups of students.

9. Provide diverse role models in the classroom and in all other sites of school instruction and activity; provide diverse role models in different field-related occupations.

10. Provide equitable quantity and quality of attention and questioning to both sexes and diverse student groups in all school instruction sites.

11. Use nonsexist, unbiased, nonderogatory language in classroom instruction and in all other school activities.

12. Provide nonsexist inclusive instruction and learning climate through teacher example, expectation, and support; through classroom materials, media, software, and bulletin boards; through integrated instructional groupings, assignments, and varied teaching and evaluation methods.

13. Infuse instruction with unbiased career information that includes the status of female students, students of color, and students with disabilities in each field of study.

14. Vary methods of teaching concepts, skills, and problem solving to meet the needs of diverse students, to develop interpersonal and intergroup interaction skills, and to provide practice in citizenship and social action.

CLASSROOM APPLICATIONS

The following ideas for classroom implementation in several different content areas are not designed to be a complete curriculum guide. These applications represent some possibilities for exposing students to basic equity education concepts and competencies, rather than precise directive lesson plans about what and how to teach. Use your own knowledge, skills, and resources as you begin to implement a nonsexist, inclusive curriculum. Be guided by your students' interests and imagination, by their needs and experiences. Involve them in goal setting and selection of materials and activities. Classroom strategies and resources are provided in the guidelines for use as starting points for planning and implementing a nonsexist, inclusive curriculum.

Incorporation of nonsexist, inclusive education key concepts, goals, and objectives into various curriculum strands is critical to do to insure that they are not just "added on" to the curriculum but become an integral part of the education program. Teacher strategies and resources are provided, as well as classroom examples and activities for students, with helpful hints for the teacher involved in a particular content area. These strategies and examples are easily adaptable for different grade levels.

Visual Arts

Goal   To understand self and others as cultural beings acting within a cultural context.

Objectives   To understand that people are both alike and different; to distinguish between the similarities that define us as human and the differences that make us unique.

Strategies

1. View, discuss, and compare the works and artistic styles of many different ethnic artists, artists with disabilities, including males and female artists in all groups.
2. Have a schoolwide exhibit of all children's artwork. During the exhibit encourage peer interaction and receptivity to their peers' ideas and to a broadened view of art.

Teacher Resources

Carson, J. 1985. Tell me about your picture. *Instructor*, 94, 40. [Emphasizes how art lessons can develop students' self-confidence when time is provided for discussing their art work.]

Chalmers, F. G. 1996. *Celebrating pluralism: Art education and cultural diversity.* Los Angeles: The J. Paul Getty Trust. [Provides a historical context for multicultural art education and explores the implications for discipline-based art education of the broad themes found in art across cultures.]

Objective   To understand the significance of cultural perspective in understanding self and others.

Strategies

1. Students study the various forms of artistic expression of people/students who represent diversity along the lines of race, ethnicity, gender, disability status, socioeconomic class, rural/urban location; observe and discuss similarities and differences of themes or content and of artistic style such as use of color, symbols, texture, form, and line.
2. Students create a cooperative wall mural using mixed media on the theme of homes and housing in urban and rural parts of the United States.

Teacher Resources

Paley, N. 1995. *Finding art's place—Experiments in contemporary education and culture.* New York: Routledge. [See chapter 2, where Tim Rollins shares experiences and successes generated from his teaching art with inner-city students, the majority of whom were minorities and had been labeled as having a learning disability or emotional/behavioral disorder.]

Rozelle, R., A. Wardlaw, and M. McKenna, eds. 1990. *Black art ancestral legacy—The African impulse in African-American art.* Dallas: Museum of Art and New York: Harry N. Abrams.

Language Arts, Interdisciplinary Arts

Goal   To understand how group membership helps determine values, attitudes, and behaviors.

Objective   To trace specific influences of gender, culture, social class, and disability status on verbal and nonverbal interaction styles.

Strategies

1. Students read stories, poems, and plays written by and about different gender, cultural, social class, and ability/disability groups. A good choice for secondary students is the play "Fires in the Mirror," by playwright Anna DeVeare Smith, the story of the conflict between African Americans and a group of Jews in Crown Heights, New York. Another recently produced play, "Having Our Say—

The Delany Sisters' First 100 Years," is by playwright and producer Emily Mann, based on the book by the same title. It is the story of two African American sisters told in the tradition of African griots. For younger students, role play characters in the selections you choose.

Teacher Resources

Allen, P. G. 1992, 1986. *The sacred hoop—Recovering the feminine in American Indian traditions.* Boston: Beacon.

Delany, S. L., and A. E. Delany (with A. H. Hearth). 1993. *Having our say: The Delany sisters' first 100 years.* New York: Dell.

Fries, K., ed. 1997. *Staring back: The disability experience from inside out.* New York: Plume/Penguin Books.

Maitino, J. R., and D. R. Peck. 1996. *Teaching American ethnic literatures.* Albuquerque: University of New Mexico Press.

2. Study the relationship between music and religion among African Americans. Use audio and video tapes of their music and invite appropriate guest speakers.

Teacher Resources

Allen-Sommerville, L. 2000. African American "church music" in the classroom: A cultural portrait. In *Multicultural education: Awareness, strategies, and activities* (2nd ed.). Edited by T. McCormick and L. Allen-Sommerville. Dubuque, Iowa: Kendall/Hunt, 75–80.

History, Art, Media

Goal   To understand the dynamics of discrimination, bias, prejudice, and stereotyping.

Objective   To understand that neither sex nor any cultural or ability/disability group is inherently superior or inferior.

Strategies

1. In small groups, have students examine photographs of artwork by women of different cultural, age, and ability/disability groups in various popular magazines, including art magazines. Research the historic exclusion of women artists, artists with disabilities, and artists of color in museums, exhibits, and books.

2. Read about the artistic contributions and history of several of these artists: Elizabeth Layton, Faith Ringgold, Frida Kahlo, Helen Frankenthaler, Juanita Martinez, Isabel Bishop, Blanche Lazzell, Georgia O'Keefe, John Biggers, Edward A. Love, and Richmond Barthe.

Teacher Resources

Cahan, S., and Z. Kocur, eds. 1996. *Contemporary art and multicultural education.* New York: Routledge.

Kent, D., and K. Quinlan. 1996. *Extraordinary people with disabilities.* New York: Children's Press/Grolier Publishing.

Turner, R. M. 1993. *Faith Ringgold: Portraits of women artists for children.* Boston: Little, Brown.

Performing Arts, Dance

Goal   To demonstrate skills for effective social action and interaction among gender, racial, ethnic, and ability/disability groups.

Objective   To extend own cross-gender and cross-cultural experience and understandings.

Strategies

1. Students learn that all cultural groups have contributed to dance in the United States. Dance and other performance arts have been vehicles through which many marginalized people have expressed resistance to oppression in their lives and, in some cases, have used their performance to bring about social change. Invite a folk dance troupe to perform at the school and to conduct dance workshops.

2. Guide the students in exploring dance as employed in theater arts with its varied cultural and regional influences. Research these groups for their contributions to dance: Dance Theater of Harlem, Martha Graham Dance Company, or the Ko-Thi Dance Company.

3. Arrange for performers with disabilities to speak or perform or show a videotape highlighting performers with disabilities.

Teacher Resources

Ko-Thi Dance Company, "A Milwaukee Treasure," established in 1969, is the only professional arts organization in Wisconsin dedicated to African, African American, and Caribbean traditional dance and music.

Weiner, J., and J. Lidstone. 1969. *Creative movement for children.* New York: Van Nostrand Reinhold.

Physical Education, Health

Goal   To understand self and others as cultural beings acting within a cultural context.

Objective   To choose and use a variety of interaction and learning styles as tools for self-actualization and for functioning across genders, abilities, and cultures.

Strategies

1. Students play a cooperative game in which there are no winners or losers based on physical abilities. A good game is called "Knots" where the objective is to "untie" a chain of people using physical and verbal cooperation. After the knot is untied, facilitate a discussion about the students' feelings about this cooperative game.

2. Students attend a game of wheelchair basketball or tennis or invite athletes with disabilities to speak to the class.

Teacher Resources

Michaelis, B., and D. Michaelis. 1977. *Learning through noncompetitive activities and play.* Palo Alto, Calif.: Education Today Co. ["Knots" is described in this book, 75–76.]

Sapon-Shevin, M. 1999. *Because we can change the world: A practical guide to building cooperative, inclusive class-room communities.* Boston: Allyn & Bacon.

Vace, N.A., S. B. DeVaney, and J. Wittmer. 1995. *Experiencing and counseling diverse populations.* Bristol, Pa.: Accelerated Development.

Sociology, Health, Media

Goal   To understand the dynamics of discrimination, bias, prejudice, and stereotyping.

Objective   To analyze own feelings and behaviors toward those who are different from ourselves.

Strategies

1. Students conduct interviews with low-income families that are headed by single females or families that have a member who has a disability. Develop interview questions regarding health needs, foods, and how nutritional and other requirements are met on a limited budget. Different kinds of questions will need to be developed according to the type of discrimination being addressed. For example, a question for a low-income family that has a member with a disability: "Does he/she have special dietary needs?" If so, then ask, "How much will these foods cost?" Then plan a week of menus and prepare a shopping list (actual grocery store prices of items needed

to prepare the meals) for a low-income family of one adult and two preschool children, one of whom has a physical disability, on a budget of twenty dollars.

2. Assign research projects on different forms of health care, including the perspective that current concepts and practices of health care are culturally conditioned. Discuss folk medicine, remedies, and practices (e.g., midwifery) that still affect the health of people with disabilities, poor people, and men and women and different ethnic and cultural groups.

Teacher Resources

Doane, N. 1980–1985. *Indian doctor book: Nature's method of curing and preventing disease according to the Indians.* Charlotte, N.C.: Aerial Photography Services.

Krotoski, D., M. Nosek, and M. Turk, eds. 1996. *Women with physical disabilities: Achieving and maintaining health and well being.* Baltimore: Paul H. Brookes.

Takaki, R. 1994. *From different shores: Perspectives on race and ethnicity in America.* New York: Oxford University Press. [See part 5, "Gender," 161–213.]

Thiederman, S. 1986. Ethnocentrism: A barrier to effective health care. *Nurse Practitioner,* 10(8):52–59.

Goal   To demonstrate skills for effective social action and interaction among gender, racial, ethnic, ability/disability, and cultural groups.

Objective   To consider nonsexist, multicultural issues in problem solving and in decision making.

Strategies

1. Students monitor local newspaper coverage and television coverage of the participation of male and female people of color and people/students with disabilities in sports events, in political races, in crime reports. Evaluate whether there is bias or balance and proportionality in the media coverage. Devise an action plan to address any imbalances or biases found in the media coverage (e.g., reporting more cases of black male crime than white male crime in a community that is 97 percent white). The plan might include a letter-writing campaign to the local television stations and newspapers to share the results of the students' surveys and then a call for more accurate reporting.

2. Students collect a file of advertisements for health care products and services. Assess them for fair and unbiased inclusion of females,

people of color, and people with disabilities in illustrations, language, and content. Redesign the ads in class, then write letters to the advertisers making suggestions for changes where bias is found.

Teacher Resources

Collins, T., M. Schneider, and S. Kroger. 1995, Fall. (Dis)Abling images. *Radical Teacher* 47:11–14.

Gitlin, T. ed. 1986. *Watching television: A pantheon guide to popular culture.* New York: Random House.

MEDIA WATCH, 1803 Mission St., Suite 7, Santa Cruz, Cal. (408) 423–6355. A watch dog group that monitors media advertising industry for bias; contact, Ann Simonton.

Olson, A. M., C. Parr, and D. Parr, eds. 1991. *Video icons and values.* Albany: State University of New York Press.

SUMMARY

This chapter provides background information on a continuum of curriculum and instruction models. The frameworks of feminist, disability, and critical multiculturalist theory and pedagogy are provided to give a foundation for the transformative curriculum model for nonsexist inclusive education. Its characteristics are described; then the key concepts, goals, and objectives are delineated; and finally, classroom applications in six discipline clusters (with teacher strategies and resources) are detailed.

REFERENCES

Banks, J. A. 1997. *Teaching strategies for ethnic studies.* Boston: Allyn and Bacon.

Belenky, M., B. Clinchy, N. Goldberger, and J. Tarule. 1986. *Women's ways of knowing.* New York: Basic Books.

Bloom, L. R. 1998. *Under the sign of hope—Feminist methodology and narrative interpretation.* Albany: State University of New York Press.

Cassuto, L. 1999, March 19. Whose field is it, anyway? Disability studies in the academy. *The Chronicle of Higher Education,* XLV(28):A60.

Code, L. 1991. *What can she know? Feminist theory and the construction of knowledge.* Ithaca, N.Y.: Cornell University Press.

Collins, P. H. 1990. *Black feminist thought: Knowledge, consciousness, and the politics of empowerment.* New York and London: Routledge.

———. 1998. *Fighting words—Black women and the search for justice.* Minneapolis: University of Minnesota Press.

Darling-Hammond, L. 1990. *Restructuring education: Women's work.* Keynote paper presented at the sixteenth annual conference of Research on Women and Education (Special Interest Group of American Educational Research Association), Milwaukee.

Davis, L., and S. Linton. 1995. Disability studies: Introduction. *Radical Teacher* 47:2.

Gill, C. 1995, Fall. A psychological view of disability culture. *Disability Studies Quarterly*, 15 (4):16–19.

Gilligan, C. 1982. *In a different voice—Psychological theory and women's development*. Cambridge: Harvard University Press.

Gollnick, D. M., and P. C. Chinn. 1998. *Multicultural education in a pluralistic society*. Upper Saddle, N.J.: Prentice-Hall.

Grant, C. A., and J. M. Sachs. 1995. Multicultural education and postmodernism: Movement toward a dialogue. In *Critical multiculturalism: Uncommon voices in a common struggle*. Edited by B. Kanpol and P. McLaren. Westport, Conn.: Bergin and Garvey, 89–105.

Kanpol, B., and P. McLaren, eds. 1995. *Critical multiculturalism: Uncommon voices in a common struggle*. Westport, Conn.: Bergin and Garvey.

Laird, S. 1988. Reforming "woman's true profession": A case for "feminist pedagogy" in teacher education? *Harvard Educational Review* 58(4):449–463.

Linton, S. [1998] *Claiming disability: Knowledge and identity*. New York and London: New York University Press.

Mairs, N. 1997. Body, mind, and soul: An interview with Nancy Mairs. Interviewed by Susan Skubik. *The World: The Journal of the Unitarian Universalist Association* 11(5):14–19.

Martin, J. R. 1984. Bring women into educational thought. *Educational Theory* 34:341–354.

McCormick, T. E. 1982. *A comparison of key multicultural education concepts used by theorists, practitioners and education organizations*. Unpublished dissertation. West Virginia University.

———. 1984, Spring. Multiculturalism: Some principles and issues. *Theory into Practice* 23(2):93–97.

———. 1990. The multicultural life of the child. In *Early childhood social studies*. Edited by C. Sunal. Columbus: Merrill, 107–129.

———. 1994. *Creating the nonsexist classroom: A multicultural approach*. New York: Teachers College Press.

McGuiness, D. 1985. *When children don't learn*. New York: Basic Books.

Noddings, N. 1990. Feminist critiques in the professions. In *Review of Research in Education* 393–424. Edited by C. Cazden. Washington, D.C.: American Educational Research Association.

———. 1992. *The challenge to care in schools: An alternative approach to education*. New York: Teachers College Press.

Schubert, W. H. 1993. Curriculum reform. In *Challenges and achievements in American education*. Edited by G. Cawelti. Alexandria, Va.: Association for Supervision and Curriculum Development, 80–115.

Sleeter, C. E., and C. A. Grant. 1994. *Making choices for multicultural education: Five approaches to race, class, and gender*. New York: Merrill.

Takaki, R. 1994. *From different shores: Perspectives on race and ethnicity in America*. New York and Oxford: Oxford University Press.

Warren, K. 1989. Rewriting the future: The feminist challenge to the male-stream curriculum. *Feminist Teacher* 4:46–52.

Welch, O. M. 1995. Exceptional children from diverse cultures: An overlooked population in the movement toward inclusion. In *Developing multicultural teacher education curricula*, 247–258. Edited by J. M. Larkin and C. E. Sleeter. Albany: State University of New York Press.

CHAPTER 11

Uncovering Bias in the Classroom:
A Personal Journey

Maryann Wickett

The school at which I teach is located in northern San Diego County, California, about seventy miles from the U.S.-Mexico border. We have eleven hundred students. The class I describe in this chapter was a multi-grade third- and fourth-grade class with thirty-two students, sixteen boys and sixteen girls. My fourth-grade students had been with me as third graders and made up about half the class. The students spoke several primary languages. About half spoke English as their first language, a quarter spoke Spanish, one Russian, one French, one Arabic, one Japanese, and two Tagalog. There were four students who participated in the Resource Specialist Program, a pull-out program to meet the needs of children with average or above average IQs but who are not performing academically as expected. There were two gifted students. About two-thirds of the class was eligible for Title I assistance.

I had participated in two statewide mathematics education projects: the California Elementary Mathematics Initiative and the Equity in Mathematics Education Project. Both emphasized the importance of teachers reflecting on their classroom practices to improve educational opportunities for all children. The issues of equity and access were important to me. I decided to take a careful look at what was going on in my classroom, so I could improve the educational experience of all my students.

One hears about issues of gender equity frequently. While I hoped, even tried to believe, this was not the situation in my classroom, it was something I had wondered about. Are my girls being cheated in mathematics? If so, are my boys being cheated in language arts? Who else is being cheated? What about my students receiving special education services? My students who are nonnative English speakers? Why are some students more reluctant than others? Am I unaware of practices I use during classroom discussions that systematically silence some students? Have my behaviors hindered some while giving greater access to others?

SEARCHING FOR ANSWERS

What I am about to share is an intimate look at myself and my practices as I searched for answers to these questions. No one is born prejudiced. All forms of bias, from extreme bigotry to cultural biases of which we are unaware, are acquired by (actually imposed on) the young person and are dysfunctional (Weissglass, 1997). To become aware of how my biases were affecting my classroom practices, I had to understand how my own life experiences have affected who I am and, consequently, the development of my own biases. As a participant in the Equity in Mathematics Education Project, I had the opportunity to do this. I listened as people shared their stories. I had the chance to share mine. As a result, I began to discover how my biases were affecting my classroom practices. I discovered I had the power to make changes as I gained a deeper understanding of myself. As a result of this examination, I could make positive changes by considering various practices, keeping those that made sense, and altering those that needed to be changed. Educational change must be grounded in personal and concrete understandings (Weissglass, 1997). The focus of my self-reflection was to gain personal insights that would enable me to become a more effective teacher. For me, becoming a more effective teacher meant giving access, support, and respect to all students during whole group discussion.

Gathering information about my classroom practices posed a problem. I had considered videotaping my teaching to find out what I was doing. I was concerned, however, that if I knew I was being taped I would be on my "best behavior." I wanted information on what I was doing subconsciously, day-in and day-out. Audiotaping and peer scripting of my lessons posed the same problem as videotaping. As I pursued my self-study, however, I found research that contradicted these beliefs. This research indicated that even when one knows the camera is on, videotaping will show many teachers unintentionally but systematically demonstrating their biases (Kaplan and Aronson, 1994). Despite these research findings, I still had my doubts and concerns.

RECORDING CLASS DISCUSSIONS

As part of my classroom routine, I record students' responses on charts as the discussion progresses. A student's contribution is recorded word for word with that student's name noted after the contribution. (In the beginning, I ask students for their permission to record their contribution. Students have the right to revise their ideas or ask that their response not be recorded.) Recording students' contributions has several benefits. First, writing student responses gives a context for modeling correct punctuation, capitalization, and spelling. Next, it helps students see the relationship between the spoken and written word and provides auditory and visual modes of presentation. Also, it gives me a written record of student contributions I can use for reflection after the lesson. Relatedly, it allows students to review and reflect on past experiences, enabling them to make connections from one activity to another. Most important, my recording shows students that I respect their contributions and that their ideas are important enough to be recorded. My intent is to show students respect, build confidence, and encourage thinking, sharing, and listening to create an inclusive, supportive learning environment.

This practice of recording provided me with the information I needed to examine my practices. Because I had charts that covered several weeks of discussions, I could use the information they provided to take an objective look at the dynamics of whole group discussions in my classroom. I would be able to make deliberate changes in my instructional behavior that would help ensure more equitable teaching.

What I Found

Examining these charts, I found that in most cases I called on two boys before calling on a girl. Overall, I called on more girls (52 percent of the time), but boys were provided the first opportunity to respond. In addition, I found that I tended to include students who were nonnative English speakers, who received special education services, or who were shy or reluctant only toward the end of a discussion, and I found that I often did not probe or ask additional questions of these students. When I did ask them follow-up questions, the questions were more knowledge based, compared to the higher-level, application-type questions I asked boys and more verbal students. In short, I found unexpected patterns of bias that were personally upsetting to me.

I had to consider why this was happening. It was usually the same small group of boys who gained initial recognition. They were bright, enthusiastic, verbal, and wriggly. Their behavior caught my attention more quickly than the quieter, reflective students. I may have called on them partly to control their behavior. I believed the other students—the girls, students who were nonnative English speakers, students receiving special education services, and those students who needed a few extra moments to respond—would wait. I also believed these boys had a lot to contribute to the discussion and often their comments triggered ideas for other students.

I value my students' opinions and frequently tell them what I am thinking and ask them for their thoughts. One morning I began class by explaining I was interested in my habits as a teacher and wanted their input about what they thought I was doing. I asked them who they thought I called on first in math, boys or girls. I gave them a few minutes to consider their answers. They were given the following choices as answers: "boys called on first," "girls called on first," "it seemed about equal," or "they didn't know." Students raised their hands to indicate their opinion. I also used this process to gather information about language arts. Their responses were interesting. In language arts, they felt I called on girls first, but in math, I called on boys first. Their perception matched the reality recorded on the class discussion charts. While disappointed in myself, this information provided an opportunity to make positive changes in the way I ran class discussions.

While the charts captured an important part of discourse in my classroom, they didn't capture everything. I was only recording students' responses, not who was volunteering but not being called on, my questioning, my responses, my body language, and so forth. This was not intended to be a scientific study but rather an expanded use of a recording method I already had in place to look at my own biases. I had enough information that I could make changes yet not so much information that I felt overwhelmed and defeated. The idea to use the class discussion charts for this purpose occurred to me after I had established them as an ongoing practice. Other possible sources of information I could have used were student reflections on what happened in class, including journal entries, group projects, reflections, responses to such questions as "How did you feel about your learning?" or "How do you feel about this discussion?"

THE PROCESS OF CHANGE

By examining my practices honestly, without condemning myself, I was able to try new ideas with my students' best interests in mind. Some of the changes I've made as a result of this process are given below.

Use of Dyads

I make certain to use dyads whenever possible. In a dyad, students are paired, and each receives an equal amount of time to talk while the other student listens without interruption (Weissglass, 1996). Dyads offer all students the opportunity to be heard, to listen, to consider other ideas, and to have their ideas considered. They build self-esteem and give students the chance to clarify their thoughts and build confidence. In addition, dyads keep students engaged and thinking about the topic at hand and afford all students the chance to think about topics or issues before they participate in a class discussion or undertake a written assignment.

Equitable Attention

I now make a conscious effort to give all children opportunities to respond first and equally in all class discussions. Whenever possible, I have visitors or my student teachers script class discussions. I continue to monitor my behavior through the charted recordings of class discussions. Before calling on a child, I pause to consider who has been heard and who is still waiting to be heard. Not only does this pause enable me to make better decisions about whom to call upon, but it also allows students additional time to think about their, responses. This additional time gives students who process information more slowly an opportunity to formulate their thoughts, thereby allowing them greater access to class discussions.

Challenge All Students to Think Deeply about Issues

Besides making a conscious effort to give all students equal opportunity in and access to class discussions, I also consider the types of questions I ask all students. Because my goal is not only to ensure equity and access to discussions but also to teach them how to think deeply about issues, I routinely ask questions that require explanation or justification of their thinking process. Students are encouraged to question or state their agreement or disagreement with each other or me. Encouraging discussion, providing response time, and asking questions that require students to explain their thought process both show students that I value their input and reinforce their use of thinking strategies.

ENCOURAGING THE MATHEMATICIAN
IN ALL CHILDREN

As I consciously work to correct my biases and encourage children to share their thoughts, conversations such as the one that follows become more routine. Note how the children interact respectfully with one another. One morning I began math with my fourth-grade students by showing them two numbers, 48 and 12. I instructed them to write a story problem that could be solved by multiplication using these numbers. They were to estimate the product and justify their estimation. They quickly shared their work with a partner, then we began the following class discussion:

> AUTUMN: This is the story problem I wrote. There were 48 kids in a pet shop. Each kid wanted 12 goldfish. If each kid gets 12 goldfish, about how many goldfish would the storekeeper get out?

> JUAN: You could make 48 into 50 by rounding to the nearest 10. You could make 12 into 10 by rounding to the nearest 10 too. 50 X 10 would equal 500. I think it would be about 500 fish.

> ALISA: In a way mine is sort of like Juan's. I did it by drawing a picture. I put a 1 in a circle and that equaled 50. I got 50 by rounding, like Juan. Then I put the two circles together and made pairs that equaled 100. There were six pairs and that would equal 600. So I think it would be about 600 fish. (As assigned, Alisa had written her own problem that involved children at the playground. Her drawing indicates this. However, the discussion could take place even though different problems were written as all students used the same numbers and the same operation.)

> LORI: Juan and Alisa sort of did the same thing, like they rounded 48 to 50, but they got different answers. I don't get why.

FIGURE 11.1

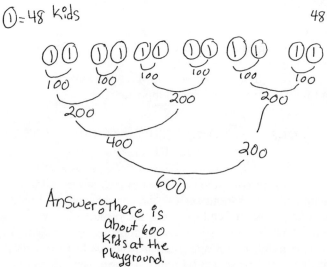

BERNITA: I think it's because Juan rounded 12 to 10 and Alisa used all twelve. That's how she got the six pairs of 50.

ALISA: Bernita's right. I didn't round the 12 to 10. I didn't think to do it.

BETH: I rounded 48 to 50 like Juan and Alisa. Then I thought, hmm . . . 50 X 12. I see a basic fact, 12 X 5. That makes 60. I know that if 12 X 5 equals 60 then 12 X 50 equals 600 because it is multiples of ten.

RICK: I thought of just multiplying 48 X 10. That equals 480.

SARA: I did it by division.

TODD: How come you always do the opposite? You solve multiplication by division and division by multiplication. Why don't you just do it straight instead of crossing back and forth like that?

SARA: You interrupted me. I like to do the opposite because it makes it more interesting. Anyway, I guessed that the product of 48 X 12 would be 400. So I divided 400 by 50, and it only equaled 8. I knew 400 wasn't big enough. It was missing 2 50s or 100, so I added 100 to 400 to equal 500 then divided 500 by 50, and it equaled 10, which is what 12 rounds to.

ANA: I just did repeated addition in my head. I thought of 48 as 50 and 12 as 10 and counted in my brain by 50s ten times, and it equaled 500. But I also just added two more 50s to make 12, which is 600 because it was easy, and I could get a better estimate that way.

MIKE: When Ana said what she did, I thought I could do it sort of the same and sort of opposite of what she did. Others were estimating 500, so I started at 500 and counted backwards by 50, and it took 10 times to get to 0.

DON: I was looking at the numbers, and I don't know if this always works, but I did it anyway. I took 2 ones away from 12 and that made 10. Then I added the 2 ones from the 12 to the 48 and that made 48 equal 50. Then I did what Juan did.

Why is this a valuable activity to do with children? In terms of math, it develops number sense. Students must justify their thinking, which develops voice. They gain confidence by sharing their ideas while considering different ways to think about problems as a result of listening to their peers. In terms of giving all children access, students carried on the above conversation with little intervention from me. Included in the conversation were girls, boys, students who were nonnative English speakers, students receiving special education services, and gifted students. They responded to each other adding their own thoughts and opinions respectfully.

All children have "mathematical promise." Alisa, Rick, and Sara fit the typical definition of mathematical promise, but also clearly showing evidence of mathematical promise are Lori, Beth, Juan, and Don, students who have been identified as needing special education services, and Bernita, who is a nonnative English speaker. The content focus of my examination of my teaching practices has been on mathematics, but what I learned carries across all subject areas and grade levels. As educators, it is our responsibility to carefully examine our practices, constantly searching for better ways to reach and include all children. It is their right and our responsibility.

NOTE

Much of this chapter was taken from Wickett, M. (1997), *Uncovering bias in the classroom: A personal journey*, in J. Trentacosta and M. J. Kenney (Eds.), Multicultural and gender equity in mathematics classroom—The gift of diversity. Published by the National Council of Teachers in Mathematics (Reston, VA). Used here with permission of the publisher.

REFERENCES

Kaplan, J., and D. Aronson. 1994. The numbers gap. *Teaching Tolerance*, 20–27.

Weissglass, J. 1996. Transforming schools into caring learning communities: The social and psychological dimensions of educational change. *Journal of a Just and Caring Education* 2 (2), 175–89.

Weissglass, J. 1997. *Ripples of hope: Building relationships for educational change*. Santa Barbara, Calif.: Center for Educational Change in Mathematics and Science.

SECTION III

Gender Issues in the Education of Students with Disabilities

CHAPTER 12

Research on Gender Bias in Special Education Services

Michael L. Wehmeyer and Michelle Schwartz

The primary purpose of this book is to introduce teachers (or teachers in training) working with students with disabilities to issues pertaining to gender equity and the impact of gender bias in the educational process. As far as we are aware, the book is unique in this focus, in part because, despite the importance of gender equity issues in educational reform efforts over the past several decades, there has been little research on gender equity and bias in the education of students with disabilities. We do know, as reviewed by chapters in the first two sections of this text, there is abundant evidence of gender inequity in the education of nondisabled girls and young women. We also know, as evidenced by the comprehensive review of the literature related to vocational and employment outcomes for women with disabilities presented in chapter 13 (Doren and Benz), that there is ample data suggesting that young women with disabilities leave school to less successful outcomes than both males with disabilities and nondisabled men and women. While recognizing that multiple and complex factors contribute to postsecondary outcomes, it seems a viable assumption that at least one factor contributing to these less desirable outcomes is gender bias in the education of students with disabilities. There is no reason to believe that girls and young women with disabilities do not experience many of the same biases and stereotypes based on gender that impact the educational experiences of nondisabled girls. This chapter examines what is known about gender bias in the education of students with disabilities and introduces an inservice training program to provide information on gender equity for teachers working with students with disabilities.

What Do We Know?

In 1986, Kratovil and Bailey made the following observation, from which the title of this text was drawn: "Little attention has been given to the 'double jeopardy' that confronts disabled students when bias and stereotyping based on sex and on disabling condition interact. Consequently, disabled students may face unacknowledged barriers to equitable education—barriers that are products of stereotyping and bias based both on sex and on disabling condition" (pp. 250–56). Unfortunately, as this text is being prepared, fully fifteen years later, Kratovil and Bailey's statement remains largely true. We can still assert (albeit regretfully) that little attention has been given to the double jeopardy of disability and gender in the education of students with disabilities.

The chapters in this book describe a number of ways we have come to "know" that gender bias impacts the education of girls and young women, from differences in teacher interactions or curriculum, gaps in math and science between boys and girls, or the experiences of sexual harassment and its devastating consequences. The header of this section asks, rhetorically, what do we "know" about gender bias and its impact on girls and boys who receive special education services and supports? While we may extrapolate from what we know about gender bias and the educational experiences of all girls and reasonably posit that these same experiences impact girls and young women with disabilities in similar ways, the truth is that according to research-based knowledge, we can answer that question quite succinctly: not much.

Singer and Osborn (1970) concluded three decades ago that some combination of social class, age, and sex were affecting differences in the numbers of males and females with mental retardation admitted into treatment centers. They posed some of the following hypotheses about males and females with mental retardation: (1) societal expectations are higher for males than females; (2) accomplishments are more important for males than for females; and (3) IQ differences between males and females at time of admission to special education services hint at lowered expectations for the women. While these authors' assumptions about the superiority of males is reminiscent of earlier eras, they were among the first to note an important factor affecting gender equity for students with disabilities: societal expectations by gender play an important role in determining what happens to people on the margins of the education system. That is, if society as a whole places less value on the role of women while setting low expectations for people with disabilities, then the expectations for women with disabilities will be very low indeed.

In 1974, Gillespie and Fink suggested that special education curricular and course materials are heavily sex-role stereotyped and hypothesized that vocational choices for students with and without disabilities may be forfeited due to stereotyping based on traditional sex roles. For example, Gillespie and Fink pointed out that certain curricular programs lead females to learn to be housewives, while males can learn carpentry or mechanical skills (Gillespie and Fink, 1974). More than a decade later, Kratovil and Bailey (1986) reviewed the extant literature in equity in special education and suggested that males with disabilities were identified for special education services (1) more frequently, (2) at a younger age, (3) with a higher level of intelligence and that (4) males with disabilities more easily and more frequently received related and support services once in special education. These earlier studies were largely speculative or based on anecdotal reports. The 1985 summary of "sex differences in educating the handicapped" prepared by Williamson-Ige and McKitric exemplifies the lack of research-based information on gender bias and stereotyping in the education of students with disabilities at that time by identifying only three studies in this area and summarizing the knowledge base with the following statement: "While handicapped [sic] students in general receive inferior vocational training, handicapped [sic] females are subjected to the worst violations in this area" (p. 73).

Moreover, until recently the primary focus of investigations of issues pertaining to gender discrimination in the education of students with disabilities were in the areas of vocational education and vocational outcomes. Because vocational issues are comprehensively examined elsewhere in this volume (Doren and Benz), as are teacher-student interactions (Grayson), we will not address those findings here. Instead, we examine research findings that contribute to the larger base of "what we know" about gender bias and special education.

GENDER BIAS AND SPECIAL EDUCATION SERVICES

*Gender Bias in Referral and Admission
to Special Education Services*

There is one area, bias in admission and referral to special education services, that has generated enough of a research base over the last fifteen years to warrant an overview. The issue has been a focal point for investigation primarily because of the link between admission and referral practices and the single most consistent characteristic of special education in the past two decades; the disproportionate number of males served (Anderson, 1997; Andrews, Wisniewski, and Mulick, 1997; Harmon, Stockton, and Contrucci, 1992; Lloyd, 1991; McIntyre, 1988; Reschly, 1996; Russo and Talbert-Johnson, 1997; Shinn, Tindal, and Spira, 1987). Many reports have documented that boys receiving special education services outnumber girls two to one. For example, the 1992 Report to Congress on the implementation of IDEA reported that more than two-thirds (68.5 percent) of secondary age students served in special education were males, even though the percentage of school-age nondisabled males was 49.7 percent. Males were disproportionately represented in every disability category except for deaf-blindness. Learning and emotional disabilities were the most disproportionate categories, with males comprising 73.4 percent and 76.4 percent of each, respectively.

Three hypotheses have been forwarded to explain the preponderance of males in special education: biology, behavior, and bias. First, overrepresentation is attributable to biological factors because boys are more vulnerable to some genetically determined disorders and predisposed to have some specific learning disabilities, particularly those related to reading disorders where males outnumber females five to one (Lyon, 1996; Reschly, 1996). It is established that females have some biological advantages over males, such as fewer biologically based disabilities at birth and more rapid maturation (Harmon et al., 1992). Second, because boys are more active and likely misbehave, researchers have also suggested that the overrepresentation of males is a function of behavior problems. Although genetic, biological, or neurophysiological differences may contribute to levels of activity for boys, behavior problems based on early learning may also influence referral and placement decisions. Kedar-Voivodas (1983) noted that child rearing practice, sex role modeling, imitation, socialization, and a student's reaction to school influence the repertoire of behavior of girls and boys in the classroom. Boys may learn early that adults are tolerant of their active behavior, while girls are encouraged to behave in more inhibited ways, passive, quiet, obedient, and pleasant (Blackorby and Wagner, 1996). As such, male overrepresentation may be a function of referral bias. Referral bias is the degree to which persons responsible for referring students for evaluation for eligibility in special education, typically teachers in regular education classrooms, make such referrals based upon personal and professional opinions rather than objective indicators.

Shaywitz and colleagues (1996) suggested that referral bias indicates that "teachers' perceptions of what constitutes inappropriate behavior enter into the decision and that, in particular, over-activity and behavioral difficulties are likely to be disruptive to a classroom and to influence decisions regarding such children" (p. 1002). Research suggests, however, that the problem is more complex than simply teachers referring males due to behavior problems. Shinn, Tindall, and Spira (1987) noted two types of errors possible in teacher referrals: (1) bias and (2) teacher inaccuracy or "the extent to which teachers' appraisal of pupil performance is confirmed by objective criteria" (p. 33). These authors identified all students in a district referred for special education because of a reading problem during one school year. They administered a measure of reading to each referred student and then determined the local norms for reading level using the same measure with students in the general population. Teacher accuracy was determined by whether referrals were accurate or inaccurate when compared with the objective measure of reading ability. Teacher bias was determined by using student achievement data as a dependent measure and documenting the proportion of referred students as a function of sex and ethnicity. Referred males and females were equivalent in performance on measures of their reading skills, but relative to the population base-rates of poor readers, there were significantly more males than females referred.

Shinn and colleagues' (1987) examination of teacher accuracy concluded that teachers were, in fact, quite accurate about the reading abilities of students they referred. Across all grades and all analyses, referred students had significant reading problems when compared with local norms. However, the distribution of achievement scores for the referred students fell within the normative distribution for the measure, and Shinn and colleagues noted that "for every referred student, a substantial number of others in the normative population performed similarly" (p. 39). These authors suggested, given the reality of limited teaching resources, teachers decide that not all low readers need to be referred, but instead only those who are poor readers and have some associated school problems, such as hyperactivity or aggression, or those that "do not meet the biases of the teacher" (p. 39).

MacMillan and colleagues (1996) studied the nomination of students to prereferral interventions in California, where students having difficulty are identified for efforts to remedy the problem in the child's typical classroom. They administered a battery of assessments to 150 students, grades two through four, who had been nominated for prereferral interventions. This sample was 60 percent male and 40 percent female. There was no significant difference by gender on intelligence or achievement tests for this sample, although teachers rated females as having higher academic competence, and there were statistical differences for gender on two teacher ratings of problem behaviors and social skills. Males were rated as exhibiting more problem behaviors and lower levels of social skills than females on one scale and were scored higher on scales measuring conduct problems, hyperactivity, and inattentiveness on the other instrument. These authors suggested that the combination of more, and more severe, behavior problems combined with poor achievement led to their referral.

A third reason for the disproportionate number of males (i.e., in addition to biologically based differences and the greater likelihood of boys displaying behavior problems), suggested by Kratovil and Bailey (1986), was influences of gender bias on the referral, classification, and placement process. We should note that gender equitable education does not mean, a priori, that there will or should be an equal number of males and females receiving special education services. Gender equity or fairness, used interchangeably here, refers to conditions in which one's position, conclusion, or behavior is impartial, free from discrimination, prejudice, or judgment based on gender (Reber, 1985). Equitable practices are those in which both males and females who qualify for and can benefit from special education are served (Rousso and Wehmeyer, 2000).

We acknowledge it is too simplistic to suggest that any one of these factors accounts exclusively for male overrepresentation. For example, issues of referral due to behavior and referral due to bias and stereotypes related to race and ethnicity are confounded. Males from African American families are disproportionately represented in special education services. This is partly due to cultural biases in testing, a lack of cultural competence and understanding on the part of referring teachers, and stereotypes about males from minority backgrounds. However, it is fair to note that too few efforts have been made to parcel out the impact of gender bias on referral, placement, and admission to special education services. Wehmeyer and Schwartz (in press) attempted to address this gap by conducting a records review of every student, six years of age and older, who had been admitted to special education for the first time during a one-year span at three different school districts. There were a total of 695 students admitted to receive special education during the time period examined. Consistent with national norms, males outnumbered girls almost exactly 2 to 1 (462 males, 233 females). We collected demographic data and indicators of the contribution (if any) of each of the three factors (biology, behavior, and bias) on admission. Data related to sex-linked conditions, severe health conditions, sensory disorders, co-occurrence of reading problems and nonconforming behavior (disorders of conduct, disorders of overactivity and/or aggression) were collected to provide some information about the presence of biological or behavioral factors. Data were also collected about students' gender, ethnicity, and date of admission to special education services, the person who referred the student for eligibility examination, primary and secondary disability category, placement (regular classroom, resource room, self-contained classroom, separate campus, other), and standardized intelligence and adaptive behavior scores used at time of admission.

To account as much as possible for those disorders with identified biological explanations, we gathered information on each student's diagnosis, and students with conditions with biological correlates were then eliminated from further analysis. To examine the impact of behavior on admission, we collected data from a referral document completed by general education teachers who referred the student for examination for eligibility for special education services. This information was uniformly available from one district only, resulting in a sample of 115 student referral sheets (74 males, 41 females). From the referral sheet, we gathered data about gender, the reason for referral, and information about the student's grade. In addition, referring teachers completed a classroom observation form quantifying the student's receptive and expressive language skills, emotional/behavioral/social skills, motor coordination, and academic characteristics.

To examine gender equitable admission practices, we considered bias due to gender stereotyping and examined several of the indicators suggested by Kratovil and Bailey (1986), Gillespie and Fink (1974), and National Longitudinal Transition Study data (Valdes, Williamson, and Wagner, 1990), as indicative of gender bias in special education. The first was the age at which students were admitted to special education. Kratovil and Bailey (1986) cited anecdotal evidence that girls are older when admitted to special education, suggesting they wait longer to receive assistance. A second indicator we examined was differences by gender on IQ scores. Again, the suggestion raised by Kratovil and Bailey (1986) was that girls must have more significant deficits in order to receive special education services and supports. In the early 1970s researchers noted that boys tended to "dominate the ranks of the referred and treated" and when admitted for special services, were found to have higher IQs than did females admitted (Gillespie and Fink, 1974; Singer and Osborn, 1970). Mercer (1973) points out similar discoveries on a clinical case register and suggests that, among other explanations, these findings may reflect a willingness for schools, families, and society in general to tolerate lower functioning among girls based on sex-role stereotypes: "Could it be that society is able to tolerate a greater amount of intellectual subnormality in a woman than in a man? If only the most visible subnormal females [sic] are referred and labeled, this factor could account for our finding that labeled females have lower IQ test scores than labeled males" (p. 72). The third indicator was type of placement. Data from the NTLS (1974) suggests that girls, once admitted for special education services, are more likely to be placed in more segregated and restrictive classroom settings.

We found that from a total of 695 new admissions to special education, 97 student records indicated a biological explanation. For the remaining 598 students, the gender proportion remained almost two-thirds males (65 percent males, 35 percent females). Upon examination of the three indicators of gender bias, there were significant differences in two. First, females obtained lower scores on standardized I.Q. tests at the time of their first admission for special education services. Second, females were disproportionately more likely than males to be placed in self-contained classrooms as a result of their admission for special education services. It also appeared that behavioral factors were influencing referral, even when we excluded cases where higher levels of over-activity, aggression, or nonconforming behaviors had been documented. In fact, only one female (2.5 percent of females) record outlined behavioral reasons for her referral, while nearly 20 percent of males had behavioral reasons listed on the referral sheets. Six males had only behavior reasons provided.

We concluded, based on these findings and a review of other studies pertaining to referral for special education services, that the present system is inequitable, not necessarily because more boys than girls are being served, but because girls who have equivalent educational needs are not provided access to supports and services that might address those needs. This study supports the observation that girls with disabilities must have more significant deficits to access special educational services and supports, and that when admitted, they are more likely than boys to be placed in more restrictive settings. Most of boys referred for special education services had genuine academic needs, yet the primary reason they were referred appeared to be behavioral. The suggestion from these findings is that girls who are not as likely to be acting out are not likely to be referred for learning problems, and thus they will have to experience more significant problems to gain the support they need.

Presumably, there are girls in the classes who have academic needs that are comparable to the boys, but they are not referred. Girls who experience learning problems may actually be displaying more passive or withdrawn behaviors, deficits in social skills, more fearful and anxious behavior, or more obedient and conforming behaviors; therefore they may be disregarded as needing educational interventions, especially when they are "only" having math problems (Grossman and Grossman, 1994; Lyon, 1996). Lyon (1996) points out that early and overreferral is preferable to late or nonreferral; students identified as needing educational supports as late as third or fourth grades have experienced several years of school failures already and in all likelihood some losses in motivation and positive self-concept. As such, the problem at hand may not be male overrepresentation but, indeed, female underrepresentation. Caseau, Luckasson, and Kroth (1994) add weight to this argument in a study in which they looked at students identified with serious emotional disturbances (SED) across two settings, the public school and a private psychiatric hospital. Students identified as SED and served in the public schools setting were, as is the general norm, predominantly male. Likewise, students identified by the school system as SED but served in the private psychiatric hospital were predominantly male. However, a third group of students receiving services through the psychiatric hospital were students who were not identified as SED by the school (despite living in the school district boundaries and attending a school in that district). The preponderance of those students were female. These authors concluded that there was gender bias in who was identified by the schools as SED and, thus, who received supports and services. They also concluded that there was a subset of females who could have been identified as SED and receiving public school services but were not.

Gender Bias in Transition and Vocational Education Materials

Although research has been conducted to examine instructional materials for use in both general and special education (Scott and Schau, 1985; Sadker and Sadker, 1982; Kratovil and Bailey, 1986), some of the more recent educational reform studies have not examined instructional materials for issues related to gender fairness as noted by Shaffer and Shevitz (this volume). To further address the even more limited attention given to the topic of gender bias and students with disabilities, we examined the degree to which instructional materials used in the transition and vocational education process are gender fair (Wehmeyer and Schwartz, in press). Vocational and transition-related study (classroom and experiential) during high school may be providing students with disabilities their most concentrated and influential source of information and preparation to enter the workforce. Given the influence of this content area, the curricular materials should be written to present the most balanced, varied, and gender-role-expanding view possible so that both females and males with disabilities recognize and appreciate a wider range of opportunities and possibilities, both traditional and nontraditional.

We obtained (from school districts) a sample of textbooks, teacher guides, and workbooks used in career development, job skills training, and living skills development classes for students with cognitive and developmental disabilities. Overall, the identified materials were products written to teach basic skills in language, social behavior, money and time management, career development (including job selection, job seeking, and job maintenance strategies) and communication skills development. After a review of the literature, we selected the seven forms of bias identified by Sadker, Sadker and Linn (1993) as the lens through which to assess the degree to which vocational or transition-related curricular materials are conveying positive (or negative) gender lessons to students with disabilities. The seven forms of bias (see Shaffer and Shevitz in this volume) are invisibility, stereotyping, imbalance/selectivity, unreality/superficiality, fragmentation/isolation, linguistic bias, cosmetic factors (Sadker and Sadker, 1977; Sadker, Sadker, and Linn, 1993).

To illustrate our findings, we discuss two particular resources we reviewed. The first is a training program to teach young adults how to interview for a job. One program module includes thirty illustrations featuring both men and women (females twenty-two, males thirty-five) performing various kinds of work. We discovered that 57 percent of the illustrations feature only nondisabled men working while 30 percent feature only nondisabled women working. No person with a disability is shown working—they are invisible. Women and men are shown:

1. Females: assembly line (food, electronics), clerical, day care, dry cleaning clerk, groundskeeper, painter, parking ticket officer, potter, food preparation.

2. Males: automotive repair, bell person, bus driver, carpenter, forester, hospital attendant, machinist, machine operator, construction worker, sales person, supermarket worker, ticket taker, truck driver, warehouse worker, wholesaler (food).

3. Both Females and Males: cleaning/janitorial.

As is apparent, males are featured performing a greater variety of jobs. Based upon the visual "lessons" reflected here, the user of this resource might conclude (1) if you have a disability, you will be invisible in the workforce, (2) men perform a greater number and greater variety of jobs than do women, and (3) women and men rarely work together, unless both are cleaning. The resource was published in 1995.

A second vocationally oriented curricular material we examined is a career development textbook that provides students with information about kinds of jobs, job related skills and attitudes, job search strategies, and job maintenance attitudes and behaviors. The most pointed discussion of any topic related to gender equity issues was about sexual harassment to which the authors devoted just over one-half of a page. In contrast to the one mentioned earlier, this resource devotes more text content (more than 16 pages) to girls or women than boys or men, as the central figure in dialogue, discussions, exercises, or examples (females 16.66 pages, males 12.41 pages). Yet we noted that a number of the illustrations, stories, and examples present girls and women in less powerful or less desirable roles than do similar stories featuring boys and men. For example, as two seniors discuss their future, the male states that he has decided to talk to his older brother who might help him generate ideas about future employment. The female contributes to this dialogue by stating that the older brother is "cute." In a second dialogue between a male and a female, the female expresses that she aspires to be a nurse or artist, while the male character expresses that he wants to be the city mayor. In both examples the female character assumes the more traditional, modest, or less ambitious role. The text was published in 1994.

Differences in Course Work

There has been quite a bit of scrutiny in special education services on the participation of girls and young women with disabilities in vocational education. This topic has been comprehensively discussed by Doren and Benz (this volume), and we will not repeat those findings here. However, in summary, both girls and boys with disabilities appear to take roughly equal numbers of vocational education courses but differ in the types of courses they are enrolled in, with girls taking more female-stereotyped courses (home economics) or preparing for female-stereotyped jobs (cashier, child care worker) and boys enrolled in courses leading to more traditionally "male" roles, such as auto mechanics or carpentry (Lichtenstein, 1996; Wagner, 1991). Figure 12.1, taken from data for students with mental retardation in the National Longitudinal Transition Study (Wagner, 1991) shows the types of vocational courses in which students were enrolled by gender. Not insignificantly, these courses also prepare attendees for higher-paying jobs, which may account for the wage gap found for males and females with disabilities (Lichtenstein, 1996).

FIGURE 12.1
Enrollment in Vocational Education by Gender

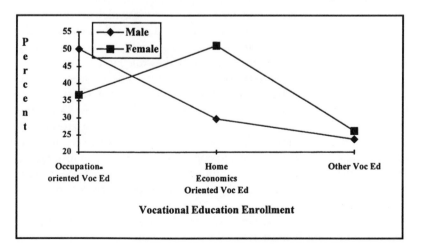

WHAT DO WE NEED TO KNOW?

If the answer to the question What do we know about gender equity for students with disabilities? is Not much, the answer to the question What do we need to know? is, logically, Quite a lot! In the final chapter of this text, Wehmeyer and Rousso discuss the issues of education, gender equity, and disability within the context of the future of "special education," and we would refer the reader to that chapter for a more in depth discussion of topics such as gender equity, students with disabilities, and access to the general curriculum or the importance of addressing gender equity issues in inclusive settings. The starting point for examining and addressing gender equity for students with disabilities must be to learn more about the impact of variables that impact all girls, variables we have covered in this text such as teacher-student interactions, sexual harassment, or gender stereotyping in curricular materials and assessment. As we amplify in the final chapter, however, this work needs to be accomplished within the context of the general education classroom. There is limited utility to conducting research to understand teacher interactions with students with disabilities who are served in separate classrooms and who are homogeneously grouped if, as we believe is the case, those types of settings are being replaced as the optimal learning environments for students with disabilities.

So, the first step is to understand how the factors that are by now oft-acknowledged as contributing to gender stereotyping and bias impact girls with disabilities. However, such research needs to be conducted with an eye toward the potential cumulative effective of bias and stereotyping based on gender and disability, the double jeopardy we have referred to, on the education of these girls and young women. In fact, some of the factors that lead to gender bias, such as differential teacher interactions or biased and stereotyped curricular materials, also exist as factors that contribute to bias and stereotypes about disability. If it is true that women are underrepresented as role models in textbooks or that their contribution to history is either not acknowledged or is presented in an "isn't-that-special" manner, so too is it true for the visibility of all people with disabilities, males and females. As more and more students with disabilities are served in general education classrooms, the absence of disabled individuals in textbooks, as role models or simply to acknowledge the contributions of people with disabilities in history, science, or other fields, will become more of an issue. Indeed, the scarcity of people with disabilities as role models as teachers will be an important issue to address.

Not only must this research address the double jeopardy of gender and disability, but it must also take into account issues related to race or ethnicity. There is, for many students receiving special education services, a triple jeopardy. African American youth are and have historically been overrepresented in special education, particularly African American males (Artiles, 1998; Daniels, 1998; MacMillan and Reschly, 1998; Patton, 1998; Valles, 1998). This phenomenon is exacerbated in areas, such as urban schools, where students from racial/ethnic minorities come from socioeconomically depressed communities. The higher number of African American students reflects the fact that more African American than white students have been diagnosed with mild mental retardation according to some researchers (Reschly, 1996, p. 48). In contrast, Hispanic and Asian students are disproportionately underrepresented in special education programs. Cultural bias, poverty, low birth weight, and inherent differences have all been suggested as explanations for such findings although the data does not fully explain or support these hypotheses (Reschly, 1996, p. 48). Gender, disability status, race and ethnicity, and socioeconomic status are not orthogonal variables that impact the educational process, and research needs to move from treating them as such. Male overrepresentation in special education services is partially a function of minority overrepresentation and partly a function, we suggest, of gender bias and the resulting female underrepresentation. We need to be more purposeful in our efforts to identify the variables that contribute to bias and discrimination and to recognize there are multiple components to the problem and, thus, the solution.

There are populations of students with disabilities about which we know almost nothing. Students with developmental disabilities and mental retardation have, by and large, been ignored even in the limited existing research. For many of these students, there are societal stereotypes that they cannot or will not achieve those outcomes typically associated with adulthood, such as employment, independent living, or marriage and parenthood. As a result of this ability stereotyping, students with developmental disabilities and mental retardation, male and female alike, are subject to low expectations. This low ceiling may, in essence, mask the impact of any gender bias and stereotyping, although the literature suggests that the impact of discrimination based on gender seems to emerge as youth move into employment and vocational outcomes. There is a need to make sure that all students are held to high expectations and that the negative impact of gender bias and stereotyping in education is given equal weight, independent of the type or frequency of the disabling condition.

Finally, we need to focus more attention on teacher preparation programs to ensure that teachers in training obtain information about gender bias. That is the intent of this text. Additionally, we need to focus attention on inservice training to ensure that teachers who don't receive the information in their preservice training programs are provided such information in the context of their teaching experience. We have developed and field tested such a resource, titled *Gender Matters: An Inservice Training Program for All Educators Working with Students with Disabilities* (Rousso and Wehmeyer, 2000). *Gender Matters* was developed with support from the Women's Educational Equity Act (WEEA) Program and the Office of Special Education and Rehabilitation Services (OSERS), both part of the U.S. Department of Education. The program consists of four distinct modules that flow sequentially from general to specific issues in gender equity in education and from attitudinal awareness to acquisition of knowledge and skills, and to the development of an action plan. The first module provides an overview of gender and disability biases in society as a whole and provides special educators with an opportunity to explore their own attitudes. The second module focuses on gender bias in general education settings and the major federal law prohibiting gender bias in school, Title IX. The third module addresses the unique aspects of gender bias and its interaction with disability bias in special education settings and provides the tools for detecting gender and disability biases in curricula and classroom interactions. The fourth module focuses on the development of an action plan to insure both the continuation of learning and the translation of that learning into concrete strategies and introduces actions to combat gender and disability bias, as well as the acquisition of skills to teach gender equity to students and parents.

Each module takes about two hours' training time and can be used separately or in some combination with the others. Ideally, special educators would have the opportunity to participate in all four modules, during a full day or two half days of training. However, each module is self-contained, and inservice trainers can use the modules to meet particular learning needs or interests.

The inservice training on gender equity was designed for use by a person who provides training (workshop, small group, preconference) to special educators, including coordinators, directors, principals, assistant principals, or grade-level or instructional content consultants. Each module provides step by step instructions on how to conduct the training so that even those trainers without prior knowledge of gender equity can succeed. Given the nature of the training, it is strongly encouraged that at least one person with a disability, preferably a woman, who has a disability rights perspective, serve as a co-trainer. The materials were field tested and validated with teachers in several states.

REFERENCES

Anderson, K. G. 1997. Gender bias and special education referrals. *Annals of Dyslexia* 47:151–162.

Andrews, T. J., J. J. Wisniewski, and J. A. Mulick. 1997. Variables influencing teachers' decisions to refer children for school psychological assessment services. *Psychology in the Schools* 34(3):239–244.

Artiles, A. J. 1998. The dilemma of difference: Enriching the disproportionality discourse with theory and context. *The Journal of Special Education* 32(1):21–36.

Blackorby, J., and M. Wagner. 1996. Longitudinal postschool outcomes of youth with disabilities: Findings from the national longitudinal transition study. *Exceptional Children* 62(5):399–413.

Caseau, D., R. Luckusson, and J. Kroth. 1994. Special education services for girls with serious emotional disturbance: A case of gender bias? *Behavioral Disorders* 20:51–60.

Daniels, V. I. 1998. Minority students in gifted and special education programs: The case for educational equity. *The Journal of Special Education* 32(1):41–43.

Gillespie, P. H., and A. H. Fink. 1974. The influence of sexism on the education of handicapped children. *Exceptional Children* 41:155–162.

Grossman, H., and S. H. Grossman. 1994. *Gender issues in education.* Boston: Allyn and Bacon.

Harmon, J. A., S. Stockton, and C. Contrucci. 1992. *Gender disparities in special education.* Research Report 143. Available from Bureau for Exceptional Children, Wisconsin Department of Public Instruction, 125 South Webster St., P. O. Box 7841, Madison, Wisc. ERIC Identifier: ED358631.

Kedar-Voivodas, G. 1983, Fall. The impact of elementary children's school roles and sex roles on teacher attitudes: An interactional analysis. *Review of Educational Research* 53(3):415–437.

Kratovil, J., and S. M. Bailey 1986. Sex equity and disabled students. *Theory into Practice* 25:250–256.

Lichtenstein, S. 1996. Gender differences in the education and employment of young adults: Implications for special education. *Remedial and Special Education* 17:4–20.

Lloyd, J. W. 1991. Why do teachers refer pupils for special education? An analysis of referral records. *Exceptionality: A Research Journal* 2(3):115–126.

Lyon, G. R. 1996, Spring. Learning disabilities. *The Future of Children: Special Education for Students with Disabilities* 6(1):54–76.

Maccoby, E. E., and C. N. Jacklin. 1978. *The psychology of sex differences.* Stanford, Calif.: Stanford University Press.

MacMillan, D. L., and D. J. Reschly. 1998. Overrepresentation of minority students: The case for greater specificity or reconsideration of the variables examined. *The Journal of Special Education* 32(1):15–24.

MacMillan, D. L., F. M. Gresham, M. F. Lopez, and K. M. Bocian. 1996. Comparison of students nominated for prereferral interventions by ethnicity and gender. *The Journal of Special Education* 30:133–151.

McIntyre, L. L. 1988. Teacher gender: A predictor of special education referral? *Journal of Learning Disabilities* 21:382–383.

Mercer, J. R. 1973. *Labeling the mentally retarded.* Berkeley, Calif.: University of California Press.

Patton, J. E. 1998. The disproportionate representation of African Americans in special education: Looking behind the curtain for understanding and solutions. *The Journal of Special Education* 32(1):25–31.

Reber, A. S. 1985. *Dictionary of psychology.* England: London, Penguin books.

Reschly, S. J. 1996. Identification and assessment of students with disabilities. *The Future of Children* 6(1):40–53.

Rousso, H., and M. L. Wehmeyer. 2000. *Gender matters: An inservice training program for all educators working with students.* Boston: Women's Educational Equity Act Publishing Center.

Russo, C. J., and C. Talbert-Johnson. 1997. The overrepresentation of African American children in special education: Resegregation of educational programming? *Education and Urban Society* 29(2):136–148.

Sadker, M., and D. Sadker. 1977. *Content Analysis of Sexism in Texts in Teacher Education (CASTTE) and Rater's Manual.* Unpublished instrument.

Sadker, M. P., and D. M. Sadker. 1982. Between teacher and student: Overcoming sex bias in classroom interaction. In *Sex Equity Handbook for Schools.* New York: Longman.

Sadker, M., E. Sadker, and E. Linn. 1993. Fair and square: Creating a non-sexist classroom. *Instructor* 102:44–46.

Schau, C. G., and C. G. Scott. 1984. Impact of gender characteristics of instructional materials: An integration of the research literature. *Journal of Educational Psychology,* 76 (2):183–193.

Scott, K. P, and C. G. Schau. 1985. Sex equity and bias in instructional materials. In *Handbook for achieving sex equity through education.* Edited by S. S. Klein. Baltimore, Md.: Johns Hopkins University Press.

Shaywitz, S. E., B. A. Shaywitz, J. M. Fletcher, and M. D. Escobar. 1996. Prevalence of reading disability in boys and girls: Results of the Connecticut Longitudinal Study. *Journal of the American Medical Association* 264:998–1002.

Shinn, M. R., G. A. Tindal, and D. A. Spira. 1987. Special education referrals as an index of teacher tolerance: Are teachers imperfect tests? *Exceptional Children* 54:32–40.

Singer, B. D., and R. W. Osborn. 1970. Social class and sex differences in admission patterns of the mentally retarded. *American Journal of Mental Deficiency* 75(2):160–162.

Valdes, K., C. Williamson, and M. Wagner, 1990. The National Longitudinal Transition Study of special education students. *Statistical Almanac, Volume 5: Youth categorized as mentally retarded.* Menlo Park, Calif.: SRI International.

Valles, E. C. 1998. The disproportionate representation of minority students in special education: Responding to the problem. *The Journal of Special Education* 32(1):52–54.

Willianson-Ige, D., and E. J. McKitric. 1985. An analysis of sex differences in educating the handicapped. *Journal of Research and Development in Education* 18:72–78.

Wisniewski, J. J., and Andrews, T. J. 1995. Objective and subjective factors in the disproportionate referral of children for academic problems. *Journal of Consulting and Clinical Psychology* 63(6):1032–1036.

CHAPTER 13

Gender Equity Issues in the Vocational and Transition Services and Employment Outcomes Experienced by Young Women with Disabilities

Bonnie Doren
and Michael Benz

Our nation has been engaged for several years in efforts to improve postschool outcomes of all youth, including youth with disabilities. The impetus for these efforts can be traced to national reports documenting an alarming gap between the demand for highly skilled employees in the workplace and the decreasing skill levels of many high school graduates (e.g., NCEE, 1990; William T. Grant Foundation, 1988; U.S. Department of Labor, 1991). The framework for these improvement efforts can be found in recent educational reform legislation (e.g., the GOALS 2000: Educate America Act of 1994; the School to Work Opportunities Act of 1994).

For students receiving special education services, there has also been a national fifteen-year effort to develop effective secondary and transition practices to improve postschool outcomes. Since 1984, when a federal policy emphasis on school-to-work transition for disabled youth was initiated by the U.S. Department of Education, hundreds of research, demonstration, and training projects have been funded to improve the school experiences and postschool outcomes of youth with disabilities (Rusch, Kohler, and Hughes, 1992).

The ultimate goal of these efforts has been to prepare *all* youth for brighter futures. Of course, reforms that are purported to be important for all youth in the abstract may not be equally beneficial for specific groups of youth. If we are to achieve our goal, we must understand (a) whether certain groups of youth experience poorer outcomes after leaving school, (b) why these groups are more vulnerable to failure, and (c) what can be done to help these groups to succeed (Traustadottir, 1990).

Gender equity issues often have been overlooked in the general and special education reform efforts of the past 15 years (American Association of University Women [AAUW], 1998; Fulton and Sabornie, 1994). Failure to understand and address the unique needs of young women, particularly young women with disabilities, may be placing them at risk for both school and community failure. As we will discuss in this chapter, a pattern of research findings is emerging that suggests the postschool outcomes of disabled women, as a whole, are much worse than those of any other referent group, including disabled men and nondisabled women and men. These findings also suggest that the postschool disadvantages many women with disabilities experience may have their roots in the secondary education services they receive.

In this chapter, we will focus on employment outcomes and employment-related school programs and transition services, realizing that employment is but one of many desirable transition and adult life outcomes. Yet one important goal for most people in America is to obtain and retain a job that is enjoyable and stimulating, provides a sufficient income to meet one's needs, and offers opportunities for promotion and advancement. However, the literature suggests that the benefits accruing from having a stable, fulfilling job have gone largely unrealized by people with disabilities (Braddock and Bachelder, 1994; National Organization on Disability, 1994; 1998). In preparation for this chapter, we explored the literature in (a) transition, school-to-work, vocational education, and career development in both general and special education; (b) vocational rehabilitation and general employment for people with disabilities; and (c) psychosocial issues for women with and without disabilities. We identified a total of thirty-four studies that included empirical information on gender, disability, and employment outcomes; these spanned from 1972 to 1998. A large number were follow-up or follow-along studies that examined the status of students with disabilities after they had exited high school. (See Appendix A for list of studies.)

In this chapter we first summarize information on postschool employment outcomes, focusing specifically on the employment experiences of young women with disabilities. Second, we summarize factors that may contribute to the employment experiences of women with disabilities. Finally, we offer recommendations, guidelines, and implications for practice in the context of current reform efforts. Several of the studies reviewed examined these three issues for disabled women relative to nondisabled women and disabled and nondisabled men. Where possible, we will add this dimension to our discussion as well. Few studies, however, examined whether women with disabilities experienced differential outcomes based on their disability type or ethnicity, so we will not address such differences.

One final note regarding our format. It is easy to become lost in a maze of details whenever an extensive literature review is presented. In an attempt to stay focused on the "big picture," we start each section with an overall conclusion and then describe the relevant findings across studies that led us to our conclusion. The specific areas of findings addressed by each study are summarized at the end of this chapter.

WHAT ARE THE EMPLOYMENT OUTCOMES FOR WOMEN WITH DISABILITIES?

The studies we reviewed included a number of employment-related dimensions. We organize our presentation of employment outcomes around the following five employment dimensions: (a) employment rates, (b) earnings, (c) type of occupation, (d) hours per week, and (e) job stability.

Employment Rates

Major finding: Women with disabilities are less likely to be employed than women without disabilities and men with and without disabilities. A majority of the studies we reviewed examined employment rates and differences related to gender. The direction of findings indicates consistently that disabled women are less likely to be employed during the transition years than any other referent group: nondisabled young women and young disabled and nondisabled men. The magnitude of the gender differences reported across the twenty-three studies ranges from 4 percent (Kranstover, Thurlow, and Bruininks, 1989) to 60 percent (D'Amico and Marder, 1991). Well over half of the studies we reviewed reported a 20 percent to 30 percent lower employment rate for women with disabilities than women without disabilities or men with or without disabilities.

It is important to note that three studies found no difference in employment rates between *women* and *men* with disabilities. Sitlington and Frank (1993) found no differences in competitive employment rates for women and men with mental retardation three years after high school. Wagner and colleagues (1993) found no differences between disabled women and men up to three years after exiting high school when controlling for parenting. DeLoach (1989) found no gender differences in employment rates for women and men with precollege disabilities who attended a four-year college during a forty-year span of time from 1948 to 1988. Interestingly, however, in that same study large differences in employment rates are found between women graduates with disabilities and women with disabilities in general. The employment rate for women graduates is approximately 70 percent higher than for women with disabilities in general.

Hourly Earnings

Major finding: Women with disabilities earn substantially less than men with disabilities, and the wage gap between women and men with disabilities increases as the time since exiting high school increases. Across the studies, we found that young women with disabilities earn between 3 percent and 78 percent less than young men with disabilities during the first two years after high school. The wage gap in favor of men with disabilities increases the longer the time since exiting secondary school and continues into and throughout adulthood (Blackorby & Wagner, 1996; Sitlington and Frank, 1993; Wagner, 1992; Wagner et al., 1993). These findings hold true across regions across the country, and educational levels (e.g., for high school and college graduates).

Some studies in this area found that, as a group, disabled and nondisabled women earn less than men as a group, and that disabled men earn less than nondisabled men. These findings may be partly explained by one study that examined wage differentials that could be attributed to discrimination based on gender and disability status. Johnson and Lambrinos (1985) found that disability discrimination accounts for a 40 percent wage differential between nondisabled and disabled women, a 33 percent wage differential between nondisabled and disabled men, and that gender discrimination accounts for 17 percent of the wage differential between disabled men and women.

Types of Occupations

Major finding: Women with disabilities are more likely than men with disabilities to be employed in low status occupations. Type or status of an occupation is closely related to the amount one earns, whether or not one receives benefits, and one's opportunities for promotion. Several studies examined gender differences in the types of occupations in which disabled women and men are employed. With only one exception (i.e., Fourqurean et al., 1991), all of the studies found that women with disabilities are *overrepresented* in lower-skill occupations, such as service, clerical/secretarial and helping occupations, and *underrepresented* in higher-skill jobs, such as labor, managerial, technical, and administrative occupations.

The overrepresentation of disabled women in lower-status occupations appears to hold across the transition and adult years. Sitlington and Frank (1993) reported that (a) 43 percent *more* women than men are employed as service workers, (b) 28 percent *fewer* women than men are employed as laborers, and (c) 15 percent *fewer* women than men are employed in higher-status jobs. DeLoach (1989) reported that 28 percent more women than men with disabilities who graduated from a four-year college are in lower-skill occupations (e.g., clerical or helping professions), and 52 percent *fewer* women than men are in higher-skill jobs (e.g., administrative, managerial, technical positions). This trend is consistent in recent studies as well. Harlan and Robert (1995) reported that the average job grade for disabled women in state jobs is five grades lower than that of disabled men.

Hours Worked Per Week

Major finding: Women with disabilities are less likely to be engaged in full-time employment than their male peers. Studies examining gender differences in hours worked per week all found that on average disabled women work fewer hours per week than disabled men. Across the studies in this area, disabled women were 11 percent (Wagner, 1992) to 49 percent (Hasazi et al., 1989) less likely than disabled men to be engaged in full-time employment. Gender differences in the number of hours disabled women and men work per week appear to increase over time. Wagner (1992) found that within two years of leaving school young disabled women were 11 percent less likely than men to be employed full time. The employment gap between young women and men increases to 30 percent by the time these two groups are three to five years out of high school.

Job Stability

Major finding: Women with disabilities are less likely to be engaged in uninterrupted employment than men with disabilities. A few studies examined gender differences in job stability. All found that disabled women are less likely than disabled men to experience stable employment over time. Across these studies, disabled women were 15 percent (Hill et al., 1985) to 72 percent (D'Amico and Marder, 1991) less likely than disabled men to be employed continuously from six months to two years after high school.

Summary of Employment Outcomes

Findings from these studies indicate that women with disabilities experience poorer employment outcomes overall than women without disabilities and men with and without disabilities. Poor employment outcomes for disabled women occur across a number of employment-related dimensions, including employment rates, earnings, type of occupation, hours worked, and job stability. The findings also indicate that employment outcomes for *nondisabled* women are poor when compared to those of disabled and nondisabled men. Together, these findings suggest that being a woman *and* a woman with disability seems to have a more detrimental effect on employment outcomes than being a man with or without a disability, although men with disabilities do experience poorer outcomes than their peers without disabilities.

WHY DO WOMEN WITH DISABILITIES
EXPERIENCE POORER EMPLOYMENT OUTCOMES?

In this section, we explore differences in the experiences of disabled women and men in (a) in-school experiences, (b) early marriage and parenting responsibilities, (c) family income, (d) use of social networks and mentors, (e) self-esteem and career expectations, and (f) involvement with vocational rehabilitation.

In-School Experiences

Major finding: Differential school experiences in vocational course participation and work experience leave young women with disabilities less prepared than their male peers for high-skill, high-wage employment opportunities once they leave school. Compared to young men, young women with disabilities enroll in fewer occupational vocational courses while they are in high school, and, when they do participate, they earn fewer credits (Blackorby, 1993; Hasazi et al., 1985; Lombard, Hazelkorn, and Neubert, 1992; Wagner, 1992). Young disabled women who participate in vocational education courses are significantly less likely than their male peers to participate in occupational training in a particular area (Blackorby, 1993). In addition, young disabled women are *more* likely than young disabled men to be receiving training in health occupations, home economics, and office occupations. Similarly, female students with disabilities are *less* likely than their male peers to receive training in agriculture and trade and industry courses (Blackorby, 1993; Lombard, Hazelkorn, and Neubert, 1992; Wagner, 1992).

The gender-differentiated occupational training young women with disabilities experience in high school also may be occurring for the general population of female high school students and for young women with and without disabilities in college. Milgram and Watkins (1994) studied fifteen early school-to-work demonstration sites. They found in all sites except one that young women are clustered in allied health and education careers, careers that are traditionally female and traditionally lower paying. At the postsecondary level, DeLoach (1989) found that female students with disabilities who attended a four-year college are more likely than their male peers to choose majors in allied health, clerical, and service occupations. Male students with disabilities, on the other hand, are more likely to choose majors in administration, management, engineering, law, and business.

Related to vocational preparation in school is the amount and type of work experience that students receive while they are still in school. A number of studies have found a positive relationship between employment during high school and employment out of school. Many of these same studies also document that young women with disabilities leave school with less work experience than their male peers (e.g., Doren and Benz, 1998; Hasazi, Gordon, and Roe, 1985; Hasazi et al., 1985; Wagner, 1992).

Early Marriage and Parenting Responsibilities

Major finding: Women with disabilities are more likely than men with disabilities to be married and/or to have parenting responsibilities after exiting high school. Young women with disabilities who have parenting responsibilities have lower employment rates after exiting school than young women with disabilities who do not have parenting responsibilities, and this gap in employment rates increases the longer these young women are out of school. Researchers have speculated that the high underemployment and unemployment rate of females in general and disabled females in particular is closely related to early marriage and parenting responsibilities. Wagner (1992) found that young disabled women are more likely to be married (12 percent) than their male counterparts (4 percent) during the first two years out of school, and young disabled women experience a greater increase in marriage rates (30 percent) than men (22 percent) between three and five years out of school. Wagner (1992) also noted that young disabled women are significantly more likely to have parenting responsibilities (41 percent) than young disabled men (16 percent) *and* nondisabled young men (14 percent) and women (28 percent). The higher rate of parenting by young women with disabilities was reported also by Edgar and Murray (1995).

There is a clear link between employment outcomes and parenting responsibilities. Wagner (1992) found that raising children and household responsibilities are the reasons given by almost half (42 percent) of young women with disabilities in her study who are not working outside of the home and who also are not looking for work. These reasons are given by only 2 percent of unemployed young men with disabilities in her study. Wagner and colleagues (1993) reported that mothers with disabilities are 6 percent less likely than young women with disabilities who are not parents to be involved in work and other activities outside of the home during the first two years after high school. This employment gap more than triples (up to 22 percent) when these two groups of young women are three to five years out of high school. Finally, Edgar and Murray (1995) found that disabled mothers are more likely to be receiving public assistance and less likely to be working than nondisabled mothers.

The gender differences in marriage and parenting rates, and the high early parenting rates experienced by young disabled women in particular, is alarming. The link of early marriage and parenting to less favorable employment outcomes clearly places young disabled women at a disadvantage compared to peers during the years after high school when important career-related building blocks are often put into place.

Family Income

Major finding: Young women with disabilities from low income families are less likely than their female and male peers from higher-income families to be employed out of school. Young women from low-income family backgrounds also have lower educational plans and occupational aspirations. Research has long documented a link between family income and other indicators of socioeconomic status and a variety of important school achievement and outcome measures. It appears that family income, gender, and employment outcomes also may be linked. Doren and Benz (1998) found that young women with disabilities from families with an annual household income of less than twenty-five thousand dollars are less likely to be competitively employed one year after school than young women with disabilities whose family's annual income is higher. The relationship among family income, gender, and employment success appears also in the general population of students.

Mortimer, Dennehy, and Lee (1992) examined relationships between family income and educational plans and occupational aspirations of high school students and found that females from low-income families have lower educational plans and occupational aspirations than females from high-income families. Similarly, Davey and Stoppard (1993) found that female high school students from low-income families expect to have less prestigious occupations, whereas young women from high-income families expect to have more prestigious occupations. Family income is not related to occupational aspirations for the young men in these studies.

Use of Social Networks and Mentors

Major finding: The likelihood of finding a job is increased when social networks and mentors are used, and young women with disabilities are less likely than their male peers to use these strategies. There is a clear, positive link between using social networks (e.g., family, friends, co-workers) and workplace mentors and finding employment for women and men with disabilities. Doren and Benz (1998) found that young disabled women and men who use a social network are more likely than youth who do not to be competitively employed one year after leaving high school. Similarly, Harlan and Roberts (1995), in their study of disabled women in state employment, found that connections through friends, relatives, politicians, and institutional networks such as rehabilitation agencies and the public employment service offices are important resources in obtaining state jobs. In addition, networking with these resources also is important in helping disabled women obtain promotions in the state system. Finally, in their study of successful women with disabilities in the workforce, Slappo and Katz (1989) found that the majority of women interviewed attribute their career success to the availability and use of workplace mentors who were like them.

Despite these positive relationships, research suggests that young women with disabilities use social networks and mentors less often and less effectively than young men with disabilities (Doren and Benz, 1998; Hasazi, Gordon, and Roe, 1985; Hanna and Rogovosky, 1992; Kranstover, Thurlow, and Brutninks, 1989; Milgran and Watkins, 1994). It is possible that young women with disabilities do not cultivate and use a social support network because they feel that constituents in their network do not support their career aspirations.

Johnson and Lambrinos (1985) reported that a contributor to wage discrimination found for women with disabilities seems to be a result of their employers' low expectations of their work productivity and ability. Similarly, disabled women in professional and skilled/semiskilled occupations report the attitudes of others to be one of the largest problems in establishing their careers (Slappo and Katz, 1989). Harlan and Roberts (1995) found that women with disabilities working in state jobs have strong perceptions that their supervisors and co-workers hold negative attitudes about them, in particular that they are weak and submissive.

Stereotypical attitudes about occupational abilities also impact nondisabled women. In a study of school-to-work and occupational preparation programs, female students in secondary and postsecondary education indicate that both peers and teachers hold stereotypical attitudes about the types of programs in which they should enroll and the types of occupations to which they should aspire (Way and Rossmann, 1996).

Self-esteem and Career Expectations

Major finding: Young women with and without disabilities have lower self-esteem than their male peers, and this seems to have a detrimental effect on postschool employment outcomes. There are differences between young women and men in the general population of students in areas such as self-esteem, self-efficacy, and expectations for future employment. In general, young women have lower self-esteem and self-confidence and lower career expectations than their male counterparts (AAUW, 1992; 1995; Orenstein, 1994; Sadker and Sadker, 1994). The Advocacy Press (1996) reported on the results of a survey completed by one thousand American teenagers that covered academic achievement and self-esteem. Even though young women report earning higher grades than young men, they score lower on all measures of self-esteem. Sixty-one percent of young women report a lack of self-confidence; more than half report having trouble handling criticism, are worried about how others feel at the expense of their own feelings, have a hard time saying what is really on their minds, and wish they could stand up for themselves more often.

It is possible that these differences are both a function of the differential experiences young women have in school and a contributing factor to the poorer outcomes they experience after leaving school. Low self-esteem and self-confidence have been attributed to the lower enrollment rates of young women without disabilities in high-level science and math courses and in nontraditional occupational programs while they are in high school. In addition, young women are less likely to pursue further education in these areas than their male peers (AAUW, 1992; Orenstein, 1994; Sadker and Sadker, 1994; Advocacy Press, 1996).

Self-esteem also can influence the extent to which students believe they are capable of reaching certain goals. Mortimer and colleagues (1992) found the young men had higher self-efficacy than the young women in their study. Young men are much more likely than their female peers to believe they will actually obtain a well-paying job after leaving school. Doren and Benz (1998) found that young women with disabilities leave school with significantly lower levels of self-esteem than their male counterparts (47 percent vs. 28 percent, respectively). Young women with low levels of self-esteem are *less* likely to be competitively employed one year out of school than young women with disabilities leaving school with high levels of self-esteem. Self-esteem did not influence the likelihood of postsecondary employment for young men with disabilities in this study.

Vocational Rehabilitation Services and Outcomes

Major finding: Adult women with disabilities receive different types of services while in vocational rehabilitation (VR) and are more likely than men to be closed into low-paying jobs or as unpaid homemakers. Both legislation and best practice require schools to establish linkages with community agencies to support students' transition goals and postschool training needs. Vocational planning and assistance are the continuing needs identified most often for youth in transition from school to the community (Marder, Wechsler, and Valdes, 1993), and vocational rehabilitation is the agency contacted most frequently by schools on behalf of students because of the range of vocationally related services it is able to provide to eligible clients (Cameto, 1993).

For these reasons, we attempted to explore gender equity issues in vocational rehabilitation services and outcomes for youth in transition. Unfortunately, this search did not take us very far.

The most comprehensive examination of transition issues for youth with disabilities to date is the National Longitudinal Transition Study (NLTS), which gathered general information on vocational rehabilitation services and outcomes for disabled youth (Cameto, 1993; Marder, 1993; Wagner and Cox, 1991; Wine, Hayward, and Wagner, 1993). The NTLS found no differences in the extent to which young disabled women and men were referred to vocational rehabilitation by schools or in the likelihood of being determined eligible for vocational rehabilitation services. This could be attributable to the fact that youth with learning disabilities or emotional disabilities are much less likely to apply for vocational rehabilitation than youth in all other disability categories. Overall, youth with disabilities who receive VR services are much more likely than those who do not to be competitively employed or enrolled in postsecondary education or training. However, we could find no information on whether young women and men benefit equally from participation in VR.

There was interest in women with disabilities in vocational rehabilitation throughout the 1980s, as researchers realized that the needs of this group may be different from men (Danek, 1992). Studies conducted during this period suggest that disabled women are likely to receive training and services that prepare them for sex-stereotyped occupations. Cowen and Ford (1986) found females less likely than males to receive vocational evaluation, on-the-job training, work-adjustment training, and job placement. Menz and colleagues (1989) examined rehabilitation outcomes over a thirteen-year period and found that services provided to female and male clients do *not* differ in average cost, length, or number. Yet women are more likely to receive training in clerical occupations, while men were provided with training in industrial occupations.

Services have a direct influence on placement outcomes. Several studies noted that females are overwhelmingly employed at closure in clerical, sales, and service positions, or they are closed as homemakers even when this was not their original goal (Cowen and Ford, 1986;

Danek and Lawrence,1985; Menz et al., 1989). Males are most often closed in professional, technical, or managerial positions. These findings hold regardless of educational level. As a result, men have higher weekly earnings than women, and more women than men are likely to be on public assistance (Cowen and Ford, 1986; Menz et al., 1989).

Summary of Factors Influencing Employment Outcomes

There are a number of factors that may contribute to the poor employment outcomes of young women with disabilities. Young women with disabilities do not participate in vocational courses or receive work experience opportunities while they are in high school at a level comparable to disabled young men. When disabled women do participate in such courses, they often are sex-stereotyped training programs associated with lower-paying jobs. This appears to be true for *nondisabled* young women as well. Finally, postsecondary training opportunities available to disabled women through continuing education, college, and vocational rehabilitation appear to be concentrated in traditionally female occupations that result in limited or low-paying jobs.

The likelihood of obtaining and advancing in a job is increased through the use of social networks and workplace mentors. Women with disabilities do not appear to use social networks or mentors effectively. In part, this may be due to stereotypical attitudes about disabled women. Stereotypical attitudes that limit occupational options appear also to be an issue for young women in general.

Disabled women are more likely than nondisabled women and disabled and nondisabled men to experience early marriage and parenting responsibilities. Mothers with disabilities are especially vulnerable to poor employment outcomes, and these disadvantages grow the longer they are out of high school.

Young women with disabilities from low-income families are less likely to be employed after leaving high school than young women with disabilities from families with higher household incomes. Similarly, young women in general who come from low-income families appear to have lower educational goals and career aspirations than young women from high-income families. For disabled and nondisabled women, educational goals and career expectations also appear to be adversely affected by issues of low self-esteem and self-efficacy.

WHAT CAN WE DO TO BRIDGE THE GAP?

Individually and collectively, the studies revealed that school, agency, workplace, family, peers, and personal variables are all important and interrelated influences of the postsecondary employment outcomes experienced by young women with disabilities. Reform efforts and legislative mandates provide a framework to build connections between and among schools, agencies, businesses, students, and families. The concept of collaboration is evident in transition and school-to-work programs and within other, broader school restructuring efforts, such as building inclusive schools. Collaborative efforts have the promise to produce results that will be more powerful and significant than the results would be of individual efforts.

Through collaborative efforts and accountability, the ultimate goal for each of us may finally be reached—to prepare our children for the best future that they can have. Developing and incorporating equitable practices into programs and services should assure that each student is provided with the necessary supports and services that he or she needs to be successful. Students are not a homogenous group, and different supports and services may be required based on a student's unique set of needs. This chapter has focused on the needs of young women with disabilities in gaining positive employment outcomes. Thus far, the findings suggest that these needs are not being met.

IMPLICATIONS FOR PRACTICE

Career Awareness and Development

Change Recruitment Strategies and the Environment of Occupational Vocational Programs The findings suggest that young women with disabilities do not receive the same type or amount of vocational training as their male peers, leaving them less prepared for the world of work. Nonstereotypical career awareness and recruitment activities may assist young women in choosing to enroll in occupational courses that will lead to high-skill, high-wage employment opportunities. A nonstereotypical environment within these courses may assist young women in choosing to remain in these courses and to take a concentration of courses in a specific occupational area that will leave them better prepared for high-wage, high-skill jobs once they leave school.

Change in Career Exploration Activities/Programs In-school programs need to develop collaborations among schools, agencies, and higher education and prioritize the development of programs that are relevant for all students and meet the unique needs of differing student groups, such as young disabled women. These collaborations should provide opportunities for true career awareness activities for all students, including the provision of current and accurate information about the nature of different careers and occupations, career preparation, training, and lines of progression leading to job advancement. Programs need to enable all students to examine how gender role socialization impacts their career goals. In-school programs should include methods for all students to explore higher-paying nontraditional careers through exposure to a wide variety of work environments using videos, work site visits, job shadowing, workplace mentors, and diverse work experiences.

Change in In-School Programs   Young women with disabilities should be recruited to participate in training in all occupations. Training should include occupationally specific math and science, hands-on learning, tool identification, and job-related physical conditioning. These activities will increase students' self-efficacy in accomplishing workplace skills (Milgram and Watkins, 1994).

Change in Career Assessment   Many assessment/career exploration tools evaluate interests and aptitudes based on past experience. Young women tend to screen out of many careers. Assessments should draw out interests and skills that young women presently have (Milgran and Watkins, 1994). The use of alternative assessments such as those developed recently within self-directed transition planning programs (Clark and Patton, 1997; Halpern et al., 1997; Martin and Huber Marshall, 1995) may provide a more relevant assessment of career interests and skills that can be used to develop career and other life goals. However, given ingrained gender-role learning, assessments should be followed by exposure to information about a variety of careers, role models, work site visits, and job shadowing experiences (Milgran and Watkins, 1994).

Support within Nontraditional Occupational Programs   Other types of skills and awareness may be required for young women with disabilities enrolled in nontraditional occupational programs. The acquisition of coping strategies may assist both young women and men with disabilities to deal with an unwelcome or hostile work environment. Fostering peer support and the use of peer-tutoring models may assist students to learn job skills and behaviors. The use of women mentors can provide support and foster awareness and respect for women in the workforce. Sexual harassment prevention awareness and skills should be incorporated into programs, and employers should be recruited to be a part of these programs. Student support groups can provide an opportunity for young women to discuss unique issues they face and strategies for addressing these issues.

Professional Development

Many teachers, counselors, employers, parents, and students need to change how they think about people and occupational attainment. They may not know any women with disabilities in nontraditional careers or other high-paying, high-skill jobs and may believe that disabled women cannot perform or do not want these jobs. These attitudes probably impact young women's own attitudes about what they can and cannot do and what type of career they should pursue. Key stakeholders (including students) need to examine their attitudes and biases.

In-Service Training

In-service training and classroom activities may help stakeholders gain an awareness and understanding of attitudes and biases and their negative impact. In-service training can include information about nontraditional jobs, instruction on how to present nontraditional career options to young women, and role models from the community. In addition, information about and practice in how to eliminate sex bias and stereotyping in instructional and counseling activities should be provided. A supportive, nonbiased liaison between young women with disabilities and their parents, teachers, and employers can be developed in which workplace issues are addressed. A good place for this type of liaison to be formed is within the context of students' IEP teams.

Training programs should also be provided to employees, supervisors, and managers to educate them on how to build a work environment including an accepting social climate. Education on the unique issues that face women and people with disabilities in the workplace should be provided. Training should also include information about illegal harassment and legal rights of employees.

Changes in School and Workplace Culture

Reform efforts in schools, agencies, and the workplace should include procedures to enhance the productivity of all students and employees by teachers, administrators, and managers having high expectations for all persons. Structures and procedures should be in place within classroom and work environments that promote accessibility, flexibility, and productivity for all students and employees. School personnel, employers, managers, students, and employees can all participate in how this environment may look and how to create it.

Collaborations among schools, agencies, and businesses can develop strategies to promote the recruitment, hiring, and retention of young women with disabilities in a variety of occupations. Technical assistance can be provided to businesses that provide work experience to young disabled women, as well as to the young women themselves through such mechanisms as job coaches (Benz and Lindstrom, 1997) and mentors.

Employers should apply unbiased, specific performance standards for all employees. They should improve dissemination efforts and accessibility to information about promotions in their organization and provide continuing education opportunities for all employees. Finally, support for nondiscriminatory employment practices should come from the highest levels of an organization and be embedded in the workplace culture. In turn, nondiscriminatory teaching practices should come from the highest levels of the educational administration and be embedded in the culture of schools.

Finally, our findings suggest that young women in general and young women with disabilities in particular are very sensitive to what others feel at the expense of their own feelings (Orenstein, 1994; Advocacy Press, 1996). In addition, working women cite internal attributes (e.g., the need to prove to others) as a major career problem (Harlan and Roberts, 1995). This makes them more vulnerable to internalizing the attitudes and stereotypical beliefs of those around them. As an alternative, we believe that exposure to positive role models, attitudes, and support from others can pave the way to increased self-efficacy, self-confidence, and esteem, which will lay the foundation for young women to begin taking a step toward developing and implementing career goals that are in their own best interest.

REFERENCES

Advocacy Press. 1996. *Pass it on.* Santa Barbara, Calif.: Girls Incorporated of Greater Santa Barbara.

American Association of University Women (AAUW). 1992. *How schools shortchange girls: A study of major findings on girls and education.* Washington, D.C.: Author.

———. 1995. *Growing smart: What's working for girls in school.* Washington, D.C.: Author.

———. 1998. *Gender gaps: Where schools still fail our children.* Washington D.C.: Author.

Benz, M. R., and L. E. Lindstrom. 1997. *Building school-to-work programs: Strategies for youth with special needs.* Austin, Tex.: Pro-Ed.

Blackorby, J. 1993. Participation in vocational education by students with disabilities. *The secondary school programs of students with disabilities.* Edited by M. Wagner. Menlo Park, Calif.: SRI International.

Blackorby, J., and M. Wagner. 1996. Longitudinal postschool outcomes of youth with disabilities: Findings from the National Longitudinal Transition Study. *Exceptional Children* 62, 399–413.

Braddock, D., and L. Bachelder. 1994. *The glass ceiling and persons with disabilities.* (NARIC Document Reproduction Service No. O11563).

Brolin, D. 1972. Value of rehabilitation services and correlates of vocational success with the mentally retarded. *American Journal of Mental Deficiency* 76, 644–651.

Bucher, D. E., D. E. Brolin and J. T. Kunce. 1987. Importance of life-centered career education for special education students: The parent's perspective. *Journal of Career Development* 13, 63–69.

Cameto, R. 1993. Support services provided by secondary schools. In *The secondary school programs of students with disabilities: A report from the National Longitudinal Transition Study of Special Education Students.* Edited by M. Wagner. Menlo Park, Calif.: SRI International.

Clark, G. M., and J. R. Patton. 1997. *Transition planning inventory.* Austin, Tex.: Pro-Ed.

Cowen, B., and M. Ford. 1986. *Women's initiative study: Access, services, and outcomes for women with disabilities in vocational rehabilitation.* (ERIC Document Reproduction Service No. ED 294 000).

D'Amcio, R., and C. Marder. 1991. *The early work experiences of youth with disabilities: Trends in employment rates and job characteristics.* Menlo Park, Calif.: SRI International.

Danek, M. M. 1992. The status of women with disabilities revisited. *Journal of Applied Rehabilitation Counseling* 23, 7–13.

Danek, M. M., and R. E. Lawrence. 1985. Women in rehabilitation: An analysis of state agency services to disabled women. *Journal of Applied Rehabilitation Counseling* 16, 16–18.

Davey, F. H., and J. M. Stoppard. 1993. Some factors affecting the occupational expectations of female adolescents. *Journal of Vocational Behavior* 43, 235–250.

DeLoach, C. P. 1989. Gender, career choice and occupational outcomes among college alumni with disabilities. *Journal of Applied Rehabilitation Counseling* 20, 8–12.

Doren, B., and M. R. Benz. 1998. Employment inequality revisited: Predictors of better employment outcomes for young women with disabilities in transition. *The Journal of Special Education* 31, 425–442.

Edgar, E., and C. Murray. 1995. The post-school status of high school graduates with learning disabilities a decade after graduation. In *The first decade after graduation: Final Report.* Edited by E. Edgar. (ERIC Document Reproduction Service No. ED 397 573).

Fourqurean, J. M., C. Meisgeier, P. R. Swank, and R. E. Williams. 1991. Correlates of postsecondary employment outcomes for young adults with learning disabilities. *Journal of Learning Disabilities* 24, 400–405.

Frank, A. R., P. L. Sitlington, and R. Carson. 1991. Transition of adolescents with behavioral disorders—Is it successful? *Behavioral Disorders* 13, 180–191.

Frank, A. R., P. Sitlington, L. Cooper, and V. Cool. 1990. Adult adjustment of recent graduates of Iowa mental disabilities programs. *Education and Training in Mental Retardation* 25, 62–75.

Fulton, S. A., and E. J. Sabornie. 1994. Evidence of employment inequality among females with disabilities. *The Journal of Special Education* 28, 149–165.

Girls Incorporated. 1996. *Pass it on . . .* Santa Barbara, Calif.: Girls Incorporated of Greater Santa Barbara, Advocacy Press.

306   BONNIE DOREN AND MICHAEL BENZ

Goals 2000: Educate America Act of 1994. [On-line]. Available at *http://www. ed.gov/legislation/GOALS2000/TheACT/.*

Halpern, A., C. Herr, N. Wolf, B. Doren, M. Johhnson, and J. Lawson. 1997. *NEXT S.T.EP.: Student Transition and Educational Planning.* Austin, TX: PRO-ED.

Hanna, W. J., and E. Rogovsky. 1992. On the situation of African-American women with physical disabilities. *Journal of Applied Rehabilitation Counseling* 23, 39–45.

Haring, K. A., and D. L. Lovett. 1990. A follow-up study of special education graduates. *The Journal of Special Education* 24, 463–477.

Harlan, S. L., and P. M. Robert. 1995. *Disability in work organizations: Barriers to employment opportunity. Final report.* (NARIC Document Reproduction Service No. R07002).

Hasazi, S. B., L. R. Gordon, and C. A. Roe. 1985. Factors associated with the employment status of handicapped youth exiting high school from 1979 to 1983. *Exceptional Children* 51, 455–469.

Hasazi, S. B., L. R. Gordon, C. A. Roe, M. Hull, K. Finck, and G. Salembier. 1985. A statewide follow-up on post high school employment and residential status of students labeled mentally retarded. *Education and Training of the Mentally Retarded* 20, 222–234.

Hasazi, S. B., R. E. Johnson, J. E. Hasazi, L. R. Gordon, and M. Hull. 1989. Employment of youth with and without handicaps following high school: Outcomes and correlates. *The Journal of Special Education* 23, 243–255.

Hill, J. W., M. Hill, P. Wehman, P. D. Banks, P. Pendleton, and C. Britt. 1985. Demographic analyses related to successful job retention for competitively employed persons who are mentally retarded. In *Competitive employment for persons with mental retardation: From research to practice* 1. Edited by P. Wehman and J. W. Hills, 65–88.

Johnson, W. G., and J. Lambrinos. 1985. Wage discrimination against handicapped men and women. *Journal of Human Resources* 20, 264–277.

Kranstover, L. L., M. L. Thurlow, and R. H. Bruininks. 1989. Special education graduates versus nongraduates: A longitudinal study of outcomes. *Career Development for Exceptional Individuals* 12, 153–166.

Lombard, R. C., M. N. Hazelkorn, and D. A. Neubert. 1992. A survey of accessibility to secondary vocational education programs and transition services for students with disabilities in Wisconsin. *Career Development for Exceptional Individuals* 15, 179–188.

Marder, C., M. Wechsler, M., and K. Valdes. 1993. *Services for youth with disabilities after secondary school: A special topic report from the national longitudinal transition study of special education students.* Menlo Park, Calif.: SRI International.

Martin, J. E., and Huber Marshall, L. 1995. Choicemaker: A comprehensive self-determination transition program. *Intervention in School and Clinic* 30, 147–156.

Menz, F. E., G. Hansen, H. Smith, C. Brown, M. Ford, and G. McCrowey. 1989. Gender equity in access, services and benefits from vocational rehabilitation. *Journal of Rehabilitation* 55, 31–40.

Milgram, D., and K. Watkins. 1994. *Ensuring quality school-to-work opportunities for young women*. Washington, D.C.: Wider Opportunities for Women.

Mortimer, J. T., K. Dennehy, and C. Lee. 1992. Influences on adolescents' vocational development. (ERIC Document Reproduction Service No. ED 352 555).

National Center on Education and the Economy (NCEE). 1990. *America's choice: High skills or low wages*. Rochester, N.Y.: National Center on Education and the Economy.

National Organization on Disability. 1994. *N.O.D. / Survey of Americans with disabilities*. Washington, D.C.: Author.

———. 1998. *N.O.D. / Harris survey of Americans with disabilities*. Washington, D.C.: Author.

Orenstein, P. 1994. *School girls: Young women, self-esteem, and the confidence gap*. New York: Doubleday.

Rusch, F.R., P. D. Kohler, and C. Hughes. 1992. An analysis of OSERS'-sponsored secondary special education and transitional services research. *Career Development for Exceptional Individuals* 15, 121–143.

Russo, N. F., and M. A. Jansen. 1988. Women, work, and disability: Opportunities and challenges. *Women with disabilities: Essays in psychology, culture, and politics*. Edited by M. Fine and A. Asch. Philadelphia, Penn.: Temple University Press.

Sadker, M., and D. Sadker. 1994. *Failing at fairness: How America's schools cheat girls*. New York: C. Scribner's Sons.

Schalock, R. L., B. Wolzen, I. Ross, B. Elliot, G. Werbel, and K. Peterson. 1986. Post-secondary community placement of handicapped students: A five-year follow-up. *Learning Disability Quarterly* 9, 295–303.

School-to-Work Opportunities Act of 1994. [On-line]. Available: *http://www.stw.ed.gov/factsht/act.htm*.

Scuccimarra, D. J., and D. L. Speece. 1990. Employment outcomes and social integration of students with mild disabilities: The quality of life two years after high school. *Journal of Learning Disabilities* 23, 213–219.

Sitlington, P. L., and A. R. Frank. 1990. Are adolescents with learning disabilities successfully crossing the bridge into adult life? *Learning Disability Quarterly*, 13, 97–111.

———. 1993. Success as an adult: Does gender make a difference for graduates with mental disabilities? *Career Development for Exceptional Individuals* 16, 171–182.

Slappo, J., and L. J. Katz. 1989. A survey of women with disabilities in nontraditional careers. *Journal of Rehabilitation* 55, 31–40.

Traustadottir, R. 1990. *Women with disabilities: Issues, resources, connections*. Syracuse, N.Y.: Syracuse University Center of Human Policy. (Eric Document Reproduction Service No. ED 337 921).

U.S. Department of Labor. 1991. *What work requires of schools*. Washington, D.C.: U.S. Department of Labor, the Secretary's Commission on Achieving Necessary Skills. U.S. Government Printing Office.

Wagner, M. 1992. *Being female: A secondary disability? Gender differences in the transition experiences of young people with disabilities*. Menlo Park, Calif.: SRI International.

Wagner, M., J. Blackorby, R. Cameto, and L. Newman. 1993. *What makes a difference? Influences on postschool outcomes of youth with disabilities.* Menlo Park, Calif.: SRI International.

Wagner, M., and R. Cox. 1991. *Parents' reports of students' involvement with vocational rehabilitation agencies in the first years after secondary school: A report from the national longitudinal transition study of special education students.* Menlo Park, Calif.: SRI International.

Way, W. L., and M. M. Rossmann. 1996. *Lessons from life's first teacher: The role of the family in adolescent and adult readiness for school-to-work transition.* Berkeley, Calif.: National Center for Research in Vocational Education (NCVRE).

William T. Grant Foundation. 1988. *The forgotten half: Pathways to success for America's youth and young families* (Final Report). Washington, D.C.: Author.

Wine, J. S., B. J. Hayward, and M. Wagner. 1993. *Vocational rehabilitation services and outcomes of transitional youth* (Final Report). (Available from Research Triangle Institute, Research Triangle Park North Carolina.)

Summary of Studies by Category of Findings

Gender Equity Studies	Employment Outcomes					Contributing Factors					
	Employment Rates	Hourly Wages	Type of Occupation	Weekly Hours	Job Stability	School Experience	Early Parenting	Family Income	Networks	Self-esteem	VR
Blackorby (1993)	X					X					
Blackorby & Wagner (1996)	X	X									
Brolin (1972)	X								X		
Bucher, Brolin & Kunce (1987)	X					X					
Cowen & Ford (1986)	X	X	X	X							X
D'Amico & Marder (1991)	X	X			X						
Danek & Lawrence (1985)			X								
DeLoach (1989)	X	X	X	X						X	
Doren & Benz (1998)	X					X		X	X	X	
Edgar & Murray (1995)	X						X				
Fourqurean, Meisgeier, Swank & Williams (1991)	X		X		X						

(continued on next page)

APPENDIX A *(continued)*

Gender Equity Studies	Employment Outcomes					Contributing Factors					
	Employment Rates	Hourly Wages	Type of Occupation	Weekly Hours	Job Stability	School Experience	Early Parenting	Family Income	Networks	Self-esteem	VR
Frank, Sitlington & Carson (1991)	X	X	X								
Frank, Sitlington, Cooper & Cool (1990)	X	X									
Hanna & Rogovsky (1992)	X								X		
Harlan & Roberts (1995)			X						X		
Hasazi, Gordon & Roe (1985)	X				X	X					
Hasazi, Gordon, Roe, Hull, Finck & Salembier (1985)	X					X	X				
Hasazi, Johnson, Hasazi, Gordon & Hull (1989)	X			X	X						
Hill, Hill, Wehman, Banks, Pendleton & Britt (1985)					X						
Johnson & Lambrinos (1985)		X							X		

(continued on next page)

APPENDIX A (continued)

Gender Equity Studies	Employment Outcomes					Contributing Factors					
	Employment Rates	Hourly Wages	Type of Occupation	Weekly Hours	Job Stability	School Experience	Early Parenting	Family Income	Networks	Self-esteem	VR
Kranstover, Thurlow & Bruininks (1989)	X	X		X						X	
Lombard, Hazelkorn & Neubert (1992)						X					
Menz, Hansen, Smith, Brown, Ford & McCrowey (1989)	X	X	X								X
National Organization on Disability (1998)	X										
Russo & Jansen (1988)	X	X	X								
Schalock, Wolzen, Ross, Elliot, Werbel & Peterson (1986)				X							
Scuccimarra & Speece (1990)	X	X		X							

(continued on next page)

APPENDIX A *(continued)*

Gender Equity Studies	Employment Outcomes					Contributing Factors					
	Employment Rates	Hourly Wages	Type of Occupation	Weekly Hours	Job Stability	School Experience	Early Parenting	Family Income	Networks	Self-esteem	VR
Sitlington & Frank (1990)	X	X		X							
Sitlington & Frank (1993)	X	X	X								
Wagner (1992)	X	X		X		X					
Wagner, Blackorby, Cameto & Newman (1993)	X	X					X				

CHAPTER 14

Nothing to Do after School: More of an Issue for Girls

Merle Froschl, Harilyn Rousso, and Ellen Rubin

Being in an afterschool program with nondisabled kids was a real eye-opener. The other girls weren't all that different from me. We all complained about our mothers and went crazy over cute boys. And we learned all this stuff. It made me feel smart.

—Student

Participating in afterschool programs provides young people with a range of skills and experiences that enhance learning in school and opportunities for success upon leaving school. Unfortunately, young people with disabilities have limited access to such programs, especially integrated programs serving both disabled and nondisabled youth. Diverse attitudinal, architectural, communication, and transportation barriers conspire to exclude them. For disabled girls, the barriers are compounded, restricting access still further. In this chapter, we explore the benefits to all youth of afterschool programs, inequitable access among various groups of youth, barriers to full participation by girls (and boys) with disabilities, costs to these youth of such exclusion, and one strategy developed in New York City to break down the barriers.[1]

While by definition afterschool programs operate after school hours and hence are not usually the direct responsibility of educators, educators can play an important role in advocating for the inclusion of students with disabilities in such programs, some of which are housed in school buildings. To this end, we include strategies that educators can use to foster inclusion. The authors of this chapter have worked together

313

for more than a decade to promote the inclusion of all young people with disabilities in community-based youth programs. In the course of our work, we have learned a great deal about the unique challenges to participation facing girls and young women with disabilities and what is needed to enable them to take on the challenges. We share our knowledge of girls' issues in the context of barriers to access for both genders. We hope this will stimulate research in and public awareness of an inequitable situation that until now has been largely invisible.

WHY ARE AFTER SCHOOL PROGRAMS IMPORTANT?

Adolescence is a time of tremendous physical, mental, social, and intellectual growth. The experiences and activities young people undertake, the skills, attitudes, and habits they acquire all influence their goals, decisions, and choices, as well as their successes and failures in school and beyond. To achieve healthy development, young people need support from their family, school, and community. Strong community-based organizations and programs for youth are an essential part of this support system. Among its many benefits, participation in community-based programs offers protection against the risks inherent in large amounts of unstructured time. Research suggests that only 60 percent of young people's time is structured with school, homework, eating, chores, or paid employment. The remaining 40 percent is discretionary and can be used either in growth enhancing or potentially destructive ways (Carnegie Corporation, 1992, p. 10). Young people unsupervised after school are at greater risk of truancy, stress, poor grades, risk-taking behavior, and substance abuse (Dwyer et al., 1990). Studies conducted by the juvenile justice system and youth advocacy groups indicate that violent juvenile crime is two to three times higher between the hours of 2 P.M. and 8 P.M. on school days than either before or after those hours (Fox and Newman, 1997; U.S. Departments of Education and Justice, 1998).

According to the 1988 National Educational Longitudinal Study, 27 percent of eighth graders spent two or more hours home alone; those from poorer families were likely to spend even more time alone (Carnegie Corporation, 1992, p. 33). Most youth indicate they would prefer not to be left alone; they prefer positive social contact with peers and caring adults, protection from risks, and opportunities to build skills and contribute to their communities (Carnegie Corporation, 1992).

Youth-serving agencies and programs offer just such protection from risk, as well as opportunities for skill building and positive development. According to a 1990 survey done by the Task Force on Youth Development and Community Programs of the Carnegie Council on Adolescent Development, the more than seventeen thousand organizations nationwide that offer community-based youth programs provide activities and opportunities designed to meet diverse adolescent needs, including socialization with peers and adults, skill building, opportunities to contribute to the community, belonging, and feelings of competence and positive self-esteem (Carnegie Corporation, 1992).

Afterschool programs offer a range of benefits to participants and the larger community. These include reducing risk-taking behaviors and vulnerability to crime that interfere with healthy development and promoting positive behaviors that facilitate academic, vocational, and social success (Carnegie Corporation, 1992; U.S. Departments of Education and Justice, 1998). As the Departments of Education and Justice report sums it up, afterschool programs enable young people to be "safe and smart."

In the arena of keeping young people "safe," research indicates that participants in afterschool programs are less likely to cut school or to engage in delinquent and criminal behavior and have lower rates of juvenile arrest, drug use, and teen pregnancy. Also, participation may produce a greater sense of safety and lower victimization rates. In addition, involvement in afterschool programs cuts down on television watching by providing an alternative, thereby lessening its negative impact. (U.S. Departments of Education and Justice, 1998; National Institute on Out-of-School Time, 1998; The National Community Education Association et al., 1997; Carnegie Corporation, 1992).

Aside from directly helping participants, afterschool programs offer benefits to communities and schools that house them. Studies suggest that communities in which afterschool programs are located experience lower juvenile crime, drug use, and child victimization rates, and schools housing afterschool programs report decreased vandalism (Carnegie Corporation, 1992; U.S. Departments of Education and Justice, 1998; National Institute on Out-of-School Time, 1998).

In terms of enabling young people to become "smart," some of the documented benefits of young people's participation in afterschool programs include higher grades and academic achievement in a range of subjects, including math and reading; increased interest and ability in reading; the development of new skills and interest in educational areas; improved quality of homework; improved attendance and lower drop out rates; lower grade retention rates; higher educational and vocational aspirations; and higher high school graduation and college enrollment rates (Carnegie Corporation, 1992; U.S. Departments of Education and Justice, 1998).

Other benefits that may be interrelated with the reduction of risk behaviors and the increase in academic achievement include decreased behavioral problems; increased social skills, including the ability to establish friendships, resolve conflicts, and relate cooperatively; improved self-esteem and self-confidence; and expanded social networks of peers and adults (U.S. Departments of Education and Justice, 1998).

WHO HAS ACCESS TO YOUTH PROGRAMS?

Despite the potential benefits of afterschool programs, not all young people have equal access. Nor are existing programs designed to meet the needs of youth representing diversity along the lines of gender, race, ethnicity, culture, disability status, class, and sexual orientation, among others.

If one could match up all the youth who should have access to afterschool programs with the programs available, a large number of youth would be "left over," including most young women with disabilities. First, there are inequities in access among youth in general. For example, youth from upper-income families are considerably more likely to participate than youth from lower-income groups (Carnegie Corporation, 1992). Second, although there has been limited research, anecdotal accounts suggest that few programs are accessible to youth with disabilities, particularly youth with physical or sensory disabilities (Community Resource Exchange, 1997); and those that do exist tend to be segregated rather than inclusive programs.

Third, while there is some indication that boys and girls may be equally likely to participate in afterschool programs, the types of programs and activities they participate in vary considerably based on gender (Carnegie Corporation, 1992) and, according to recent surveys, few programs address the needs of girls, disabled or nondisabled (Ms. Foundation for Women, 1993; Academy for Educational Development, 1997). For example, in the Ms. Foundation survey of 112 programs nationwide that serve girls either exclusively or in co-educational settings, only 36 percent provided a separate time and place for girls in which they could share and address their own unique concerns. Only 10 percent served girls between the ages of nine and fifteen, which according to some experts may be a period of heightened vulnerability to the strains of sexism and loss of self-esteem for girls (Gilligan, Lyons, and Hammer, 1990; AAUW, 1991; 1992). And most programs and services for girls focused on eliminating problems—teen pregnancy, drug abuse—rather than building strengths and resilience (Ms. Foundation, 1993). These surveys also revealed that except for one or two programs that stand out as exceptions (see descriptions of the Networking Project for Disabled Women and Girls and the Living Out Loud program elsewhere in this text), there are almost no programs directed specifically to needs of girls with disabilities. In addition, most programs specifically geared to girls are not inclusive of girls with disabilities, particularly girls with visible disabilities. Given this situation, it is no exaggeration to say that young women with disabilities have been systematically excluded from the afterschool experiences essential to later education and careers.

THE PRICE OF EXCLUSION

We have described above some of the benefits to all youth of participating in afterschool programs, and, by implication, the disadvantages of nonparticipation. For girls and young women with disabilities who face double discrimination out in the world, the price of exclusion is particularly high. The Individuals with Disabilities Education Act requires that all students with disabilities age fourteen and older have a written plan to set goals and establish support for their transition from secondary school to adult life (U.S. Department of Education, 1998). Research documents the considerable difficulty that youth with disabilities have experienced during this transition and thus their need for assistance, as evidenced by low graduation and employment rates and limited involvement in postsecondary education (Hasazi, Gordon, and Roe, 1985; Mithaug, Horiuchi, and Fanning, 1985; Edgar et al., 1988, all reported in Wagner, 1992; Wagner, et al., 1992; National Education Goals Panel, 1994).

This situation is exacerbated for young women with disabilities, who have lower levels of participation in work and other activities outside the home upon leaving school than disabled young men or nondisabled young women (see Doren and Benz, this volume, for a fuller discussion). For example, Wagner (1992) found that two years after leaving secondary school, women with disabilities are significantly less likely to be employed than men with disabilities (32 percent versus 52 percent), and are also less likely to be engaged in volunteer, job training or postsecondary education (51 percent versus 69 percent). While women and men with disabilities participate equally in social and community activities during the first two years following high school, women's participation declines markedly in the next few years (from 29 percent to 17 percent), and, in general, women are less likely than men to see friends socially (40 percent versus 57 percent). These statistics certainly do not fit the general population stereotype of females as being more socially involved than males.

Researchers hypothesize that lower involvement of females with disabilities in occupationally specific vocational education may explain their lower employment rates upon leaving school. However, it is also through experiences outside the classroom that young people receive valuable training in social and vocational skills, as we described above, and participation in these experiences during high school years differs for disabled students based on gender. Female students are involved in fewer activities outside of school, including socializing with friends, participating in community programs, and having jobs (Wagner, 1992).

The Barriers to Inclusion for Youth with Disabilities

To give a context for understanding the barriers facing girls and young women, let us first consider why youth with disabilities of both genders are excluded from afterschool programs. The Americans with Disabilities Act (ADA) prohibits discrimination based on disability in areas such as employment, state and local government, public accommodations, and transportation. Title III of the act—the public accommodations title prohibiting discrimination in diverse facilities owned by private entities, from hotels to grocery stores to community agencies providing recreational, sports, or educational programs—paves the way for inclusion of all children in the broadest range of interdisciplinary informal educational experiences. Yet when it comes to afterschool programs, the law has been implemented far too infrequently.

Prior to the passage of the Education for All Handicapped Children Act in 1975 (now IDEA), the exclusion of youth with disabilities from afterschool programs was perhaps a logical extension of segregated (or nonexistent) schooling and exclusion from classes and schools serving nondisabled youth. With IDEA, more students with disabilities have been integrated into local schools, yet a similar trend has not occurred in afterschool programs. In our experience, afterschool programs, when available for youth with disabilities, have been largely segregated. However, students with less visible and/or less significant disabilities may be somewhat better integrated into community programs (AMYD, 1989; Community Resource Exchange, 1997), partly because they are less likely to need accommodations, and when they do, the need may not be apparent until these youth are well ensconced in the program. At least they can get in the door.

Do afterschool programs really need to be integrated? If there were enough segregated programs so that all youth with disabilities could participate—and now, as far as we can tell, there are not—would that suffice? We suggest not. While separate afterschool programs should be an option for youth with disabilities and their families who want them, they should not be the only option. Separate programs run counter to the spirit of the ADA and other disability rights legislation, and, as with the argument for integrated education, separate is not equal. We have found no studies that compare the benefits of segregated versus integrated afterschool programming. However, the young people with disabilities we worked with have made many compelling arguments about the value of their participation in inclusive afterschool programs, enabling them to recognize commonalities with their nondisabled peers and preparing them to live in an integrated world. Derrick, a young man with cerebral palsy, remarked: "The mainstreaming experience has given me a chance to know about different people, to express and share my experiences of being a young person with a disability and hear how nondisabled young people feel." We want to emphasize that young people with disabilities are not the only beneficiaries. Nondisabled youth are also enriched by participation in inclusive afterschool programs that can challenge their own disability stereotypes and open learning to new and creative ways of doing things (AMYD, 1989; 1996).

So given the benefits, why aren't more afterschool programs inclusive of young people with disabilities? Fear, lack of knowledge, lack of exposure to people with disabilities, and stereotypical attitudes on the part of youth-serving agencies are among the factors that appear to foster exclusion. More specifically, through research we have conducted with the Alliance for Mainstreaming Youth with Disabilities (AMYD, 1994; Community Resource Exchange, 1997) described below, and a recent survey we conducted of leaders in youth agencies that support inclusion (Rubin, 1999), we have identified and critiqued some of the reasons youth agencies give for exclusion.

There Are No Young People with Disabilities Knocking on Our Door
Many youth agencies insist they do not exclude young people with disabilities, but rather these young people simply do not show up. This appears to be a "Catch 22" situation in that disabled young people and their families, accustomed to being denied access, simply quit trying and hence become "invisible." Programs that include young people with disabilities indicate the need to break this cycle through creative outreach strategies. These include incorporating photos of youth with and without disabilities and information about access on program brochures; providing brochures in alternative formats; and using young people with disabilities involved in the program as recruiters.

It Costs Too Much   It is frequently assumed that there are exorbitant costs associated with accommodating disability related needs, costs that youth programs cannot afford. While inclusion may sometimes require more staff and more money, too often, lack of funds becomes the "excuse" to keep disabled youth out. In truth, many accommodations such as a TTY, a small ramp, or an adjustment in the height of furniture require minimal cost.

It is important to acknowledge that many programs are housed in old, inaccessible facilities. The ADA does not require community programs to be located in accessible buildings, particularly if the buildings were built before the law went into effect. But it does require that barriers be removed where such removal is "readily achievable," that is, without much difficulty and expense. In response, some programs have built a ramp into a community center that has one or two steps or made wider aisles for everyone to pass through, or removed a door jam or frame. Others have sought to hold aspects of their programs, like teen rap sessions, in accessible spaces outside their usual facility. While there are architectural barriers that a considerable number of afterschool programs face—some housed in old facilities may never become barrier free without major renovations—these realities sometimes become a rationalization for excluding youth with all types of disabilities, including those that do not require physical access. Lack of knowledge and negative attitudes may come into play here. It may be assumed that "disability" means "use of wheelchairs or crutches," with no understanding of the diversity of disabilities that young people have.

Our Staff Is Not Properly Trained to Deal with Those Young People
Program directors and staff are often convinced they need detailed information on a broad range of disabilities to serve any disabled youth. The lack of funds and time to provide such training becomes the reason to exclude young people with disabilities. What they fail to realize is that youth with and without disabilities are more similar than different and share many common experiences so that much of what staff members already know about working with young people is applicable. While in some cases it may be useful for staff to have disability related information, this is often obtainable from young people themselves, who are usually experts on their own disabilities, or from their parents.

How Could They Possibly Participate?   Attitudes of personnel working in youth programs are often the greatest barrier. Stereotypical thinking is usually a greater impediment to inclusion than lack of disability-specific information. "How can she do painting if she can't see?" "How can he join the team if he's so poorly coordinated?" While some disabilities can prevent a young person from doing things in the same way as a nondisabled peer, most barriers can be overcome with some problem solving. This is where staff training is useful, to help staff confront their negative attitudes and put their own creativity and resourcefulness to work.

Nondisabled Youth Will Leave   Many agencies express the concern that if they encourage youth with disabilities to participate, nondisabled participants in the program will feel uncomfortable and/or resentful and ultimately leave. Our research experiences go counter to this claim (AMYD, 1994; 1996). Nondisabled youth in afterschool programs are often far more receptive to inclusion than adult staff. As an example, representatives of AMYD once made a presentation on inclusion to the youth council of a community agency. Without a moment's hesitation, the teens that were members of the council made a commitment to do outreach to youth with disabilities in their community. We should add, though, that even if some nondisabled youth are not welcoming, this should not become the basis for exclusion. Youth agencies should not tolerate the ableist attitudes of some youth any more than they should tolerate the racist or sexist attitudes of others.

They Can't Get Here   Transportation can be a barrier to participation for youth with some types of disabilities but does not explain the broad pattern of exclusion that exists. Most youth agencies do not provide transportation, yet youth with disabilities may need transportation arrangements to attend, particularly if they live in communities that lack a fully accessible transportation system. The problem is compounded when youth with disabilities have special, publicly funded transportation arrangements to and from school. Often, these arrangements are unduly rigid, so that a young person cannot stay late at school to attend an in-house afterschool activity, nor can she/he be taken to a community-based program rather than home after school. While disability rights laws and strong advocacy efforts are working to challenge and change these practices, they remain a reality for at least some young people with disabilities. There are no easy answers here. Sometimes resourcefulness can lead to creative solutions, such as advocating with schools to be more flexible in transportation arrangements, or with parents to provide transportation themselves, or to allow their child to use partially accessible transportation, such as taxis, which may be workable albeit imperfect for young people with some disabilities and can be considerably cheaper for the agency than fully accessible vans or buses.

It's Not Worth Another Battle!   Parental attitudes can also be a barrier to inclusion. While many parents of youth with disabilities are ardent advocates for inclusive formal education, they may be far less invested in ensuring their child's involvement in afterschool programs. Having fought hard for an appropriate education for their child, they may lack the stamina for yet another battle, lack knowledge about just how important afterschool programs can be, or lack faith, often based on experience, that afterschool programs will make needed accommodations. And parents have their own stereotypical attitudes about people with disabilities. They may perceive their child as too vulnerable and/or limited to survive and thrive in afterschool programs; it may seem safer to keep them at home. This may be particularly the case for parents of daughters with disabilities.

The Barriers to Inclusion for
Girls and Young Women with Disabilities

The barriers discussed above affect both boys and girls with disabilities. However, there are some factors that have a significant impact on girls. These, too, are often based on stereotypical attitudes, with disability stereotypes reinforcing gender stereotypes so that it is assumed that young girls with disabilities could not, should not, or would not want to participate in afterschool programs, or if they could, their participation would need to be quite restricted.

It's Not Safe   Safety on the streets is an issue facing many youth and their parents today. There are real dangers, such as crime or drug abuse, which warrant concern and precautions. But sometime fears and assumptions about the vulnerability of youth compound the picture. Both girls and youth with disabilities are often seen as particularly vulnerable to danger, like physical and sexual abuse. Girls with disabilities are perceived as doubly vulnerable by parents, youth workers, and others who assume, for example, that they can't fight back, have impaired judgment, are seen as easy victims, or are simply physically fragile and prone to accidents. This limits the participation of girls with disabilities in afterschool programs. Parents may be reluctant to let their daughters out of the house after school. Many of the informants in our surveys identify parental overprotection as a major impediment to afterschool involvement. Fear of sexual abuse may be a particular source of concern to parents. While disabled girls are often perceived as asexual, they are also perceived as sexually vulnerable. There is some reality here about their vulnerability to abuse. Research suggests that youth with disabilities have higher rates of physical and sexual abuse than nondisabled youth and that girls have higher rates of abuse than boys (Sobsey, 1994; Waxman-Fiduccia, 1998; Linn and Rousso, this volume). However, in the opinion of our informants, parental fears may go well beyond facts, so that even when there will be close supervision, parents are reluctant to let go of daughters. They may be more at ease about sons, who they assume can better fend for themselves. We might add that because of parental concerns about safety, the transportation barriers noted earlier may have more restrictive ramifications for girls. In our experience, while boys who are wheelchair users might be allowed to roll a considerable distance on their own or to try out a bus route, for girls such experimentation may be deemed too dangerous. For agency staff, concerns about safety may translate into discouraging disabled girls who do show up from joining the program at all—"You'll hurt yourself, and our insurance won't cover your being here"—or at least from joining activities that don't seem safe and sedate—"Instead of participating in the race, why don't you help me keep time?" Often this means tracking girls with disabilities into stereotypical female activities—arts and crafts rather than sports and science—so that their participation in the community program reinforces the gender biases they face elsewhere.

She Doesn't Need It   Stereotypes about disabled women as incompetent and asexual lead to the presumption that women with disabilities cannot take on the roles of wife/ partner, mother, worker, or contributor to the community (Fine and Asch, 1981, 1988) but, rather, will be cared for at home upon leaving school. For parents who hold such a vision, enrolling their daughters in afterschool programs designed to prepare them for a productive adult life may seem irrelevant or even harmful, setting up expectations for a life they will never lead. Even for parents with a more positive vision, misconceptions that afterschool programs mainly provide opportunities for sports and roughhousing, combined with the stereotype that sports is not for girls, particularly not for girls with disabilities, may keep girls at home. Staff of afterschool programs may harbor some of these assumptions and misconceptions about the future of girls with disabilities and their potential, leading them to restrict the range of activities available to girls with disabilities.

She Is Not Ready and Doesn't Want It   While many parents struggle with seeing their children as separate and independent, when a child is disabled and female, the struggle may become intensified. Particularly when young people must depend on parents or others to meet their disability-related needs, and/or when they look or act younger as the result of developmental differences, it is easy to overlook their thrust toward independence. For disabled girls, parental concerns about their future and safety, as well as their own gender socialization toward passivity and compliance, may reinforce the view of them as younger than they are chronologically or developmentally. With such a perception, parents may fear that their daughters are not ready for the level of self-sufficiency required in an afterschool program. Also, they may not recognize the need for peer contact and exploration of budding social and sexual interests. One young woman said, "My mom's clueless. She thinks I'm still interested in dolls when what I'm really interested in is guys." Of course, it may not be that her mother doesn't know, but that she is afraid to know.

In summary, when we seek to understand why girls with disabilities are excluded from afterschool programs, we must conclude that a complex set of factors involving parents, community agencies, and society preclude equal participation for girls with disabilities. The stereotypical view that disabled girls are dependent, incompetent, and lacking in leadership potential have translated into a series of barriers that must be overturned.

Despite the closed doors and stereotypical images they face, many of the young women with disabilities we have met have been impressively resilient and resourceful in overturning those barriers. Sometimes they find their way in through the back door, literally and figuratively. When one young woman who used a wheelchair attended a holiday party at a youth program where her nondisabled friend was a member, she had to enter through the locked back entrance, where the garbage bin was stored, since it was the only entrance without steps. Once there, she started coming back and eventually became a "regular," continuing long after her friend had left. She had to nudge staff members to keep the back door unlocked and to move the garbage to another location, which they eventually did. This young woman was a strong advocate, but she explained she couldn't do it without her friend being there as an ally, at least initially. Young women and young men with disabilities need allies in the struggle for inclusion.

STRATEGIES TO CONFRONT THE BARRIERS

The Alliance for Mainstreaming Youth with Disabilities (AMYD), a New York City–based coalition of organizations and individuals committed to inclusion, developed strategies to promote inclusion of youth with disabilities in afterschool programs. One particularly effective strategy, the Youth Leadership Training Program (YLTP), involved the empowerment of disabled and nondisabled young people as advocates for inclusion. While neither AMYD nor the YLTP specifically focused on the inclusion of girls with disabilities, both recognized and addressed the particular barriers facing girls, as well as broader issues of multiple discrimination. The YLTP provides a model to foster the inclusion of girls with disabilities in afterschool programs that can be adapted by educators to help ensure equitable opportunities for this group of students.

AMYD was founded in 1987 to ensure that all youth-serving agencies in New York City fully integrate youth with disabilities into their programs. Until its dissolution in 1997 due to lack of funds, it was one of the few disability rights/advocacy organizations throughout the country specifically focused on community-based youth programs. For the first five years of its existence, AMYD focused on two major strategies to promote inclusion. One strategy was to provide training and technical assistance to youth-serving agencies in New York City. The second strategy was to advocate with public officials to develop policies and practices to promote inclusion. Despite strides made with some youth-serving agencies and policymakers, however, AMYD's dual approach did not significantly increase the access of disabled youth to youth programs. To more fully identify and address the barriers to full inclusion, AMYD carried out a research project to determine what else was needed to make the inclusion of youth with disabilities a priority in New York City (AMYD, 1994). Interviews were conducted with policymakers, funders, youth agency staff, parents, and youth with and without disabilities to determine the barriers to inclusion, the catalysts that foster inclusion, the features of successful inclusive programs, and the steps needed to put inclusion on the public agenda.

One of the key findings was that policymakers, funders, and youth agencies were not facing any external pressure to ensure inclusion and hence did not see it as a pressing issue. Even though many recognized inclusion as "the right thing," as well as a legal requirement, they acknowledged they would not take action without pressure, given the many other priorities they faced. Another finding was that disabled youth, their nondisabled friends, and their parents saw inclusion as essential yet rarely encountered any truly inclusive programs. Few, if any, had engaged in collective action to promote inclusion, partly because no organizing mechanisms existed. Some young people and parents had advocated for inclusion on an individual basis, with varying degrees of success. What emerged, then, was the need for an external force to demand inclusion and a set of constituency groups—youth and parents—with a strong vested interest in serving as that force.

Based on these findings, AMYD embarked on a new strategy. Youth development programs from other arenas had demonstrated that youth could be effective advocates on their own behalf and could successfully serve both as educators and as mentors for peers, as well as catalysts for change (AMYD, 1994; Roach, Sullivan, and Wheeler, 1999). AMYD's intent was to draw on the energy, eloquence, and insistence of youth with and without disabilities to convince youth agencies, funders, and policymakers to make a commitment to inclusion.

AMYD Youth Leadership Training Program

The AMYD Youth Leadership Training Program (YLTP) was started in 1995. The initial planning for the YLTP, including the establishment of

broad goals, curriculum topics, and recruitment methods, was conducted by AMYD's Youth Committee, which consisted of young people
already involved in the governance of AMYD, other youth they recommended, and a few adults from AMYD experienced in youth development. Input from youth was the highest priority. The objective of the
program, as defined by the planners, was to provide youth with and
without disabilities with the knowledge, attitudes, and skills necessary
to educate and advocate with peers, youth service providers, policymakers, and funders about inclusion. The goal was to increase participation of youth with disabilities in inclusive, community-based youth
programs, and ultimately to ensure that youth with disabilities had
access to every youth program in the city.

The program was committed to training both disabled and nondisabled youth as leaders in the struggle for inclusion, based on the belief
and knowledge that inclusion based on disability status, like integration
based on race, ethnicity, and other aspects of diversity, benefited all
youth. In the selection of participants for the YLTP, other dimensions of
diversity in addition to disability status—gender, race, ethnicity, age
(originally twelve to eighteen, ultimately shifting upwards as the participants aged), and geography—were identified as key. The youth leaders
needed to reflect at least part of the rich diversity of the youth population in New York City. AMYD was eager to insure the inclusion of
young women with disabilities, since they would be particularly effective spokespersons for the multiple barriers faced by disabled girls. Also,
by their very presence, they would challenge the stereotypical view that
girls with disabilities were dependent, incompetent, and lacking in leadership potential. Engaging female participants proved a formidable task.

Participants were recruited in a variety of ways, including an ad in
the youth-run newspaper *New Youth Connections*; presentations by
youth and adult planners at schools, youth agencies, and summer
camps; and mailing fliers. Recruits sometimes came from unexpected
sources. Prior to active recruitment efforts, a nondisabled young
woman, Evelyn, who worked as a reporter for *New Youth Connections*,
interviewed one of the authors (Rubin) for an article on inclusion in
school. She had decided to write the article when a boy who used a
wheelchair joined one of her classes, and she realized she felt afraid and
uncomfortable in his presence. In the course of the interview, Evelyn
learned about the YLTP and not only joined the program herself but
also recruited several of her nondisabled girlfriends. This taught us that
inviting potential recruits to bring their friends could be an important
recruitment strategy. Particularly for some of the younger girls, participating in the YLTP with a girlfriend was exactly the assurance that their
parents needed to allow them to participate.

Through extensive outreach, twenty young people were recruited. There were an equal number of disabled and nondisabled participants, although members with disabilities participated on a more consistent basis, and about twice as many girls as boys. The majority of participants were young people of color. The disabled members of the group represented a range of physical and sensory disabilities and were nearly gender-balanced, with four girls and six boys to start, suggesting that we may have been successful in countering some of the typical barriers that prevent girls with disabilities from initiating involvement—although our sample was admittedly small. However, the program was less successful in sustaining the involvement of the girls; only one attended consistently. The other three girls attended sporadically and ultimately left for some reasons related to gender and disability-specific factors—such as parental overprotectiveness in one case, and a lengthy hospitalization in another—and others more typical of youth, that is, competing demands on time.

Among the nondisabled participants, all were girls. No nondisabled boys even filled out applications. We hypothesize that both gender and disability stereotypes may have played a role in this. First, the nature of the program—community service rather than sports/recreation—may have appealed more to girls than to boys. Second, nondisabled youth who heard about the program may have assumed that nondisabled participants would be required to teach, counsel, and/or take care of disabled members, consistent with the stereotype that disabled people are dependent and needy. Since caretaking is more in keeping with the female gender role, nondisabled girls may have been more readily attracted.

The Youth Committee planners set broad guidelines for the YLTP curriculum, wanting to leave sufficient leeway for the youth participants, in collaboration with the facilitators (Rousso and Rubin), to set the agenda. The goal of promoting inclusion in afterschool programs dictated the need to provide youth leaders with knowledge about the need, importance, and barriers to inclusion and leadership skills and related attitudes needed to translate this knowledge into education and advocacy strategies for use with peers and adults.

The YLTP evolved into a fifteen-session training program, with each session approximately 3 hours in length, held every two to three weeks over a one-year period. Each session consisted of activities from several components, which emphasized active learning rather than passive listening as the primary strategy for engagement. The program culminated in the development of a peer workshop, which would be implemented by the youth leaders toward the end of building an "army" of youth advocates.

The underlying philosophy and principles that guided the development of the curriculum for both the training program and the teen workshop included the following:

1. Young people each have their own unique identity yet have a great deal in common that cuts across differences based on disability status, gender, race/ethnicity, class, sexual orientation, and other factors.

2. Teenagers all face barriers and injustices that they need to confront and address on their own behalf and on behalf of one another; when some young people are excluded, all young people lose out.

3. Young people with disabilities face barriers to their full participation in afterschool programs based on their disability status; sometimes these barriers are compounded by their gender, race/ethnicity, and other factors.

4. Such exclusion not only hurts disabled young people but also deprives nondisabled youth of the opportunity to work, play, and learn from their disabled peers.

5. All young people must fight for the inclusion of disabled youth in afterschool programs.

The various training program components are discussed below (AMYD, 1996).

Warm-up Activities   A warm-up activity was provided at the start of each session to help participants to connect to one another and the program. After a few sessions, individual members or pairs of participants were asked to develop their own warm-up activities to present to the group, thus affording them an opportunity to develop their program design skills. An example, developed by one of the participants, was called "Stop the Press." It began with participants writing down on a note card the name of a person they admired, such as a famous person, family member, or friend. The cards were then collected, mixed up, and redistributed. Next, group members mingled with one another, trying to locate the person who had written the card they were holding. When someone found a "match," he or she would shout "Stop the Press"; all the action in the room would stop, and the author of the card would explain why she/he looked up to the person he/she listed on the card.

Identity Activities   The participants represented diversity along many dimensions, including disability status, gender, and race/ethnicity. To be sufficiently comfortable with one another to work together and to advocate for the common cause of inclusion, they needed to appreciate their commonalities while not devaluing their differences and, at times, differing needs. An example of an identity exercise was a go-around in which each participant responded to the questions "What's great about being a teenager today? What's tough?" Hearing one another give similar answers across disability, gender, race/ethnicity, and class lines had a strong impact on participants, so much so that they chose to include this "Common Bonds" exercise in their workshop for peers.

Discrimination/Injustice Activities   To enable participants to understand the discriminatory nature of the exclusion of disabled youth from afterschool programs, it proved helpful to put such disability bias in the larger context of various forms of discrimination, such as gender bias, racism and homophobia, and to encourage activism against all types of discrimination. Activities in this section included an exercise to define stereotypes and identify ways in which one's own life had been stereotyped; problem solving around discriminatory situations, for example, "How would you handle it if your teacher only called on the boys?" and a discussion of the links between different forms of bias. This section of the curriculum afforded an opportunity to address the double discrimination that young women with disabilities face in afterschool programs and other aspects of their lives.

Disability Rights and Culture   To enable participants to make the case for inclusion, they needed to understand not only the illegal nature of exclusion but also the benefits of inclusion for all youth, disabled or not. Hence information was provided on both disability rights laws and disability culture. For example, participants met with a guest speaker who gave a history of the disability rights movement and the ADA; they learned to critique disability-related advertisements and images in the media; they also obtained information on famous disabled people in history. The young people shared with one another the ways that their lives had been enriched by inclusive opportunities and the losses they had experienced as the result of exclusion.

Leadership Skills   To educate and advocate with peers, participants needed a range of leadership skills, including the ability to communicate, to facilitate a group, to handle differences of opinion and conflict, to problem solve new situations, and to plan and implement a strategy for social change. While opportunities to develop some of these skills were incorporated into the components described above, the curriculum contained some activities primarily focused on the development of leadership skills. These included an exercise in which participants identified the skills and attributes of leaders they admired; a review of a set of guidelines for leading a group discussion; a practice session to strengthen interviewing skills; and an opportunity to reflect on situations in which each participant had been an effective advocate at home, school, or in the community.

Workshop Development   Throughout the training program, participants were asked to consider ways that they could translate their newly developing knowledge and skills into widespread advocacy efforts on behalf of inclusion. About halfway through the YLTP, the participants decided to develop a workshop on inclusion for peers with and without disabilities. Much of the remaining half of the training program was focused on facilitating the young people's development, fine-tuning, and implementation of the workshop. They began by establishing goals for their peer workshop, then identifying activities to use with peers to achieve these goals. Most of the activities were selected from the existing YLTP curriculum, although some new aspects were developed, such as an action plan that concluded the workshop. The workshop format that the young people developed included not only exercises but also instructions on how to conduct them so that other young people could implement the workshop as well. A description of the workshop is provided below:

Peer Workshop Description   The goals of the workshop, as defined by its youth developers, included the following:

1. to show the commonalities between disabled and nondisabled teens;
2. to develop respect and understanding between disabled and nondisabled teens and show they can learn from one another;
3. to make disabled people more visible as role models;
4. to identify the stereotypes that disabled and nondisabled youth face;
5. to demonstrate the benefits of inclusion to all youth; and
6. to get workshop participants to commit to inclusion.

Peer Workshop Contents   The workshop included the following components:

1. *Introduction*: The goals of the workshop, the ground rules for participation, and a definition of "inclusion" (or "mainstreaming," as it was called at the time).
2. *Warm-up activity*: "The Name Game," a go-around in which participants gave their first name and an adjective revealing something about themselves that started with the same letter as their first name and then recalled the names and the corresponding adjectives of all participants that preceded them.

3. *Common bond activity*: An exploration of what was difficult and easy about being a teen today, thus enabling participants to recognize the similarities in feeling and experience of all young people in the room, despite differences based on disability status, gender, race, ethnicity, and so on.

4. *Activity on stereotypes*: An examination of the definition and meaning of stereotypes, enabling the young people to recognize and challenge disability stereotypes and to make the link between stereotyping and discriminatory practices, such as exclusion from afterschool programs.

5. *Personal stories on inclusion/exclusion*: Personal stories by youth leaders and participants about the benefits of participating in an inclusive afterschool program or the negative consequences of exclusion.

6. *Action plan*: A written check-off list of next steps by which participants could commit themselves to continue to work on inclusion after the workshop was over. Possibilities included talking to others about inclusion, challenging disability-biased language, speaking with the director of a local afterschool program about inclusion, encouraging young people with disabilities to go to afterschool programs in their community, and signing up for further training on inclusion to become a youth leader.

As designed, the peer workshop was about two hours in length and was to be conducted by two youth leaders, one disabled and the other nondisabled, for a group of fifteen to twenty young people with and without disabilities. In reality, there was much variability in the length of time allotted, the size of the group, and the disability status of both the leaders and the participants. Partly because the YLTP curriculum addressed variability and unpredictability as a fact of life for trainers, the youth trainers were able to "go with the flow," conducting workshops under a range of situations.

The original vision for the YLTP was that the initial group of youth leaders would conduct peer workshops on an ongoing basis throughout the city and that the YLTP would itself be repeated with regularity, first by AMYD to perfect the curriculum, then by an ever-increasing group of youth agencies, with technical assistance from AMYD. Thus diverse organizations would acquire their own in-house group of youth advocates to spread the word about inclusion within the agency and beyond. Through this multilayer, multiplier strategy, more and more youth and youth agencies throughout New York City would make the commitment to inclusion of youth with disabilities in afterschool programs. Unfortunately, AMYD's loss of funds after the first training cycle prevented the vision from becoming a reality. Pairs of the initial "graduates" conducted the peer workshop in only a handful of agencies. However, information from evaluation forms, informal feedback, and observations by the adult facilitators from the first set of workshops suggested that the YLTP had considerable potential to promote inclusion and to positively affect the lives of youth leaders.

That the leadership and advocacy skills carried over was demonstrated by follow-up activities of a few of the young people. Angelina, a young woman with cerebral palsy, became an advocate for inclusion among funders of youth programs, speaking at a national funders' conference, and was selected as a member of the board of directors of a new national fund by and for young women. Derrick, a wheelchair user who began college several months after completing the program, campaigned for a more accessible dorm room and for lighter entrance doors in classroom buildings, benefiting not only himself but many other students. Evelyn, the nondisabled reporter mentioned earlier, advocated for inclusion in an afterschool program in her college town.

PROMOTING INCLUSION FOR YOUNG WOMEN (AND YOUNG MEN) WITH DISABILITIES: WHAT CAN EDUCATORS DO?

Although not often directly involved in afterschool programs, educators working with students with disabilities can become advocates for their inclusion in these programs. And they can make sure that their advocacy efforts take into account the particular barriers facing young women. Here are some strategies to promote inclusion.

- Educators can raise the awareness of young women and men with disabilities in their classes, as well as their parents, about the importance of afterschool participation. It is particularly important to have in-depth discussions with parents of young women with disabilities, challenging their misperceptions about the nature and benefits of participation and problem solving concerns about safety, transportation, and so on.

- Educators can include participation in afterschool activities in their students' IEP and/or transitional plan, using as a rationale the growing body of literature on the benefits of afterschool participation for all students and the research suggesting a link between lack of participation and disappointing postsecondary outcomes for young women with disabilities in particular.

- Educators can start a Youth Leadership Training Program to engage students with and without disabilities to become advocates for inclusion. With minor alterations, a YLTP can be a particularly effective vehicle for promoting the inclusion of girls with disabilities in afterschool programs. Such alterations include involving a higher percentage of disabled girls and expanding the curriculum to address girls' issues more fully. Particularly if the program is conducted during school hours, more young women with disabilities are likely to participate and become active advocates for themselves and other young women.

- To the extent that a rigid transportation system for disabled students precludes their participation in afterschool activities at the school itself or in other locations, educators can advocate for a more flexible system, evoking disability rights laws such as IDEA or the ADA if necessary. Parents and students can also be engaged in such advocacy so that there is collective pressure from multiple fronts.

- When schools house afterschool programs in their own facilities, educators can advocate for the inclusion of disabled students and facilitate the engagement of girls with disabilities in particular.

- In collaboration with students with disabilities and parents, educators can identify one or two community-based youth programs offering activities and develop an advocacy strategy to promote inclusion. This could be part of the work of a youth leadership training program, if such a program is developed.

- Educators can raise the awareness of their peers and school administrators about the benefits of afterschool participation and the barriers that students with disabilities, particularly girls, face and engage the whole school, and perhaps the entire school district, in an advocacy campaign.

Like all youth, young women with disabilities need the opportunity to develop new skills, expand their options, build friendships and networks, find refuge from danger, and just have fun through participation in afterschool programs. Yet they are as likely as not to remain home during the afterschool hours, depriving them of tools they will need for survival and success upon leaving school. While educators are not responsible for the pattern of exclusion that these young women face, they can take a stand against it. When young women with disabilities bring their life experiences into the arena of afterschool programs, all young people benefit. As one nondisabled youth said, "Having an inclusive attitude makes an activity more fulfilling for everyone. I never realized there were so many ways to take on a problem or task. I've learned so much."

NOTE

1. All the quotes from youth that appear in this chapter come from participants in the AMYD Youth Leadership Training Program. Names, where they appear, have been changed to ensure confidentiality.

REFERENCES

Academy for Educational Development. 1997. *Growing girls! A report on programming for the girls of New York City.* New York: Author, for the New York Women's Foundation.

Alliance for Mainstreaming Youth with Disabilities (AMYD). 1989. *Policy statement.* Unpublished paper commissioned by Educational Equity Concepts, Inc., coordinating agency for AMYD.

AMYD. 1994. *Crafting an agenda for citywide mainstreaming.* Unpublished report.

————. 1996. *Youth leadership training program manual.* Unpublished resource developed for the Youth Leadership Training Program of AMYD.

American Association of University Women (AAUW). 1991. *Shortchanging girls, shortchanging America: A call to action.* Washington, D.C.: Author.

————. 1992. *The AAUW report: How schools shortchange girls.* Washington, D.C.: Author.

Carnegie Corporation of New York, Carnegie Council on Adolescent Development. 1992. *A matter of time: Risk and opportunity in the nonschool hours: Report of the task force on youth development and community programs.* New York: Author.

Community Resource Exchange. 1997. *The Alliance for Mainstreaming Youth with Disabilities: Feasibility study.* Unpublished study commissioned by AMYD.

Dwyer, K. M., J. L. Richardson, K. L. Danley, W. B. Hansen, S. Y., Sussman, B. Brannon, C. W. Dent, C. A. Johnson, and B. R. Flay. 1990. Characteristics of eighth-grade students who initiate self-care in elementary and junior high school. *Pediatrics* 86:448–454. Reported in National Institute on Out-of-School Time, 1998. Fact sheet on school-age children's out-of-school time, Wellesley, Mass.: Center for Research on Women, Wellesley College.

Edgar, E., P. Levine, R. Levine, and M. Dubey. 1988. Washington state follow up studies 1983–1987 students in transition: Final report. Seattle, Wash.: Networking and Evaluation Team, Experimental Education Unit, University of Washington. Reported in M. Wagner. 1992. *Being female: A secondary disability? Gender differences in the transition experiences of young people with disabilities.* Menlo Park, Calif.: SRI International.

Fine, M., and A. Asch. 1981. Disabled women: Sexism without the pedestal, *Journal of Sociology and Social Welfare* 8(2):65–80.

Fine, M., and A. Asch, eds. 1988. Introduction: Beyond pedestals. In *Women with disabilities: Essays in psychology, politics and culture.* Philadelphia: Temple University Press, 1–37.

Fox, J. A., and S. A. Newman. 1997. Afterschool crime or afterschool programs. Report to the U.S. Attorney General. Washington, D.C.: Fight Crime Invest in Kids. Reported in National Institute on Out-of-School Time, *1998: Fact sheet on school-age children's out-of-school time.* Wellesley, Mass.: Center for Research on Women, Wellesley College.

Gilligan, C., N. Lyons, and T. Hammer, eds. 1990. *Making connections: The relational worlds of adolescent girls at the Emma Willard School.* Cambridge, Mass.: Harvard University Press/

Hasazi, S. B., L. R. Gordon, and C. A. Roe. 1985. Factors associated with the employment status of handicapped youth exiting high school from 1979–1983. *Exceptional children* 51:455–469. As reported in M. Wagner. 1992. *Being female: A secondary disability? Gender differences in the transition experiences of young people with disabilities.* Menlo Park, Calif.: SRI International.

Mithaug, D., C. Horiuchi, and P. Fanning. 1985. A report on the Colorado statewide follow-up survey of special education students. *Exceptional Children* 51:394–404.

Ms. Foundation for Women. 1993. *Programmed neglect: Not seen, not heard. Report on girls programming in the United States.* New York: Author.

National Community Education Association, the U.S. Department of Education, Policy Studies, Associates, and the American Bar Association, Division of Public Education, July 1997. Keeping schools open as community learning centers: The benefits of schools as community learning centers. Available online at http://inet.ed.gov/pubs/LearnCenters/benefits.html.

National Educational Goals Panel. 1994. The national education goals report: Building a nation of learners. Washington, D.C.: Author. Reported in U.S. Department of Education. 1998. *To assure the free appropriate public education of all children with disabilities.* Twentieth report to Congress on the implementation of the Individuals with Disabilities Education Act. Washington, D.C.: Author.

National Institute on Out-of-School Time. 1998. *Fact sheet on school-age children's out-of-school time.* Wellesley, Mass.: Center for Research on Women, Wellesley College.

Roach, C., L. Y. Sullivan, and W. Wheeler. 1999. *Youth leadership for development: Civic activism as a component of youth development programming.* Chevy Chase, Md.: Nation 4–H Council's Innovation Center for Community and Youth Development.

Rubin, E. 1999. *Factors that help and hinder inclusive afterschool programming: An informal survey.* Unpublished paper.

Sobsey, D. 1994. *Violence and abuse in the lives of people with disabilities: The end of silent acceptance?* Baltimore: Paul H. Brookes.

U.S. Department of Education and U.S. Department of Justice. 1998. *Safe and smart: Making the afterschool hours work for kids.* Washington, D.C.: Authors.

Wagner, M. 1992. *Being female: A secondary disability? Gender differences in the transition experiences of young people with disabilities.* Menlo Park, Calif.: SRI International.

Wagner, M., R. D'Amico, C. Marder, L. Newman, and J. Blackorby. 1992. *What happens next? Trends in postschool outcomes of youth with disabilities: The second comprehensive report from the National Longitudinal Transition Study of Special Education Students.* Menlo Park, Calif.: SRI International.

Waxman-Fiduccia, B. 1998. *Disabled women and violence fact sheet.* Unpublished position paper developed for the National Task Force on Violence against Women of the National Organization for Women (NOW) Legal Defense and Education Fund, Washington, D.C.

CHAPTER 15

What Do Frida Kahlo, Wilma Mankiller, and Harriet Tubman Have in Common? Providing Role Models for Girls with (and without) Disabilities

Harilyn Rousso

In 1984, I had the opportunity to develop a mentoring and role model program for adolescent girls with physical and sensory disabilities, the Networking Project for Disabled Women and Girls. Started at the YWCA of the City of New York and replicated in other locations throughout the country, the project sought to increase the educational, vocational, and social aspirations of young women with disabilities and to foster their ability to become independent, productive adults. This chapter describes the need for, evolution of, and contributions of the Networking Project[1] and offers suggestions for adapting aspects of the project to school and classroom settings.

PERSONAL BASIS FOR THE NETWORKING PROJECT

The Networking Project for Disabled Women and Girls developed not only out of my professional knowledge as an educator, social worker, psychotherapist, and disability rights activist, but also out of my personal experiences as a woman growing up with a disability, cerebral palsy.[2]

During my childhood and adolescence, I did not know any children or adults with disabilities. Partly this was because I attended public

337

schools in New York City in the 1950s and 1960s, when most students with disabilities were in segregated schools, on home instruction, or not educated at all. My disability was relatively mild, requiring few accommodations, and my mother was a strong advocate, so I was fully included in general education classes before there were legal mandates in that direction. But far more important than the lack of disabled peers in school was my determination to stay away from other disabled people. My disability had caused me so many painful experiences—people teasing, staring, disliking me because I had cerebral palsy—that I did not want to be associated with the very characteristic that had caused me such distress. It never occurred to me that there might be people with disabilities out in the world who were interesting, smart, attractive, funny, or successful. At least I had never met any.

When I was twenty-two, I had an unexpected, important experience. I worked one summer for a prominent economist, Betty, who happened to have cerebral palsy. I was shocked when I met her at the job interview. It was like looking at a mirror image of myself sitting across the table. Betty had quite a powerful effect on me. I was impressed that a woman with cerebral palsy, not a very socially acceptable disability, could make it in a man's field (antitrust economics). Another thing that impressed me, perhaps more than her career success, was that she was married. When I was growing up, my parents and I accepted the societal myth that women with disabilities were asexual and that they could not lead socially and sexually fulfilling lives. Based on this myth, I put aside any hope of dating, finding a partner, or having children. Instead, I concentrated on my studies and career. Betty's lifestyle and her marriage to an interesting, dynamic man made me reconsider the assumptions I had made about my social potential. She planted the seeds of positive possibilities that I took with me when later on I began to explore the social scene. Later in our intergenerational friendship, which lasted more than thirty years, she told me that she had learned a great deal from me as well. Although she was fifty-five when we met, I was the first person she had ever talked with about the effect of her disability on her life. Until then, the fact that she had cerebral palsy had been a visible yet unspoken reality in her life. Our conversations enabled her to reclaim a hidden part of herself and begin to obtain more of the accommodations she needed.

Meeting Betty enabled me to challenge stereotypes and develop a more positive image of my future. Later on, contact with people with disabilities continued to be a powerful influence. After college, I decided to become a psychotherapist. When the school I was attending terminated me on the grounds that a person with my disability could not succeed in the profession, it was with the support of a group of therapists with disabilities who had "been there—done that" and knew that I could, that I was able to take legal action against the school for discrimination. Thanks to them, I began a dual career as psychotherapist and disability activist.

Betty and the succession of strong, proud women and men with disabilities whom I have met subsequently have had a profound effect on my life. I only wish that I had met them when I was younger and more fully immersed in making educational, career, and life decisions. The Networking Project developed out of my commitment to ensure that future generations of girls and young women with disabilities would have access to successful women with disabilities like Betty at earlier, more strategic moments in their development.

THE INVISIBILITY OF SUCCESSFUL WOMEN WITH DISABILITIES

My lack of contact with or knowledge about successful women with disabilities when I was growing up is still typical of girls and young women with disabilities. Although many disabled women have made contributions to society, such as Jane Addams, Alicia Alonso, Frida Kahlo, Dorothea Lange, Juliet Gordon Low, Wilma Mankiller, Wilma Rudolph and Harriet Tubman[3] the fact that they have disabilities is largely unknown.

Because of stereotypes about disability and womanhood, women with disabilities who are successful are no longer perceived as disabled (Women and Disability Awareness Project, 1984, p. 20). The more familiar myths about disabled people—that they are sick, helpless, dependent, childlike, and asexual—are incompatible with success. Until recently, being a woman seemed inconsistent with high achievement. Successful women were perceived as manlike, seeking a career because they could not "catch a man," that is, because they were not "true women" (Women and Disability Awareness Project, 1984, p. 20). So it is not surprising that the accomplishments of women with disabilities are often disregarded on two counts: disability and gender.

For disabled women of color, disabled lesbians, and disabled women who are members of other oppressed groups, there is an additional layer of stereotyping that is incompatible with success. Successful women from these groups are particularly invisible in society.

This situation may be changing. As a result of the disability rights movement and the passage of disability rights legislation, such as the ADA, people with disabilities are literally more visible in the streets, participating more fully in their communities, and their stories and images appear with greater frequency in the media. Yet such changes are relatively new and may not yet be sufficiently intense or focused to counteract the stereotypical images of disabled women and the lack of positive role models.

While school curricula could counterbalance this lack of role models, too often they reinforce it by excluding the contributions and accomplishments of women with disabilities (Women and Disability Awareness Project, 1984; Resource Center on Educational Equity/ CCSSO, 1986). Stories of successful men with disabilities appear somewhat more often, but not significantly so; by and large, disability history is overlooked (Linton, 1998). Educational resources include few images and examples involving disabled women and girls; when present, such examples tend to reinforce negative stereotypes.

As a result, disabled women and girls do not have access to successful women with disabilities who could serve as positive role models, helping them develop positive, realistic expectations and aspirations. This limits their educational, vocational, and social choices. As one deaf woman explained: "I never knew what would happen when I left school. It scared me. I used to believe that when I graduated, I'd die or live with my family forever. That was because I'd never met a deaf woman" (O'Toole, 1979, p. 55).

Fine and Asch (1981) noted that because of the myths and stereotypes about disabled women, there are few socially sanctioned roles for them to fill. They are perceived as inadequate to fulfill either the nurturing roles of wife and mother, the traditional roles reserved for women, or the economically productive roles of breadwinner considered appropriate for men. As a result, they often experience what Fine and Asch described as rolelessness—a lack of clarity about who and what to be and to become. This lack of socially acceptable roles is a severely limiting condition in disabled women's lives, often more limiting than the disability itself.

How children learn social roles is a complex phenomenon. Parents teach roles directly and indirectly and serve as role models themselves. When considering the absence of socially sanctioned roles for girls and women with disabilities, it is important to appreciate the dilemmas facing parents of disabled daughters (Rousso, 1984; 1985). They often do not know what to expect and may be uncertain if their daughters can follow in their footsteps in work or in their social lives. Like most people, they tend to be unaware of successful disabled women in the present or past. As a result, parents of disabled girls too often remain focused on the present, failing to communicate positive expectations to their daughters. Their daughters may misinterpret the parental silence to mean there is no future, at least not a productive, satisfying one. Alternatively, parents may set low expectations because they have accepted stereotypical images about who people with disabilities can be (Rousso, 1988). The net result can be profoundly damaging, contributing to the unemployment, underemployment, and social isolation of young women with disabilities upon leaving school.

The lack of positive role models, of course, has been a problem for all young women, as well as young people of color, low-income youth, and gay youth of both genders. Various strategies, such as mentoring programs, media campaigns highlighting successful women or people of color, or more inclusive curricula have been developed to address this issue. Mentoring projects have proliferated since the 1980s to address the need for positive role models and greater adult contact by youth (Public/Private Ventures, 1996). They seek to limit "risk" behaviors, such as dropping out of school, adolescent pregnancy, and drug problems, and to promote healthy development and expanded educational and career options.

Unfortunately, the widespread recognition of the need for role models by youth has not encompassed awareness of similar needs of disabled youth, and few mentoring programs have made an active attempt to include disabled young people. Until recently, their need for role models, particularly among girls with disabilities, has been as invisible as successful disabled women themselves.

THE NETWORKING PROJECT: START-UP

The major goal of the Networking Project for Disabled Women and Girls was to develop a program for adolescent girls with physical and sensory disabilities that would address the absence of role models by providing them with varied opportunities to meet diverse, successful women with disabilities. In addition, since no other role model program of this type existed, we hoped to encourage replication by offering technical assistance to community groups nationwide interested in developing a similar project and to develop materials to assist in replication. It was of great value to be able to operate the Networking Project in the YWCA of the City of New York, a community-based organization focused on women's issues and needs. It reinforced a basic tenet of the project that disabled women and girls are a minority group of women who face double discrimination. Indeed, underlying all aspects of the Networking Project was the assumption that the major issues facing disabled women and girls were civil rights issues and that prejudice and discrimination often impeded their success to a greater extent than physical or sensory limitations.

What Does It Mean to Be a Role Model?

Although I knew from my own experiences that girls with disabilities were limited by their lack of access to role models, at the program's start I was not yet sure what it meant for disabled women to serve as role models. What exactly were they to do? What role should they play? By her very presence, a woman serving as a role model could offer the hopeful message "You can be like me." But alone, this could encourage imitation without taking into account the unique talents of the young person; at worst, it could deteriorate into "You must be like me." We wanted the adult women to provide a range of options and positive possibilities, but we also wanted to facilitate the girls' discovery of their own potential. Some of what we sought seemed encompassed by the notion of "mentor," which includes teaching, guidance, advice, and encouragement, fostering the stance of "I will help you be whoever you wish to be."

So the adult women with disabilities in the Networking Project would be role models and mentors, as well as older friends, kindly aunts, and more. This was an evolving concept, based on our growing understanding of the needs of the girls and the interests and capacities of the women. Indeed, clarifying the intergenerational relationship became an important part of the project and one determinant of its success.

Developing Networks of Disabled Women and Girls

One of the first tasks in the development of the Networking Project was to establish a network of women with disabilities living in the community. There was a strong commitment to make this network as diverse as possible in terms of career area, educational background, ethnicity, lifestyle, and disability type. For example, we were eager to ensure that the women invited to join the network were not all "super achievers," but rather worked in jobs involving a range of educational requirements, from on-the-job training or vocational training programs to professional degrees. Some of the job areas represented included jewelry making, photography, court interpreting, computer programming, medicine, social work, community organizing, sales, private investigation, and carpentry. Ensuring inclusion of disabled women from varied racial and ethnic groups was another challenge. We sought to develop a mentor network in which the cultural backgrounds of the members matched the racial and ethnic mix of the young people involved in the program. Other factors we considered were age of onset of disability and attitudes toward disability status and womanhood. It was beneficial to include as many women as possible who had become disabled before or during adolescence, so they could share their experiences growing up with a disability. Also, it was crucial to choose mentors who felt positive about themselves as women and as disabled people and could send positive messages to the girls. We attempted to include women who were active in the disability rights and/or women's movements, assuming they would have pride in those aspects of their identity that formed the basis of their activism.

Members of the network were recruited in varied ways: from disability groups, women's groups, professional organizations, advocacy groups, corporations, educational institutions (including disabled students' services on campuses), and governmental agencies. Some mentoring programs have sought to recruit all their mentors from one company or organization, for the sake of efficiency and accountability (One to One Publication, 1994) but this was not an option for us since few companies, particularly those not specifically working in the field of disability or rehabilitation, could provide the diverse cadre of disabled women we sought. One unanticipated problem was that companies and organizations did not necessarily know which of their employees or members had a disability, or if they did, they were reluctant to "single them out," based on disability status. The Networking Project was started before the passage of the Americans with Disabilities Act, so in the absence of federal protection against discrimination, many employees or organizational members were reluctant to disclose disability-related needs. Publicizing the project in agency and company newsletters so that employees or members could contact the project directly was our way around the disclosure issue. We found women with disabilities eager to participate, partly because many recognized the lack of role models in their own lives. It was considerably harder to recruit the girls.

There were many barriers to recruiting girls with disabilities for the Networking Project. Some girls, not surprisingly, were not future-oriented or had limited expectations for their adult lives, so they could not see a need for a program to expand their career and social options. For example, during one recruitment presentation to a group of high school students at a local high school (the administrator insisted there was no way to convene only girls), the majority of the boys were eager to join and annoyed at their exclusion, whereas few girls showed any interest. In the ensuing discussion, the boys seemed considerably more concerned than the girls about independence, postsecondary education, and careers and recognized the program as a stepping stone to those outcomes. For other girls, the social stigma of disability and segregated special education classes made them reluctant to join a program only for disabled youth. Still others, eager for contact with boys, were not interested in a girls-only program. "Why not invite boys? We want to meet boys," some advocated.

In addition, some parents were overprotective; accustomed to having their daughters at home during after-school hours, they discouraged them from joining the program. Parental concerns were not necessarily unfounded. One mother indicated that two of her sons had been shot and killed in the neighborhood, and she was not about to let her daughter, who had a mobility disability that greatly limited the pace of her walking, out of her sight. Practical problems, such as lack of accessible public transportation and some girls' obligation to care for younger siblings at home, compounded the difficulties. Such barriers required creative outreach techniques, such as using appealing young women with disabilities with whom potential participants could identify as recruiters; setting up information meetings with parents to allay their fears; and providing free accessible transportation. Only after several home visits by project staff and the guarantee of door-to-door transportation would the mother who had lost two sons allow her daughter to participate. Through recruitment in schools and agencies serving youth with disabilities, the project was successful in engaging about thirty girls between the ages of thirteen and twenty-five, with a range of physical and sensory disabilities, including amputation, cerebral palsy, muscular dystrophy, spina bifida, spinal cord injury, speech disability, blindness, and deafness.

Limiting the project to girls with physical and sensory disabilities was, we felt, a necessary compromise. There are many commonalties across a broader range of disability types and using an expanded definition that included, for example, intellectual, cognitive, learning, and emotional disabilities could have enabled women and girls with diverse disabilities to break down their stereotypes of one another and see themselves as part of an inclusive group. However, there is a hierarchy of socially acceptable disabilities (Saflios-Rothschild, 1982), and we were concerned that with too broad a definition, women and girls on different ends of the hierarchy might be reluctant to identify with one another. While not an unworkable problem, this would have required consciousness raising and other training to break down barriers. There was also the question of whether and how participants with differing disabling conditions might need different programming to address the range of capacities and skills. Clearly, an inclusive definition of disability raises questions and issues regarding the development of a role model and mentoring project that are worth pursuing. Given the challenges of starting a new program, we chose to avoid further complexity by initially limiting our definition of disability. As the project evolved, young women with multiple disabilities, including cognitive and learning disabilities also participated, and some of the replication efforts used more expansive definitions.

Networking Conference for Women

After developing a network of women with disabilities to serve as mentors and role models, a day-long networking conference was held to achieve two purposes. One was to provide an orientation to the Networking Project, including a full explanation of its goals so that the women could decide whether and to what extent they wanted to participate. Project staff would also have an opportunity to assess the interests, strengths, limitations, and training needs of the women. The second major purpose was to enable the women to determine the types of attitudes, information, and skills they wanted to pass along to the girls. We believed they would be the best judge of what was most important in their lives for younger people to know.

To assist with this, participants were given questions about various aspects of their lives across a variety of settings: in school, at work, with their families, and in social circles. They discussed these with one another in small groups. Questions included: "What kinds of educational, work, and social aspirations did your parents have for you while you were growing up?" "What were your hurdles in getting your first job?" Such discussions enabled the women to identify factors that helped and hindered their personal and professional development, to examine the impact of being female and disabled on their life choices and experiences, and to consider the implications of these for their role as mentors.

For most participants this was their first opportunity to talk with other women with disabilities about their lives and to recognize what they had in common. For example, Edith, a sixty-three-year-old pediatrician who walked with leg braces and crutches as the result of childhood polio, had been one of the few women, much less women with disabilities, in her medical school class. She had survived and succeeded in her career by downplaying her disability and gender status and had little contact with other disabled people prior to the conference. She initially balked at the prospect of spending a whole day at a conference talking with other disabled women. "What in the world will we talk about?" she demanded to know. But at the end of the day, she was reluctant to leave and became one of the most committed mentors in the project, remaining for several years until her retirement and move to another city, where she helped establish a similar project.

Networking Conference for Women and Girls

After the women's gathering, the mentoring process was started by bringing together mentors, girls, and parents for a day-long networking conference. Girls were encouraged, though not required, to bring their parents, with the understanding that they would have opportunities to meet apart from them, thereby ensuring their privacy.

The first part of the conference was designed exclusively for girls and their parents and served as the counterpart to the separate women's networking meeting described previously. It introduced girls and their parents to the project and provided an opportunity to share and reflect on their life experiences, as well as to consider the kinds of questions they would like to ask their mentors. The orientation was conducted with girls and parents together and included a panel presentation by several women with diverse disabilities talking about their experiences growing up with a disability. This was followed by separate small group meetings for girls and parents. The girls talked about their interests, future plans, the experience of being female and disabled, and questions they might like to ask adult women with disabilities. Some of the discussion questions included "Do you think it is harder or easier to get a good job if you are a woman or a man?" "How about if you are disabled or nondisabled?" "What types of jobs interest you, and why?" Are you interested in getting involved in a long-term romantic relationship, such as marriage or having children when you get older?" Discussion topics in the parents' groups focused on their vision for their daughter's future and barriers she might face. Questions included "What are some of your concerns for your daughter's future? How are these similar to or different from your concerns for your other children?"

In the second half of the conference, the network of women joined the girls and parents to begin the mentoring process. Through structured small group sessions, girls had opportunities to ask questions and express concerns about their future. "How can you flirt if you can't see?" asked one teen girl who was blind. "How did you talk your mother into letting you move out of the house?" asked another, relieved that her mother was in another group and not within hearing distance. The adult women answered the girls' often burning questions with stories of their own lives designed to allay fears, where appropriate, but also to acknowledge some difficult realities related to being female and disabled. The networking conference helped identify major areas of concern for girls with disabilities that would become the focal point of future meetings and set the stage for the mentoring activities that would follow.

INTERGENERATIONAL ACTIVITIES

The Networking Project hosted numerous intergenerational activities, including large and small group sessions, field trips, and one-to-one encounters. The varied project components offered girls the chance to meet diverse women and explore a range of themes affecting their lives, from mother-daughter relationships to friendships and romantic relationships, independent living, and career choices. Some activity was held every other week to provide continuity and build group cohesion. Not everyone participated in all aspects of the program. Factors such as need, interest, and practical realities influenced the extent and nature of each younger and older member's involvement. Some of the key activities are briefly described below.

Work-Site Visits

What does it mean to be a court reporter or a neurochemist or a carpenter? Most young women know little about the meaning of a job title or the reality of what adults do at work. Young women with disabilities have even less information about the range of job possibilities or about the types of disability-related accommodations available. Work site visits were designed to expand girls' sense of job possibilities for women with different disabilities and to give them a taste of what it is like to perform a particular job. Small groups of girls, and sometimes their parents, would meet with an adult woman with a disability at her place of employment. The visits, lasting from two hours to a whole day, would include first watching the mentor carry out some of her typical job activities and then talking with the mentor about her job, for example, how she made her career choice, the education and training she needed, the pros and cons of her work, the barriers she faced as a woman with a disability, and her relationships with co-workers. On-site observations elicited interesting questions, such as "Didn't your boyfriend mind that you were a good carpenter? Isn't that a man's job?" or (to a social worker who was blind) "How do you pick up nonverbal cues from your clients if you cannot see them?" Some mentors found themselves gaining new insights into the basis of their own career decisions by offering explanations to the girls.

Mentor Panels on Careers and Lifestyles

Mentor panels consisted of several women with disabilities talking with girls about some aspect of their work, social, or community life, thus introducing girls to an expanded range of career or lifestyle options. One career panel on women in science included a nurse's aide, lab technician, high school science teacher, and researcher in marine biology. Another consisted of small business owners, including a woman who owned a private investigation company, a psychotherapist in private practice, a jewelry maker with her own store, and a free-lance word processor. One of the lifestyle panels on partners and parenting included a single woman with no children, another single women who had just adopted a baby, two married women—one with, the other without children— and a lesbian mother in a long-term relationship. Panelists addressed the advantages and disadvantages of their career and lifestyle choices; the factors, including gender and disability, that contributed to their choices; the barriers they faced as disabled women in their work or way of life and strategies they used to address these barriers; and ways they sought to balance their career or lifestyle choices with other aspects of their lives.

Special Events Celebrating the Accomplishments of Disabled Women

One strategy for expanding the array of positive images available to girls with disabilities was organizing special events highlighting the artistic achievements of women with disabilities. We held an art exhibit in the YWCA gallery that featured paintings, drawings, sculpture, and crafts of women artists with disabilities. Young project participants not only saw the exhibit, but they also participated in hands-on workshops conducted by the artists. Girls learned a jeweler's techniques of melting and molding fine metals while seated in a wheelchair and a painter's strategy of holding her paintbrush between her teeth since she had limited use of her hands. The exhibit remained open for several weeks, thereby providing an opportunity for public education as well.

Another event, in honor of Women's History Month, was a reading in the public library of literary works by women writers with disabilities. This included the works of historic and contemporary, published and unpublished writers.[4] Girls were involved as listeners and also as readers of some of the pieces, including (in a few instances) girls reading their own works. All works were read by women or girls with disabilities.

Theme-Centered Workshops

All adolescents grapple with issues such as sexuality, body image, and independence. Being disabled and female often compounds the resolution of such issues. For example, how can a disabled young woman loosen her ties to her parents when she is dependent on them to provide transportation or to meet her physical needs, such as assistance with eating or using the bathroom? The project developed theme-centered workshops, so girls could discuss some of the "hot topics" on their minds with older women with disabilities. Each workshop focused on one topic, determined by the girls, and included questions to facilitate intergenerational conversation. For example, at the workshop on independence, each mentor was asked to describe when and how she moved out of her parents' house, how she felt, and what she wishes she had known then. Occasionally, outside speakers who were knowledgeable about the topic also attended. In a workshop on transportation, the executive director of an independent living center known for helping people develop skills to use public transportation, who happened to be a young man with muscular dystrophy, was invited to kick off the discussion. Because he had a sister with the same disability, he was in a unique position to comment on the role of gender in parental attitudes. He described how his parents allowed him to use the new accessible public buses at any time of the day or night but only allowed his sister to use paratransit, a separate system that ran on a limited schedule. His comments led to a lively discussion of the widespread parental resistance to the girls' use of public transportation. This led to a follow-up session for parents, girls, and mentors on transportation, resulting in some of the parents agreeing to let their daughters receive travel training.

One-to-One Mentoring

In the one-to-one mentoring component, women and girls were paired and asked to meet on a regular basis over a one- to two-year time period to provide each girl with more individualized, focused adult attention than would be possible in large or small group activities. This component was one of the most labor intensive aspects of the project, but when it worked well, it was gratifying to both participants.

Girls and women were matched using a variety of variables, including career interests, personality, communication style, disability type, race, ethnicity, socioeconomic group, and geographic proximity. Yet, according to an assessment of the component (Campbell, 1987), many of these variables were irrelevant. Despite our efforts, fewer than half the pairs kept meeting beyond a few months. What distinguished successful from unsuccessful matches was the mentor's ability to be a good listener—"I can tell her things I can't tell my mom"—and the pair's ability to have fun together—"We just can laugh and have a good time." Existing research on mentoring reframes our experience in slightly different language, indicating that the mentor's ability to build trust may be more important than any commonality between the pair (Public/Private Ventures, 1996).

One of the longest lasting mentor pairs was between the oldest women and youngest girl in the project who were of different racial, socioeconomic, and disability groups and lived on the opposite ends of the city. They did share an interest in medicine, but perhaps more significant was the commitment of the mentor to meet with her mentee frequently, to call her between visits, to be deeply interested in the girl's life and future, and to be willing to forge a relationship without imposing her adult agenda on the young woman.

Mentors and mentees were expected to meet every four to six weeks in one another's homes, at restaurants, movie theaters, museums, or other locations, or at events held at the YWCA. Telephone contact was encouraged between sessions. More frequent meetings would have been preferable, particularly when the mentoring relationship was just forming, but logistical problems, such as lack of accessible transportation and time and energy restrictions on the part of disabled women who already had highly demanding schedules, made even monthly visits a challenge. Coupling mentor-mentee visits with Networking Project events held at the YWCA helped to lessen at least some of the barriers.

An important ingredient in sustaining the one-to-one component was providing mentors with ongoing training and support to enhance the mentoring relationship and troubleshoot problems. Research suggests that support for mentors is an essential ingredient for any successful mentoring program (Public/Private Ventures, 1996, p. 9). In addition to the initial Networking Conference for Women, we held mentor training sessions every six to eight weeks to discuss roles and expectations, provide information and skills, and address common problems that were emerging in the mentoring relationship. Early on, an overview of adolescent development was provided, with particular emphasis on the role of such factors as gender, disability, race, ethnicity, and socioeconomic class. Such information was particularly useful for mentors who had not had recent experience with adolescents and thus were inadequately prepared for the emotional ups and downs that their mentees might be facing. Many of the mentors, regardless of experience, were struck by the difficulties involved in engaging young women in conversation, particularly by phone. One-word answers to their thoughtful questions and long silences on the end of the telephone line were a source of considerable frustration to mentors. Encouraging the women to persist, be consistent, and stay connected long enough to build the trust needed to lessen the silence was an important part of the training.

Another issue addressed in training was giving and receiving help. An important survival skill for girls with disabilities—and all youth and adults, to a degree—is the ability to ask for and receive precisely the help they need. A girl's ability to control the type and quantity of help she receives, rather than being at the mercy of caregivers, is an important aspect of her becoming independent. Unfortunately, asking for help is stigmatized in our culture. From childhood, most people are taught to "do it themselves" regardless of cost, and at the same time, to appreciate whatever help they receive regardless of whether they want or need it. For people with disability-related limitations, following the cultural prohibition against asking for help may be particularly damaging. We had hoped that our mentors would be able to model effective strategies for obtaining needed help. We found, however, that particularly for older women who had grown up when there was more of a charity rather than a civil rights model of disability, their career success had depended on disavowing their disability-related needs and minimizing their requests for help. Thus, we devoted a training session to the topic of asking for help, if not to change the mentors' attitudes, then at least to raise their awareness. For some of the mentors, these sessions greatly increased their ability to ask for help in their own lives.

Engaging the mentors in critiquing the training sessions proved invaluable. While our inclination was to address broad topics relevant to the lives of girls, the mentors reminded us that they also needed practical advice, such as where to take their mentees and how to establish appropriate relationships with parents.

Most of our training efforts were focused on the mentors, but ongoing training sessions for the girls would also have been useful. Aside from the initial intergenerational Networking Conference, we held one formal orientation session. This was designed to help girls explore their hopes, dreams, and fears about the mentoring relationship and to understand the practical aspects of their participation. What became increasingly apparent as the project evolved was that the girls were uncertain how to relate to an older woman in an unfamiliar role. As one of the girls asked, "What should I do with her?" Also, there were issues about whether mentors could be trusted not to reveal confidences to mothers or just be trusted to really care about them. Many girls had difficult relationships with their mothers, as well as problematic histories with community agencies in which professionals had betrayed their trust. All of these factors spoke to the need for ongoing support for the girls so that they could risk letting a relative stranger become an active participant in their lives.

Work with Parents

Parents are an important influence on the future expectations and life goals of all young people. Their vision of the future may be particularly important for girls with disabilities, who may have access to fewer outside influences than their nondisabled female or disabled male peers. Thus, an important goal of the Networking Project was to enable parents to develop positive, realistic expectations for their disabled daughters through contact with successful disabled women.

One strategy was to invite parents to some events that their daughters were attending, such as mentor panels, worksite visits, and celebrations of the accomplishments of disabled women. Recognizing the girls' need for their own space, we were selective in choosing events that parents could attend and, where appropriate, had separate discussion groups for parents. We also held parent workshops on topics salient to the lives of girls, such as independent living and social/sexual issues, and open-ended discussion groups in which parents were encouraged to voice concerns about their daughters' futures. Despite active outreach efforts, we were never successful in engaging more than a handful of parents. For some parents, overloaded with other responsibilities, attending project events became one more burden they were unwilling to assume. Also, many parents had been negotiating with agencies to get needed services for their daughter since her birth, so by her adolescence, they were mistrustful of such encounters or were just burned out. Parents seemed most willing to attend project events that were relaxed, nondemanding, and with no formal agenda. A mother/daughter barbecue and a picnic in Central Park were particularly successful.

BENEFITS OF THE PROJECT

Did the girls benefit from participation in the Networking Project? We used a variety of strategies to attempt to answer this question, including staff observations, feedback forms filled out by participants after various events, and anecdotal information from girls who had "graduated" from the project. Three years after the project began, we hired an outside evaluator to conduct a project evaluation involving written questionnaires for all girls in the project and telephone interviews with some youth and adult participants in the one-to-one component. Based on the information that was gathered, we reached some tentative conclusions.

The Project Fostered the Independence of Youth Participants

For some of the girls, contact with women with disabilities living on their own gave them the vision that they, too, could lead independent lives. As one young woman stated: "The project network helped me change because before I was part of it, I thought I had to live with my parents for the rest of my life. I thought there was no such thing as a handicapped person living alone and having a job. Now I have the confidence to do all the things I want to do" (Campbell, 1987, p. 5).

During the course of their involvement, several young women began to use public transportation and/or make their own arrangements for car services. For a few of the girls involved in the one-to-one component, their mentors went with them on their maiden voyages on public buses, showing them how to use the wheelchair lift, to request from the driver a lowering of the front steps, and to develop a sense of security and safety when in the bus. As one of the girls said, "My mentor had me get on and off five different buses during one of our visits. By the end of the day, I felt almost wrecked—it was scary, you know—but I had it down pat."

For a few of the older girls, participation in the project facilitated the process of moving out of their parents' house into college dorms or apartments with peers. For one young woman, a college freshman who had been convinced by her family that as a wheelchair user she could never survive dorm life, stories by some of the mentors of successfully living on college campuses and concrete advice on what skills she needed to live independently enabled her to move on campus by the middle of her sophomore year. As she explained, "I wound up moving by myself on a public bus, but now my family's come around. They see I can do it."

The Project Enabled Some Girls to Expand Career Goals or Pursue Dreams That Seemed Unobtainable

For example, Diana was a good science student who entered the program with a conviction that she could never pursue her interest in medicine because she had cerebral palsy and used a wheelchair. She ultimately entered college as a premed student, largely as the result of encouragement and a recommendation she received from her mentor, a pediatrician, and the advocacy provided by project staff with the vocational education counselor.

Kim, an Asian American young woman who was discouraged at every turn from pursuing her desired career in social work because of her mobility disability—"How will you climb stairs to make home visits?" one of her relatives repeatedly asked—finally entered a social work program when her mentor, a social worker who used crutches, helped her problem solve the issue of meeting with clients in inaccessible locations and served as a counterbalance to all the negative opinions.

To Benefit, Girls Needed to Be Actively Engaged and Connected

Not every girl's experience with the project was a success story. Factors that appeared to contribute to successful outcomes for girls were regular attendance, evidence of real engagement with the project (for example a willingness to help plan events or to contribute to discussions), and an attachment to at least one adult staff member and/or mentor.

Mentors Benefited as Well

Mentors were gratified at being able to share survival strategies and expertise. One woman stated: "I like the satisfaction of knowing what I had to share made a difference." Some obtained new skills and self-assurance that enhanced their own lives. One mentor described greater freedom in asking for help: "I couldn't lift Ellen's [her mentee's] wheelchair to put in my car, so, since I am a do-it-yourself-or-not-at-all person, I concluded we would have to stay in the neighborhood. But to my surprise, Ellen recruited a stranger off the street to give us a hand. It was no big deal, and next time, I did the recruiting." Another mentor noted greater freedom in speaking about taboo topics: "The girls unabashedly asked questions about everything. I became much more open about myself, my disability, and my sexuality; not only with them but with my family and friends. It was a gift to have the conspiracy of silence thwarted at last."

In addition, the girls, by sharing their dilemmas about drugs, violence, and sex, for example, educated the women about what it was like to be a teen today and highlighted the differences between the generations. As one of the women said, "These girls are so much more street smart than I ever was. I really admire their spunk and ability to survive in their world. I'm not sure I could." And clearly, for many of the women, even those with broad networks of family, friends, and colleagues, being exclusively among women and girls with disabilities offered a unique sense of community. "Being here, I can be totally me," commented one mentor.

Role Models and Mentors Help, but They May Not Be Enough

One of our findings was that girls with disabilities not only need a more positive vision of who they can be and become but also a diverse set of skills needed to implement that vision. These skills include decision making, problem solving, future planning, information gathering, identifying relevant resources, communication, and self-advocacy, among others. A young woman may decide that she wants to become an electrician, as one of our young participants did, but then she will need to investigate prerequisite skills and courses, advocate with her vocational counselor and parents, problem solve adaptations to address her disability-related limitations, and so forth. Access to role models and mentors can provide the vision but not necessarily all the skills.

One strategy that we developed well into the program was to add a skills development component consisting of a series of workshops for the girls to build what we called "pre-employment skills." Broken into five major life areas—work, social life, parents, housing and transportation—these were essentially hands-on workshops in which we would use experiential techniques such as role-playing, small group discussions, and brainstorming to teach skills and foster awareness of relevant community resources. Mentors were sometimes invited to co-lead or sit in on sessions, but the primary emphasis was on fostering skills rather than mentoring.

THE NETWORKING PROJECT: WHAT DOES IT MEAN FOR TEACHERS?

After the Networking Project was developed in New York City, efforts were made to replicate it in whole or in part in various cities throughout the country, including Albany, Los Angeles, Philadelphia, Pittsburgh, Spokane, and Westchester County (New York). Resources were developed to assist with the replication process. While most of the sponsoring organizations at the replication sites were community agencies, such as a YWCA or independent living center, aspects of the project can be implemented in schools as well. The following subsections address some simple strategies for capturing the intent, spirit, and hopefully some of the benefits of the Networking Project.

Strategy 1

Incorporate into educational materials lessons and assignments that highlight the accomplishments and issues of women and girls with disabilities. There is a growing number of books and videos by and about disabled women. Select materials that represent diversity in terms of race, ethnicity, disability type, educational level, career choice, and lifestyle. Early on in the school year, invite students to brainstorm the names of famous disabled women they know or to identify the contributions of a list of women with disabilities. This is a good way to pique curiosity and lay the groundwork for further study.

Strategy 2

Advocate that school-wide events, for example career fairs or events in honor of Black History Month or Women's History Month include women with disabilities as presenters, and incorporate materials that reflect the lives and issues of disabled women.

Strategy 3

Work with students to hold grade-wide or school-wide events celebrating the accomplishments of disabled women, such as a poetry reading or film festival.

Strategy 4

Work with local independent living centers or other disability advocacy agencies to identify a small group of diverse women with disabilities who are willing to come into the classroom periodically to share information about their work or other aspects of their lives. Ideally, these women should be well known to the referring agency and hence can be counted on to have positive, realistic attitudes toward being disabled and female. Given our experience with the Networking Project, ongoing contact with a group of women is useful, enabling students to build relationships, although even one-time contact with a range of women can help expand options. This core group of women—and it can be just three to five women to start—can work with teachers and students to develop programs that address the students' needs and interests. These can include mentor panel presentations, theme-centered workshops, or field trips to a mentor's worksite, as described above. The state vocational rehabilitation agency may be willing to cover student travel costs for work-related field trips. As this core group of women becomes engaged, members may help recruit other disabled women to participate in classroom events. Some of the new recruits may then become part of the core.

Strategy 5

As the group of mentors expands, consider asking the agency that referred the women or the part of the school system involved in community activities to assist in providing periodic screening, orientation, training, and support sessions for mentors.

Strategy 6

Introduce a one-to-one mentoring component to take place in the classroom and/or during school hours when a system is in place to provide mentor training and support. If this proves infeasible, some of the benefits of one-to-one mentoring may be achieved by providing informal mingling time for students and mentors before or after programs. Particularly if the same group of mentors stay involved, intergenerational "hanging out," over juice, soda and cookies, perhaps, can foster the building of intergenerational relationships.

Strategy 7

Invite parents to some mentoring activities so that they have exposure to positive role models, but be selective and respectful of adolescents' need for independence. Also, if periodic meetings with parents apart from their children are held, invite some of the mentors to attend (although this should be done only with the young people's knowledge and permission).

WHAT ABOUT THE BOYS?

A common reaction when people learn about the Networking Project is "What about the boys? Don't they need mentors and role models too?" In fact, disabled youth of both genders have limited access to role models and could benefit from mentoring and role model projects. But the needs of girls with disabilities are intensified by such factors as the following:

- the greater invisibility of successful women with disabilities compared to successful men with disabilities in our curricula and culture—studies of curricula for disability-related content suggest images and stories of disabled men and boys appear more often than those of disabled women and girls;
- the more limited socially sanctioned roles available to disabled women compared to disabled men;
- the double discrimination that disabled women face out in the world, suggesting disabled girls' need to learn strategies to survive and succeed in the face of multiple barriers.
- in addition to girls' greater need, there are particular benefits to providing disabled girls with a "females only" mentoring program, providing a safe space for honest, open, intergenerational conversations about difficult, sometimes intimate issues. Several of the young women in our project initially protested the absence of boys; but as the project went on, many remarked that they felt differently. As one young woman said, "I don't think I could have shown how scared I was about going out in the world with guys around. Pretend you're strong, and that kind of thing."

Despite the benefits, developing sex-segregated mentoring programs is not always possible. You may need to develop mentoring and role model activities geared to students with disabilities of both genders. Many of the suggestions provided above can be adapted to include men with disabilities as mentors and materials about disabled men and boys. But even within a co-educational approach, it is important to address the particular role model needs of girls with disabilities. The following subsections address some possible strategies.

Strategy 1

When introducing role model materials, lessons, and exercises, choose those that highlight the accomplishments of women and girls with disabilities. By way of explanation, engage students in a direct discussion of the invisibility of successful women with disabilities. Have them look through their textbooks, popular magazines, and television programs to analyze whether and how disabled women and girls are portrayed in comparison to disabled men and boys.

Strategy 2

Make sure that disabled women are well represented as speakers and guests; take advantage of gender-specific events, such as Women's History Month, to showcase the achievements of disabled women.

Strategy 3

If both women and men with disabilities are invited into the classroom to serve as mentors, make sure at least an equal number of women, or better yet, a few more women than men, participate to counterbalance the invisibility issue. Also, consider having some activities, such as mentor panels, be gender specific, for example, consist of only female mentors, or only male mentors, to help students consider the role of gender issues in their own lives. In addition, consider providing male and female students with some opportunities to meet separately with mentors of their gender, perhaps through discussion groups.

POSITIVE POSSIBILITIES

My mentor, Betty, and I continued our relationship for more than three decades, until her death a few years ago. At some point, she stopped being my mentor and became my friend, but the seeds of positive possibilities that she gave me early on have continued to flower in my mind. I did not become like her, or even necessarily what she had expected or hoped for me, but at least partly through her, I was able to develop a vision for myself that has remained expansive rather than confining. It is a challenge for girls with disabilities to create such a vision in the world they grow up in, filled with barriers and stereotypes that restrict their choices and their dreams. For these girls, women with disabilities can provide the nurturing environment for such an act of creation.

NOTES

1. This chapter focuses on the work of the Networking Project from 1984 through 1989, when the author was director. The project remains ongoing at the YWCA/NYC at this writing, in somewhat different form and name and under different leadership.

2. Some material from this section also appears in H. Rousso, with S. G. O'Malley and M. Severance, 1988, *Disabled, Female and Proud! Stories of Ten Women with Disabilities*, Boston: Exceptional Parent Press, introduction.

3. For information on these and other famous women (and men) with disabilities, see D. Kent and K. Quinlan, 1996, *Extraordinary People with Disabilities,* Danbury, Conn.: Children's Press.

4. Sources of published works include S. E. Browne, D. Connors, and N. Stern, eds., 1986, *With the Power of Each Breath: A Disabled Women's Anthology*, Pittsburgh: Cleis Press; D. Drieger and S. Gray, eds., 1992, *Imprinting Our Image: An International Anthology by Women with Disabilities*, Canada: Gynergy Books; K. Fries, ed., 1997, *Staring Back: The Disability Experience from the Inside Out*, New York: Plume, the Penguin Group; M. Saxton and F. Howe, eds., 1987, *With Wings: An Anthology of Literature by and about Women with Disabilities*, New York: The Feminist Press at City University of New York.

REFERENCES

Campbell, P. B. 1987. *YWCA networking project for disabled women and girls: Project assessment report.* Commissioned by the YWCA of the City of New York.

Fine, M., and A. Asch. 1981. Disabled women: Sexism without the pedestal. *Journal of Sociology and Social Welfare* 8(2):65–80.

Linton, S. 1998. *Claiming disability: Knowledge and identity.* New York: New York University Press.

One to One Publication. 1994, June. Creating an institutionalized school-based mentoring program. *One to One in Focus* 3.

O'Toole, J. C. 1979. Disabled women: The case of the missing role model. *Independent* 2:55–57.

Public/Private Ventures. 1996. *Mentoring: A synthesis of P/PV's research: 1988–95.* Philadelphia: Author.

Resource Center on Educational Equity/Council of Chief State School Officers. 1986. *Achieving equity in education programs for disabled women and girls: A model workshop manual.* Washington, D.C.: Author.

Rousso, H. 1984 and 1985. Fostering healthy self-esteem, Parts I and II. *Exceptional Parent*, 14:8, pp. 9–14 (Part I), 15:1, pp. 9–12 (Part II).

————. 1988. Daughters with disabilities: Defective women or minority women? In *Women with disabilities: Essays in psychology, politics and culture*. Edited by M. Fine and A. Asch. Philadelphia: Temple University Press, 139–171.

Saflios-Rothschild, C. 1982. Social and psychological parameters of friendship and intimacy for disabled people. In *Disabled people as second class citizens*. Edited by M. G. Eisenberg, C. Griggins, and R. J. Duval. New York: Springer Publishing, 40–41.

Women and Disability Awareness Project. 1984. *Building community. A manual exploring issues of women and disability*. New York: Educational Equity Concepts, Inc.

CHAPTER 16

The Living Out Loud Program: Building Resiliency in Adolescent Girls with Disabilities

Nancy Ferreyra
and Estelle Eskenazi

I am not so different. I actually see my disability as a gift now, a different way of seeing things. I no longer limit myself to one way of doing things and therefore have created some good problem-solving skills. I am luckier than others because I can see many ways of doing things.

> —nineteen-year-old graduate
> of the Living Out Loud Program

INTRODUCTION AND PROJECT OVERVIEW

Living Out Loud was a five-year project serving adolescent girls with learning disabilities and/or physical disabilities. Located in the San Francisco Bay area, Progressive Research and Training for Action operated the project from October 1994 through December 1999. Funded by the Center for Substance Abuse Prevention, the goal of the project was to build resiliency in disabled girls, so they would not use tobacco, alcohol, or other drugs. The project sought to lessen the risk factors for substance abuse while building on the strengths and capacities of the participants, so they could become strong, successful young women.

The basic objectives of the project were to (1) design a substance abuse prevention program to meet the needs of young women with learning and/or physical disabilities and (2) gather baseline data about the attitudes and behaviors of girls with learning and/or physical disabilities to fill the information gap about this group.

The prevention program consisted of several components, including a life skills curriculum, facilitated groups, one-on-one counseling, adult disabled women as role models, integration in community events and programming, and provision of opportunities not often afforded to disabled girls. Over five years, the project served approximately three hundred girls, most of whom were Latina and African American and from low-income families.

Program Rationale and Philosophy

Adolescence is a critical time in any girl's life. Unlike boys, whose self-esteem drops during adolescence but then climbs during adulthood, girls' self-esteem drops and continues to decline for the rest of their lives (AAUW, 1991). Hence, at around age eleven, girls "lose their voice." In response to this declining self-image, research indicates that nondisabled girls use alcohol, tobacco, and other drugs to cope with depression and stress. Adolescent girls with disabilities face more challenges to maintaining their sense of self than their nondisabled peers because of social oppression and exclusion from social activities and are at risk for negative outcomes.

The Living Out Loud program was developed to enable girls with disabilities to find their voice and fulfill their potential. It was founded on the tenet that the most significant barriers that girls with disabilities face are societal barriers. Therefore, to become successful women, these girls must have a clear understanding of the context that surrounds their position in society as females and as females with disabilities. The program's philosophy drew upon feminism and the independent living model. It was a peer advocacy model, enabling girls to recognize and address their own needs and advocate on their own behalf.

Research Basis for the Program

Committed to developing a program grounded in research, we conducted a literature search on substance abuse prevention for adolescent girls with disabilities, but found no data. As an alternative, we broke the topic into three related parts. We first examined research on substance abuse among girls and, next, on substance abuse among youth with disabilities. Third, we reviewed what was known about the status and unique obstacles facing girls with disabilities, even if this information was not specifically related to substance abuse. In addition, we conducted a series of focus groups with women with diverse disabilities of various ages and ethnic backgrounds, adolescent girls with physical and/or learning disabilities, educators, and experts who had developed model programs for youth with disabilities. These focus groups provided information on factors contributing to substance abuse, barriers to developing strong self-esteem, and strategies for empowering and developing resilience in girls and young women with disabilities. The data gathered from these sources were used to craft the components of the program. Major findings and their implications for programming are presented next.

LITERATURE REVIEW

Risk Factors for Substance Abuse among Female Adolescents

The most widely documented risk for substance abuse among adolescent girls is poor body image (Bodinger-de Uriarte and Austin, 1991) and the desire to fit in with boys. Hence, the curriculum would need to address body image, including specific issues for girls with disabilities. Additionally, there was evidence of a high rate of depression among adolescent females and its correlation with substance abuse. Thus, staff would need the skills to address depression and know community resources that provide counseling services.

Risk Factors for Substance Abuse among Youth with Disabilities

A common perception is that just as youth with disabilities are isolated from mainstream activities, they are also sheltered from exposure to alcohol and other drugs. However, according to at least one study (Moore, 1992), disabled youth initiate drug use at the same time as nondisabled youth. This suggested that although Living Out Loud was intended to be a prevention program, it was likely that some of the participants might already be experimenting with alcohol or other drugs.

Another risk factor for youth with disabilities identified in the literature was "enabling" by family members and society in general (Resource Center on Substance Abuse and Disability, 1992). In their desire to have their disabled children be "normal," there is a tendency to accept behaviors (such as drinking alcohol) that are viewed as a typical adolescent rite of passage into adulthood. Similarly, other adults in a youth's life may perceive that the young person has no other options for recreation. To address this issue, the program would need to educate parents, family members, and teachers about substance abuse.

Obstacles for Girls with Disabilities

Studies on the "state" of girls with disabilities documented a range of obstacles. These included high rates of physical and sexual abuse and neglect (Cross, Kaye, and Ratnofsky, 1993), as well as teen pregnancy and poor academic achievement (Wagner, 1992). Such findings suggested the importance of addressing violence and sexuality in the curriculum. Additionally, since boys outnumbered girls two to one in special education (U.S. Department of Education, 1998) it seemed likely that the needs of disabled girls were overshadowed by those of the boys. As such, we felt that girls would benefit from focused, personal attention and the chance to meet with a group of their peers.

FOCUS GROUPS

The focus groups of women with disabilities, girls with disabilities, educators, and program developers provided a range of useful information. One common theme emerging from the various groups, further substantiated by the literature review, was the lack of role models for disabled girls (O'Toole, 1979; Fine and Asch, 1988). This made a compelling case for having women with disabilities heavily involved throughout the program.

IMPLEMENTING THE PROGRAM

Identifying Participants

The original program design was to convene groups at school-based sites, serving all disabled girls enrolled in the school, regardless of their specific disability. But it soon became apparent that this design was weak for two reasons.

First, one of the most critical aspects to the program was cultivating community among the participants. This was to be accomplished by the girls sharing common experiences and supporting each other's struggles. If the girls had different disabilities, they might share some experiences, but their various levels of emotional and cognitive development might impede any meaningful communication. In the end, in order for groups to become cohesive, it was decided that the participants needed to have the same disability.

Second, it was important that the research findings be as significant as possible. Because this population of girls had never been studied, the project had a strong commitment to produce results that would make meaningful contributions to the substance abuse field, the disability field, and the gender studies community. The larger and more specific the sample, the more meaningful the findings.

Therefore, we decided to include only girls with learning disabilities or physical disabilities and to have a separate group for each. We included girls with learning disabilities because they represented the largest percentage of students receiving special education services, and girls with physical disabilities, a relatively low incidence group, because of staff interest. If a participant had both a physical and a learning disability, she chose the group in which she wanted to participate.

Physical disability was defined broadly as any disabling condition that impaired the student's capacity to perform an activity of daily living. Most participants had cerebral palsy; others had spina bifida or spinal cord injuries. Several had speech disabilities and used augmentative communication devices. Almost half of the physically disabled girls also had learning disabilities. Participants with physical disabilities were recruited through high school special education departments, medical therapy units, disability service agencies, medical rehabilitation clinics, and by word of mouth.

Learning disability was defined as an average or above average I.Q. and a documented difference in learning style. Girls involved in the program had dyscalculia, dyslexia, dysgraphia, dysphasia, auditory processing learning disability, attention deficit disorder, social perceptual learning disability, and perceptual motor disability. Only one of the girls in the learning disability group also had a physical disability. Participants with learning disabilities were recruited through the special education departments of the high schools where the group meetings were held.

Recruiting Staff

The program recruited staff who would mirror the life experiences of the participants. Preference was given to women who (1) had a personal experience growing up as a disabled girl and (2) had a broader analysis of the societal position of females with disabilities. Staff members were also of various ethnic backgrounds to match the demographics of the participants.

Developing and Implementing the Curriculum

Drawing on research and the staff's expertise in the fields of women's and girls' issues, disability rights/culture and substance abuse, a curriculum was designed that included the core components: (1) disability identity, culture, community, and diversity; (2) disability rights/civil rights issues, including accommodations; (3) body image and changes; (4) sexual harassment, assault, and other forms of violence; (5) suicide; (6) alcohol, tobacco, and other drugs abuse and prevention; (7) self-defense; (8) transition, postsecondary education and vocation; (9) parenting; (10)

recreational options; (11) personal assistant management; (12) finances; and (13) nutrition and diet.

Counselors had the flexibility to spend more time on some components, less time on others. For instance, the group for girls with physical disabilities spent more time on civil rights under the Americans with Disabilities Act, and the group for girls with learning disabilities devoted more time to the issue of utilizing accommodations in the classroom. Some exercises in the curriculum were the same for both groups, and some differed. For instance, in the area of nutrition, while the physically disabled girls had to address the logistics of cooking, the learning disabled girls needed to focus on how to read and follow a recipe.

Once the program was underway, various components were added reflecting other needs and interests of the girls. These included entrepreneurship, where girls developed business skills; formulated plans for small businesses; made and marketed jewelry; and learned about the global marketplace, partly by establishing e-mail contact with youth in other countries; media literacy, where the girls critiqued magazines and other media and used media images to explore issues of body image and physical appearance; and videography, where participants shot, edited, and produced videos.

In addition, as we got to know the girls, we realized that certain assumptions we had made about their lives were erroneous, requiring modifications in the curriculum. For example, we assumed that participants would have some knowledge about their disability. While this assumption was true for the girls with physical disabilities, over half the girls with learning disabilities did not know the nature of their specific learning disability or its effects on their unique learning needs. A handful of these girls did not know they had a disability; they thought they were in special education because they were "slow." The curriculum was revised to include basic information on various learning disabilities and ways to accommodate them. Girls received calculators and hand-held computerized spellers and were informed that they had a right to use these tools in class and to obtain other accommodations, such as extended time for tests.

Staff also discovered that although we designed a rich educational curriculum, what kept the girls coming back was not so much the information they received, but rather the opportunities to connect with peers and engage in fun activities. Participants wanted opportunities afforded their nondisabled peers, so these were provided.

Much of the curriculum was implemented in a group format. The groups for girls with learning disabilities were convened on high school campuses during regular school hours. Generally, these groups met twice a week for one hour. The group for girls with physical disabilities met at a local independent living center three to four Saturdays a month during the regular school year. We purchased a wheelchair accessible van and transported most of the girls to and from the site.

In addition to group sessions, the program provided one-on-one counseling that was designed to address social and academic problems and provide the young women with a sense of being cared about and important. Through counseling, the staff was able to assist girls with issues that had not been anticipated at the start of the program. For example, while we knew many participants came from communities with ongoing economic challenges, we had not anticipated the extent of the need by some girls for help with basic living support, including food, clothing, and shelter, requiring an extensive outlay of staff time. Also, we had not anticipated that most of the girls' individualized education plans (IEPs) would be outdated, requiring considerable time-consuming advocacy to ensure updating.

Another aspect of the program was field trips. These fostered independence (for some of the physically disabled young women, it was their first opportunity to be out in a public setting without their parents), provided information on educational and career options (i.e., visiting local colleges), and were simply fun and recreational. For some of the girls who had not intended to go to college, the field trips to college campuses, combined with the rest of the program, helped them reconsider, apply, and enroll. As one participant stated: "Living Out Loud has taught me how to overcome some of the fear of going to college and becoming a professional. If I wasn't a participant in Living Out Loud, I would be home thinking I could not achieve anything and might have converted myself into a mother."

Another program element was access to role models, through contact with staff and visitors, providing several girls with their first opportunity to meet adult women with disabilities. Other features of the intended program included a parent support group and presentations to teachers on the substance abuse risks for girls with disabilities. Neither proved feasible due to time constraints of parents and teachers. To reach these groups, the staff established telephone contact with parents and distributed packets of information to teachers.

EVALUATION

An evaluation of the program was carried out by an independent research firm, employing both process and outcome methods. To measure the impact of the program on the individual participants, staff members conducted pre and post surveys utilizing measures of self-esteem and alcohol, tobacco, and illicit drug use patterns and behaviors. Also, a life skills survey was created to determine the level of information participants retained from the curriculum. In addition, entry and exit surveys were used to gather basic demographics on participants' family members and measure changes in expectations and academic and vocational plans.

To assess the impact of the program on participants with learning disabilities, a comparison group of learning disabled girls who did not receive program services was recruited. The comparison group, matched to the treatment group by age, ethnicity, and disability, also completed measures of self-esteem and drug/alcohol use. Because not enough physically disabled girls could be identified for a comparison group, participants with physical disabilities were interviewed to gather more information on their experiences in the program.

Each summer the preliminary findings were analyzed, and program staff members were interviewed as part of the process evaluation. Continually, it appeared the evaluation results were not capturing the impact of the program. For example, staff interviews revealed that a number of the girls were not planning on attending college at the beginning of their senior year but then went on to attend a local junior college. These data were not being recorded through the intake and exit surveys, so the surveys were revised to include items regarding postsecondary plans.

The evaluation findings included the following:

1. The program had a positive impact on the development of a positive disability identity.

2. The girls had a greater understanding of their disability and the tools to accommodate it. One participant stated: "Living Out Loud helped me address the fact that I had a disability. It helped me learn that I did not need to be ashamed, which is why I kept away from people." According to another participant: "This program taught me to advocate for myself and to deal with my learning disabilities. I really like this program because I really didn't know what kind of disabilities I had, and now I do."

3. The participants felt they were a part of a larger community, the disability community.

4. The participants had a sense of entitlement to receive their specific disability-related accommodations, and they developed the skills to advocate for themselves. For example, one young woman stated that because of the program: "I have to speak out for what I believe in . . . to make a big deal about accessibility . . . to have a voice . . . to feel comfortable saying I can't do it."

5. In terms of substance abuse prevention, program participants used alcohol, tobacco, and other drugs at a slighter lower rate than the comparison group. However, both the participant and comparison groups reported fairly low rates of use in general. Participants did learn a considerable amount about the effects of substance use on people with disabilities: "I knew about the effects of drug and alcohol use on able-bodied kids from a class I had taken in high school, but I didn't know the specifics about my population. Living Out Loud's education was more in-depth, and related the effects on us."

Some achievements seemed small by external standards yet were highly significant in the lives of participants, such as getting 100 percent correct on a spelling test for the first time or a girl having the knowledge and confidence to tell siblings that she is not stupid—she has a learning disability. According to interviews with the girls, the most valuable part of the Living Out Loud experience was spending time with other disabled girls and with an adult woman with a similar disability.

IMPLICATIONS OF LIVING OUT LOUD FOR EDUCATORS

Here are some ways that educators can draw upon the teachings and spirit of the Living Out Loud Program in their own work:

1. Educators should recognize that substance abuse is an issue facing all youth, including youth with disabilities, and that for girls and young women with disabilities, there may be some unique dimensions to the issue. They need to learn as much as they can about the topic and advocate for the inclusion of information on girls (and boys) with disabilities during in-service training sessions on substance abuse.

2. Educators might want to consider developing a Living Out Loud Program in their schools. If they do, it is a good idea to involve girls with disabilities in the planning process. Ideally, women with disabilities would run the program, or at least be available as role models. Most important, the program should be fun.

3. Educators must ensure that youth with disabilities of both genders are fully integrated in all substance abuse prevention programs and courses in their schools and that the curriculum of these programs and courses includes the needs and issues of girls with disabilities.

4. Educators should provide girls with disabilities with opportunities and experiences that build on their strengths and capacities and fos-

ter self-esteem. As the Living Out Loud Program suggests, these can include offering disabled girls opportunities to meet, share interests and concerns, and just hang out; enabling girls to learn about their disabilities and to determine and obtain the accommodations they need; inviting women with disabilities from the community to serve as role models; and organizing field trips that can expand girls' post-secondary options.

Although girls with and without disabilities tend to lose their voice in adolescence, this trend is not inevitable. Programs such as Living Out Loud enable girls with disabilities to speak what is on their minds and develop a positive sense of self. Thus they have more options from which to choose and a more hopeful future and are less likely to abuse substances and engage in other risky behaviors. To quote the final stanza of a poem written by a Living Out Loud participant:

>Sometimes it is not easy but I keep going on
>Nothing will stop me from succeeding
>Because I am a proud
>Strong
>Young Woman
>Who is on her way up!!!!

REFERENCES

American Association of University Women (AAUW). 1990. *Shortchanging girls, shortchanging America: A call to action.* Washington, D.C.: Author.

Bodinger-de Uriarte, C., and G. Austin. 1991. Substance abuse among adolescent females. *Prevention Research Update* 9. Portland, Ore.: Western Regional Center for Drug-Free Schools and Communities.

Cross, S., E. Kaye, and A. C. Ratnofsky. 1993. *A report on the maltreatment of children with disabilities.* Washington, D.C.: National Center on Child Abuse and Neglect.

Fine, M., and A. Asch, eds. 1988. *Women with disabilities: Essays in psychology, culture, and politics.* Philadelphia, Penn.: Temple University Press.

Moore, D. 1992. *Preliminary research findings.* Dayton, Ohio: Center on Wright State University.

O'Toole, C. 1979. Disabled women: The case of the missing role model. *Independent 2.*

Resource Center on Substance Abuse and Disability. 1992. *A look at alcohol and other drug abuse prevention and . . . disability and enabling: A fact sheet.* Washington, D.C.: VSA Educational Services.

U.S. Department of Education. 1998. *To assure the free appropriate public education of all children with disabilities: Twentieth annual report to Congress* on the implementation of the *Individuals with Disabilities Education Act (IDEA)*. Washington, D.C.: Author.

Wagner, M. 1992. *Being female—A secondary disability? Gender differences in the transition experiences of young people with disabilities.* Menlo Park, Calif.: SRI International.

SECTION IV

Summary and Future Directions

CHAPTER 17

Addressing Gender Equity in Special Education Services: An Agenda for the Twenty-first Century

Michael L. Wehmeyer and Harilyn Rousso

Readers who have persevered through this point in the text will have an appreciation of the complexity of addressing gender equity in the education of students with disabilities. We know far too little about the day-to-day experiences of girls with disabilities; about the curricular materials they interact with and the degree to which those reflect bias and stereotypes; about the ways teachers respond to their inquiries or call on them in class; or about sexual harassment and the other experiences and issues impacting girls in educational settings.

We do, however, know some things. Young women with disabilities graduate to less positive adult outcomes, like employment, than do their male peers with disabilities. Given that such outcomes for people with disabilities in general are fairly dismal, this places women with disabilities on the bottom rung of the ladder of success, self-reliance, and life satisfaction. As reviewed by Doren and Benz (this volume), it appears evident that one contributor to this situation is the fact that girls and young women with disabilities receive a different vocational education experience than their male counterparts, with females participating in vocational education coursework that is more gender stereotyped (e.g., child care, domestic services), leading to lower-wage jobs.

Another thing that is clear is that males outnumber females two to one in admission to special education services. As illustrated by Wehmeyer and Schwartz (this volume), the reasons for this are multiple and complex. Males are likely overreferred to special education services due to issues pertaining to behavior and race. Girls are likely underreferred because of bias and girls' tendency to remain quiet. How many girls remain unserved and, thus, struggle day to day is unknown, but one can presume that number to be significant.

There are other things that, if we don't "know" them in the sense of empirical data, we can hypothesize with a great deal of certainty. First, there are too few role models for girls with disabilities, particularly girls with developmental or cognitive disabilities. The push to ensure that girls and young women have access to coursework in math and science will ensure that more women enter nontraditional employment fields and, thus, boost the pool of women from careers in science or math. However, the commitment to equitable math and science education has not specifically included girls with disabilities, and the pool of female scientists, engineers, and mathematicians contains few women with disabilities. Add to this the fact that few women with cognitive or more significant disabilities are present in the workforce in any capacity, and the outcome is that girls with disabilities do not have role models and mentors who provide the impetus for breaking societal stereotypes and barriers. Rousso (this volume) clearly demonstrates the need for mentors and role models in the lives of girls with disabilities.

Second, we can hypothesize that sexual harassment is a part of the educational experiences of too many girls with disabilities. As Linn and Rousso (this volume) note, sexual harassment has remained an almost invisible issue for special educators. If, however, as these authors note, 85 percent of girls in high school report having been sexually harassed in their school experience, why would we not expect that a significant proportion of girls with disabilities had similar experiences? Indeed, other types of abuse data suggest that the percentage of girls with disabilities facing sexual harassment may be even higher than that of their nondisabled peers.

Third, we can hypothesize that the curriculum with which girls with disabilities interact contains sex stereotypes and biases. Wehmeyer and Schwartz (this volume) provide some preliminary support of that. It certainly seems evident that in addition to issues pertaining to the visibility of women in textbooks, there are few people with disabilities represented in traditional texts, and even fewer women with disabilities. We simply do not know to what degree curricular materials that have been developed largely for use with students with disabilities, particularly vocational and career-oriented materials, propagate gender stereotypes.

Fourth, anecdotal information suggests that limited access to after school programs may be a significant form of gender bias for young women with disabilities. Such programs foster attitudes, skills, and knowledge essential for successful adulthood. From what we can tell, disabled girls face multiple barriers to participation (see Froschl, Rousso, and Rubin, this volume). While after school programs are not part of formal education, schools can influence their development, implementation, and participation levels indirectly, through advocacy, and sometimes directly, by sponsoring and/or housing such programs. Yet schools may not be adequately using their influence to ensure the inclusion of disabled students in general and disabled girls in particular.

Fifth, we hypothesize that boys with disabilities also pay a price for gender bias in school. Flood's chapter (this volume) describes the impact of rigid gender roles and expectations on nondisabled boys and suggests how expectations related to disability status may place boys with disabilities in problematic situations in school that impede their full development and hinder learning. The reality is we don't know. Research on the impact of gender bias on nondisabled boys is relatively new. There is need to ensure the inclusion of boys with disabilities in such research while it is evolving, rather than after the fact.

There are other issues that we must conclude that we don't know anything about. For example, there is a great deal of information about the impact of teacher interactions with males or females and the degree to which these interactions impact learning (see Grayson, this volume). There simply has not been similar work done with students with disabilities. While one might hypothesize that in more traditional classrooms in which students with disabilities are served together (resource room, self-contained classroom), there might be similar patterns of teacher interactions. However, in an inclusive classroom, in which the student is the only or one of the only students with disabilities, how does the disability factor play into teacher interactions? We don't know. It could well be that girls with disabilities in such settings are, like their nondisabled counterparts, routinely ignored or provided interactions that differ qualitatively from those provided males, with and without disabilities. However, students with disabilities sometimes need more intensive supports than nondisabled students, and it could just as well be that the types and frequencies of interactions are determined more by disability status than gender, or, more likely, by some complex combination of both factors. At this point, we must say we don't know much about interaction patterns.

This illustrates the complexity of gender issues for students receiving special education services that we noted earlier. Indeed, this entity we have referred to for years as "special education" is not static, and in considering an agenda for the future, we need to recognize the factors that will affect that future. Most of the chapters in this text are written from the perspective of gender equity and with reference to the laws, research, and other aspects that influence that perspective. In considering an agenda to promote gender equity for students with disabilities in the twenty-first century, we would like to turn for a while to a perspective that will be more familiar to many readers of this text, the perspective of special education.

TRENDS IN SPECIAL EDUCATION AFFECTING GENDER EQUITY

Inclusion and Access to the General Curriculum

For much of the quarter century since the passage of Public Law 94–142, special education has been a place where children with disabilities go to receive an individualized educational program. Over the last decade, however, there has been a growing consensus, propelled by a federal commitment to ensuring the inclusion of students with disabilities in general education classrooms, that students with disabilities need to be educated in the same settings that their nondisabled peers receive their education. The inclusion debate has been one of place; where should students with disabilities receive their education? The 1997 amendments to the Individuals with Disabilities Education Act (IDEA), as the Education for All Handicapped Children Act was renamed in 1992, pushed this debate beyond one of just place to one of quality. In recent years, many educators have begun to wonder just how special special education is. Kavale and Forness (1999) conducted a meta-analysis of studies examining practice in special education. They began their analysis by noting the two interpretations of the phrase *special education* that can be emphasized. The first places the emphasis on the word *special*. In this interpretation, *special education* refers to the development of methods that are unique and exclusive to special education, presumably in response to the unique learning needs of students with disabilities. The second interpretation places the emphasis on *education* and focuses on the modification of existing general education techniques and curricula, or the accommodation thereof, to fit the needs of students with diverse disabilities and learning styles. The former, emphasizing *special* has been the dominant interpretation for much of the last three decades. Unfortunately, Kavele and Forness (1999) found only modest support for using these "special" techniques as ways of improving the educational outcomes of students with disabilities. They conclude that "special education becomes significantly more effective when the education aspect is emphasized" (p. 83).

The 1997 amendments to the IDEA put just that emphasis on special education, requiring that educators document how each student receiving special education services be provided access to the general curriculum. The field is in the early stages of determining what constitutes access and how to achieve it. Clearly, access is provided through changes to the curricular materials themselves (e.g., implementation of principles of universal design to ensure that all students can use materials). Additionally however, and particularly for students with more significant disabilities, access means more than using technology to adapt materials and must imply accommodating the curriculum to the student's unique learning needs. Thus, the educational program of students with mental retardation may be driven by the general curriculum, but students may receive only a portion of the content, or the content may be adapted to meet individual needs. Another component of access, often overlooked, may involve enhancing the curriculum to reflect the particular talents, strengths, and experiences that students with disabilities bring to the learning process so that the curriculum is truly reflective of all students along all lines of diversity, including disability. This is a shift away from the view of disability as a deficit; while not denying that a disability may impose limitations on learning, there is also recognition that aspects of the disability experience can be assets, encompassing ways of exploring and learning about the world that benefit everyone (Wahl, this volume; Rousso, 1997). Ideally, the "enhanced" curriculum would be used by disabled and nondisabled students. Additionally, we note that while access to the general curriculum moves the emphasis from the place where students receive educational services to the content of that educational program so that conceivably, students with disabilities could have access to the general curriculum outside of the typical classroom, it seems unlikely that the trend toward inclusive educational services will reverse itself.

In general, then, it seems prudent to predict that the educational experiences of students with disabilities in the twenty-first century will be more directly tied to the general curriculum and will be provided within the context of the general education classroom. Thus, the emphasis is on special *education* as a set of services and supports instead of *special* education as place. As such, efforts to promote gender equity for students with disabilities will, likely, overlap with gender equity efforts for all students. That is, when students with disabilities are present in the general education classroom and receive educational services that are driven by the general curriculum, many of the concerns that have been addressed in relation to nondisabled girls will become pertinent to girls and young women with disabilities. This may be, of course, a double-edged sword. On the one hand, materials currently used in typical classroom settings are gender biased, then simply adapting them for use with students with disabilities will only exacerbate the problem. On the other hand, if girls with disabilities are a part of the general classroom, efforts to impact that setting and to address bias inherent in the general curriculum will have direct benefit to girls with disabilities. And ideally, as students with disabilities become increasingly present in general education settings, efforts to address gender bias in the curriculum will expand to address the intersection of disability and gender bias, just as they currently address the intersection of gender with race, ethnicity, socioeconomic status, and other factors, to the benefit of all students.

This shift in emphasis from *special* education to special *education* will place additional demands on efforts to promote gender equity. First, as previously mentioned, we have no real understanding of the ways in which teachers interact with students with disabilities in general classroom settings, let alone how that might vary according to gender. Since "inclusive" classrooms are those in which students with disabilities are not disproportionately represented, most such classrooms will include only a few students with disabilities, at the most. Given the limited number of students in such classrooms, examination of biases in teacher interactions will have to be determined in contrast with other nondisabled students in the classroom, male and female, and, perhaps, through cross-classroom comparisons. Nonetheless, although it will be a challenge, it is important to understand to what degree gender impacts on the types of instruction received by students with disabilities.

Disproportionate Representation

If the educational services for students with disabilities in the twenty-first century will be characterized by inclusion in the general education classroom and access to the general curriculum, it seems likely that for the immediate future, boys will continue to be disproportionately represented among those receiving these services. There are some viable reasons for the disproportionate representation of males. Far too often, however, the literature suggests (see Wehmeyer and Schwartz, this volume), boys with disabilities have been referred for special education services in essence to get them out of the regular classroom due to their behavior. When special education can no longer be a place to which students can be removed, issues pertaining to disproportionate representation may change. Moreover, there is no assurance that girls who may currently be underrepresented will be identified and provided adequate supports. In fact, one could predict that boys' dominance of teacher attention and time due to behavior issues will continue to be a reality, and that alone will ensure that males receive special education supports disproportionately.

We must not, however, address the issue of disproportionate representation of males receiving special education services as a gender-only phenomenon, for it is not. This is one point where the issues of biases and stereotypes due to gender, disability, and race have a logical intersection. Our efforts to examine biases in referral must do a better job of identifying discrimination due to each factor and to their shared dimensions.

School to Work and Transition

One of the aspects of the traditional special education model that appears worth carrying over into the next century is its outcomes-oriented focus. The IDEA requires that, in essence, students ages fourteen and over receiving special education services must have transition-related goals included in their educational program. These transition services can focus on a broad array of postschool outcomes, including enrollment in postsecondary education, employment, residential and living outcomes, or recreation and leisure outcomes. Ideally, this links what is happening in the classroom for the last years of a student's educational program to meaningful outcomes that will ensure success and satisfaction as an adult. In recent years a similar movement has emerged within general education that places a focus on school-to-work outcomes. Again, the likely trend is that students with disabilities will, with greater and greater frequency, receive transition services and supports within the context of the general classroom and through the directive of school to work curricular and content issues. We know that the important area of vocational education is one where gender bias has been particularly evident in the education of girls and young women with disabilities, and it is imperative that we not repeat the sins of the past by forming school-to-work programs that are based on gender stereotypes and lead to less positive outcomes for women with disabilities. It is important that issues pertaining to equity in course content, curricular materials, vocational interest and aptitude assessments, job sampling practices (e.g., all students have opportunities to sample a wide array of jobs during their educational years), and other practices inherent in transition, school-to-work, and vocational education be addressed.

Technology and Assistive Devices

As was previously mentioned, one solution to providing access to the general curriculum is through technology. Students who have visual disabilities can gain access to challenging materials through computer programs that can use voice-synthesized speech to read text. Students with motor- or movement-related disabilities can participate in hands-on science experiments through the use of a variety of switches or other accommodations. The list of ways in which students might benefit from technology is endless. The 1997 amendments to IDEA require not only that the Individualized Education Program contain a statement of how the student's disability affects his or her involvement and progress in the general curriculum but also what services, program modifications, and supports are necessary to gain that access, including, specifically, whether the child requires assistive technology devices and services. The growing emphasis on technology in education introduces yet another area with potential for a wide gender gap. Limited studies of nondisabled girls and boys suggest that boys outperform girls in computer skills and that they take more and higher-level computer courses in school (Grossman and Grossman, 1994; AAUW, 1998). Why? There is certainly no reason to believe that gender differences in cognitive, motor, or perceptual skills play a role. One only has to scan the shelves of most computer software stores to see the wide array of male-oriented software programs to begin to sense that issues of bias are at work.

Access to technology will be an important component of a quality education program in the future, and we must be vigilant to ensure that girls have equal access. Assistive technology is, however, more than just computer use. Assistive devices such as hearing aids; mobility devices such as wheelchairs; augmentative and alternative communication devices, including speech synthesized communication devices; and other similar products ensure access and opportunity. There is some indication that adult women with disabilities face complex barriers to use of assistive technology; those with limited exposure to and experience with such devices may find their use more intimidating and frustrating (Scherer, 1993). Such patterns begin early. Although there is no evidence to support the supposition, one suggested outcome of gender bias in special education services that has been raised throughout the last two decades is that girls have less access to related and support services. We need to ensure that this is not the case for access to technology.

AN AGENDA FOR THE FUTURE

What can one teacher do to make a difference? While the task of addressing gender equity may seem overwhelming, there are manageable, identifiable steps that can be taken. Indeed, as Maryann Wickett's chapter shows (this volume), change occurs one teacher at a time. Margaret Mead's oft-cited adage never to doubt that a small group of dedicated people can make a difference because, indeed, that is the only way to make a difference is true here as well. Of course, we are not opposed to a widespread collective effort to eradicate gender bias, indeed all types of bias, in schools. Revolution is good. But so is individual action for social change. As a way of closing this text, we make the following suggestions for change makers of the future.

Know Thyself   Change starts with examining one's own practices and beliefs. Chapters by Wickett and by Grayson in this volume provide a model for and materials to support a self-evaluation of one's practice. Don't make assumptions about whether or not you do or do not treat students differently. Step back and examine the question in an objective manner.

Knowledge Is Power   Take advantage of resources to learn about gender equitable practices and, if possible, arrange for training opportunities for other educators. There are many national organizations such as the National Coalition on Sex Equity in Education, the American Association of University Women, and the Women's Educational Equity Resource Center, regional organizations such as the Equity Assistance Centers,[1] and local organizations that provide materials and access to training on gender equity; you could contact these to find out about training in your area. Also, there are some programs designed to promote gender equity for girls with disabilities (Froschl, Rousso, and Rubin; Rousso; Ferryra, all this volume). Use them to begin a program in your school or classroom or just to get ideas. Keep track of what works and what doesn't. Give the developers feedback, so they can develop even better programs for your use.

Cooperation and Intentional Evaluations   Margaret Mead emphasized change through a small group because it is through interaction with others who share a common vision that we are energized and empowered to act. Particularly, it can be very useful to use team-teaching circumstances to evaluate one another's practice in relation to gender equity. Such internal evaluations are very powerful but must be accomplished within a framework of trust and mutual support.

Families as Partners   Create reliable allies with parents and extended family members of children with disabilities, particularly parents of girls. Many parents of girls with disabilities share concerns about their daughters' future, and if they are made aware of the many, often subtle ways that the education system discriminates against girls, and the consequences thereof, they can become powerful agents for the system's change.

Curriculum Evaluation   Curricular materials and classroom activities need to be gender fair. Begin with your classroom. Do the materials you use reflect bias, such as that described in the Grayson and Shevitz and Shaffer chapters (this volume)? How about videos and other media? Identify materials that are not biased, or augment existing materials to ensure equity. Are classroom speakers representative of both genders and people with disabilities? You can begin by ensuring that your classroom and the instructional activities therein are gender fair. Once you have established that objective, you can take that to a district level by serving on curriculum committees or sharing your findings with district personnel responsible for the curriculum.

Title IX   Get to know Title IX and how it might be beneficial, as a means of leverage, for your students.

Students as Allies   Communicate your commitment to equity to your students and bring them on as allies in your efforts. Work with students to set classroom standards for behavior and tolerance. Work within the school to ensure that students have access to orientations on issues such as sexual harassment. Be your students' ally and advocate, and be willing to listen to students.

Women with Disabilities in the Community as Allies   Draw upon the expertise of adult women with disabilities in the community to help promote gender equity in your classroom. Depending on their background and interests, they can serve as mentors and role models for students and their parents, provide invaluable information on postsecondary options and the work of work, assist with the assessment of curricula, suggest resources that more fully promote the accomplishments of women and men with disabilities, and provide a link to the national and global disabled women's movement.

Research to Practice   While research has been the domain of universities, there is a growing movement for participatory action research, in which practitioners have an equal role in designing, conducting, and disseminating research. If you don't have a link with a research institution, form one and suggest research activities in your classroom and campus in which you can be actively involved.

Teachers can make a difference. That is the premise of this book. Indeed, we believe that the changes that need to be made to ensure gender equity for girls with disabilities will, in fact, happen one teacher at a time.

NOTE

1. Contact information: NCSEE—P.O. Box 534, Annandale NJ 08801–0534; AAUW-1111 Sixteenth Street NW, Washington, DC 20036, 202–728–7602; WEEA Equity Resource Center-55 Chapel Street, Newton, MA 02458–1060, 800–225–3088; For information on the EACs, use the following website: *http://www.umich.edu/~eqtynet/TitleIV.dacs.html.*

REFERENCES

American Association of University Women (AAUW). 1998. *Gender gaps: Where schools still fail our children.* Washington, D.C.: Author.

Grossman, H., and S. H. Grossman. 1994. *Gender issues in education.* Boston: Allyn and Bacon.

Kavale, K. A., and S. R. Forness. 1999. *Efficacy of special education and related services.* Washington, D.C.: American Association on Mental Retardation.

Rousso, H. 1997. Seeing the world anew: Science and disability. In *Thoughts and deeds: Equity in math and science education.* Edited by N. Kreinberg and E. Wahl. Washington, D.C.: Collaboration for Equity—AAAS, 131–134.

Scherer, M. J. 1993. What we know about women's technology use, avoidance and abandonment. In *Women with disabilities: Found voices.* Edited by M. Willmuth and L. Holcomb. Binghampton, N.Y.: Harrington Park Press.

INDEX